The Lowe's Katrina Cottage Series

Katrina Cottage 1, the original 308 square foot cottage, designed by Marianne Cusato. See plan on page K5.

Reprinted with permission of *Cottage Living* magazine. Photograph by Robbie Caponetto.

Table of Contents

The Lowe's Katrina Cottage Series

Hailed as the solution to housing after Hurricane Katrina, the Lowe's Katrina Cottage has evolved into a nationwide sensation finding popularity as primary housing as well as affordable housing, guesthouses, resorts and camps.

As evidenced throughout the media and in the marketplace, never before have so many people wanted to live in well-designed, smart looking homes. To meet this demand, Lowe's has teamed up with Marianne Cusato and a group of designers to offer a series of Katrina Cottages as plans and a complete line of materials for construction from foundation to fashion lighting and more.

Cottages in the Lowe's Series range from 308 square feet to 1,807 square feet. They can be clustered in villages, built as primary homes or function as accessory buildings. Several of the cottages have grow options, allowing for smaller cottages to be expanded over time.

How to Purchase a Lowe's Katrina Cottage

1. Select a Plan: The first step is to select a floor plan. Lowe's Katrina Cottages range in size from 308 to 1,807 square feet. See all the plans on pages K5 to K22 or at lowes.com/LowesKatrinaCottage. For ordering information, see page K32.

1 Select a plan

2. Research Permitting and Codes: **After selecting a floor plan, contact your local building department to check any zoning or minimum square footage requirements**. Ask your building officials about requirements for filing for a permit. This is a good time to start interviewing contractors. Some building departments will require a local engineer's stamp on the drawings. A local contractor should be able to help determine permit and code requirements in the area and direct you to a licensed professional if necessary.

To find a contractor, contact your local Chamber of Commerce or the local branch of the National Association of Home Builders (NAHB.org).

2 Research local codes

3 Select materials

3. Select Materials: Once you have received your Lowe's Katrina Cottage plan, visit the Commercial Sales desk of your local Lowe's store and work with our sales specialists to select all of your materials from foundation to finish and decorative.

4. Obtain Financing: Work through a local bank to secure construction loan for materials and labor.

4 Obtain financing

5. Make the Purchase: Visit your local Lowe's store and work with the commercial sales team to purchase all of the materials for your Katrina Cottage plan, arrange delivery and start construction.

5 Purchase a Lowe's Katrina Cottage and start building

The Lowe's

Katrina Cottage

Materials

All products and materials for the Lowe's Katrina Cottages from the foundation plate up can be purchased at Lowe's. This includes the studs, doors, windows, insulation, fixtures, cabinets, electrical, plumbing, appliances, the kitchen sink, and more are all available at Lowe's. The homeowner or contractor must supply the foundation and/or piers, connections to a sewer or septic tank, HVAC system and construction labor.

Functional, Affordable and Elegant Housing Alternatives

Lowe's Katrina Cottage is not a modular or pre-fabricated home. It is "stick built" like any other traditional home. While Lowe's in-store sales specialists can help you select and supply you with the construction materials needed, a licensed contractor is recommended for actual construction. Other pre-construction steps or requirements are the homebuilder's responsibility.

Available Features of the Lowe's Katrina Cottage

- Hardieplank® lap siding that is rot and termite resistant
- Paperless mold and mildew resistant drywall
- Metal roof
- Energy efficient windows
- Full kitchen including refrigerator, free-standing stove, built-in hood, sink and cabinets
- 9' ceilings or taller in most cottage designs
- Outdoor living space – either a front porch or stoop

The materials will arrive to the jobsite in multiple shipments directly from the Lowe's store. A store associate will work with you to develop a delivery schedule which will allow materials to arrive in different phases during the construction process.

The Lowe's Katrina Cottages are available in Lowe's stores nationwide. Stop by your local Lowe's Commercial Sales desk for more information.

plan name: KC308

plan #537-200K-KC308

Designer: Marianne Cusato

Bedrooms: 1

Bathrooms: 1

Ceiling Height: 9 ft.

Conditioned Living Area: 308 sq. ft.

Overall Dimensions (including porch):

30'-0" long x 14'-0" wide

The cottage that started it all. Small and compact, this plan is ideal for a guest cottage, studio or in-law flat in the backyard, as well as a fishing cabin or vacation cottage on a lake. This design can sleep four in bunk beds.

Note: Artist renderings and photos may vary slightly from the actual working drawings. Please refer to the floor plan for accurate layout.

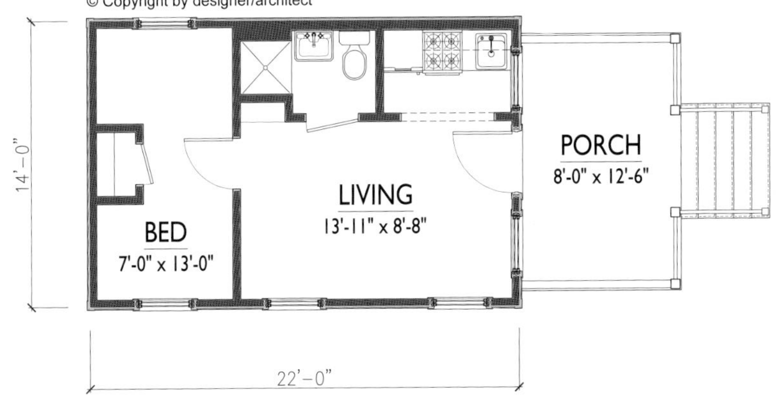

for pricing and ordering, see page K32 | call toll-free 1-877-379-3420

plan name: KC416

plan #537-200K-KC416

Designer: Marianne Cusato
Bedrooms: 1
Bathrooms: 1
Ceiling Height: 9 ft.
Conditioned Living Area: 416 sq. ft.

Overall Dimensions
(including porch):
34'-0" long x 16'-0" wide

Revised and refined, this cottage allows more room for living and sleeping. The design is perfect for a guest cottage, studio or in-law flat in the backyard, as well as a fishing cabin or vacation cottage on a lake.

Note: Artist renderings and photos may vary slightly from the actual working drawings. Please refer to the floor plan for accurate layout.

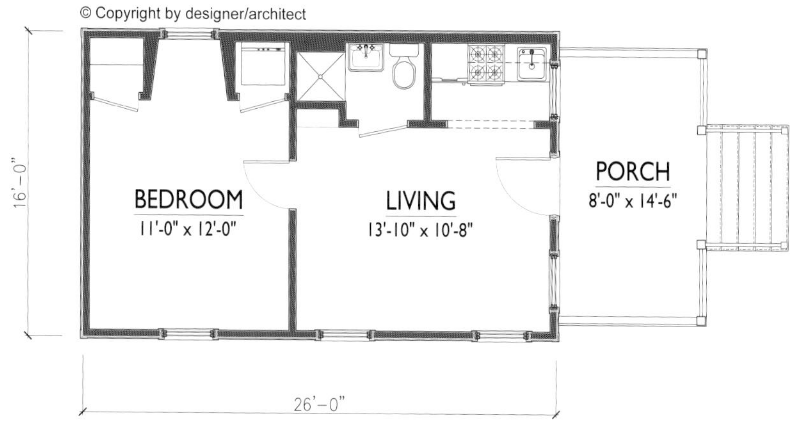

for pricing and ordering, see page K32 | call toll-free 1-877-379-3420

plan name: KC480

LOWE'S katrina cottage™

plan #537-200K-KC480

Designer: Eric Moser
Bedrooms: 2
Bathrooms: 1
Ceiling Height: 9 ft.
Conditioned Living Area: 480 sq. ft.

Overall Dimensions
(including porch):
32'-0" long x 20'-0" wide

Two bedrooms in less than 500 square feet is hard to accomplish, but this plan does so with craft. The design is ideal for a guest cottage, in-law flat or vacation home.

Note: Artist renderings and photos may vary slightly from the actual working drawings. Please refer to the floor plan for accurate layout.

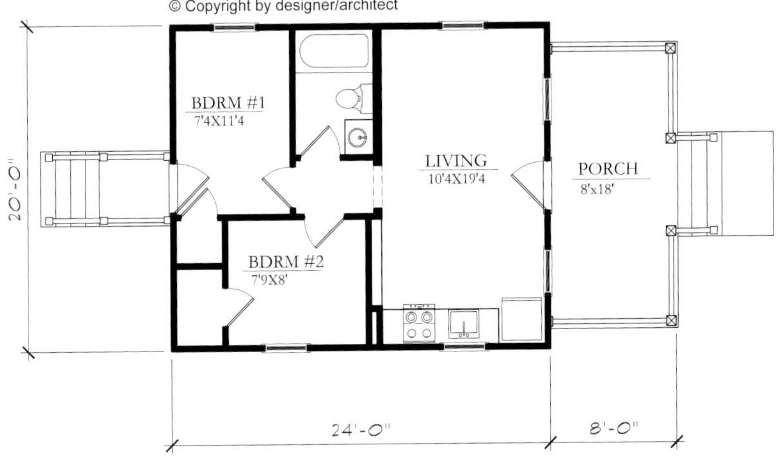

for pricing and ordering, see page K32 | call toll-free 1-877-379-3420

LOWE'S katrina cottage™

plan name: KC517

plan #537-200K-KC517

Designer: Geoffrey Mouen

Bedrooms: 1

Bathrooms: 1

Ceiling Height: 9 ft.

Conditioned Living Area: 517 sq. ft.

Overall Dimensions (including porch):
40'-0" long x 15'-8" wide

Ideal as a bunkhouse, this cottage is equipped with a generously-sized dressing area to add efficiency and comfort for the occupancy of several residents.

Note: Artist renderings and photos may vary slightly from the actual working drawings. Please refer to the floor plan for accurate layout.

for pricing and ordering, see page K32

plan name: KC544

LOWE'S katrina cottage™

plan #537-200K-KC544

Designer: Marianne Cusato

Bedrooms: 2

Bathrooms: 1

Ceiling Height: 9 ft.

Conditioned Living Area: 544 sq. ft.

Overall Dimensions (including porch):
42'-0" long x 16'-0" wide

Compact and efficiently planned, this two-bedroom cottage is perfectly sized to sit on the back of a lot as a guest house, or clustered with other cottages to create small villages.

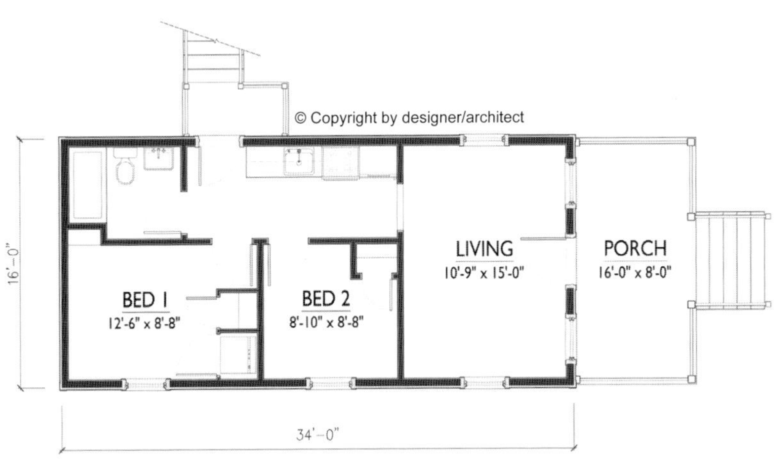

Note: Artist renderings and photos may vary slightly from the actual working drawings. Please refer to the floor plan for accurate layout.

for pricing and ordering, see page K32 | call toll-free 1-877-379-3420

LOWE'S katrina cottage™

plan name: KC576

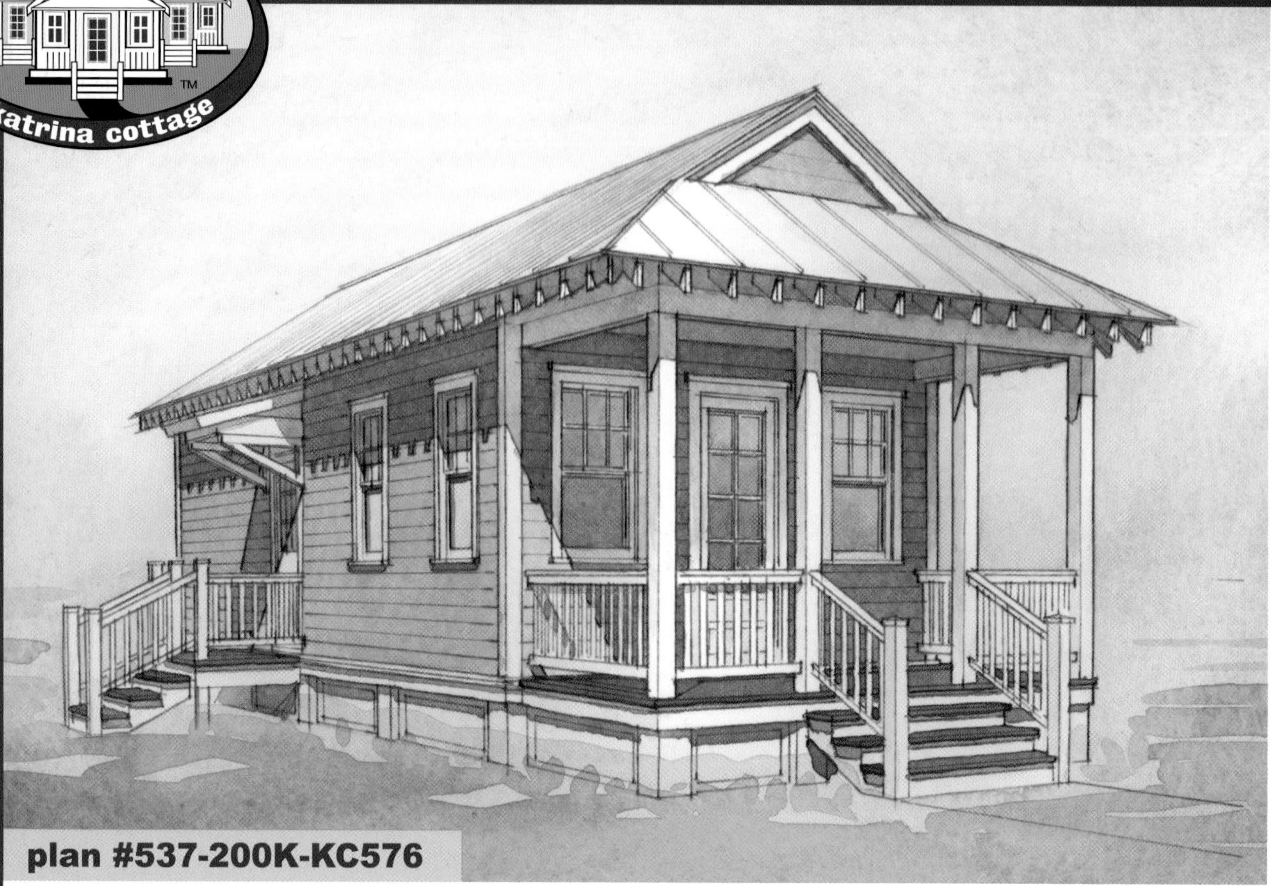

plan #537-200K-KC576

Designer: Marianne Cusato

Bedrooms: 1

Bathrooms: 1

Ceiling Height: 9 ft.

Conditioned Living Area: 576 sq. ft.

Overall Dimensions
(including porch):
44'-0" long x 16'-0" wide

Based on the principles of universal design, including appropriate turning radiuses, this one-bedroom cottage is ideal for a variety of homeowners and is designed to be handicap accessible.

Note: Artist renderings and photos may vary slightly from the actual working drawings. Please refer to the floor plan for accurate layout.

for pricing and ordering, see page K32 | call toll-free 1-877-379-3420

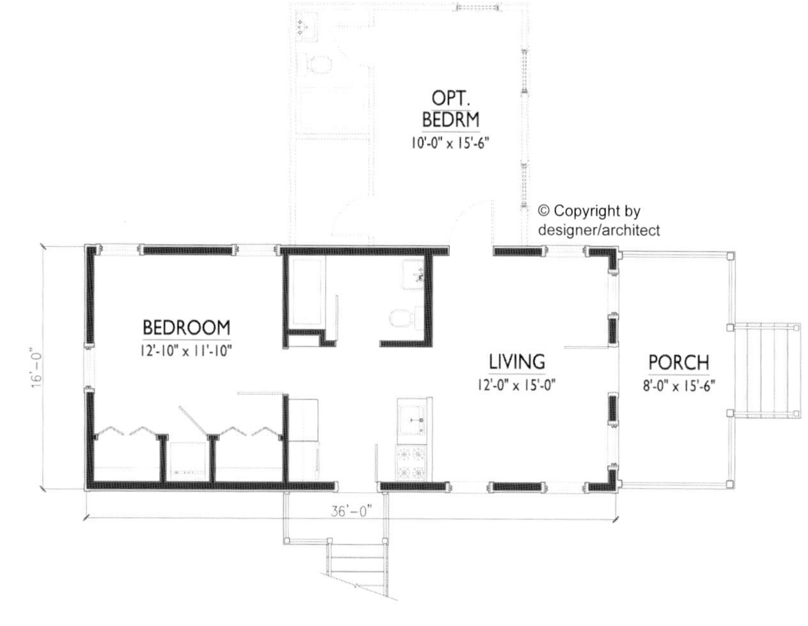

plan name: KC633

plan #537-200K-KC633

Designer: Eric Moser

Bedrooms: 1

Bathrooms: 1

Ceiling Height: 8 ft. first floor;
8 ft. second floor

Conditioned Living Area: 633 sq. ft.

Overall Dimensions (including porch):
23'-6" long x 22'-0" wide

This plan turns wide to the street so it can fit on a shallow lot or tuck into a back corner of a property. The large room across the entire second floor can be used as a generous bedroom or open studio space.

Note: Artist renderings and photos may vary slightly from the actual working drawings. Please refer to the floor plan for accurate layout.

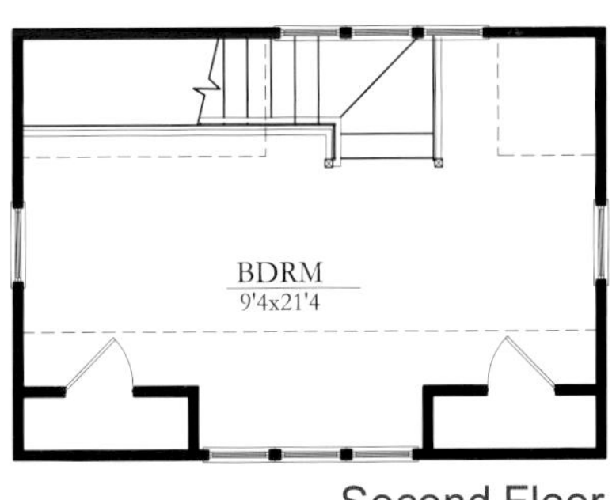

Second Floor

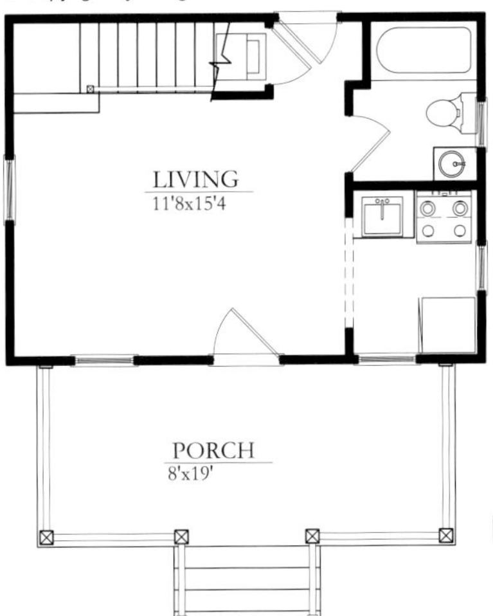

First Floor

LOWE'S katrina cottage™

plan name: KC675

Chenoweth 07

plan #537-200K-KC675

Designer: Eric Moser
Bedrooms: 2
Bathrooms: 1
Ceiling Height: 8 ft. first floor; up to 8 ft. second floor
Conditioned Living Area: 675 sq. ft.

Overall Dimensions (including porch):
32'-0" long x 15'-0" wide

This charming, 1 1/2 story cottage fits two bedrooms and a single bathroom into a compact footprint.

Note: Artist renderings and photos may vary slightly from the actual working drawings. Please refer to the floor plan for accurate layout.

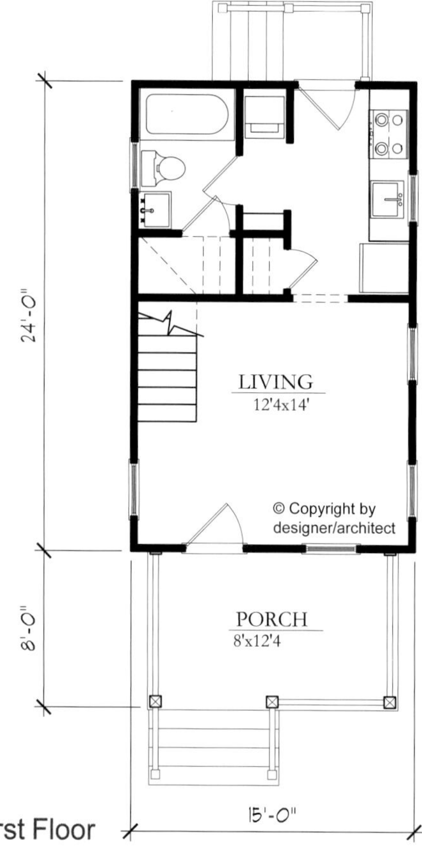

First Floor

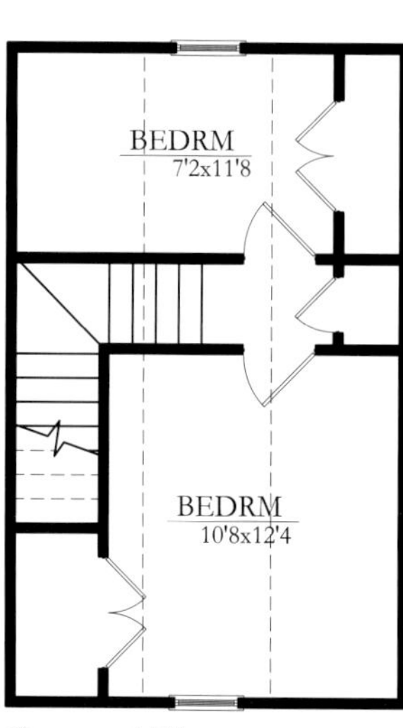

Second Floor

for pricing and ordering, see page K32 | call toll-free 1-877-379-3420

plan name: KC697

LOWE'S katrina cottage™

plan #537-200K-KC697

Designer: Eric Moser
Bedrooms: 1.5
Bathrooms: 1
Ceiling Height: Varies
Conditioned Living Area: 697 sq. ft.

Overall Dimensions (including porch):
33'-6" long x 24'-0" wide

A vaulted ceiling in the living room and sleeping loft define the open feeling of this plan, which is ideal for a starter house or vacation cabin.

Note: Artist renderings and photos may vary slightly from the actual working drawings. Please refer to the floor plan for accurate layout.

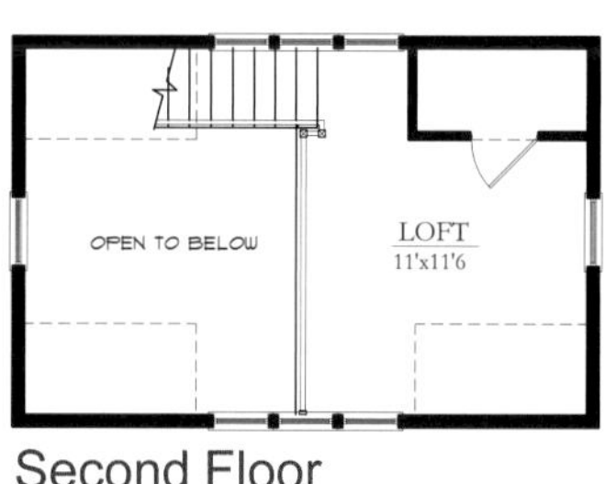

Second Floor

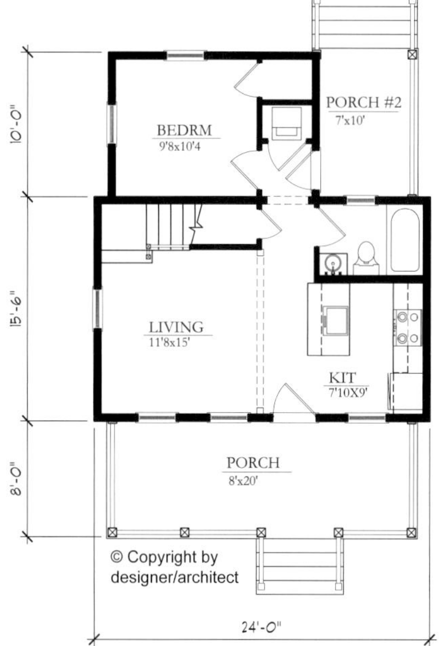

First Floor

plan name: KC612

plan #537-200K-KC612

Designer:
Duany Plater-Zyberk & Co.
Bedrooms: 2
Bathrooms: 1
Ceiling Height: 10 ft.
Conditioned Living Area: 612 sq. ft.

Overall Dimensions
(including stoop):
38'-0" long x 18'-0" wide
64'-0" long x 18'-0" wide
with optional suite

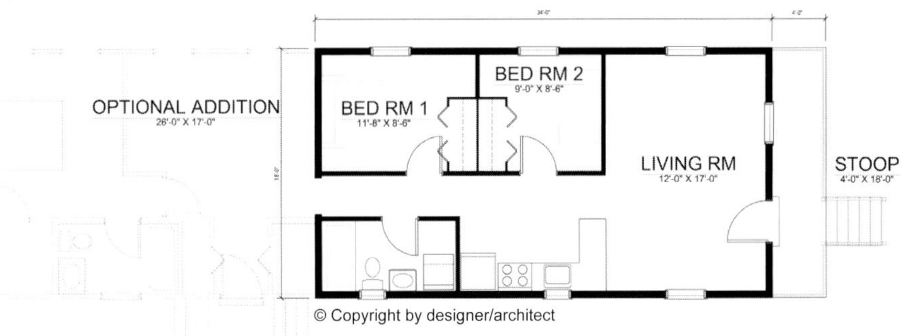

Designed to grow, this two-bedroom cottage with one bathroom starts at 612 square feet and can expand over time to a three bedroom, two bathroom 1,080 square foot house with a family room. The design is ideal for long, narrow lots.

Note: Artist renderings and photos may vary slightly from the actual working drawings.
Please refer to the floor plan for accurate layout. Material package does not include materials for optional addition.

for pricing and ordering, see page K32 | call toll-free 1-877-379-3420

plan name: KC1080

plan #537-200K-KC1080

Designer:
Duany Plater-Zyberk & Co.
Bedrooms: 3
Bathrooms: 2
Ceiling Height: 10 ft.
Conditioned Living Area:
1,080 sq. ft.

Overall Dimensions
(including porch):
63'-10" long x 18'-0" wide

This expanded plan includes three bedrooms and two bathrooms as well as a family room. KC1080 is the expanded version of KC612.

Note: Artist renderings and photos may vary slightly from the actual working drawings. Please refer to the floor plan for accurate layout.

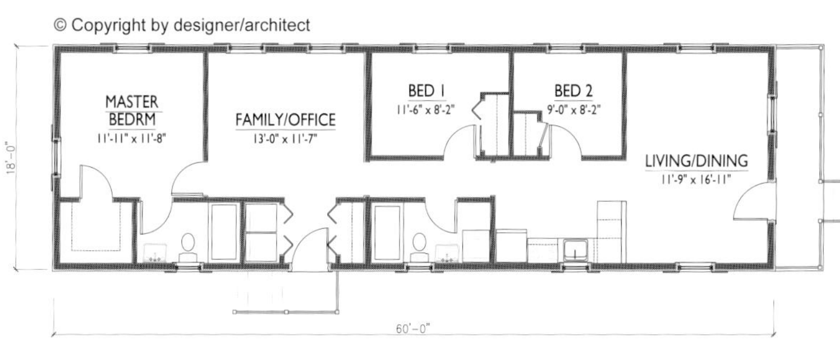

for pricing and ordering, see page K32 | call toll-free 1-877-379-3420

plan name: KC888

LOWE'S katrina cottage™

noweth 07

plan #537-200K-KC888

Designer: W.A. Lawrence
Bedrooms: 2
Bathrooms: 2
Ceiling Height: 9 ft.
Conditioned Living Area: 888 sq. ft.

Overall Dimensions (including porch):
52'-0" long x 25'-0" wide

Designed to be handicap accessible with generously-sized rooms, this quaint Acadian-style plan includes two bedrooms, each with its own bathroom. An optional bedroom addition extends this design to a 1,112 square foot, three bedroom/two bathroom house.

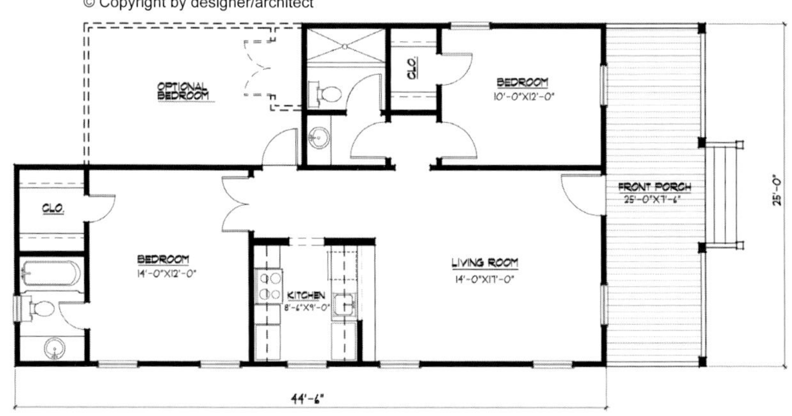

Note: Artist renderings and photos may vary slightly from the actual working drawings. Please refer to the floor plan for accurate layout.

for pricing and ordering, see page K32 | call toll-free 1-877-379-3420

plan name: KC1112

plan #537-200K-KC1112

Designer: W.A. Lawrence
Bedrooms: 3
Bathrooms: 2
Ceiling Height: 9 ft.
Conditioned Living Area:
1,112 sq. ft.

Overall Dimensions
(including porch):
52'-0" long x 25'-0" wide

BED 3
10'-0" x 12'-0"

BED 2
10'-0" x 12'-0"

PORCH
25'-0" x 7'-6"

BED 1
14'-0" x 11'-10"

LIVING ROOM
13'-9" x 16'-10"

25'-0"

44'-6"

Designed to be handicap accessible, this quaint Acadian-style plan has generously-sized rooms. It also includes three bedrooms and two bathrooms as well as a laundry room. This plan is the expanded version of KC888.

Note: Artist renderings and photos may vary slightly from the actual working drawings. Please refer to the floor plan for accurate layout.

plan name: KC910

katrina cottage

plan #537-200K-KC910

Designer: Marianne Cusato

Bedrooms: 3

Bathrooms: 1

Ceiling Height: 9 ft.

Conditioned Living Area: 910 sq. ft.

Overall Dimensions (including porch): 43'-0" long x 26'-0" wide

This three bedroom/one bathroom core cottage has the option to grow to a three bedroom/two bathroom 1,185 square foot cottage. When expanded, the second bedroom converts to a study or sitting room off the master bedroom suite.

Note: Artist renderings and photos may vary slightly from the actual working drawings. Please refer to the floor plan for accurate layout.

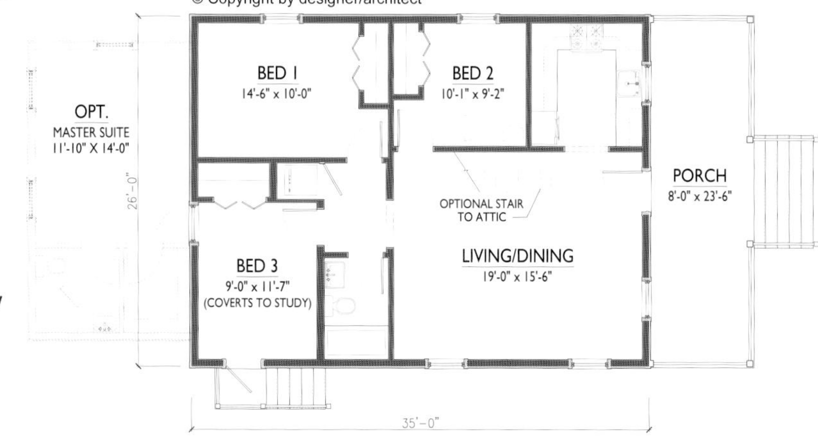

for pricing and ordering, see page K32 | call toll-free 1-877-379-3420

plan name: KC1185/KC1807

plan #537-200K-KC1185

Optional
Second Floor

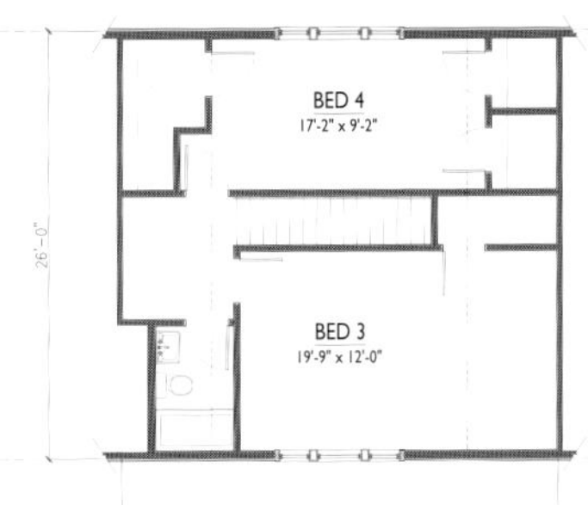

First Floor

Both versions include a study.
This plan is the extended version of KC910.

Designer: Marianne Cusato
Bedrooms: 3
Bathrooms: 2
Ceiling Height: 9 ft.
Conditioned Living Area:
1,185 sq. ft.

Overall Dimensions
(including porch):
55'-6" long x 26'-0" wide

Equipped with a master bedroom suite on the ground floor, this cottage has the ability to grow from a 1,185 square foot, three bedroom/ two bathroom cottage. By finishing the attic, the cottage becomes a 1,807 square foot, five bedroom/ three bathroom house.

Note: Artist renderings and photos may vary slightly from the actual working drawings. Please refer to the floor plan for accurate layout.

plan name: KC936

LOWE'S katrina cottage™

plan #537-200K-KC936

Designer: Marianne Cusato
Bedrooms: 2
Bathrooms: 1
Ceiling Height: 9 ft. first floor;
8 ft. second floor
Conditioned Living Area: 936 sq. ft.

Overall Dimensions
(including porch):
26'-0" long x 26'-0" wide
40'-6" long x 26'-0" wide
with optional suite

This two-story design features two bedrooms with one bathroom. It has the option of growing to a three bedroom/two bathroom 1,200 square foot home with a first floor master bedroom.

Second Floor

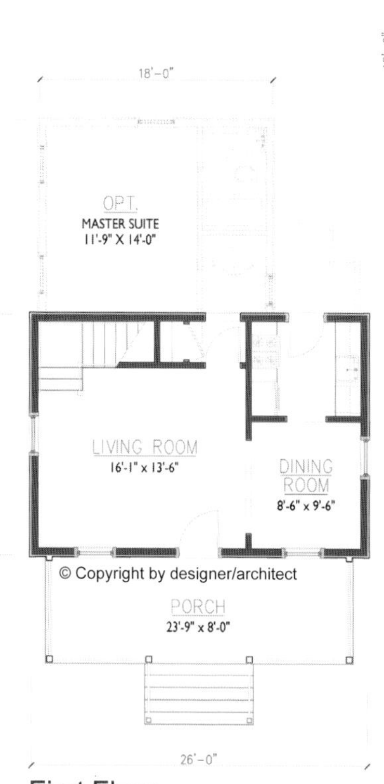

First Floor

Note: Artist renderings and photos may vary slightly from the actual working drawings. Please refer to the floor plan for accurate layout. Material package does not include materials for optional addition.

for pricing and ordering, see page K32 | **call toll-free 1-877-379-3420**

plan name: KC1200

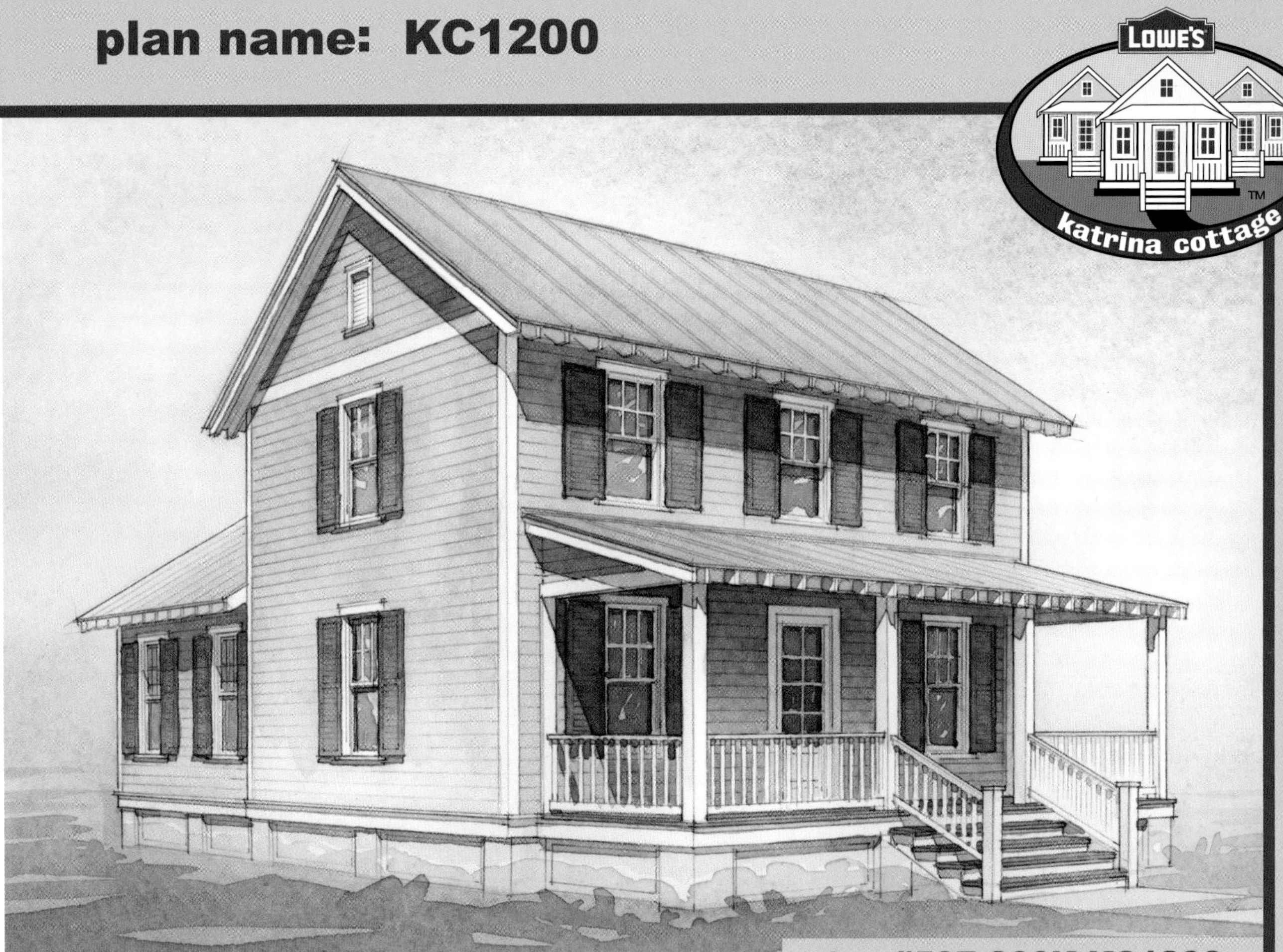

plan #537-200K-KC1200

Designer: Marianne Cusato
Bedrooms: 3
Bathrooms: 2
Ceiling Height: 9 ft. first floor;
8 ft. second floor
Conditioned Living Area:
1,200 sq. ft.

Overall Dimensions
(including porch):
40'-8" long x 26'-0" wide

This 1,200 square foot, two-story design features three bedrooms/ two bathrooms with a downstairs master bedroom. KC1200 is the expanded version of KC936.

26'-0"
18'-0"
BED 1
10'-4" x 11'-2"
BED 2
12'-0" x 9'-1"

Second Floor

18'-0"
32'-8"
14'-8"
18'-0"
MASTER SUITE
11'-9" x 14'-0"
LIVING ROOM
16'-1" x 13'-6"
DINING
8'-6" x 9'-6"
PORCH
23'-9" x 8'-0"
26'-0"

First Floor

Note: Artist renderings and photos may vary slightly from the actual working drawings. Please refer to the floor plan for accurate layout.

LOWE'S katrina cottage™

plan name: KC1175

plan #537-200K-KC1175

Designer:
Duany Plater-Zyberk & Co.
Bedrooms: 2
Bathrooms: 2
Ceiling Height: Varies
Conditioned Living Area: 1,175 sq. ft.

Overall Dimensions
(including porch):
41'-0" long x 33'-0" wide

This open plan with a 12' ceiling in the living room balances traditional vertical proportions with compact planning. A lower ceiling in the kitchen (7'-6") allows room for a second floor bedroom suite.

Note: Artist renderings and photos may vary slightly from the actual working drawings. Please refer to the floor plan for accurate layout.

Second Floor

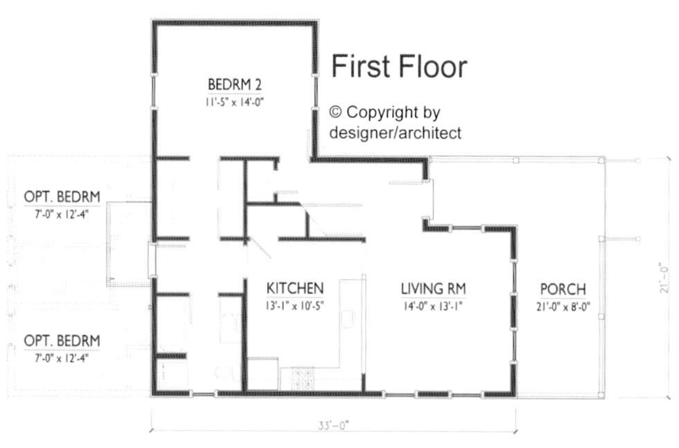

for pricing and ordering, see page K32 | call toll-free 1-877-379-3420

Free Lowe's Gift Card Offer

Lowe's Special Rebate Offer

Purchase any plan from the Lowe's Katrina Cottage Series featured on pages K5 through K22 PLUS at least $15,000 of your materials from Lowe's and receive a gift card for the purchase price of your plans.

Lowe's Katrina Cottage Series features wood framing, termite-resistant siding, metal roofing and mold- and moisture-resistant drywall. When you purchase all materials, from nails, blueprints and framing to the appliances, Lowe's will arrange delivery of the materials in multiple shipments based on the progress of construction. The builder is responsible for the foundation and any heating and air conditioning installed. Check local building codes and floor elevations to determine specific foundation requirements.

To receive the rebate:

1. Purchase any of the Katrina Cottage Series blueprints PLUS at least $15,000 of your materials to build the cottage at Lowe's before 12/31/09. Requests must be postmarked by 1/31/10. Claims postmarked after this date will not be honored.
2. Limit one gift card per set of plans.
3. Please allow 3-4 weeks for processing. If you do not receive a gift card after 4 weeks, visit www.lowes.com/rebates, or you may call 1-877-204-1223.
4. Please keep a copy of all materials submitted for your records.
5. Copy the entire sale receipt(s), including store name, location, purchase date, and invoice number, showing blueprint purchase and total amount spent.
6. Mail this complete page with your name, address and other information below, along with a copy of the receipt(s).

Name ______________________________

Street Address ______________________________

City ______________________________

State/Zip ______________________________

Daytime phone number (   ) - ______________

E-mail address ______________________________

Katrina Cottage Plan # purchased ______________________________

I purchased a
- ☐ Six-Set Plan Package
- ☐ Builder's CAD Package

MAIL TO:
Lowe's Katrina Cottage Gift Card
P.O. Box 3029
Young America, MN 55558-3029

Check the status of your rebate at www.lowes.com/rebates

Other terms and conditions. Requests from groups will not be honored. Fraudulent submission of multiple requests could result in federal prosecution under the U.S. Mail Fraud Statutes (18 USC, Section 1341 and 1342). Offer good in the U.S.A. only. Void where prohibited, taxed or restricted by law. If you do not receive your rebate within 3-4 weeks, please call 1-877-204-1223 or visit www.lowes.com/rebates. This page may not be reproduced, traded or sold. Please keep a copy for future reference.

Frequently Asked Questions

KC1185 front elevation, see plan on page K19. Reprinted with permission of *Cottage Living* magazine. Photograph by Robbie Caponetto.

Do I need to have the plans reviewed by a local engineer?

Yes. Building codes vary due to the great differences in geography and climate throughout the United States and Canada. Each state, county and municipality has its own building codes, zone requirements, ordinances and building regulations. Plans may need to be modified to comply with local requirements regarding snow loads, energy codes, hurricane, soil and seismic conditions and a wide range of other matters. Plans should be reviewed by a local professional architect or engineer prior to the start of construction to verify that they comply with all applicable codes.

How is a Katrina Cottage different from a trailer or mobile home?

The cottages are designed to the same specifications as a full-scale house. They are designed to withstand 140-MPH wind gusts and are constructed utilizing quality materials. For example, the siding is termite and rot resistant, and the wallboard is moisture, mold and mildew resistant. The only difference between the cottages and a traditional house is the size. The cottages are smaller to make them more affordable and faster to build.

Are the cottages expandable?
Some of the cottages are designed to expand with optional additions as time and funds allow.

What is included when I purchase the plan?
There are two types of plan packages that can be purchased, both include full drawings needed for construction. A six-set plan package is offered so you have enough copies for your bank, contractors and sub-contractors. We also offer a Builder's CAD Package which is a complete set of construction drawings in an electronic file format. See page K32 for a more detailed description of The Builder's CAD Package and pricing for both packages.

What materials can and can't be purchased at Lowe's to build a Katrina Cottage plan?
Products that can be purchased at Lowe's to build your home include: studs, framing material, insulation, fixtures, electrical, plumbing, appliances, decorative items and more are included. The only items that can't be purchased at Lowe's include the HVAC system and septic/ sewer system.

Will the Lowe's Katrina Cottage require ground reinforcement or a foundation?
Because Lowe's Katrina Cottages are considered permanent structures, they do require a foundation. In some cases, local ordinances may require the house to be built on piers. Make sure to follow all local building codes when constructing a Lowe's Katrina Cottage. Homeowners will need to check the flood elevation of the lot to ensure piers are set at the proper height.

Do I have to use the 140-MPH storm rated materials to build my cottage?
No. A Lowe's store can adjust the material list to include logical replacement items for your region.

How much assembly is required? Do I need my own contractor?
Lowe's Katrina Cottages are designed to be "stick built" homes, and a licensed contractor is recommended. Although much of the work can be performed by a qualified do-it-yourselfer, there are several steps in the process requiring inspection by a qualified home inspector. A licensed contractor will be well aware of how to build the cottage according to local codes. Contractors can be located through your area's chamber of commerce. A licensed electrician and structural engineer may be required.

How long does it take to build a Lowe's Katrina Cottage?
The construction time of a Lowe's Katrina Cottage is dependent on the size and type of cottage built. A cottage can be completed in as little as 6 - 8 weeks, but variables, such as weather, labor and regulatory compliance may come into play. Always talk with your contractor when scheduling build timelines.

KC1185 Living room. Reprinted with permission of *Cottage Living* magazine. Photograph by Robbie Caponetto.

Using the Katrina Cottage

Rendering by Richard Chenoweth

Lowe's Katrina Cottages can be used in several ways. They can be clustered in **villages**, built as **grow houses** – the first piece of a larger home – or used as an **accessory building** in the back of a property.

Villages

Through design, a single Lowe's Katrina Cottage creates a dignified home for an individual family. But clustered together in villages, these cottages do even more – they create a sense of place. They create communities.

The standard practice after a disaster is to provide large parks with endless rows of FEMA trailers, which display practically no traits of individuality or sense of place. Lowe's Katrina Cottages are designed to offer an alternative to not only the trailer parks in place for disaster housing, but also trailer parks established as affordable housing.

Villages of Lowe's Katrina Cottages reach all facets of life, providing options for both people looking for affordable housing as well as those who simply don't want or need a larger house.

The Grow House

Several of the Lowe's Katrina Cottage designs have the unique ability to expand and become part of a larger home constructed later. This is known as a "grow house" or "seed house." And it's often how homes were built prior to the 1950's.

Architects once designed homes with the specific intention to add to them later. When a family required an extra bedroom, it wasn't necessary to stick a "For Sale" sign in the yard and move to a new neighborhood. The family simply added a bedroom to the existing house.

For several of the Lowe's Katrina Cottages, the initial cottage is the first piece of a more expansive home. Once the cottage is constructed, an owner can choose to build other parts of the house at any time in the future. Designers of the Lowe's Katrina Cottage put much thought into where windows and doors were placed, specifically to make growing the house easier. As your need for more space grows, so can your home.

Accessory Buildings

Accessory buildings, also known as "out buildings," are freestanding structures added in the back of a property. They are commonly used as in-law flats, guest cottages, studios and hunting cabins. In areas destroyed by a hurricane, the smaller Lowe's Katrina Cottages can be built in the back of a property as an accessory building free of the footprint of the house. Once the main house is rebuilt, the cottage can be converted into a guesthouse, adding value and creating an asset. Lowe's Katrina Cottages can also be built in the backyards of existing houses for any of the uses listed above, or for an elderly parent or rental property.

New Urbanism

Applying lessons from the past to build the future

The concepts for using Lowe's Katrina Cottage are based on the principles of "New Urbanism," also known as Traditional Neighborhood Developments (TNDs). New Urbanist neighborhoods are walkable communities designed to contain a diverse range of housing and businesses. For example, a New Urbanist neighborhood might have a retail store on the first floor of a building with residential space on the upper floor. New Urbanism also supports regional planning for open space, mixed-use and mixed-income development.

These strategies could very well be the best way to reduce time people spend in traffic, to increase the supply of affordable housing and to rein in suburban sprawl. The Lowe's Katrina Cottage was born under the umbrella of New Urbanism, which is based on building compact communities that create a sense of place – a true sense of community.

Renderings by Richard Chenoweth

The Lowe's Katrina Cottage has the unique ability to be an accessory building (left) or part of a larger home that is constructed later (right).

The Design Team

The designers of the Lowe's Katrina Cottage series are leaders in the field of traditional architecture and New Urbanism. Each believes buildings can be more than shelter – they can be dignified homes. They also believe towns can be more than a collection of buildings – they can be communities.

Marianne Cusato
Designer

Reprinted with permission of *Cottage Living* magazine. Photograph by Robbie Caponetto

Acclaimed designer Marianne Cusato has received international media attention for her work on the Katrina Cottages and for her role in promoting an alternative to FEMA trailers on the Gulf Coast. In June 2006, Congress appropriated $400 million for an alternative emergency housing program, based on the idea of the Katrina Cottage. Her first cottage was the recipient of the annual People's Design Award from the Cooper-Hewitt Museum, the National Design Museum of the Smithsonian Institute.

Cusato is the principal of Cusato Cottages, LLC, a New York-based firm specializing in traditional architectural design.

Eric Moser

Geoffrey Mouen

W.A. "Bud" Lawrence

Andrés Duany
Architect

Andrés Duany and his wife, Elizabeth Plater-Zyberk, are among the most influential architects in the world today. Their town planning firm, Duany Plater-Zyberk & Company (DPZ), is recognized globally as the leader in the movement to build better communities and end suburban sprawl. Since 1980, DPZ has completed more than 300 new towns, regional plans and award-winning communities, including Seaside, Florida, dubbed by *Time* magazine as "the most astounding design achievement of its era."

Widely known as our nation's leading thinker in New Urbanism and town planning, Andrés Duany was appointed by Governor Haley Barbour to lead the Mississippi Renewal Forum. Duany and DPZ continue to play a major role in the reconstruction of hurricane-devastated areas of Louisiana and Mississippi.

Eric Moser, *Designer*

Eric Moser is the principal of Moser Design Group, Inc., located in Beaufort, South Carolina. A member of the Mississippi Renewal Forum, he specializes in the design of residential architecture for traditional neighborhoods throughout the Southeast. Moser's work has been featured in a variety of publications, including *Period Homes*, *Southern Accents* and the *Wall Street Journal*.

Geoffrey Mouen, *Architect*

Geoffrey Mouen has more than 15 years of professional design experience in architecture and New Urban town planning, including serving as town architect for Celebration 1999-2001. He designed the Builder Magazine Showcase Home for the 2005 International Builders Show and has been honored with a Palladio Award for his work in the new traditional development, Baldwin Park.

W. A. "Bud" Lawrence, *Designer*

Bud Lawrence, is the principal partner of Period Style Homes, Inc., specializing in land planning and residential design. Throughout his 34-year career, he has designed residential projects in classical, traditional and vernacular styles nationally and internationally. His designs have been published in many periodicals, won numerous regional and national awards and are featured in several neo-traditional/New Urbanism communities.

Lowe's Katrina Cottage Pre-Construction Tip List

- ☐ **Secure land making sure it meets criteria for the Lowe's Katrina Cottage plan selected**
  1. Meets building code and zoning restrictions.
  2. Deed should be researched for clear title.
  3. Survey should be completed.
  4. If septic system required, assure land will accommodate system.
  5. If on site well required, contact well drilling company for advice on water availability.

- ☐ **Secure General Contractor to construct cottage**
  1. Interview several contractors.
  2. Check references.
  3. Check with Better Business Bureau for positive/negative information.
  4. Assure contractor carries insurance (Workman's Comp and premises liability).
  5. Have any contracts reviewed by your attorney before signing.
  6. Review previous homes constructed by contractor.

- ☐ **Verify Engineering Requirements and Local Codes**
  1. Determine proper foundation according to local building codes. (Lowe's Katrina Cottage does not include house foundation.)
  2. Ensure footings are poured to local codes. (Will require inspection.) (May be handled by contractor.)

- ☐ **Secure financing**
  1. Work through a local bank to secure contruction loan financing for the materials and labor.
  2. Ensure you will have sufficient draws to pay contractor and material suppliers as construction progresses.

- ☐ **Obtain necessary building permits. (May be handled by contractor)**
  1. Be aware of all inspections that are required in your local market so each phase required has been inspected by Code Enforcement.
  2. Get permits needed for driveway connection. (May be handled by contractor.)

- ☐ **Prepare For Construction**
  1. Contact utility company to provide temporary electric power at job site. (May be handled by contractor.)
  2. Schedule well drilling (if needed) ahead of construction. (May be handled by contractor.)
  3. Have a dumpster put on site for debris collection. (May be handled by contractor.)
  4. Meet with excavator to mark off building perimeter and site prep. (May be handled by contractor.)
  5. Take out a Builder's Risk insurance policy with theft rider before construction begins. Ensure contractor notifies supplier when ready to have framing lumber shipped.

- ☐ **During Construction**
  1. Visit construction site often to review progress and answer questions.
  2. Ensure contractor has confirmed window and door delivery.
  3. Ensure contractor has contacted mechanical contractors. (Lowe's Katrina cottage does not include HVAC system.)
  4. Ensure contractor has scheduled gypsum delivery from supplier.
  5. Ensure contractor has scheduled delivery of interior trim and it is stored inside of house.
  6. Ensure contractor has scheduled delivery of cabinets, vanities, finish plumbing etc. when ready.
  7. Ensure contractor has scheduled delivery of flooring.

- ☐ **Construction Inspections**
  1. Schedule septic system installation before construction is complete. (Will require inspection.) (May be handled by contractor.)
  2. Ensure well water is tested so you will be able to obtain Certificate of Occupancy.
  3. Ensure contractor gets final inspections completed to be able to receive Certificate of Occupancy.

- ☐ **Finishing Up**
  1. Provide contractor with a list of issues found in completed structure and make sure these are taken care of.
  2. Ensure contractor completes interior and exterior clean up as well as landscaping if in original contract.
  3. Adjust insurance policy to full Homeowner's coverage.
  4. Arrange for lending institution to convert construction loan to a permanent loan.
  5. Ensure all bills have been paid and contractor has no liens pending.
  6. Move your furniture in and enjoy your Lowe's Katrina Cottage!

The purpose of this document is to provide general tips and guidelines for constructing a residential dwelling and is not intended to be all inclusive of the requirements for building a house. Consult with a professional builder/contractor/banker/attorney and the appropriate local, state, and federal governmental agencies applicable to building in your specific location.

Resources & Links

www.lowes.com/KatrinaCottage

www.cusatocottages.com

www.chamberofcommerce.com

Beyond the Home

Personalize Your Lowe's Katrina Cottage with Distinctive Outdoor Accessories

Pretty as a Picture

The right fence can make your home a focal point, much like the right frame on a picture. There are many styles to choose from – charming picket fencing, privacy fencing and low-maintenance, vinyl fencing are just a few. Consider the look you want to achieve and lifestyle needs when selecting the perfect "frame" for your cottage.

Color Me Home

Whether you prefer the lush look of a thick, green lawn or a profusion of color to greet you whenever walking outside, landscaping should be a reflection of what makes you feel good. Trees, flowers, shrubs, rock – regardless of the size of your yard, landscaping materials add beauty and interest.

Decorative Details

The possibilities are virtually endless for adding decorative touches outside your new cottage. A new rug for the front porch that's suitable for use year round; outdoor lamps, torches, rocking chairs and string lights for entertaining; garden stakes, statuaries, fountains – any of these serve to make the outdoors another "room" of your cottage.

Katrina Cottage Index

Order Form

Please send me -

PLAN NUMBER 537 - ______________________

☐ Six-Set Plan Package ($700) $________

☐ Builder's CAD Package ($950) $________

SUBTOTAL $________

Sales Tax (MO residents add 7%) $________

☐ Shipping / Handling (see chart at right) $________

TOTAL (U.S. funds only - sorry no CODs) $________

I hereby authorize HDA, Inc. to charge this purchase to my credit card account (check one):

☐  ☐  ☐  ☐ 

Credit Card Number ______________________

Expiration Date ______________________

Signature ______________________

Name ______________________
(Please print or type)

Street Address ______________________
(Please **do not** use a PO Box)

City ______________________

State ______________________

Zip ______________________

Daytime Phone Number (____) - ______________________

E-mail address ______________________

Thank you for your order!

How To Order Plans

For fastest service, Call Toll-Free 1-877-379-3420 day or night

THREE Easy Ways To Order

1. CALL toll-free 1-877-379-3420 for credit card orders. MasterCard, Visa, Discover and American Express are accepted.
2. FAX your order to 1-314-770-2226.
3. MAIL the Order Form to:

HDA, Inc.
944 Anglum Road
St. Louis, MO 63042
Attn: Customer Service Dept.

Before You Order

Builder's CAD Package - A CAD package is a complete set of construction drawings in an electronic file format. If you purchase a CAD package, you have the option to take the plan to a local design professional who uses AutoCAD or DataCAD and they can modify the plan much easier than a paper-based drawing. The Builder's CAD Package includes a one-time build copyright release, allowing you to make changes and the necessary copies needed to build your home.

Exchange Policies - Since blueprints are printed in response to your order, we cannot honor requests for refunds. However, if for some reason you find the plan purchased does not meet your requirements, you may exchange that plan for another plan in our collection within 90 days of purchase. At the time of the exchange, you will be charged a processing fee of 25% of the original plan package price, plus the difference in price between the plan packages (if applicable) and the cost to ship the new plans.

Building Codes & Requirements - At the time the construction drawings were prepared, every effort was made to ensure that plans and specifications meet nationally recognized codes. Our plans conform to most national building codes. Because building codes vary from area to area, some drawing modifications and/or the assistance of a professional designer or architect may be necessary to comply with your local codes or to accommodate specific building site conditions. We advise you to consult with local building officials for information regarding codes governing your area.

Questions?

Call Our Customer Service Number

1-877-379-3420

Katrina Blueprint Pricing

Six-Set Plan Package	$700
Builder's CAD Package	$950

Shipping & Handling Charges

U.S. Shipping - (AK and HI express only)	
Regular (allow 7-10 business days)	$17.50
Priority (allow 3-5 business days)	$30.00
Express* (allow 1-2 business days)	$45.00
Canada Shipping (to/from)† -	
Standard (allow 8-12 business days)	$40.00
Express* (allow 3-5 business days)	$75.00

* For express delivery, please call us by 11:00 a.m. Monday-Friday CST

† Orders may be subject to custom's fees and/or duties/taxes

Overseas Shipping/International - Call, fax, or e-mail (plans@hdainc.com) for shipping costs.

LOWE'S®

HOME PLANS

DISTINGUISHED SMALL HOMES

PLANS FROM THE LOWE'S LEGACY SERIES

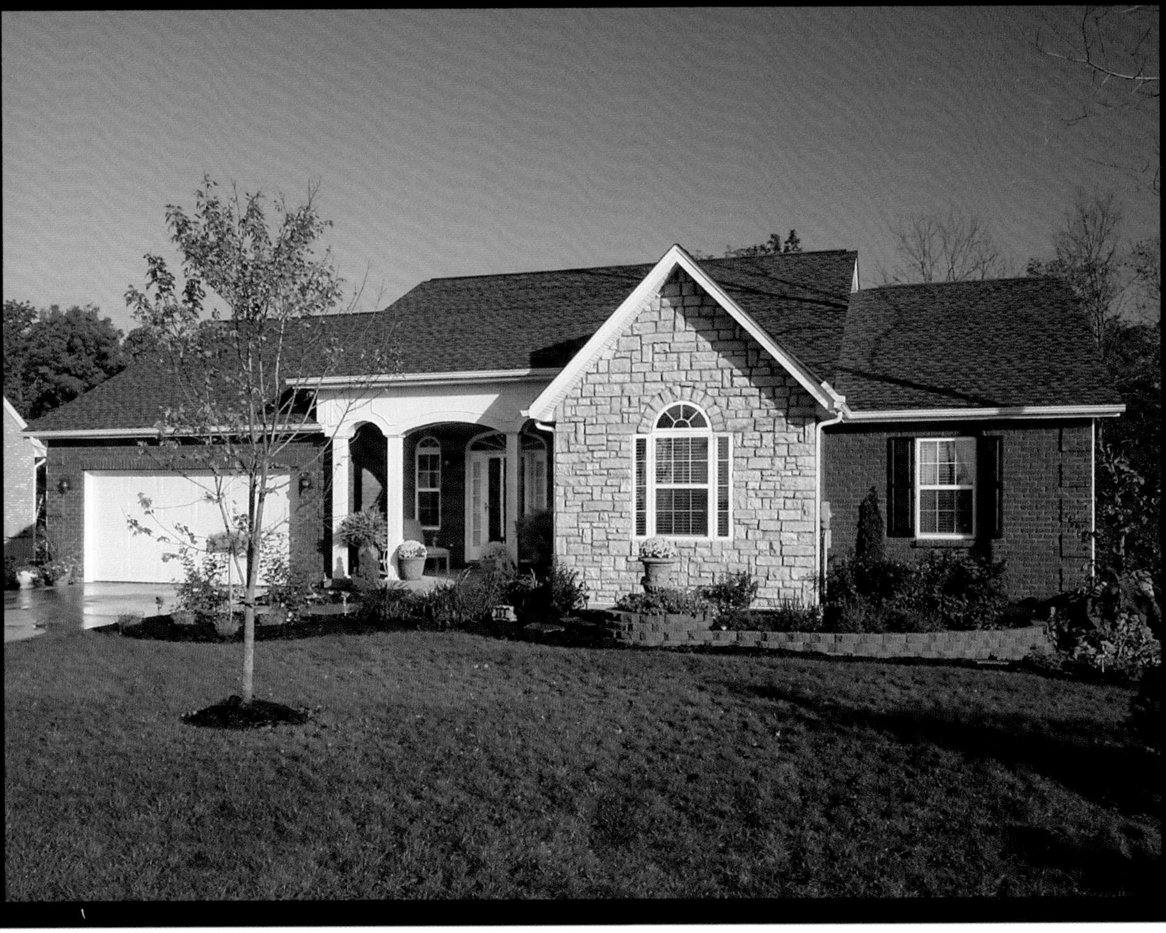

COVER HOME - The houses shown clockwise on the front cover are Plan #537-072L-0008, photo by Mark Englund; Plan #537-065L-0170, photo by Studer Residential Design; and Plan #537-200K-KC544; courtesy of Marianne Cusato. Please see Index for more information.

LOWE'S LEGACY SERIES: DISTINGUISHED SMALL HOME PLANS is published by HDA, Inc., 944 Anglum Road, St. Louis, MO, 63042. Printed in U.S.A. © 2008. Artist drawings and photos shown in this publication may vary slightly from the actual working drawings. Some photos are shown in mirror reverse. Please refer to the floor plan for accurate layout.

ISBN-13: 978-1-58678-076-0
ISBN-10: 1-58678-076-X

Current Printing

10 9 8 7 6 5 4 3 2 1

HDA, Inc.
944 Anglum Rd.
St. Louis, Missouri 63042
corporate website - www.hdainc.com

HOME PLANS

DISTINGUISHED SMALL HOMES

CONTENTS

It's what separates you from the have knots.

LESS WANE, LESS WARP, AND FEWER KNOTS.

Top Choice lumber is hand selected at the mill and quality is verified by third-party inspectors. Plus, our treated lumber has a limited lifetime warranty against rot and decay. So whether you're adding a deck or a room, insist on Top Choice for your next project.

EXCLUSIVELY AT:

LOWE'S®

Let's Build Something Together™

Making Changes To Your Plan

We understand that it is difficult to find blueprints for a home that will meet all your needs. That is why HDA, Inc. is pleased to offer home plan modification services.

Typical home plan modifications include:

- Changing foundation type
- Adding square footage to a plan
- Changing the entry into a garage
- Changing a two-car garage to a three-car garage or making a garage larger
- Redesigning kitchen, baths, and bedrooms
- Changing exterior elevations
- Or most other home plan modifications

Home plan modifications we cannot make include:

- Reversing the plans
- Adapting/engineering plans to meet your local building codes
- Combining parts of two different plans (due to copyright laws)

Our plan modification service is easy to use. Simply:

1. Decide on the modifications you want. For the most accurate quote, be as detailed as possible and refer to rooms in the same manner as the floor plan (i.e. if the floor plan refers to a "den" then use "den" in your description). Including a sketch of the modified floor plan is always helpful.

2. Complete and e-mail the modification request form that can be found online at www.houseplansandmore.com.

3. Within two business days, you will receive your quote. Quotes do not include the cost of the reproducible masters required for our designer to legally make changes.

4. Call to accept the quote and purchase the reproducible masters. For example, if your quote is $850 and the reproducible masters for your plan are $800, your order total will be $1650 plus two shipping and handling charges (one to ship the reproducible masters to our designer and one to ship the modified plans to you).

5. Our designer will send you up to three drafts to verify your initial changes. Extra costs apply after the third draft. If additional changes are made that alter the original request, extra charges may be incurred.

6. Once you approve a draft with the final changes, we then make the changes to the reproducible masters by adding additional sheets. The original reproducible masters (with no changes) plus your new changed sheets will be shipped to you.

Other Important Information:

- Plans cannot be redrawn in reverse format. All modifications will be made to match the reproducible master's original layout. Once you receive the plans, you can make reverse copies at your local blueprint shop.

- Our staff designer will provide the first draft for your review within 4 weeks (plus shipping time) of receiving your order.

- You will receive up to three drafts to review before your original changes are modified. The first draft will totally encompass all modifications based on your original request. Additional changes not included in your original request will be charged separately at an hourly rate of $75 or a flat quoted rate.

- Modifications will be drawn on a separate sheet with the changes shown and a note to see the main sheet for details. For example, a floor plan sheet from the original set (i.e. Sheet 3) would be followed by a new floor plan sheet with changes (i.e. Sheet A-3).

- Plans are drawn to meet national building codes. Modifications will not be drawn to any particular state or county codes, thus we cannot guarantee that the revisions will meet your local building codes. You may be required to have a local architect or designer review the plans in order to have them comply with your state or county building codes.

- Time and cost estimates are good for 90 calendar days.

- All modification requests need to be submitted in writing. Verbal requests will not be accepted.

2 Easy Steps for FAST Service

1. Visit www.houseplansandmore.com to download the modification request form
2. E-mail the completed form to customize@hdainc.com or fax to 913-856-7751

If you are not able to access the internet, please call 1-877-379-3420 (Monday-Friday, 8am-5pm CST)

What's The Right Plan For You?

Choosing a home plan is an exciting but difficult task. Many factors play a role in what home plan is best for you and your family. To help you get started, we have pinpointed some of the major factors to consider when searching for your dream home. Take the time to evaluate your family's needs and you will have an easier time sorting through all of the home plans offered in this book.

BUDGET: The first thing to consider is your budget. Many items take part in this budget, from ordering the blueprints to the last doorknob purchased. Once you have found your dream home plan, visit our website at www.houseplansandmore.com to get a cost-to-build estimate to ensure that the finished product is still within your cost range.

FAMILY LIFESTYLE: After your budget is deciphered, you need to assess you and your family's lifestyle needs. Think about the stage of life you are at now, and what stages you will be going through in the future. Ask yourself questions to figure out how much room you need now and if you will need room for expansion. Are you married? Do you have children? How many children do you plan on having? Are you an empty-nester?

Incorporate in your planning any frequent guests you may have, including elderly parents, grandchildren or adult children who may live with you.

Does your family entertain a lot? If so, think about the rooms you will need to do so. Will you need both formal and informal spaces? Do you need a gourmet kitchen? Do you need a game room and/or a wet bar?

FLOOR PLAN LAYOUTS: When looking through our home plans, imagine yourself walking through the house. Consider the flow from the entry to the living, sleeping and gathering areas. Does the layout ensure privacy for the master bedroom? Does the garage enter near the kitchen for easy unloading? Does the placement of the windows provide enough privacy from any neighboring properties? Do you plan on using furniture you already have? Will this furniture fit in the appropriate rooms? When you find a plan you want to purchase, be sure to picture yourself actually living in it.

Experts in the field suggest that the best way to determine your needs is to begin by listing everything you like or dislike about your current home.

EXTERIOR SPACES: There are many different home styles ranging from Traditional to Contemporary. Flip through and find which style most appeals to you and the neighborhood in which you plan to build. Also think of your site and how the entire house will fit on this site. Picture any landscaping you plan on incorporating into the design. Using your imagination is key when choosing a home plan.

Choosing a home plan can be an intimidating experience. Asking yourself these questions before you get started on the search will help you through the process. With our large selection of multiple styles we are certain you will find your dream home in the following pages.

THE LOWE'S LEGACY SERIES

LEG'A'CY: SOMETHING THAT IS HANDED DOWN OR REMAINS FOR GENERATIONS

HDA, Inc. is proud to introduce to you the Lowe's Legacy Series. The home plans in this collection carry on the Lowe's tradition of quality and expertise, and will continue to do so for many generations.

Choosing a home plan can be a daunting task. With the Legacy Series, we will set your mind at ease. Selecting a plan from this book will ensure a home designed with the Lowe's standard of excellence, creating a dream home for you and your family.

This collection of Legacy Series plans includes our most popular distinguished small home plans. Browse through the pages to discover a home with the options and special characteristics you need.

Along with one-of-a-kind craftsmanship, all Legacy Series home plans offer industry-leading material lists available for purchase. These accurate and affordable material lists will save you a considerable amount of time and money, providing you with the quantity, dimensions and descriptions of the major building materials necessary to construct your home. You'll get faster and more accurate bids from contractors and material suppliers, and you'll save money by paying for only the materials you need.

The Lowe's Legacy Series is the perfect place to start your search for the home of your dreams. You will find the expected beauty you want and the functional efficiency you need, all designed with unmatched quality.

Turn the page and begin the wonderful journey of finding your new home.

Photos clockwise from top: 537-001D-0003, page 70; 537-021D-0001, page 69; 537-021D-0011, page 72; 537-001D-0064, page 66.

LOWE'S LEGACY SERIES

Plan Number: 537-005D-0001 | Price Code: B

Special Features

- 1,400 total square feet of living area
- Master bedroom is secluded for privacy
- The large utility room has additional cabinet space
- Covered porch provides an outdoor seating area
- Roof dormers add great curb appeal
- Living room and master bedroom feature vaulted ceilings
- Oversized two-car garage has storage space
- 3 bedrooms, 2 baths, 2-car garage
- Basement foundation, drawings also include crawl space foundation

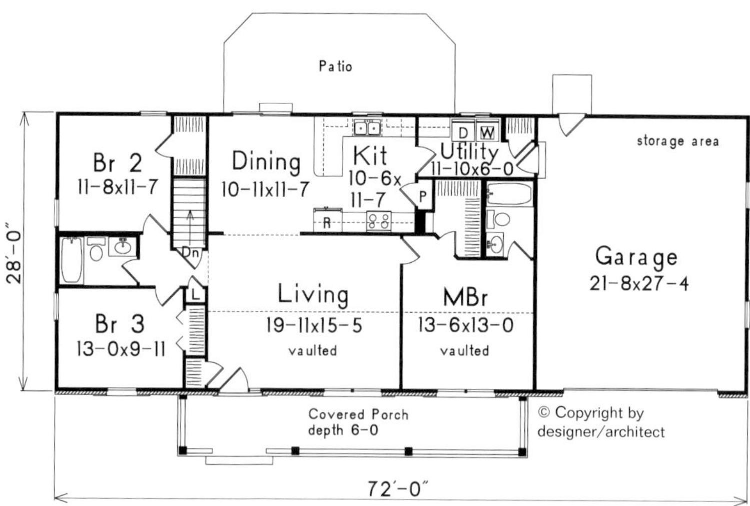

To Order See Page 288 | Call Toll-Free 1-877-379-3420

PLAN NUMBER: 537-058D-0016 | PRICE CODE: B

LOWE'S LEGACY SERIES

SPECIAL FEATURES

- 1,558 total square feet of living area
- The spacious utility room is located conveniently between the garage and kitchen/dining area
- Bedrooms are separated from the living area by a hallway
- Enormous living area with fireplace and vaulted ceiling opens to the kitchen and dining area
- Master bedroom is enhanced with a large bay window, walk-in closet and private bath
- 2" x 6" exterior walls available, please order plan #537-058D-0078
- 3 bedrooms, 2 baths, 2-car garage
- Basement foundation

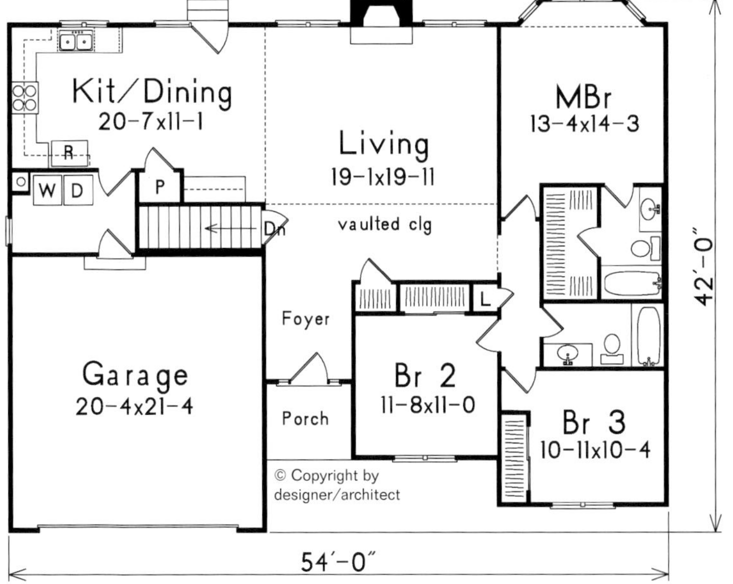

Special Features

- 962 total square feet of living area
- Both the kitchen and family room share warmth from the fireplace
- Charming facade features a covered porch on one side, screened porch on the other and attractive planter boxes
- L-shaped kitchen boasts a convenient pantry
- 2 bedrooms, 1 bath
- Crawl space foundation

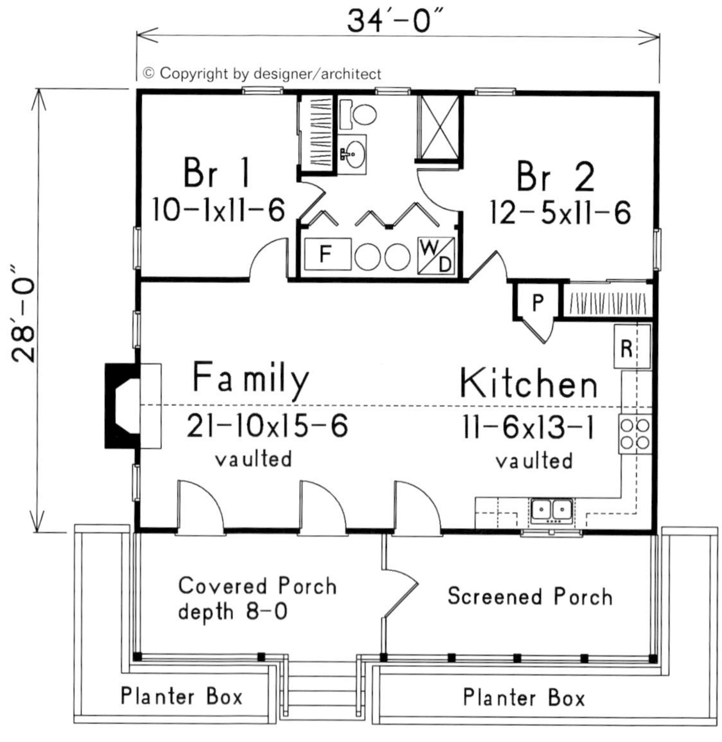

LOWE'S LEGACY SERIES

SPECIAL FEATURES

- 2,029 total square feet of living area
- Stonework, gables, roof dormer and double porches create a country flavor
- Kitchen enjoys extravagant cabinetry and counterspace in a bay, island snack bar, built-in pantry and cheery dining area with multiple tall windows
- Angled stair descends from large entry with wood columns and is open to a vaulted great room with corner fireplace
- Master bedroom boasts two walk-in closets, a private bath with double-door entry and a secluded porch
- 4 bedrooms, 2 baths, 2-car side entry garage
- Basement foundation, drawings also include crawl space and slab foundations

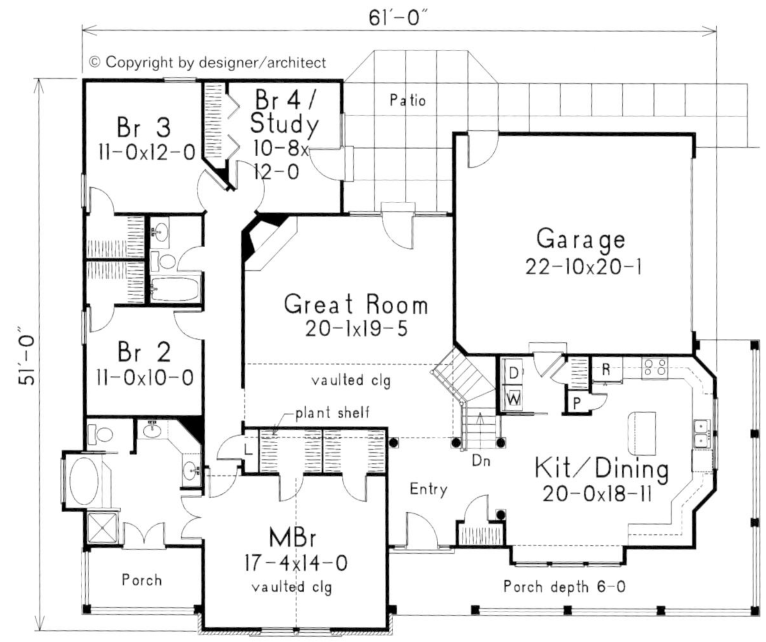

SPECIAL FEATURES

- 1,013 total square feet of living area
- Vaulted ceilings in both the family room and kitchen with dining area just beyond the breakfast bar
- Plant shelf above kitchen is a special feature
- Oversized utility room has space for a full-size washer and dryer
- Hall bath is centrally located with easy access from both bedrooms
- 2" x 6" exterior walls available, please order plan #537-058D-0073
- 2 bedrooms, 1 bath
- Slab foundation

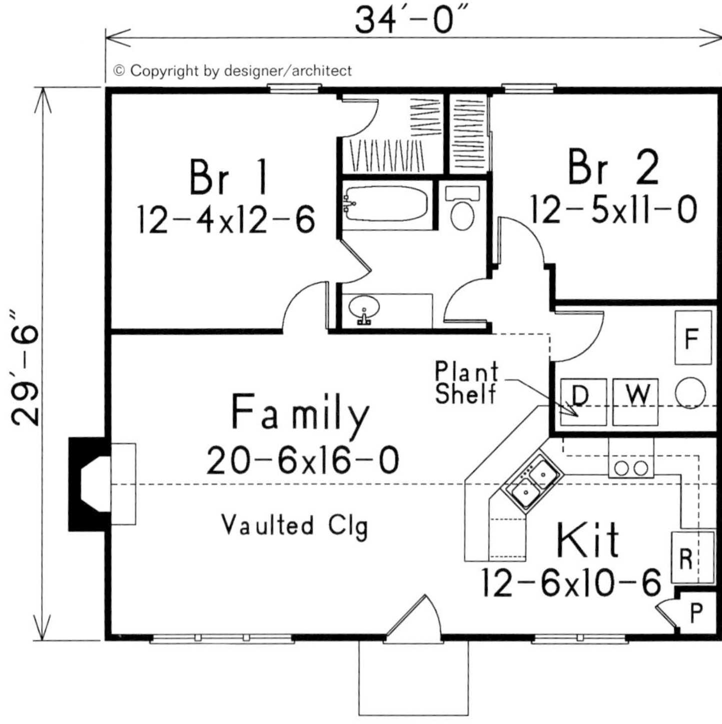

SPECIAL FEATURES

- 1,668 total square feet of living area
- Large bay windows grace the breakfast area, master bedroom and dining room
- Extensive walk-in closets and storage spaces are located throughout the home
- Handy covered entry porch
- Large living room has a fireplace, built-in bookshelves and a sloped ceiling
- 3 bedrooms, 2 baths, 2-car drive under garage
- Basement foundation

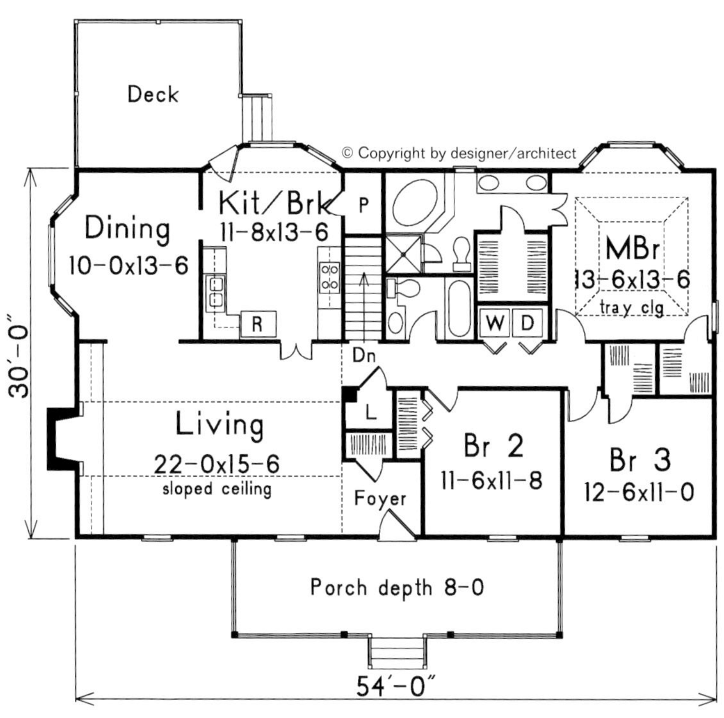

PLAN NUMBER: 537-007D-0067 | PRICE CODE: B

SPECIAL FEATURES

- 1,761 total square feet of living area
- Exterior window dressing, roof dormers and planter boxes provide visual warmth and charm
- Great room boasts a vaulted ceiling, fireplace and opens to a pass-through kitchen
- The vaulted master bedroom includes a luxury bath and walk-in closet
- Home features eight separate closets with an abundance of storage
- 4 bedrooms, 2 baths, 2-car side entry garage
- Basement foundation

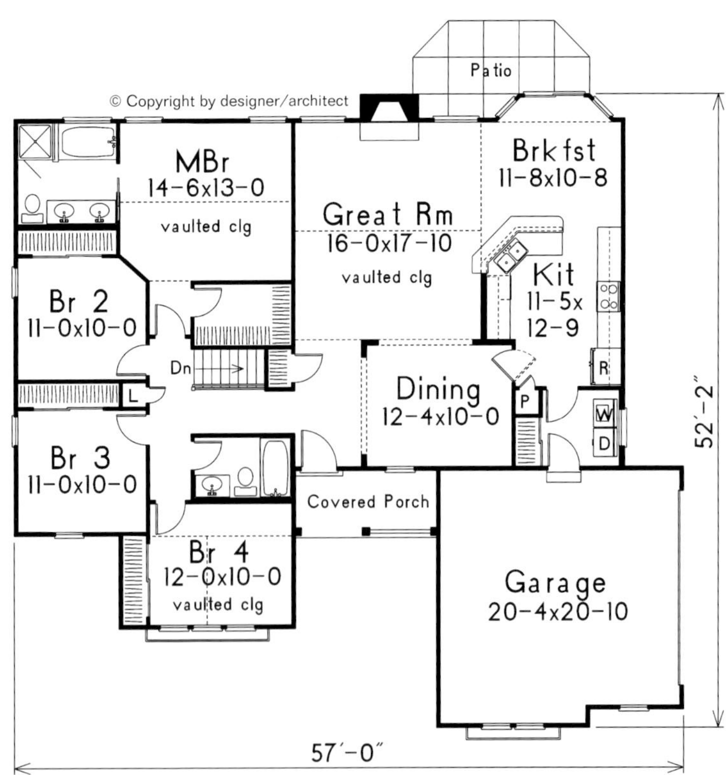

SPECIAL FEATURES

- 1,680 total square feet of living area
- Compact and efficient layout in an affordable package
- Second floor has three bedrooms all with oversized closets
- All bedrooms are located on the second floor for privacy
- 3 bedrooms, 2 1/2 baths, 2-car garage
- Basement foundation

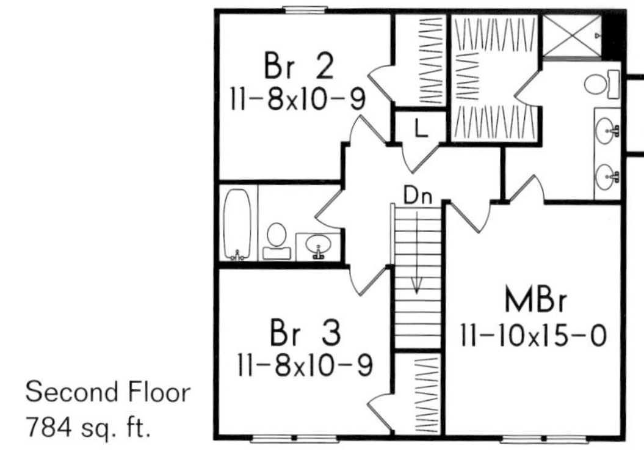

Second Floor
784 sq. ft.

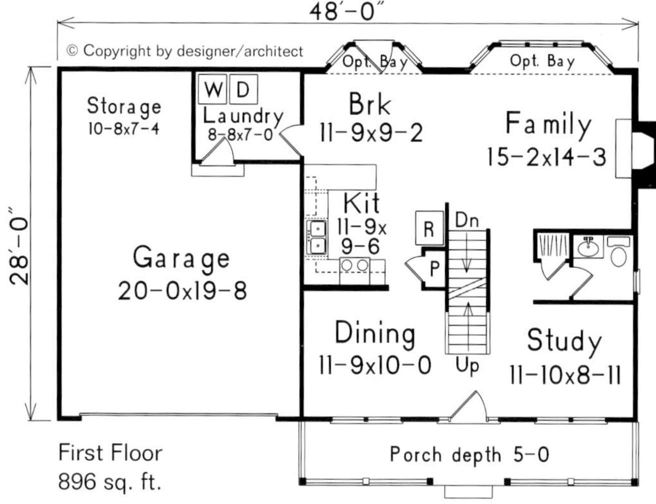

First Floor
896 sq. ft.

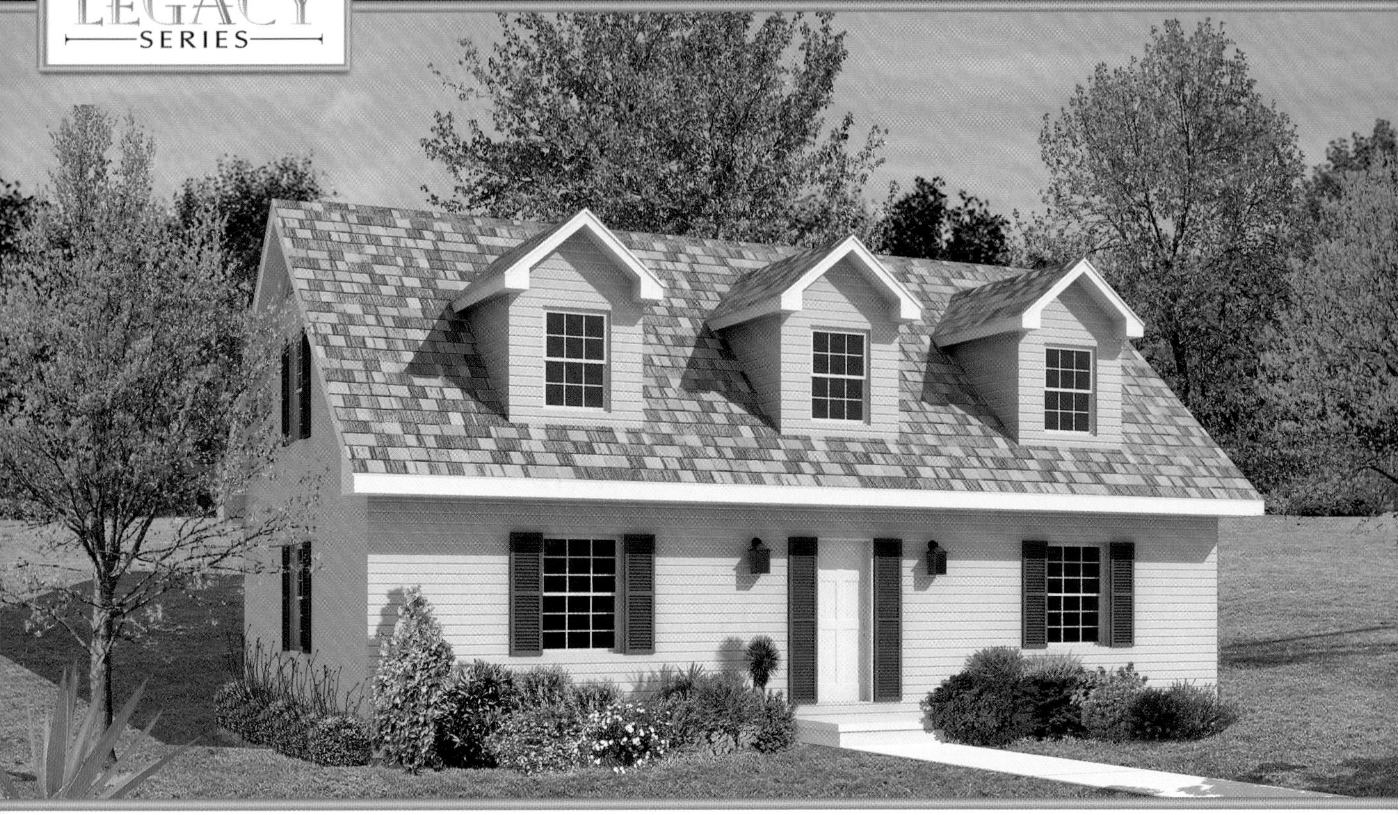

SPECIAL FEATURES

- 1,705 total square feet of living area
- Cozy design includes two bedrooms on the first floor and two bedrooms on the second floor for added privacy
- L-shaped kitchen provides easy access to the dining room and the outdoors
- Convenient first floor laundry area
- 2" x 6" exterior walls available, please order plan #537-001D-0111
- 4 bedrooms, 2 baths
- Crawl space foundation, drawings also include basement and slab foundations

Second Floor
665 sq. ft.

First Floor
1,040 sq. ft.

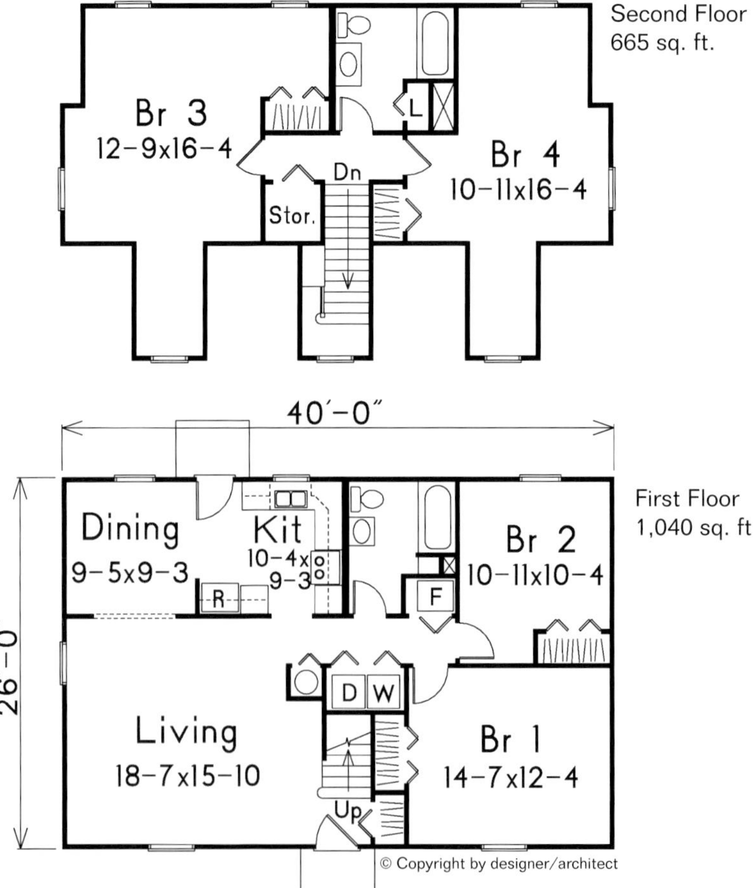

LOWE'S LEGACY SERIES

SPECIAL FEATURES

- 1,501 total square feet of living area
- Spacious kitchen with dining area is open to the outdoors
- Convenient utility room is adjacent to the garage
- Master bedroom features a private bath, dressing area and access to the large covered porch
- Large family room creates openness
- 3 bedrooms, 2 baths, 2-car side entry garage
- Basement foundation, drawings also include crawl space and slab foundations

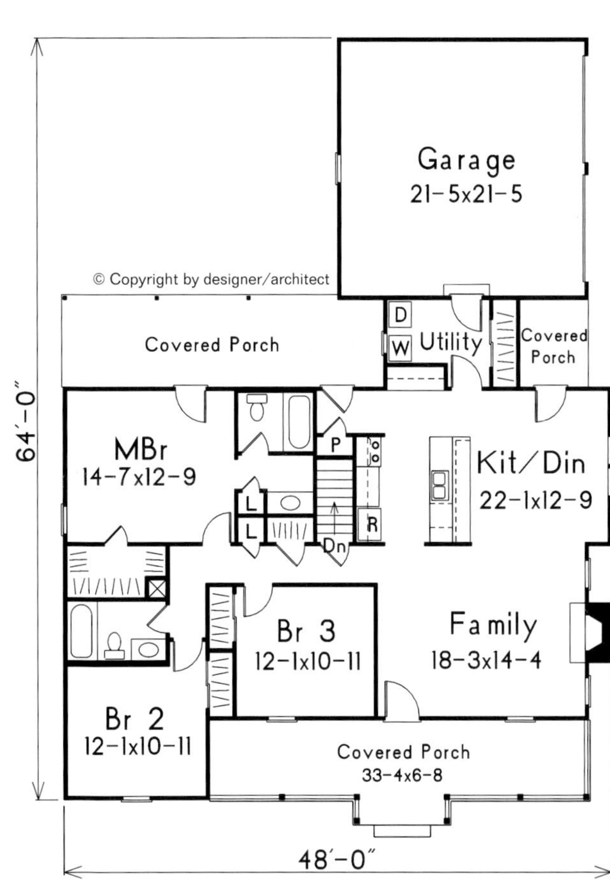

PLAN NUMBER: 537-058D-0006 | PRICE CODE: A

SPECIAL FEATURES

- 1,339 total square feet of living area
- Full-length covered porch enhances front facade
- Vaulted ceiling and stone fireplace add drama to the family room
- Walk-in closets in the bedrooms provide ample storage space
- Combined kitchen/dining area adjoins the family room for the perfect entertaining space
- 2" x 6" exterior walls available, please order plan #537-058D-0072
- 3 bedrooms, 2 1/2 baths
- Crawl space foundation

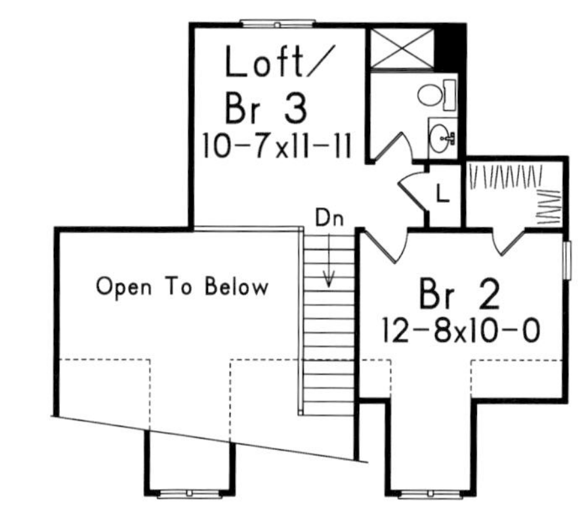

Second Floor
415 sq. ft.

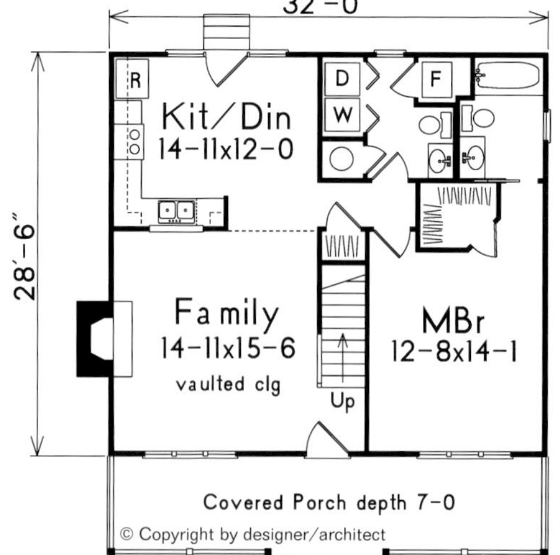

First Floor
924 sq. ft.

SPECIAL FEATURES

- 1,791 total square feet of living area
- Vaulted great room and octagon-shaped dining area enjoy a spectacular view of the covered patio
- Kitchen features a pass-through to the dining area, center island, large walk-in pantry and breakfast room with large bay window
- The master bedroom enjoys a vaulted ceiling and a sitting area
- The garage includes extra storage space
- 4 bedrooms, 2 baths, 2-car garage with storage
- Basement foundation, drawings also include crawl space and slab foundations

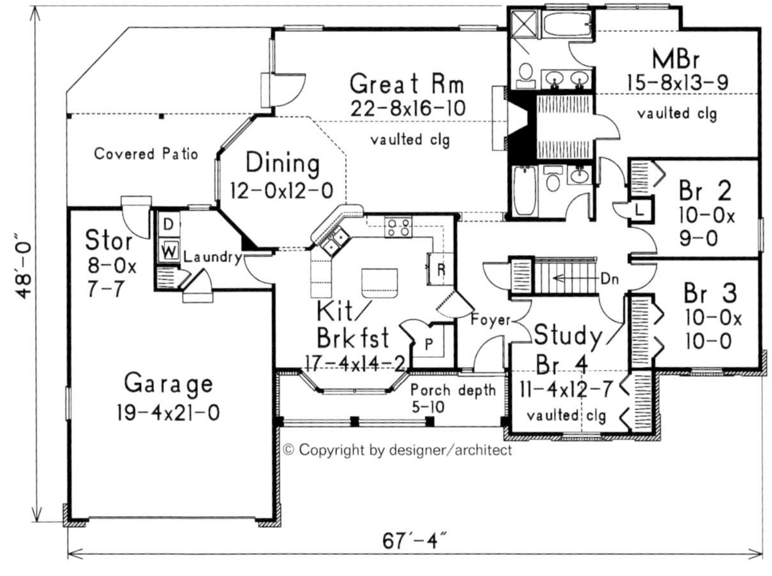

SPECIAL FEATURES

- 1,360 total square feet of living area
- Kitchen/dining room features an island workspace and plenty of dining area
- Master bedroom has a large walk-in closet and private bath
- Laundry room is adjacent to the kitchen for easy access
- Convenient workshop in garage
- Large closets in secondary bedrooms maintain organization
- 3 bedrooms, 2 baths, 2-car side entry garage
- Basement foundation, drawings also include crawl space and slab foundations

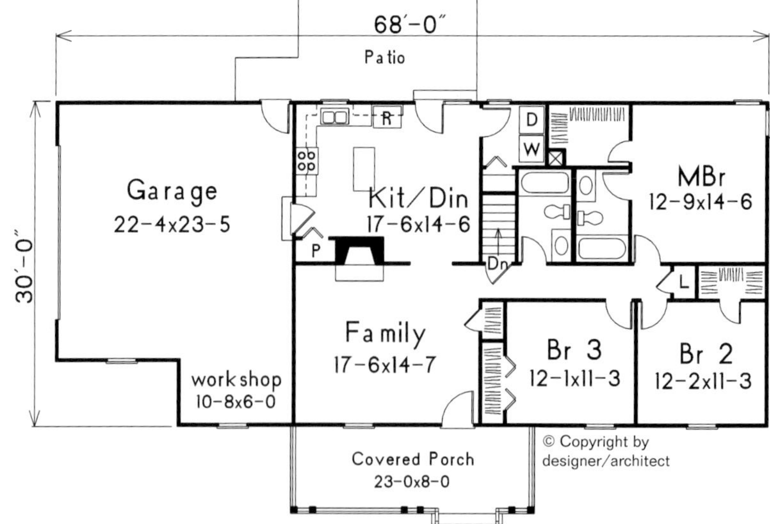

LOWE'S LEGACY SERIES

SPECIAL FEATURES

- 448 total square feet of living area
- Bedroom features a large walk-in closet ideal for storage
- Combined dining/sitting area is ideal for relaxing
- Galley-style kitchen is compact and efficient
- Covered porch adds to front facade
- 1 bedroom, 1 bath
- Slab foundation

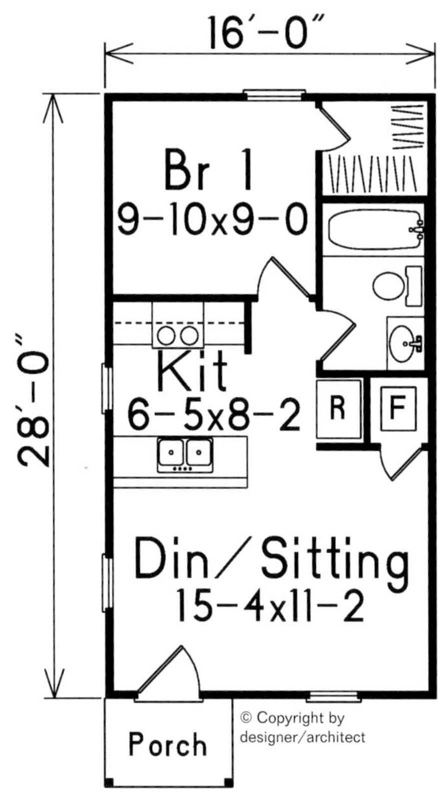

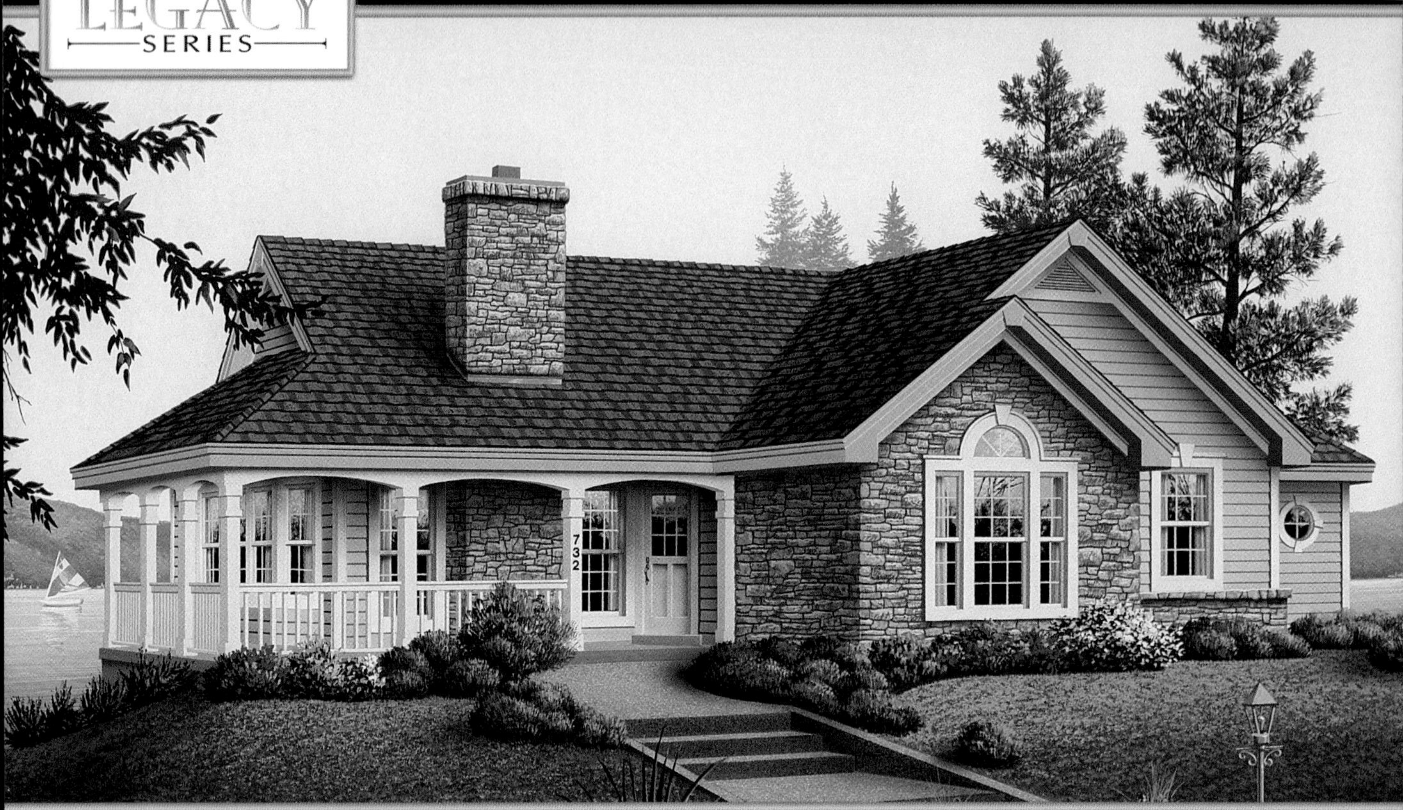

SPECIAL FEATURES

- 1,384 total square feet of living area
- Wrap-around country porch for peaceful evenings
- Vaulted great room enjoys a large bay window, stone fireplace, pass-through kitchen and awesome rear views through an atrium window wall
- Master bedroom features a double-door entry, walk-in closet and a fabulous bath
- Atrium opens to 611 square feet of optional living area below
- 2 bedrooms, 2 baths, 1-car side entry garage
- Walk-out basement foundation

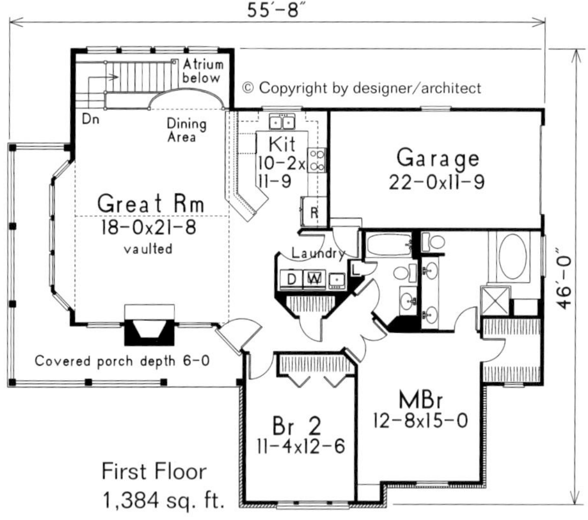

First Floor
1,384 sq. ft.

Rear View

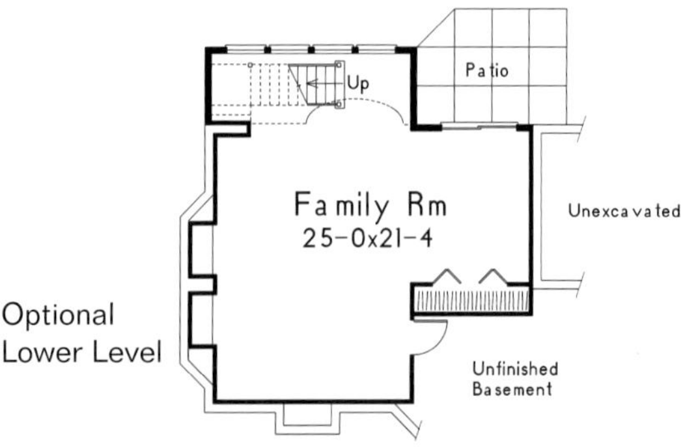

Optional
Lower Level

Plan Number: 537-007D-0036 | Price Code: A

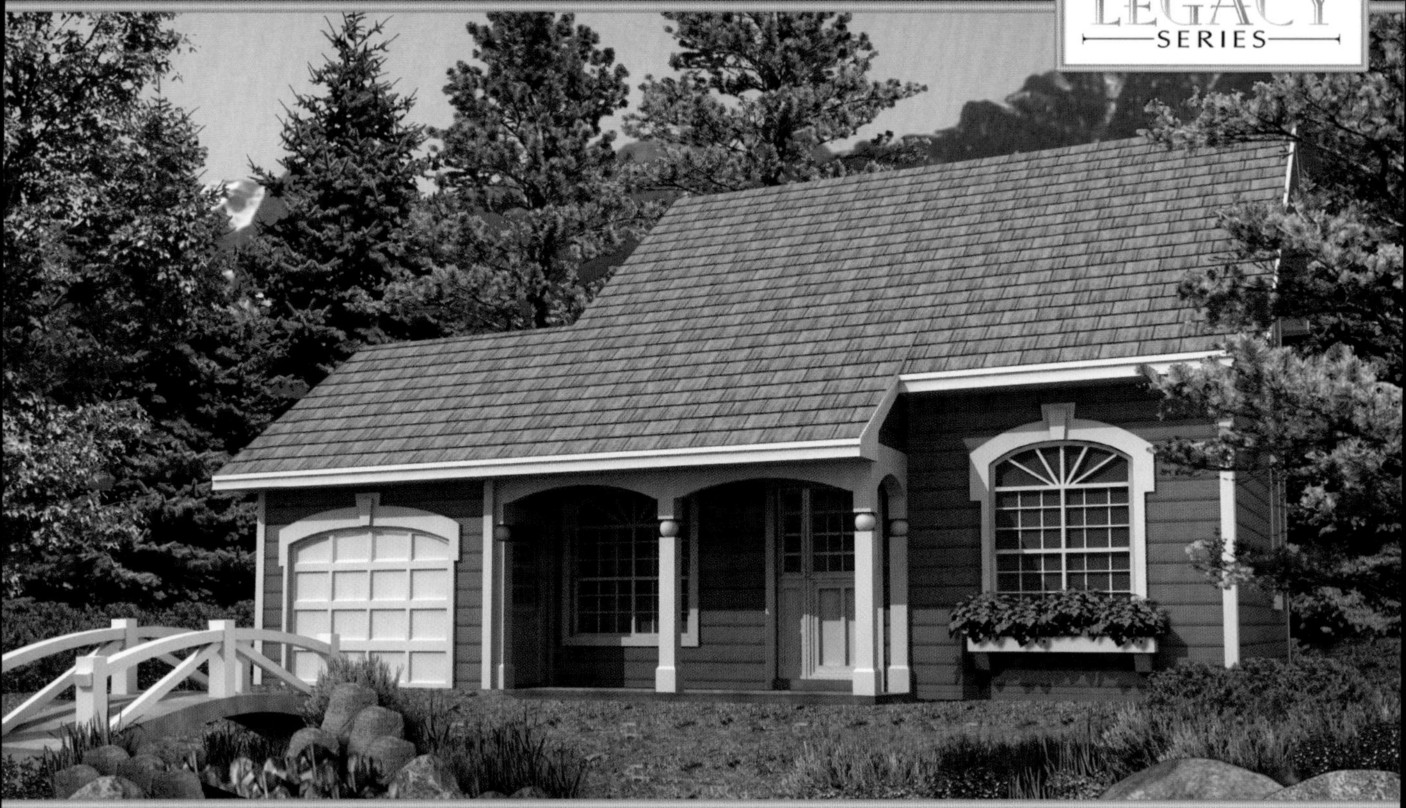

Special Features

- 1,330 total square feet of living area
- Vaulted living room is open to the bayed dining room and kitchen creating an ideal space for entertaining
- Two bedrooms, a bath and linen closet complete the first floor and are easily accessible
- The second floor offers two bedrooms with walk-in closets, a very large storage room and an opening with louvered doors which overlooks the living room
- 4 bedrooms, 2 baths, 1-car garage
- Basement foundation

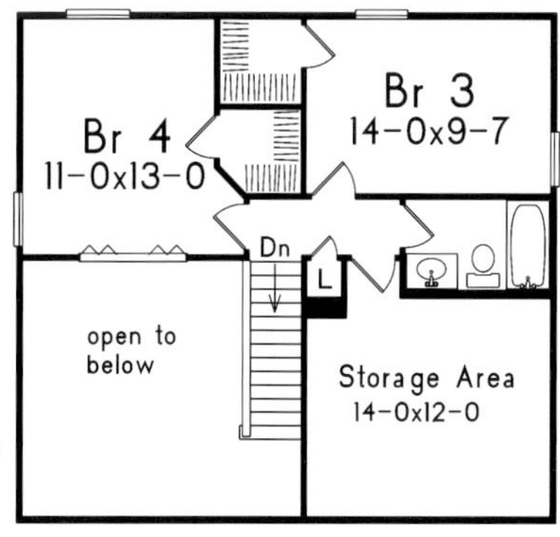

Second Floor
446 sq. ft.

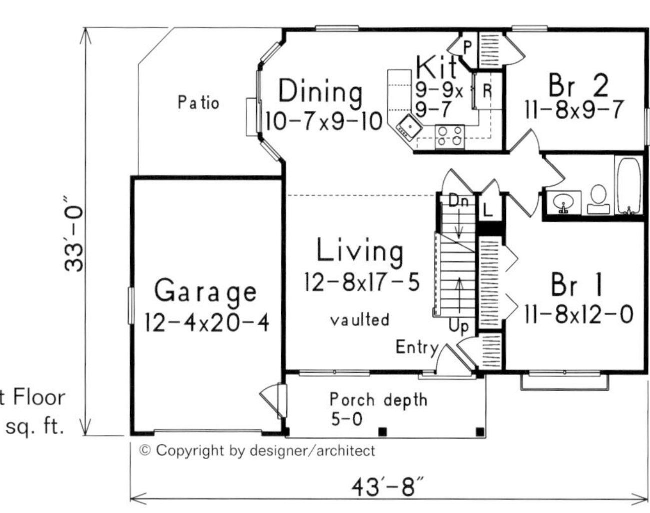

First Floor
884 sq. ft.

PLAN NUMBER: 537-033D-0012 | PRICE CODE: C

SPECIAL FEATURES

- 1,546 total square feet of living area
- Spacious, open rooms create a casual atmosphere
- Master bedroom is secluded for privacy
- Dining room features a large bay window
- Kitchen and dinette combine for added space and include access to the outdoors
- Large laundry room includes a convenient sink
- 3 bedrooms, 2 baths, 2-car garage
- Basement foundation

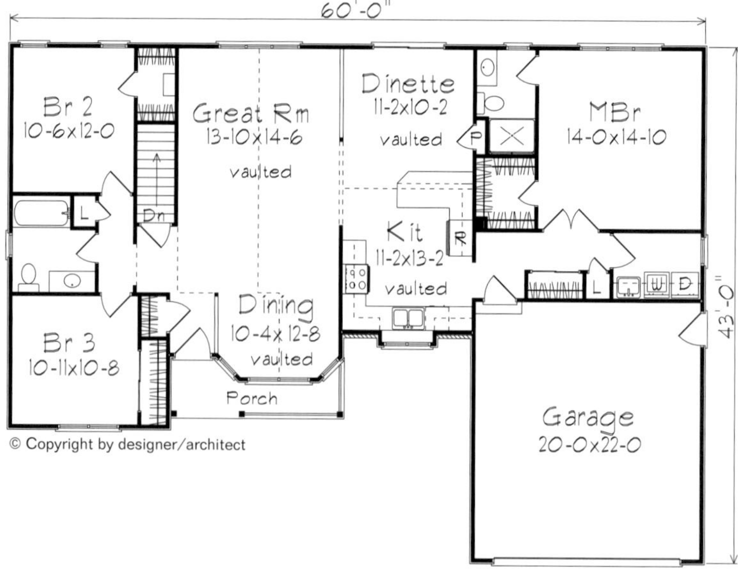

SPECIAL FEATURES

- 1,619 total square feet of living area
- Elegant home features three quaint porches and a large rear patio
- Grand-scale great room offers a dining area, fireplace with a built-in alcove and shelves for an entertainment center
- First floor master bedroom has a walk-in closet, luxury bath, bay window and access to rear patio
- Breakfast room with bay window contains a staircase that leads to the second floor bedrooms and loft
- 3 bedrooms, 2 1/2 baths, 2-car side entry garage
- Basement foundation

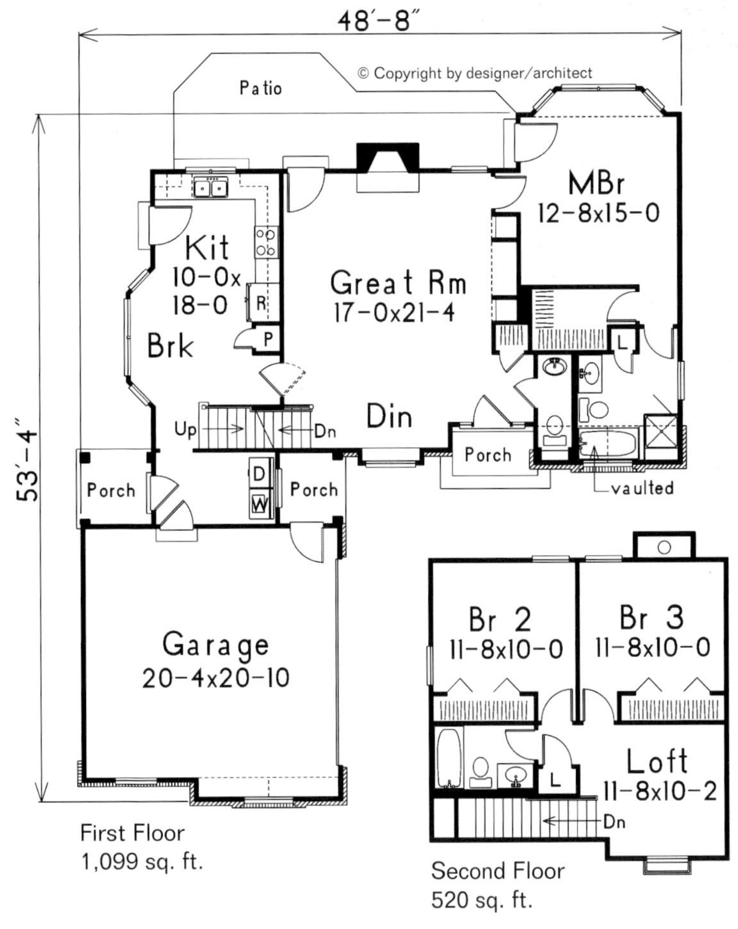

First Floor
1,099 sq. ft.

Second Floor
520 sq. ft.

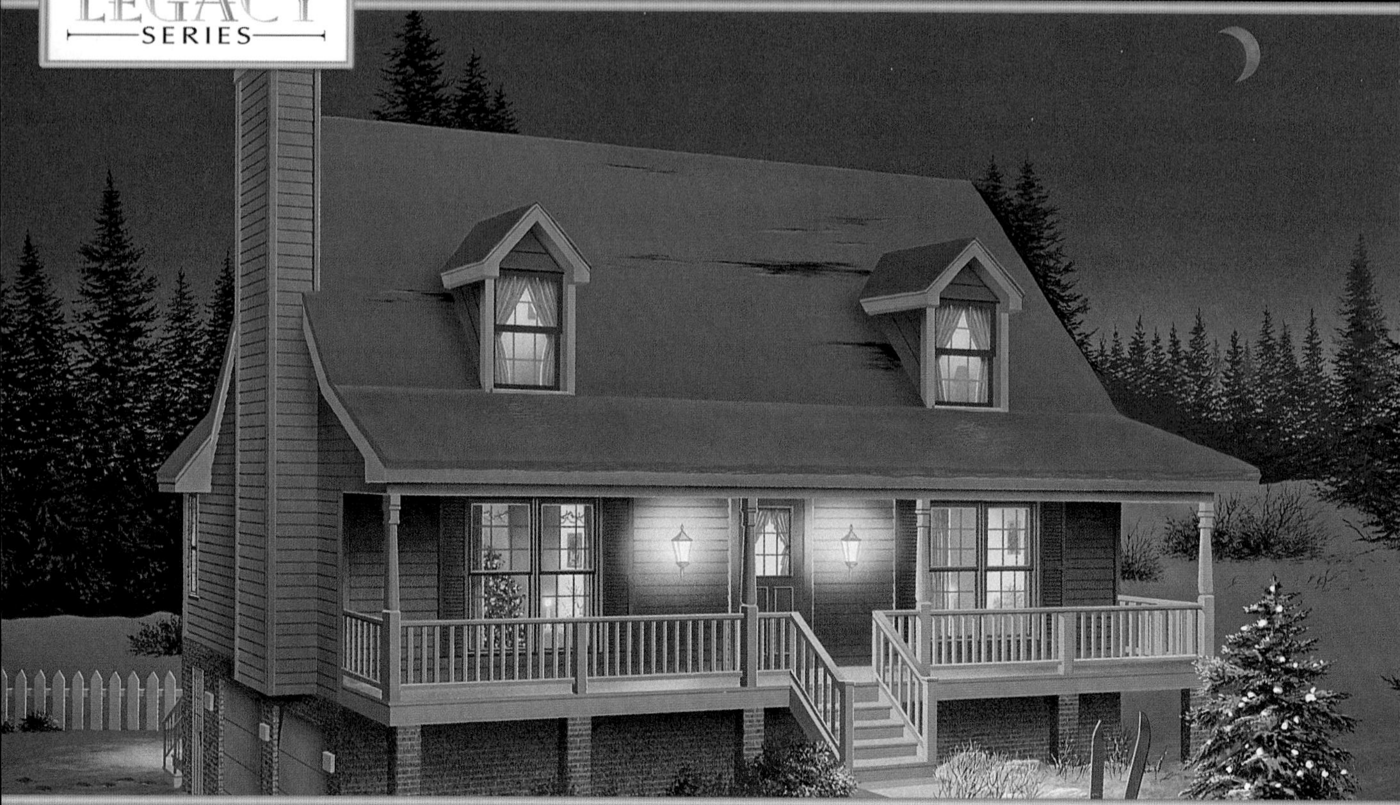

SPECIAL FEATURES

- 1,657 total square feet of living area
- Stylish pass-through between the living and dining areas
- Master bedroom is secluded from the living area for privacy
- Large windows in the breakfast and dining areas create a bright and cheerful atmosphere
- 3 bedrooms, 2 1/2 baths, 2-car drive under garage
- Basement foundation

Second Floor
611 sq. ft.

First Floor
1,046 sq. ft.

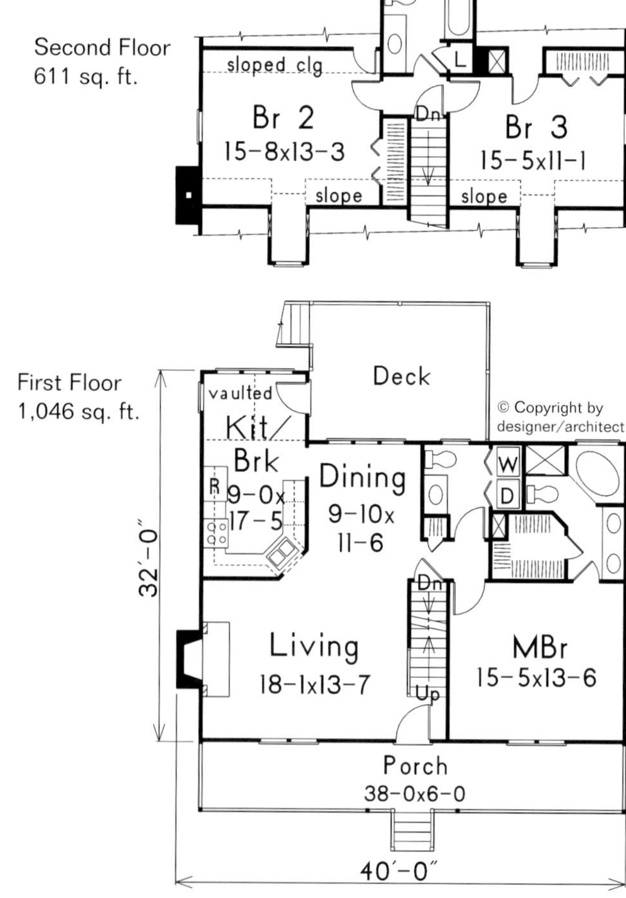

Plan Number: 537-010D-0005 | Price Code: A

Special Features

- 1,358 total square feet of living area
- Vaulted master bath has a walk-in closet, double-bowl vanity, large tub, shower and toilet area
- Galley kitchen opens to both the living room and the breakfast area
- A vaulted ceiling joins the dining and living rooms
- Breakfast room has a full wall of windows
- 3 bedrooms, 2 baths, 2-car garage
- Slab foundation

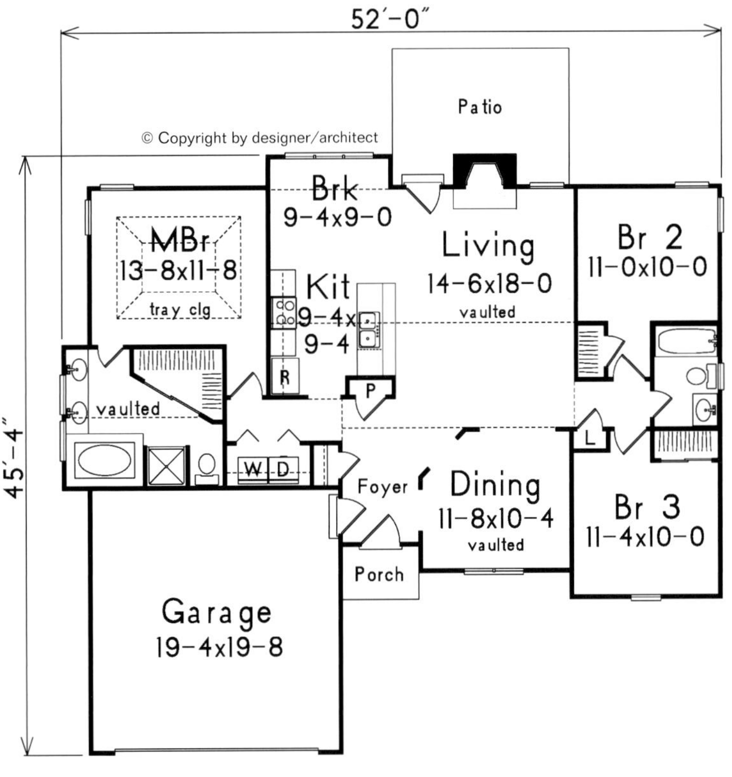

PLAN NUMBER: 537-001D-0029 | PRICE CODE: A

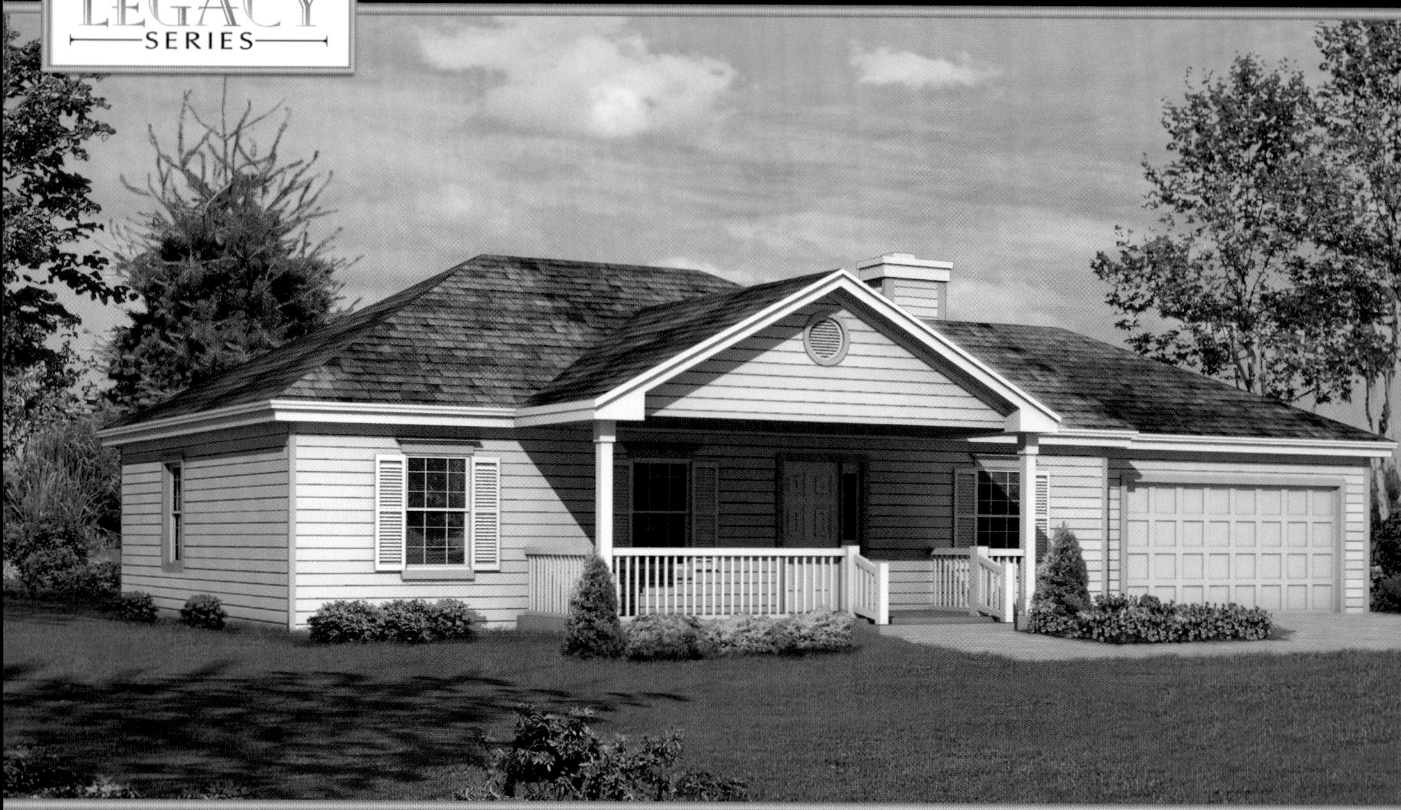

SPECIAL FEATURES

- 1,260 total square feet of living area
- Spacious kitchen and dining area features a large pantry, storage area and easy access to the garage and laundry room
- Pleasant covered front porch adds a practical touch
- Master bedroom with a private bath adjoins two other bedrooms, all with plenty of closet space
- 3 bedrooms, 2 baths, 2-car garage
- Basement foundation, drawings also include crawl space and slab foundations

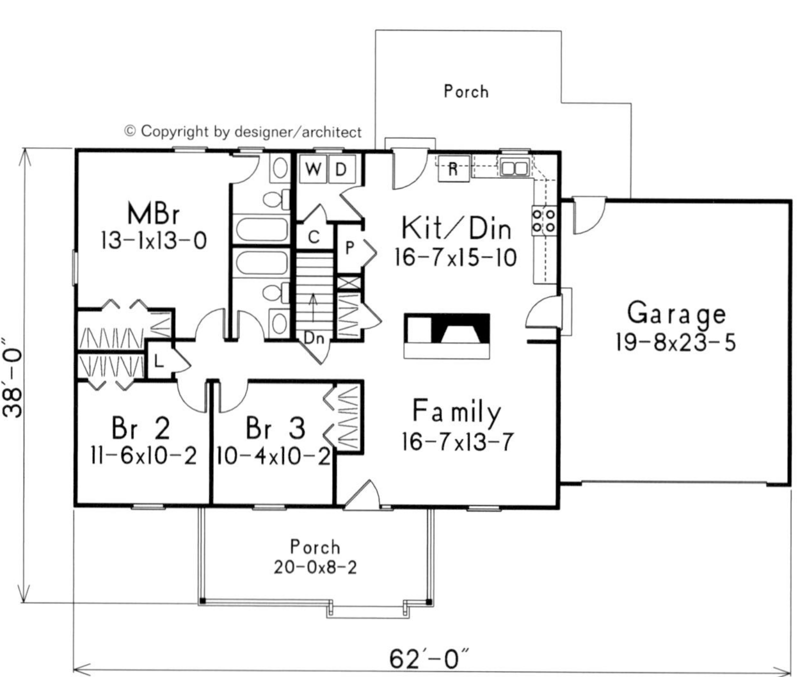

LOWE'S LEGACY SERIES

SPECIAL FEATURES

- 1,977 total square feet of living area
- Classic traditional exterior is always in style
- Spacious great room boasts a vaulted ceiling, dining area, atrium with elegant staircase and feature windows
- Atrium opens to 1,416 square feet of optional living area below which consists of a family room, two bedrooms, two baths and a study
- 4 bedrooms, 2 1/2 baths, 3-car side entry garage
- Walk-out basement foundation

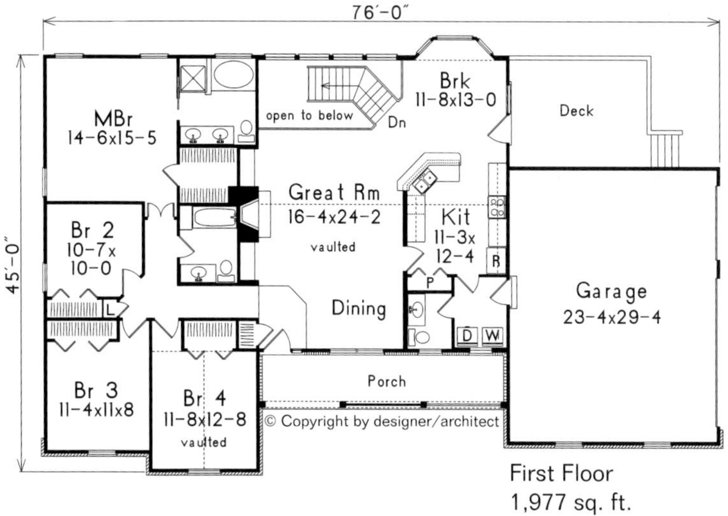

First Floor
1,977 sq. ft.

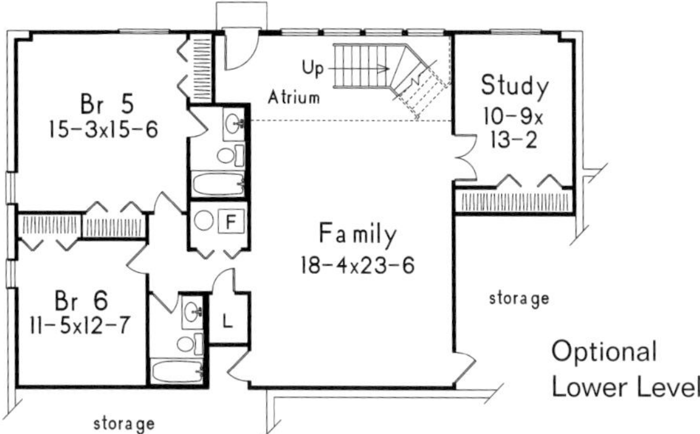

Optional
Lower Level

Plan Number: 537-017D-0007 | Price Code: C

Special Features

- 1,567 total square feet of living area
- Energy efficient home with 2" x 6" exterior walls
- Living room flows into the dining room shaped by an angled pass-through into the kitchen
- Cheerful, windowed dining area
- Master bedroom is separated from other bedrooms for privacy
- Future area available on the second floor has an additional 338 square feet of living area
- 3 bedrooms, 2 baths, 2-car side entry garage
- Partial basement/crawl space foundation, drawings also include slab foundation

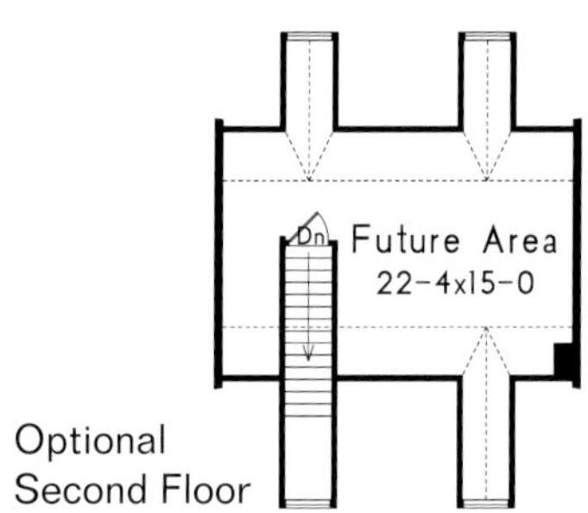

Optional Second Floor

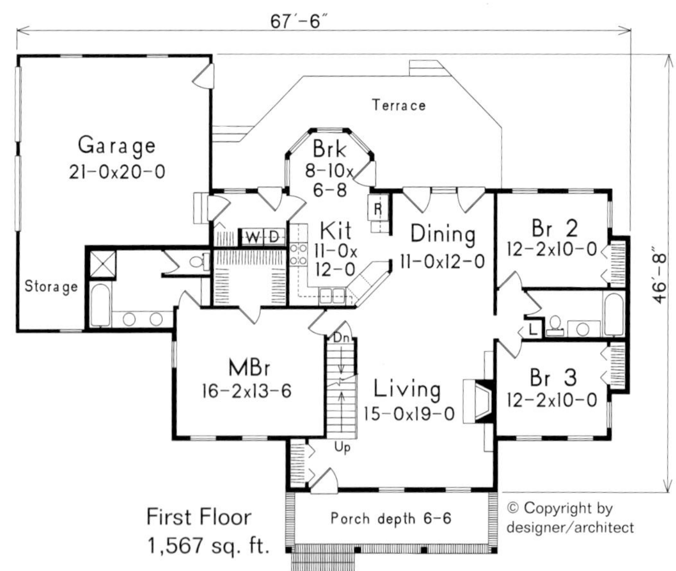

First Floor
1,567 sq. ft.

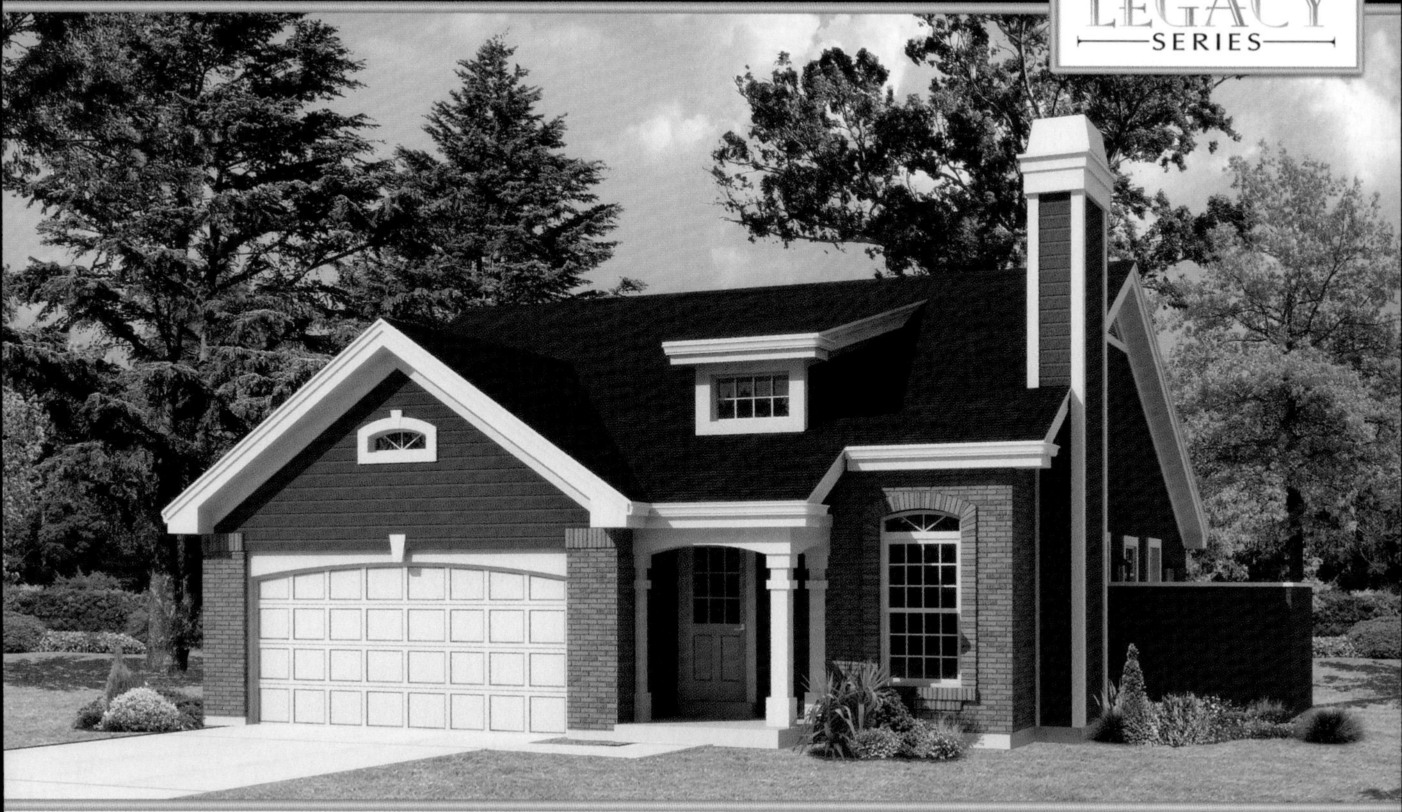

SPECIAL FEATURES

1,153 total square feet of living area

The arched windows, detailed brickwork and roof dormer all combine to create a stylish and inviting exterior

A fireplace, U-shaped kitchen with built-in pantry and dining area with view to a side fenced patio are the many features of the living room area

The master bedroom includes a private bath, walk-in closet and access to the patio area

3 bedrooms, 2 baths, 2-car garage

Basement foundation

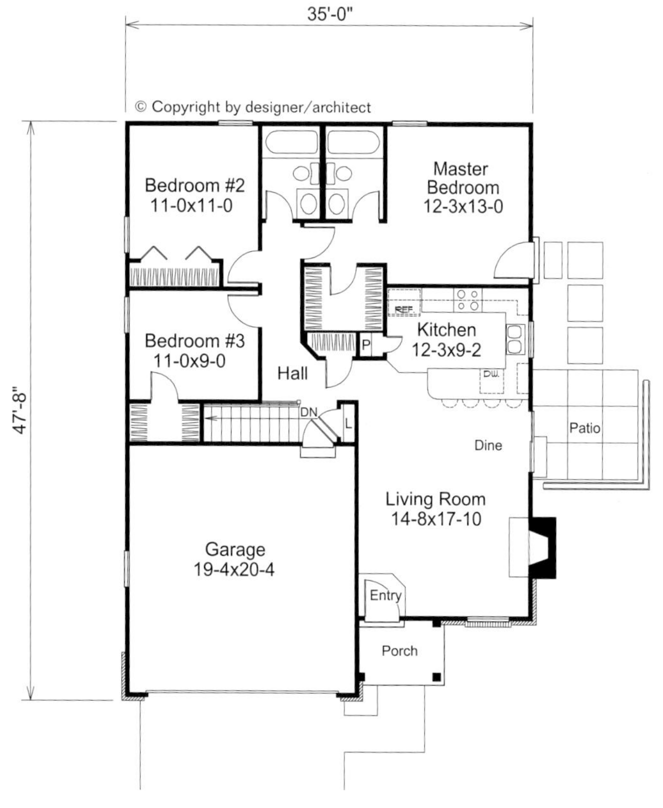

Plan Number: 537-022D-0022 | Price Code: A

Special Features

- 1,270 total square feet of living area
- Spacious living area features angled stairs, vaulted ceiling, exciting fireplace and deck access
- Master bedroom includes a walk-in closet and private bath
- Dining and living rooms join to create an open atmosphere
- Eat-in kitchen has a convenient pass-through to the dining room
- 3 bedrooms, 2 baths, 2-car garage
- Basement foundation

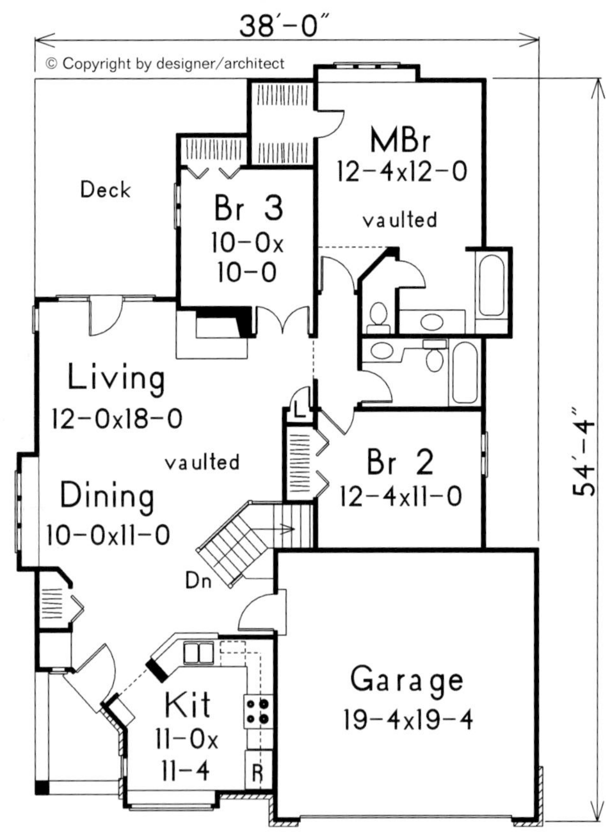

SPECIAL FEATURES

- 1,285 total square feet of living area
- Accommodating home with ranch-style porch
- Large storage area on back of home
- Master bedroom includes dressing area, private bath and built-in bookcase
- Kitchen features pantry, breakfast bar and complete view to the dining room
- 2" x 6" exterior walls available, please order plan #537-001D-0119
- 3 bedrooms, 2 baths
- Crawl space foundation, drawings also include basement and slab foundations

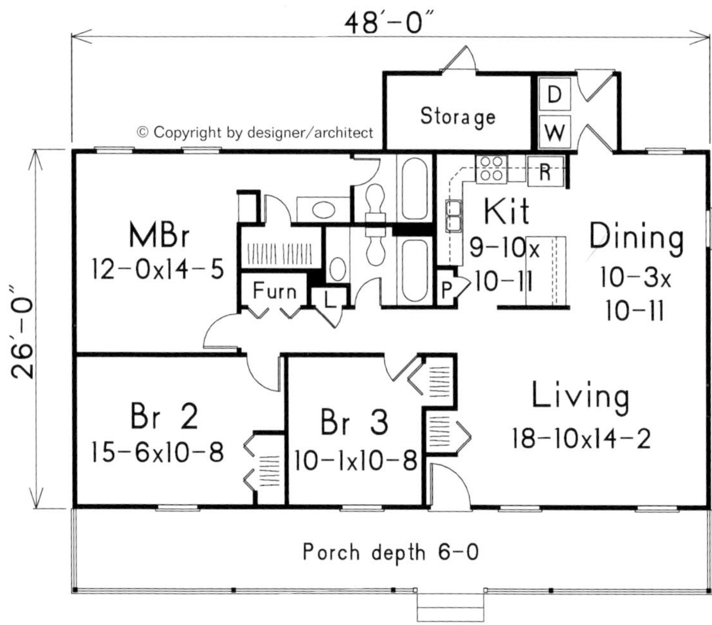

Plan Number: 537-007D-0034 | Price Code: C

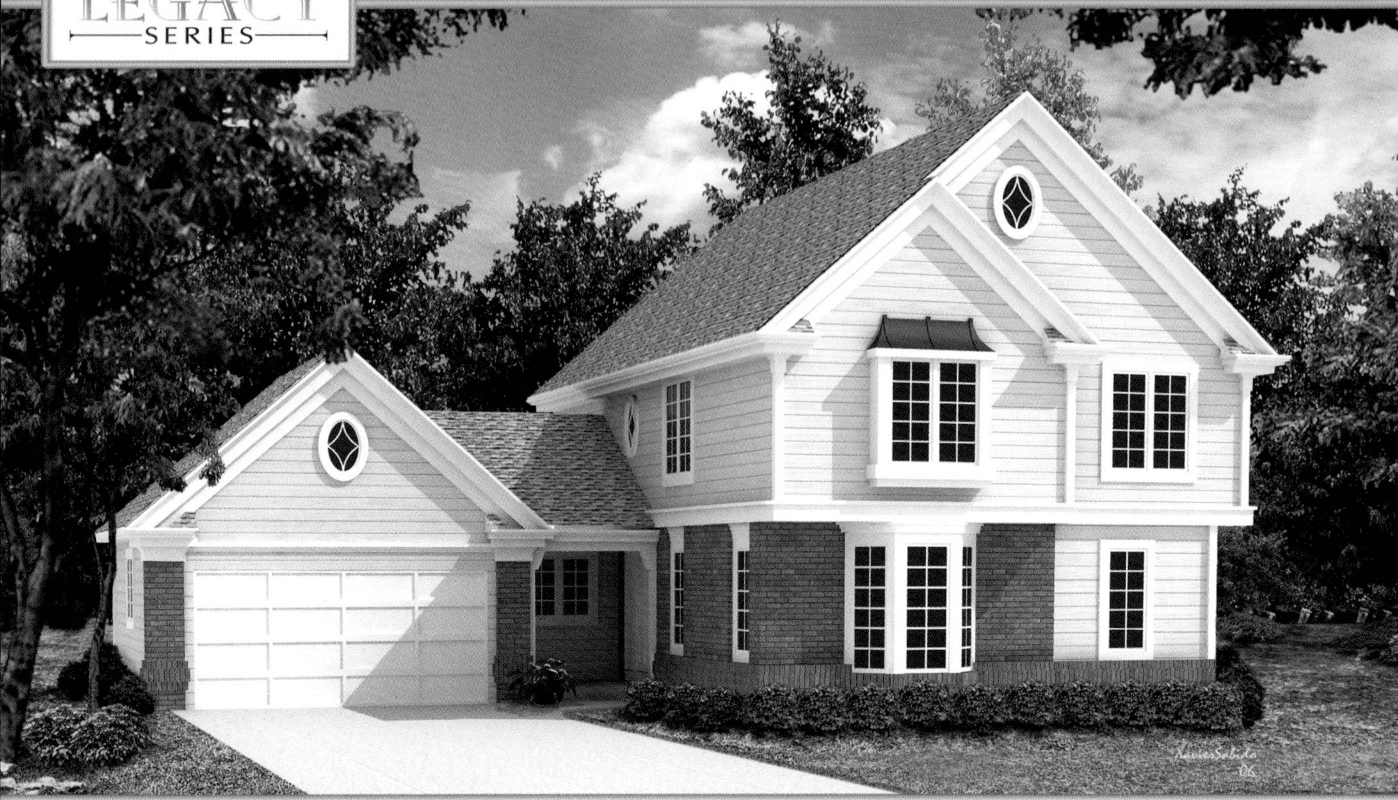

Special Features

- 2,012 total square feet of living area
- Gables, cantilevers, and box-bay windows all contribute to an elegant exterior
- Two-story entry leads to an efficient kitchen and bayed breakfast area with morning room
- Garage contains extra space for a shop, bicycles and miscellaneous storage
- 5 bedrooms, 2 1/2 baths, 2-car garage
- Basement foundation

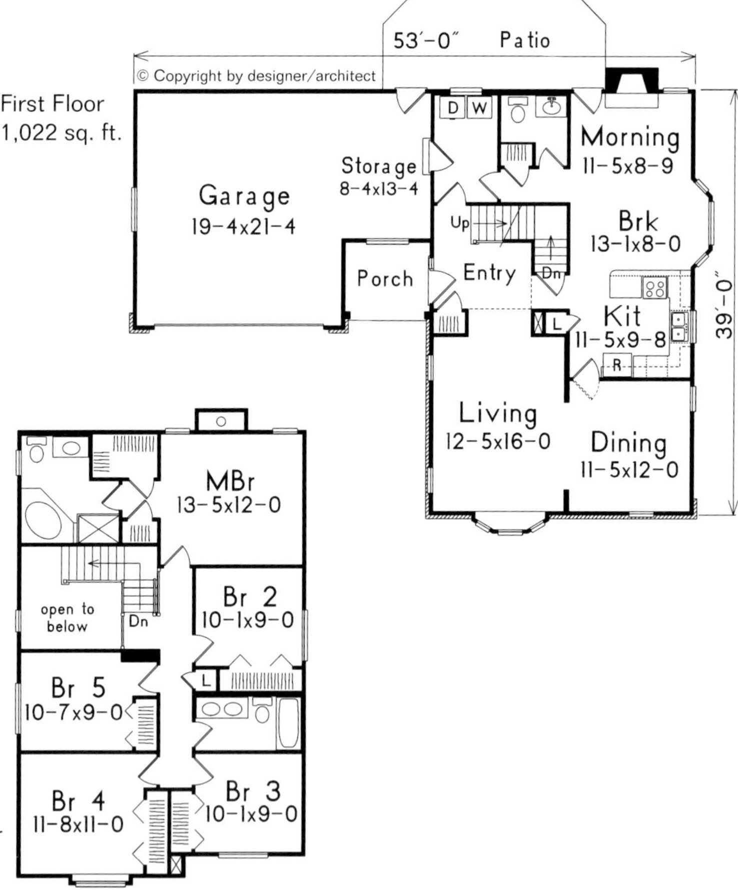

First Floor
1,022 sq. ft.

Second Floor
990 sq. ft.

Plan Number: 537-048D-0011 | Price Code: B

Lowe's Legacy Series

Special Features

- 1,550 total square feet of living area
- Alcove in the family room can be used as a cozy corner fireplace or as a media center
- Master bedroom features a large walk-in closet, skylight and separate tub and shower
- Convenient laundry closet
- Kitchen with pantry and breakfast bar connects to the family room
- Family room and master bedroom access the covered patio
- 3 bedrooms, 2 baths, 2-car garage
- Slab foundation

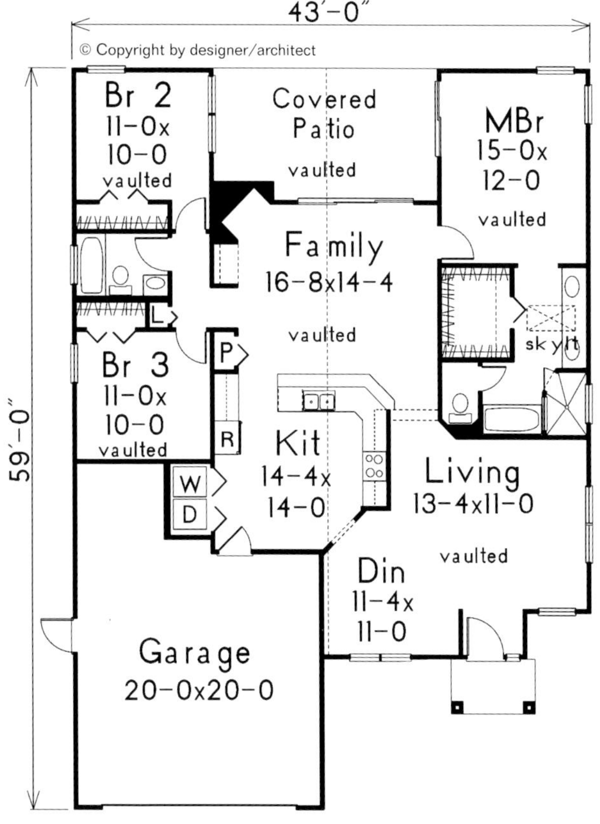

PLAN NUMBER: 537-007D-0200 | PRICE CODE: A

SPECIAL FEATURES

- 1,137 total square feet of living area
- Cleverly designed two-story is disguised as an attractive one-story home
- The spacious and dramatic entry features a vaulted ceiling, coat closet with plant shelf above and an ascending stair to the second floor
- The living room with fireplace is open to the bayed dining area and functional L-shaped kitchen furnished with an island counter and adjacent laundry room
- The optional finished lower level includes a family room, hall bath and third bedroom with walk-in closet and allows for an extra 591 square feet of living area
- 2 bedrooms, 1 1/2 baths, 2-car garage
- Walk-out basement foundation

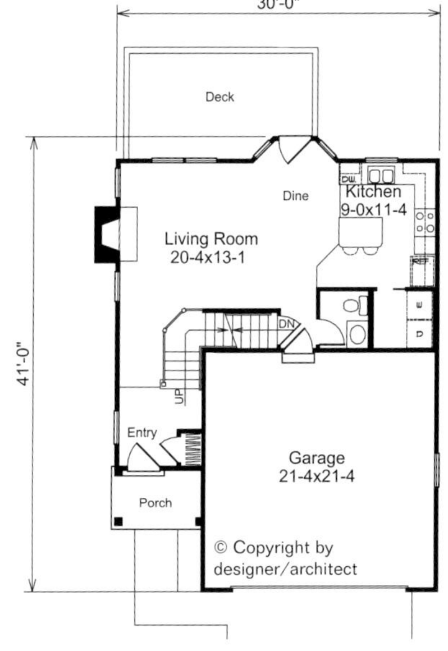

First Floor
621 sq. ft.

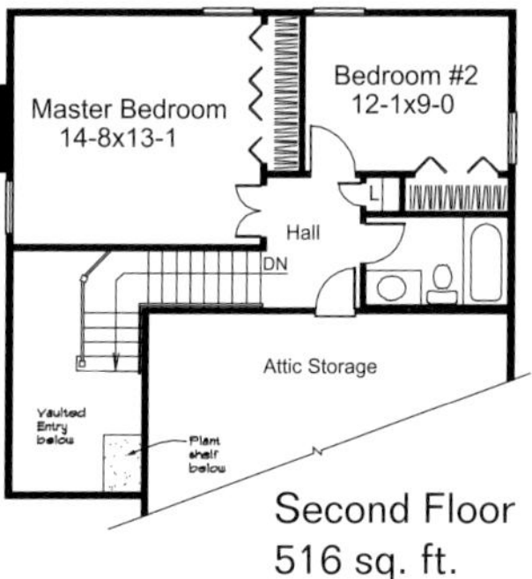

Second Floor
516 sq. ft.

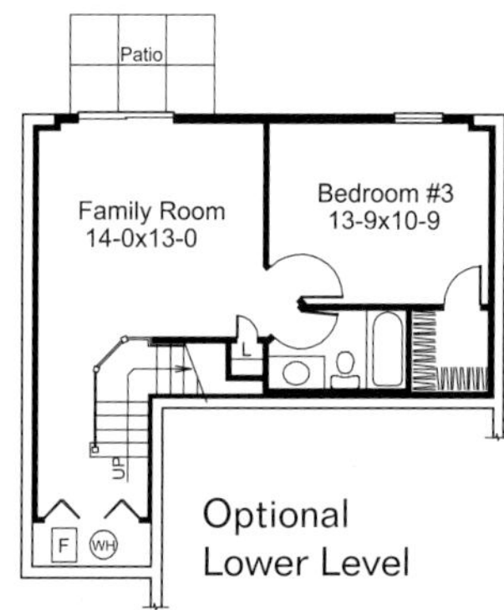

Optional
Lower Level

SPECIAL FEATURES

- 1,684 total square feet of living area
- Delightful wrap-around porch is anchored by a full masonry fireplace
- The vaulted great room includes a large bay window, fireplace, dining balcony and atrium window wall
- Double walk-in closets, large luxury bath and sliding doors to an exterior balcony are a few fantastic features of the master bedroom
- Atrium opens to 611 square feet of optional living area on the lower level
- 3 bedrooms, 2 baths, 2-car drive under rear entry garage
- Walk-out basement foundation

Rear View

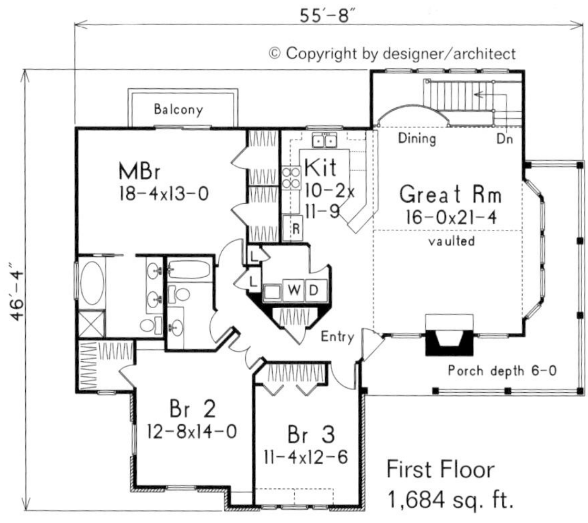

First Floor
1,684 sq. ft.

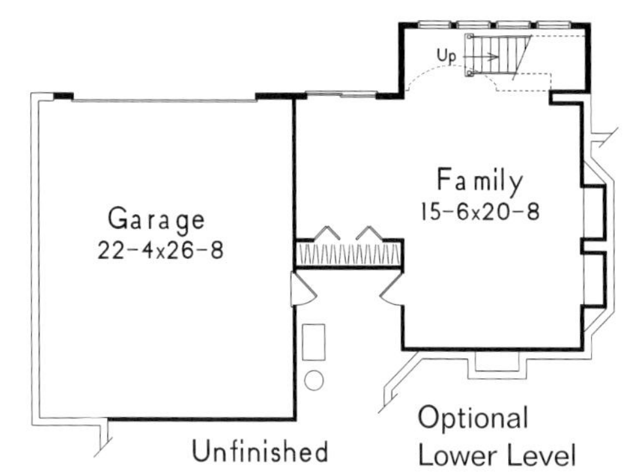

Unfinished

Optional
Lower Level

PLAN NUMBER: 537-053D-0042 | PRICE CODE: A

SPECIAL FEATURES

- 1,458 total square feet of living area
- A convenient snack bar joins the kitchen with breakfast room
- Large living room has a fireplace, plenty of windows, vaulted ceiling and nearby plant shelf
- Master bedroom offers a private bath, walk-in closet, plant shelf and coffered ceiling
- Corner windows provide abundant light in the breakfast room
- 3 bedrooms, 2 baths, 2-car garage
- Crawl space foundation, drawings also include slab foundation

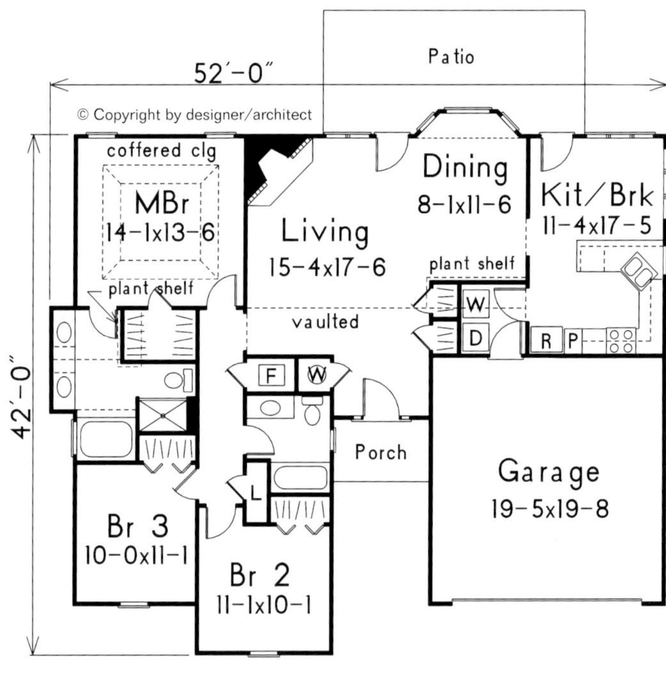

SPECIAL FEATURES

- 1,708 total square feet of living area
- Massive family room is enhanced with several windows, a fireplace and access to the porch
- Deluxe master bath is accented by a step-up corner tub flanked by double vanities
- Closets throughout maintain organized living
- Bedrooms are isolated from living areas
- 3 bedrooms, 2 baths, 2-car garage
- Basement foundation, drawings also include crawl space foundation

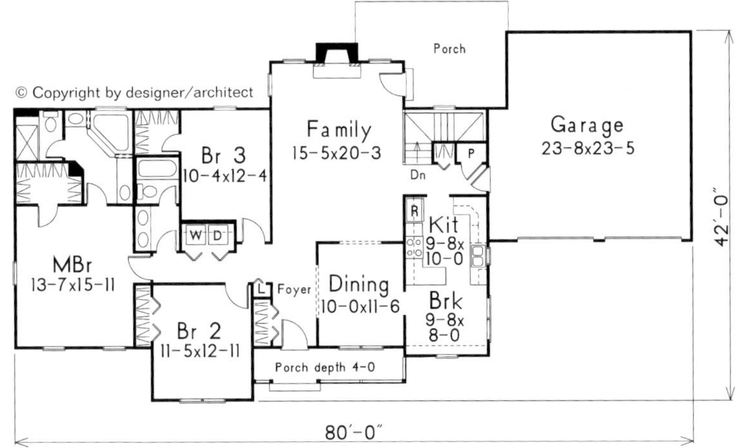

SPECIAL FEATURES

- 2,357 total square feet of living area
- 9' ceilings on the first floor
- Secluded master bedroom includes a private bath with double walk-in closets and vanity
- Balcony overlooks living room with large fireplace
- The future game room on the second floor has an additional 303 square feet of living area
- 4 bedrooms, 3 1/2 baths, 2-car side entry garage
- Slab foundation, drawings also include crawl space foundation

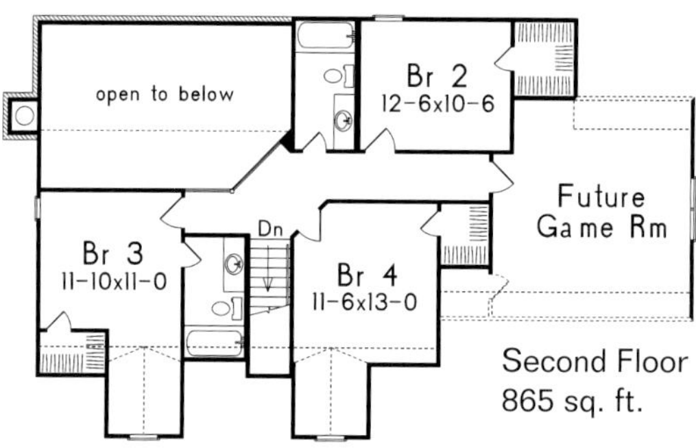

Second Floor
865 sq. ft.

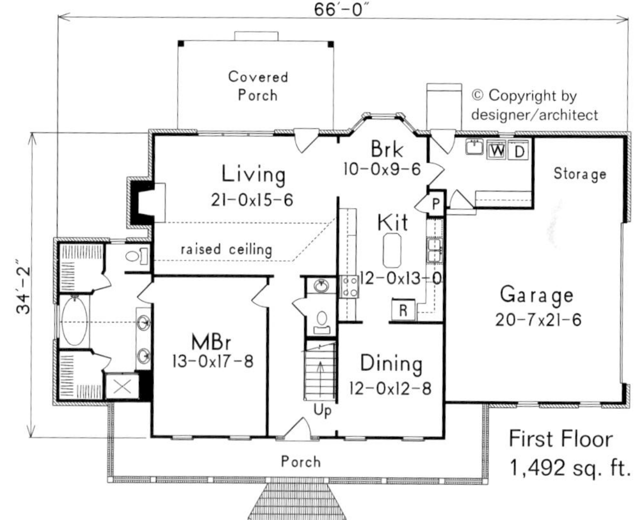

First Floor
1,492 sq. ft.

SPECIAL FEATURES

- 1,396 total square feet of living area
- Gabled front adds interest to the facade
- Living and dining rooms share a vaulted ceiling
- Master bedroom features a walk-in closet and private bath
- Functional kitchen boasts a center work island and convenient pantry
- 3 bedrooms, 2 baths, 1-car rear entry carport
- Basement foundation, drawings also include crawl space foundation

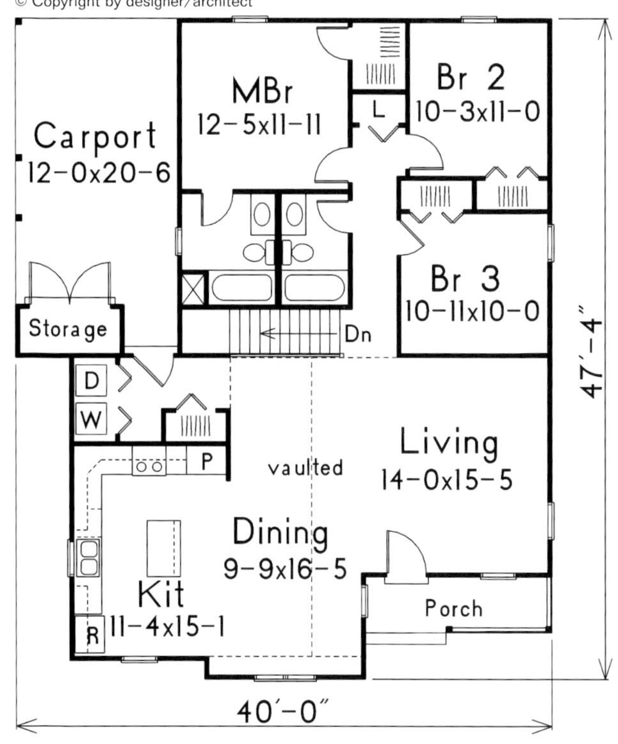

SPECIAL FEATURES

- 1,524 total square feet of living area
- Delightful balcony overlooks two-story entry illuminated by an oval window
- Roomy first floor master bedroom offers quiet privacy
- All bedrooms feature one or more walk-in closets
- 3 bedrooms, 2 1/2 baths, 2-car garage
- Basement foundation, drawings also include crawl space and slab foundations

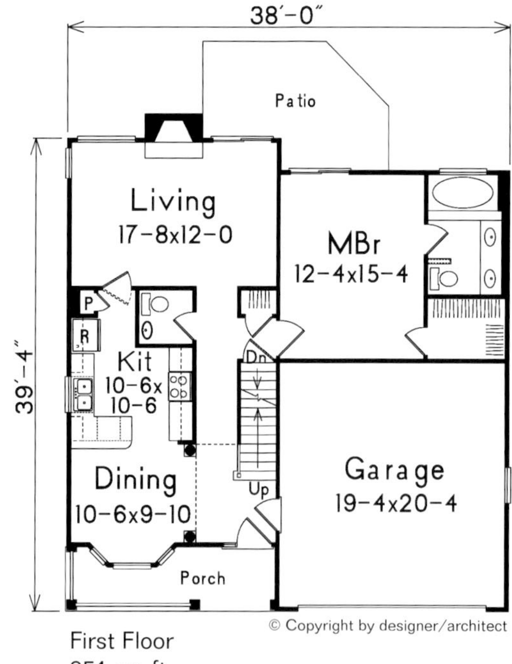

First Floor
951 sq. ft.

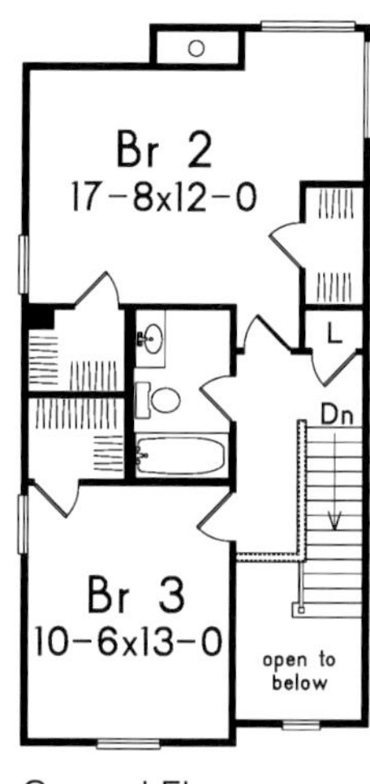

Second Floor
573 sq. ft.

PLAN NUMBER: 537-001D-0087 | PRICE CODE: A

SPECIAL FEATURES

- 1,230 total square feet of living area
- Spacious living room accesses the huge deck
- Bedroom #3 features a balcony overlooking the deck
- Kitchen with dining area accesses the outdoors
- Washer and dryer are tucked under the stairs for space efficiency
- 3 bedrooms, 1 bath
- Crawl space foundation, drawings also include slab foundation

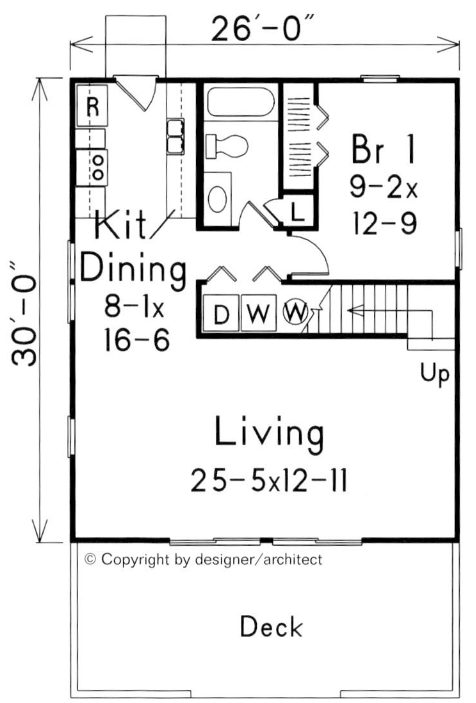

First Floor
780 sq. ft.

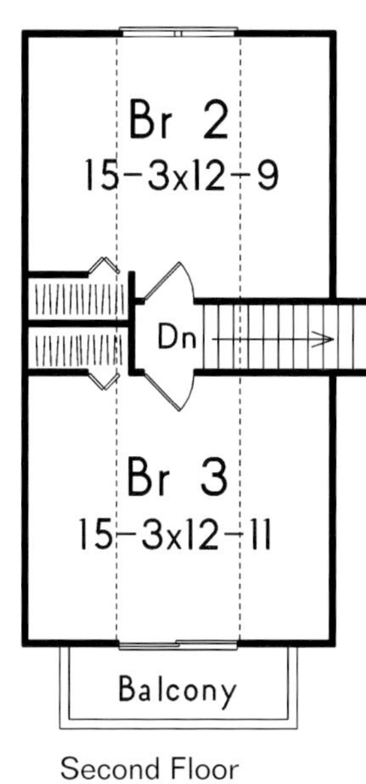

Second Floor
450 sq. ft.

SPECIAL FEATURES

- 1,600 total square feet of living area
- Energy efficient home with 2" x 6" exterior walls
- Impressive sunken living room features a massive stone fireplace and 16' vaulted ceiling
- The dining room is conveniently located next to the kitchen and divided for privacy
- Special amenities include a sewing room, glass shelves in the kitchen, a grand master bath and a large utility area
- Sunken master bedroom features a distinctive sitting room
- 3 bedrooms, 2 baths, 2-car side entry garage
- Slab foundation, drawings also include crawl space and basement foundations

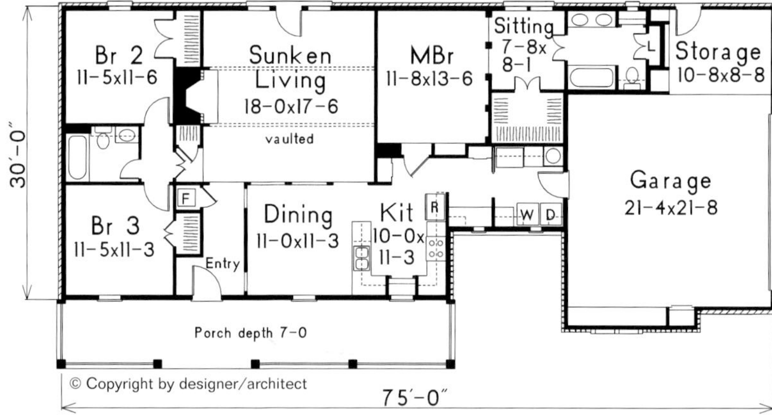

SPECIAL FEATURES

- 496 total square feet of living area
- The traditional front exterior and rear both enjoy shady porches for relaxing evenings
- The living room with bayed dining area is open to a functional L-shaped kitchen with a convenient pantry
- A full bath, large walk-in closet and access to both the rear porch and the garage are the many features of the rear bedroom
- 1 bedroom, 1 bath, 2-car garage
- Slab foundation

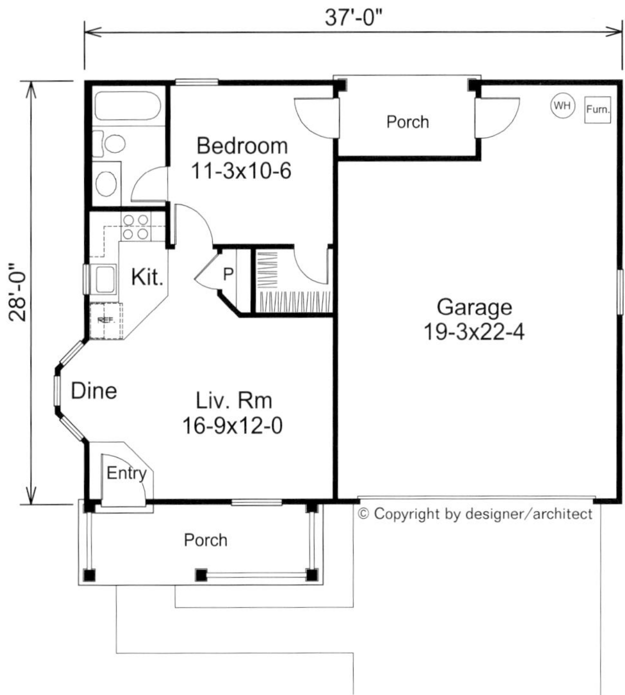

SPECIAL FEATURES

- 1,140 total square feet of living area
- Open and spacious living and dining areas for family gatherings
- Well-organized kitchen has an abundance of cabinetry and a built-in pantry
- Roomy master bath features a double-bowl vanity
- 3 bedrooms, 2 baths, 2-car drive under garage
- Basement foundation

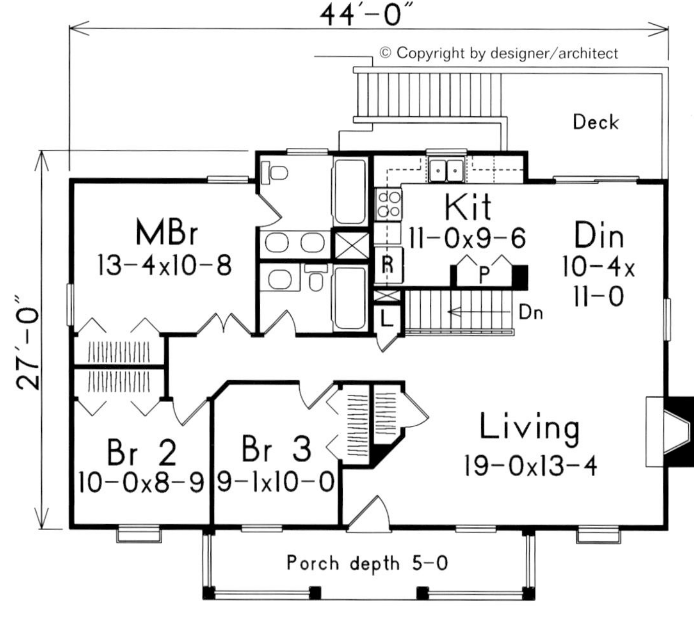

SPECIAL FEATURES

- 1,315 total square feet of living area
- Dining room has a sliding door to the rear patio
- Large storage space in garage
- Cozy eating area in the kitchen
- Kitchen has easy access to the laundry/mud room
- Large living room with double closets for storage and coats
- 3 bedrooms, 2 baths, 2-car garage
- Basement foundation, drawings also include slab foundation

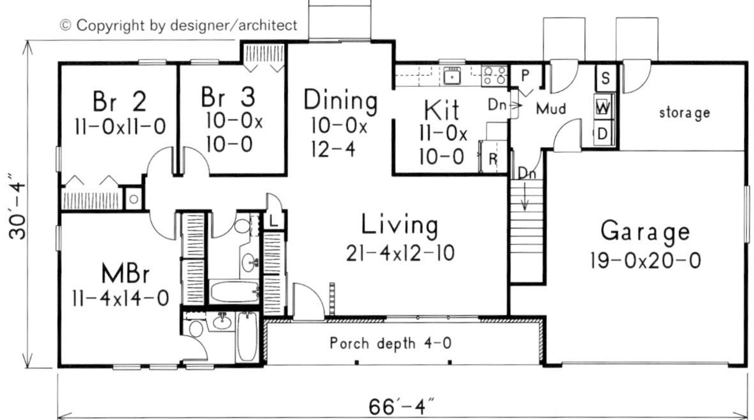

PLAN NUMBER: 537-040D-0007 | PRICE CODE: D

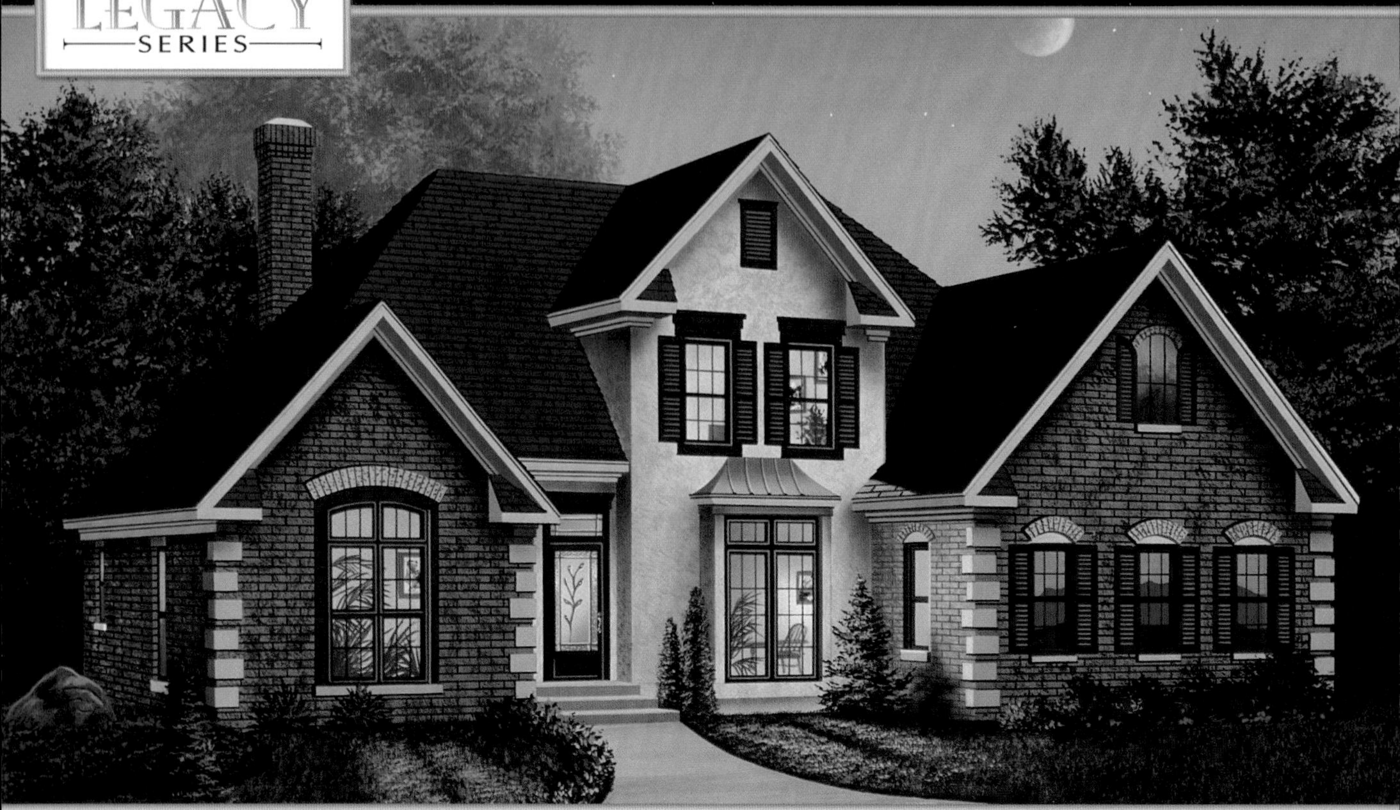

SPECIAL FEATURES

- 2,073 total square feet of living area
- Family room provides an ideal gathering area with a fireplace, large windows and a vaulted ceiling
- Private first floor master bedroom enjoys a vaulted ceiling and luxury bath
- Kitchen features an angled bar connecting it to the breakfast area
- 4 bedrooms, 2 1/2 baths, 2-car side entry garage
- Basement foundation

Second Floor
632 sq. ft.

First Floor
1,441 sq. ft.

 TO ORDER SEE PAGE 288 |

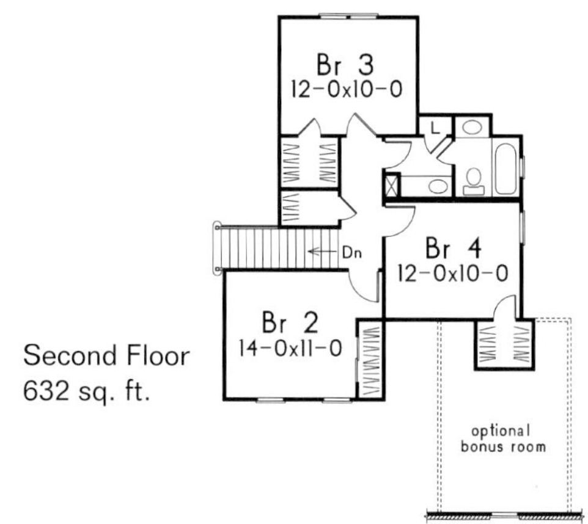

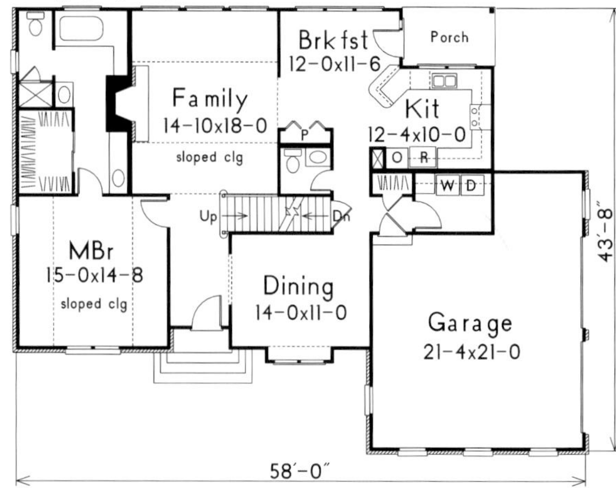

Plan Number: 537-022D-0020 | Price Code: AA

Lowe's Legacy Series

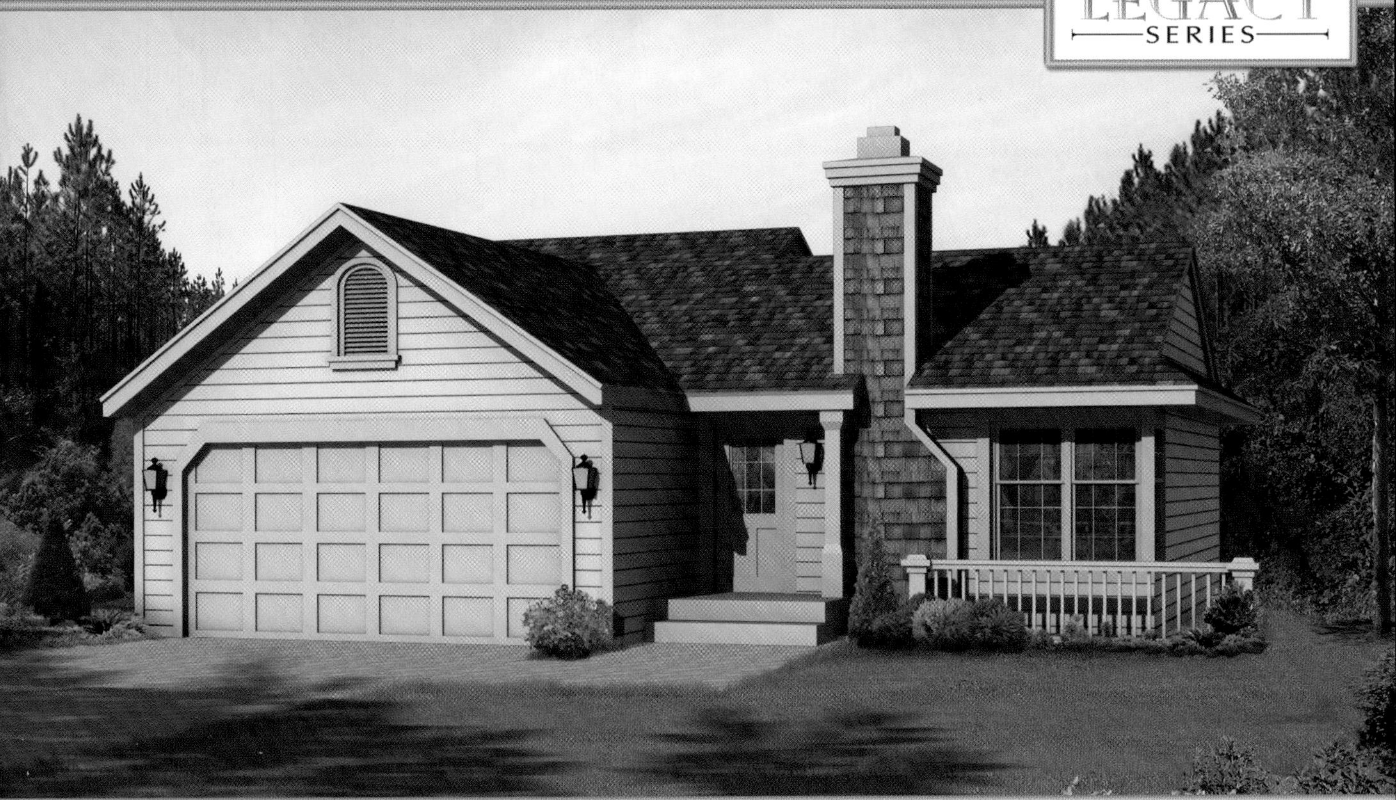

Special Features

- 988 total square feet of living area
- Great room features a corner fireplace
- Vaulted ceiling and corner windows add space and light in great room
- Eat-in kitchen with vaulted ceiling accesses deck for outdoor living
- Master bedroom features separate vanities and private access to the bath
- 2 bedrooms, 1 bath, 2-car garage
- Basement foundation

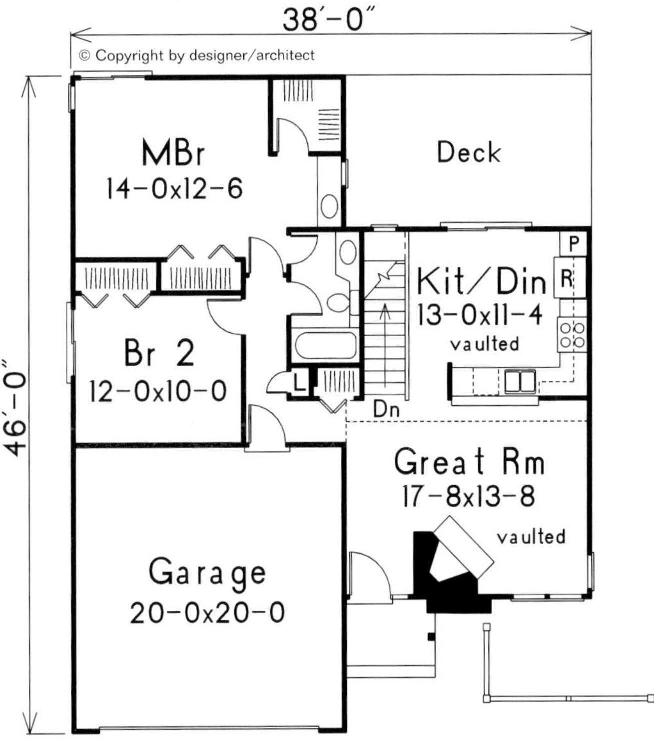

SPECIAL FEATURES

- 1,868 total square feet of living area
- Energy efficient home with 2" x 6" exterior walls
- Luxurious master bath is impressive with an angled quarter-circle tub, separate vanities and large walk-in closet
- Dining room is surrounded by a series of arched openings which complement the open feeling of this design
- Living room has a 12' ceiling accented by skylights and a large fireplace flanked by sliding doors
- Large storage areas
- 3 bedrooms, 2 baths, 2-car side entry garage
- Slab foundation, drawings also include crawl space foundation

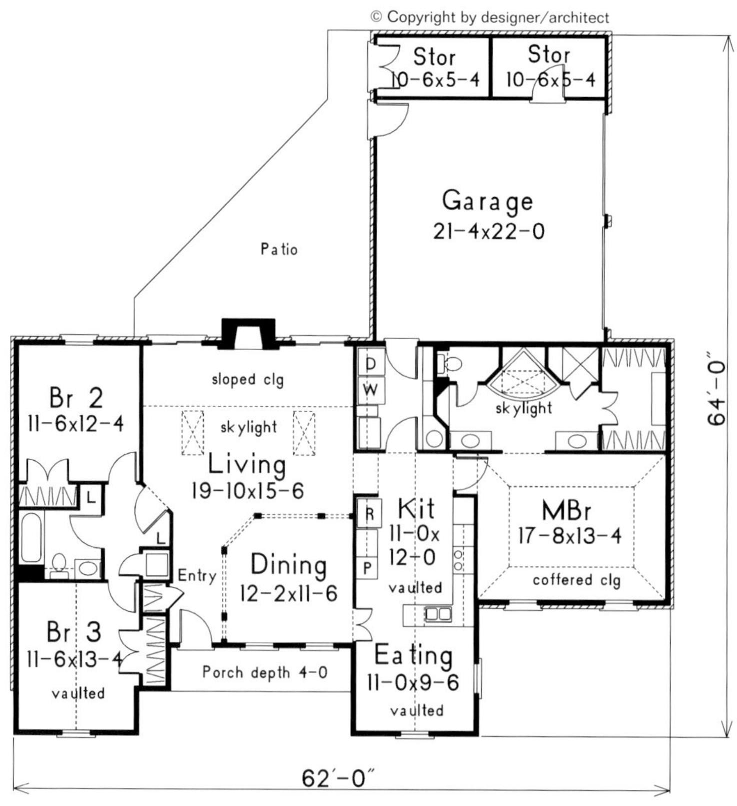

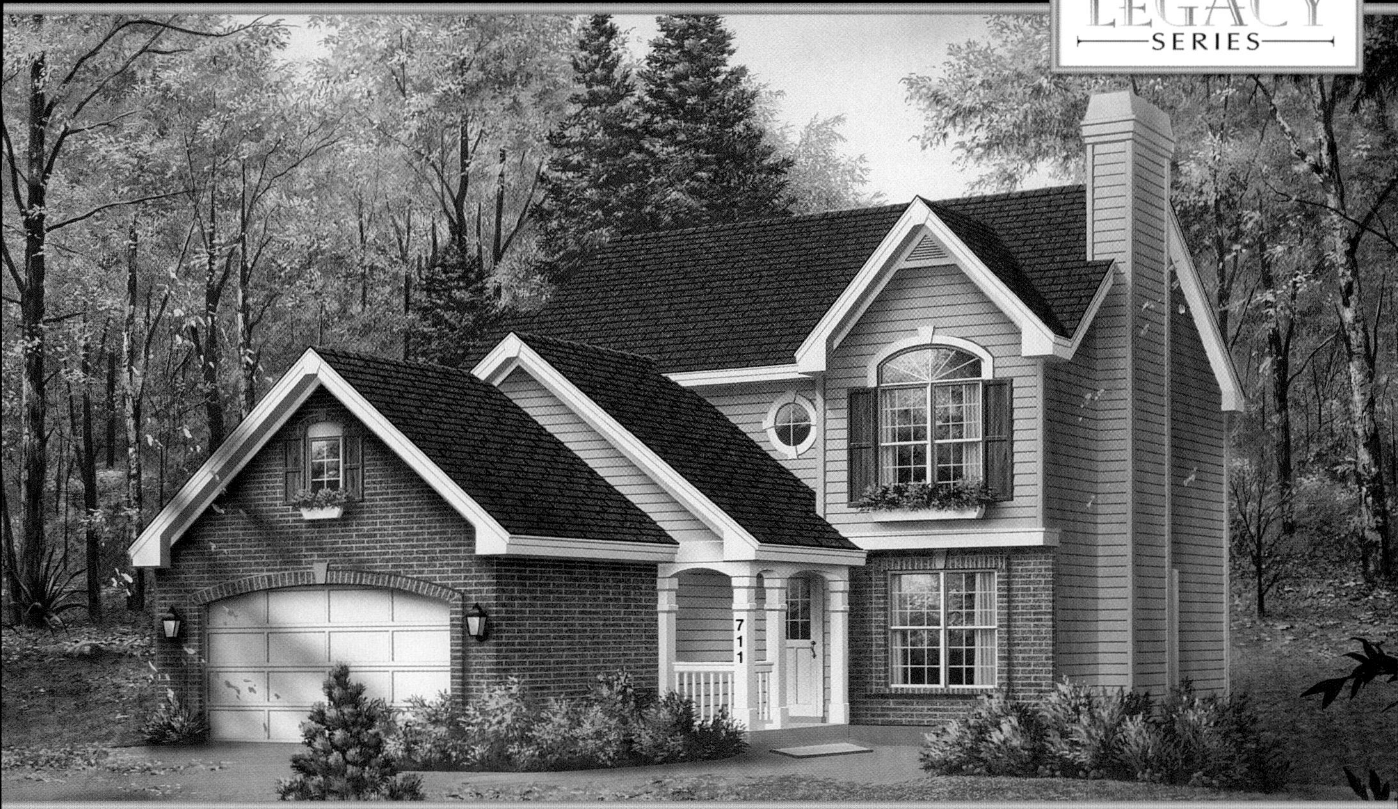

SPECIAL FEATURES

- 1,575 total square feet of living area
- Inviting porch leads to spacious living and dining rooms
- Kitchen with corner windows features an island snack bar, attractive breakfast room bay, convenient laundry area and built-in pantry
- A luxury bath and walk-in closet adorn the master bedroom suite
- 3 bedrooms, 2 1/2 baths, 2-car garage
- Basement foundation, drawings also include crawl space and slab foundations

Second Floor
773 sq. ft.

First Floor
802 sq. ft.

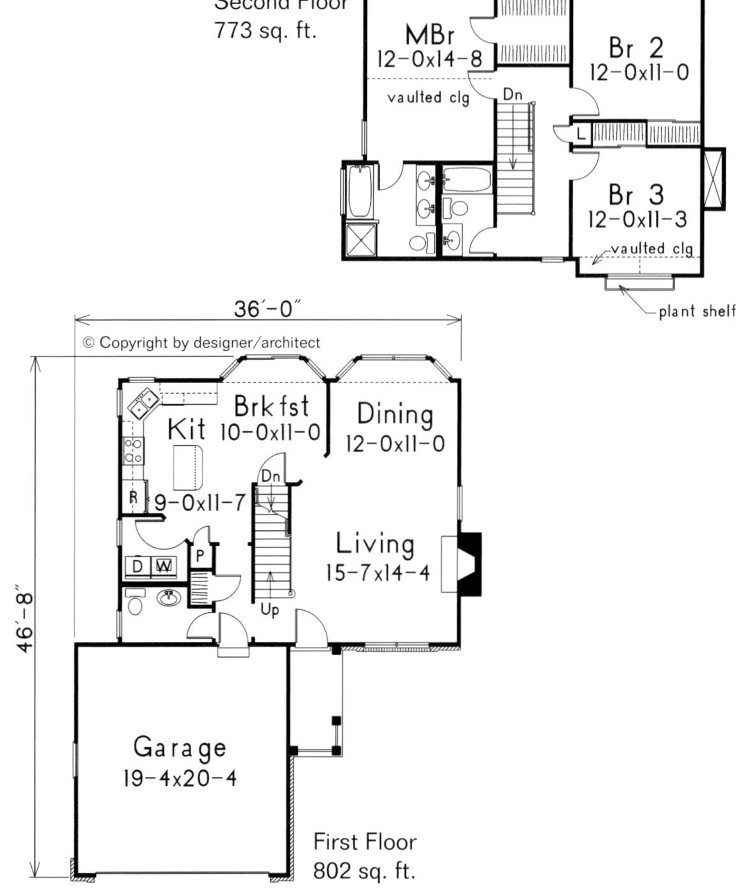

Special Features

- 1,597 total square feet of living area
- Spacious family room includes a fireplace and coat closet
- Open kitchen and dining room provide a breakfast bar and access to the outdoors
- Convenient laundry area is located near the kitchen
- Secluded master bedroom enjoys a walk-in closet and private bath
- 4 bedrooms, 2 1/2 baths, 2-car detached garage
- Basement foundation

Second Floor
615 sq. ft.

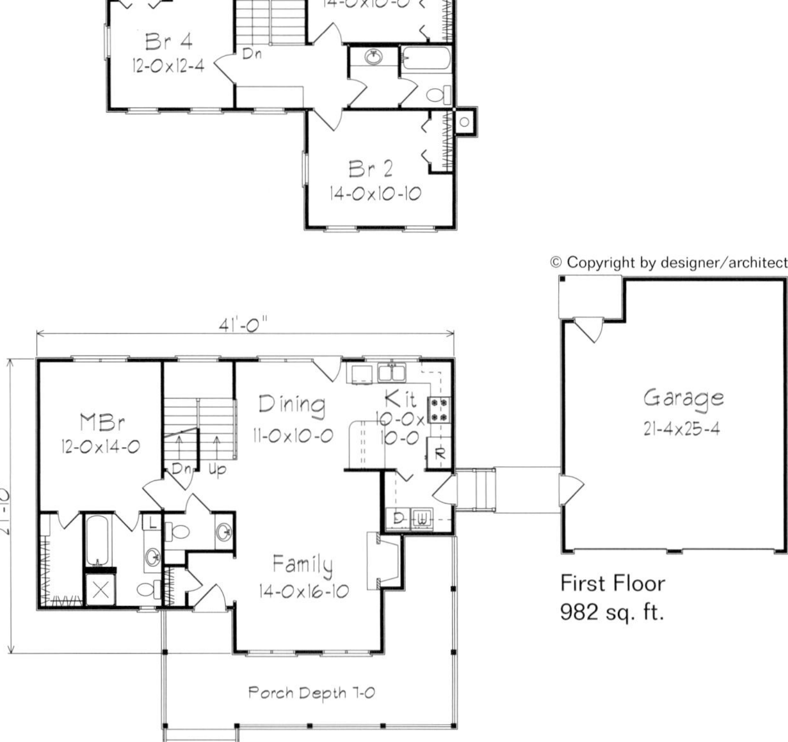

First Floor
982 sq. ft.

LOWE'S LEGACY SERIES

SPECIAL FEATURES

- 1,220 total square feet of living area
- A vaulted ceiling adds luxury to the living room and master bedroom
- Spacious living room is accented with a large fireplace and hearth
- Gracious dining area is adjacent to the convenient wrap-around kitchen
- Washer and dryer are handy to the bedrooms
- Covered porch entry adds appeal
- Rear deck adjoins dining area
- 3 bedrooms, 2 baths, 2-car drive under garage
- Basement foundation

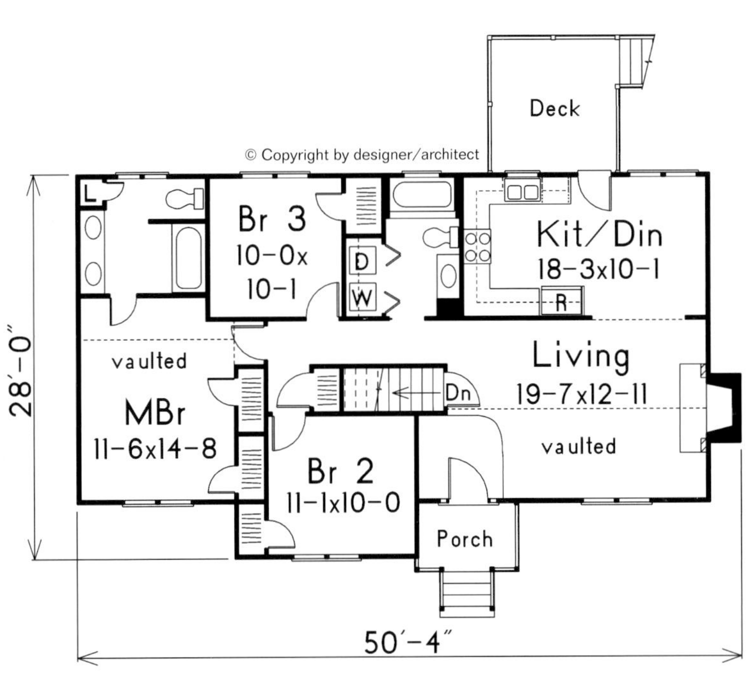

Plan Number: 537-006D-0003 | Price Code: B

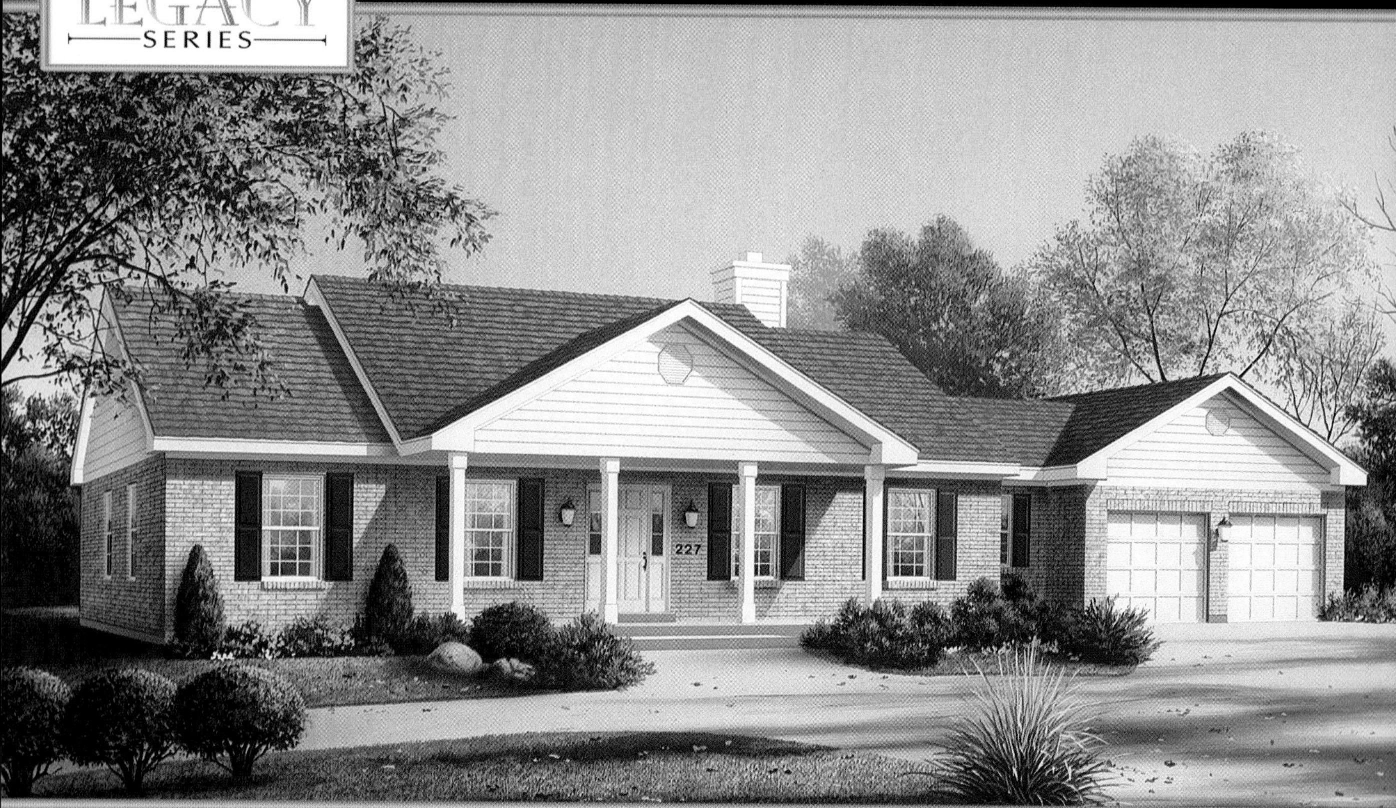

Special Features

- 1,674 total square feet of living area
- Vaulted great room, dining area and kitchen all enjoy a central fireplace and log bin
- Convenient laundry/mud room is located between the garage and the rest of the home with handy stairs to the basement
- Easily expandable screened porch and adjacent patio access the dining area
- Master bedroom features a full bath with tub, separate shower and walk-in closet
- 3 bedrooms, 2 baths, 2-car garage
- Basement foundation, drawings also include crawl space and slab foundations

To Order See Page 288 | Call Toll-Free 1-877-379-3420

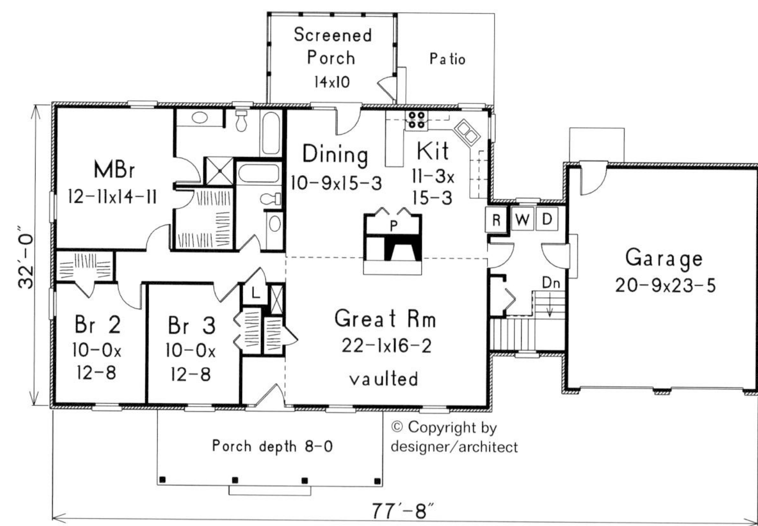

LOWE'S LEGACY SERIES

SPECIAL FEATURES

- 987 total square feet of living area
- Galley kitchen opens into the cozy breakfast room
- Convenient coat closets are located by both entrances
- Dining/living room offers an expansive open area
- Breakfast room has access to the outdoors
- Front porch is great for enjoying outdoor living
- 3 bedrooms, 1 bath
- Basement foundation

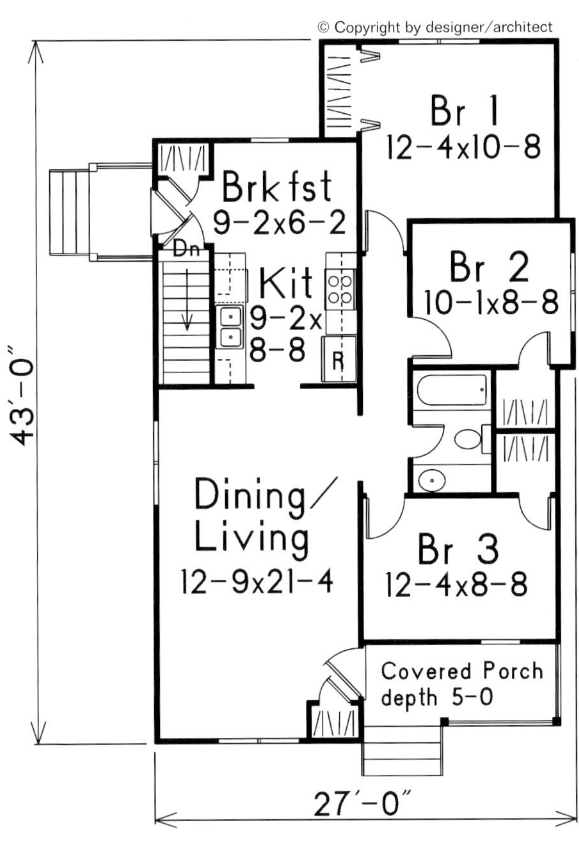

SPECIAL FEATURES

- 1,444 total square feet of living area
- 11' ceilings in the living and dining rooms combine with a central fireplace to create a large open living area
- Both secondary bedrooms have large walk-in closets
- Extra space in the garage is suitable for a workshop or play area
- Front and rear covered porches add a cozy touch
- U-shaped kitchen includes a laundry closet and serving bar
- 3 bedrooms, 2 baths, 2-car side entry garage
- Slab foundation, drawings also include crawl space foundation

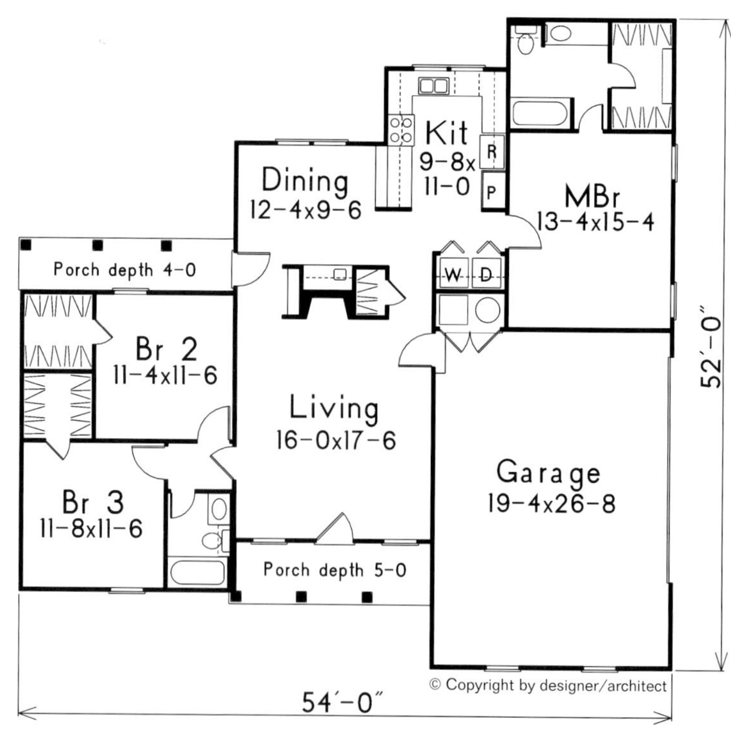

SPECIAL FEATURES

- 1,368 total square feet of living area
- Entry foyer steps down to an open living area which combines the great room and formal dining area
- Vaulted master bedroom includes a box-bay window and a bath with a large vanity, separate tub and shower
- Cozy breakfast area features direct access to the patio and pass-through kitchen
- Handy linen closet is located in the hall
- 3 bedrooms, 2 baths, 2-car garage
- Basement foundation

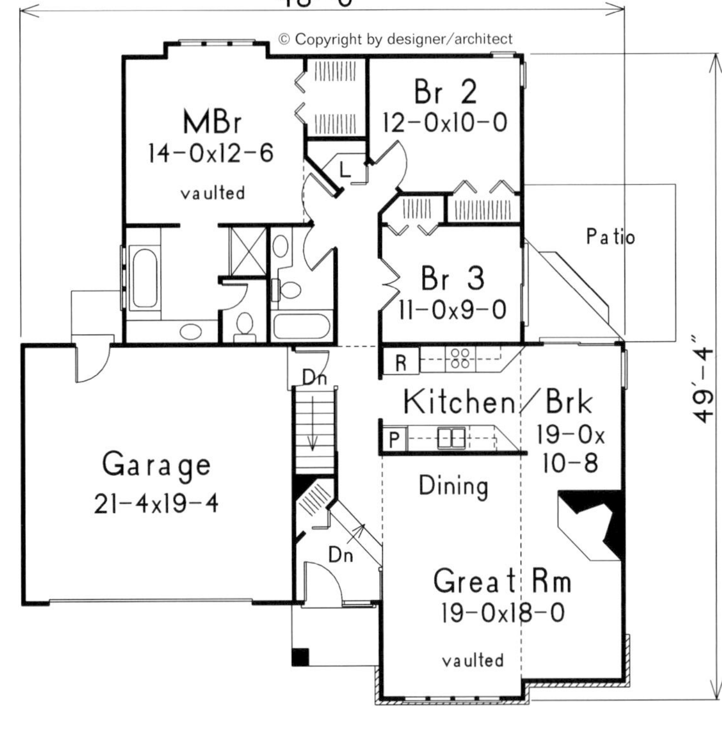

Plan Number: 537-007D-0060 | Price Code: B

Special Features

- 1,268 total square feet of living area
- Multiple gables, large porch and arched windows create a classy exterior
- Innovative design provides openness in the great room, kitchen and breakfast room
- Secondary bedrooms have private hall with bath
- 3 bedrooms, 2 baths, 2-car garage
- Basement foundation, drawings also include crawl space and slab foundations

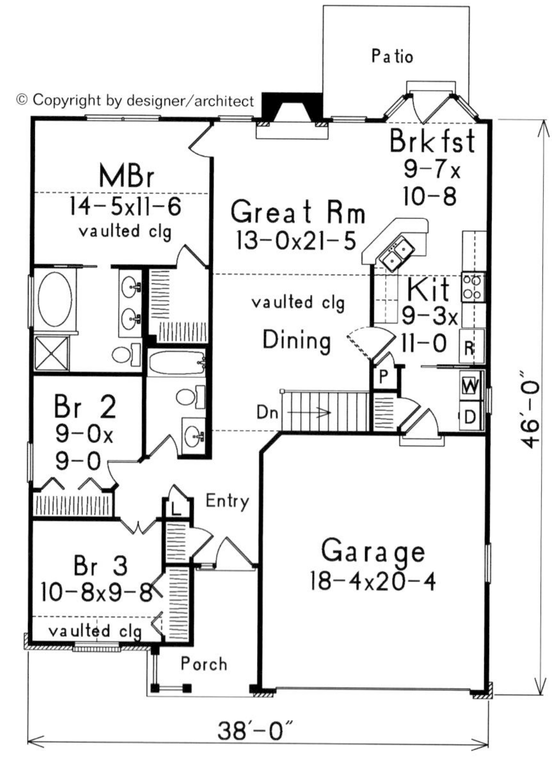

SPECIAL FEATURES

- 1,882 total square feet of living area
- Wide, handsome entrance opens to the vaulted great room with fireplace
- Living and dining areas are conveniently joined but still allow privacy
- Private covered porch extends breakfast area
- Practical passageway runs through the laundry room from the garage to the kitchen
- Vaulted ceiling in the master bedroom
- 3 bedrooms, 2 baths, 2-car garage
- Basement foundation

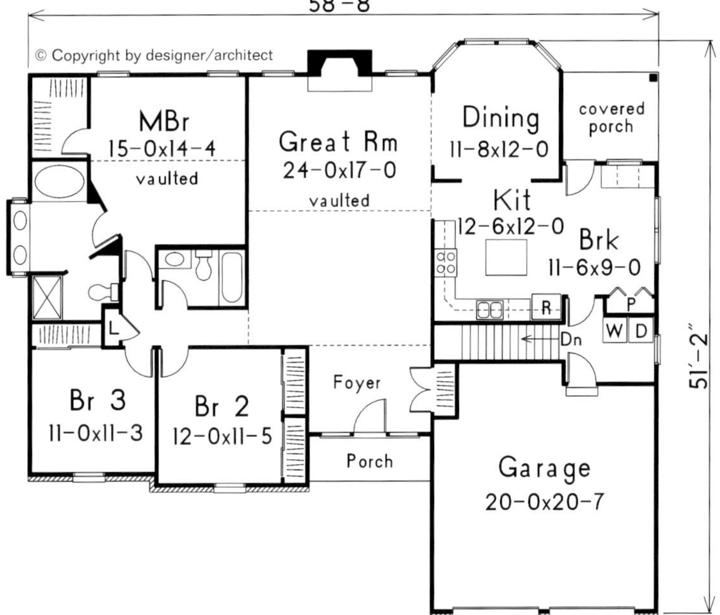

SPECIAL FEATURES

- 1,475 total square feet of living area
- Family room features a high ceiling and prominent corner fireplace
- Kitchen with island counter and garden window makes a convenient connection between the family and dining rooms
- Hallway leads to three bedrooms all with large walk-in closets
- Covered breezeway joins the main house and garage
- Full-width covered porch entry lends a country touch
- 3 bedrooms, 2 baths, 2-car detached side entry garage
- Slab foundation, drawings also include crawl space foundation

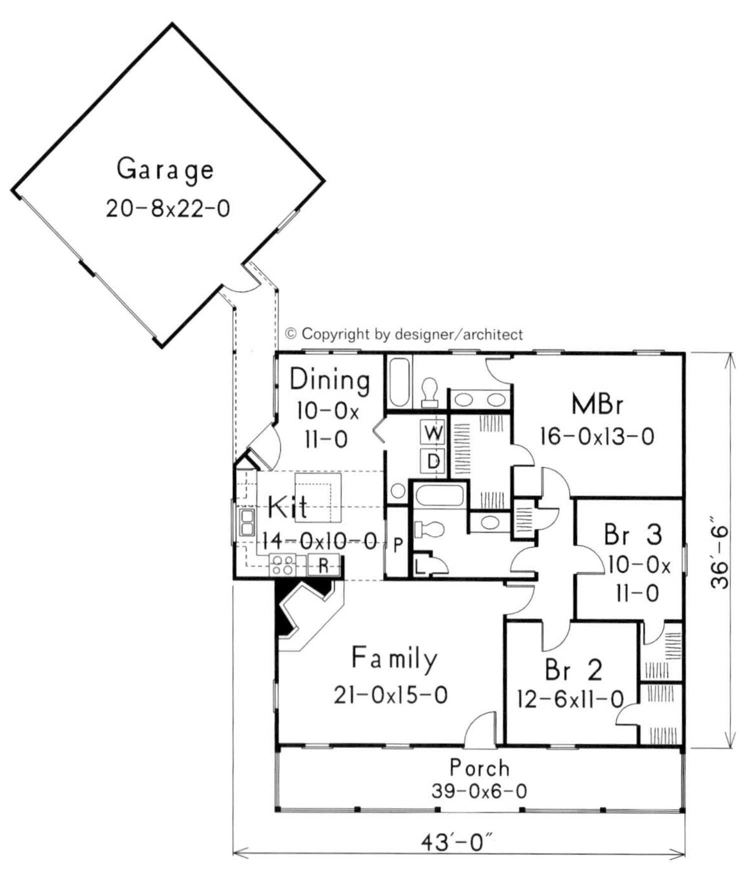

SPECIAL FEATURES

- 1,721 total square feet of living area
- Roof dormers add great curb appeal
- Vaulted dining and great rooms are immersed in light from window wall
- Breakfast room opens onto the covered porch
- 3 bedrooms, 2 baths, 3-car garage
- Walk-out basement foundation, drawings also include crawl space and slab foundations
- 1,604 square feet on the first floor and 117 square feet on the lower level atrium

Rear View

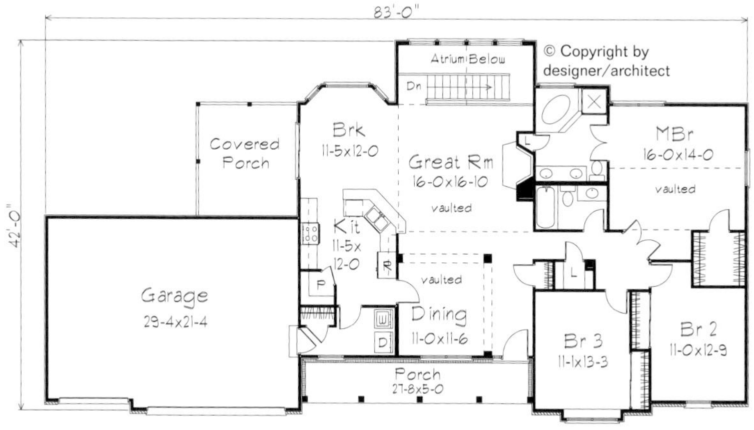

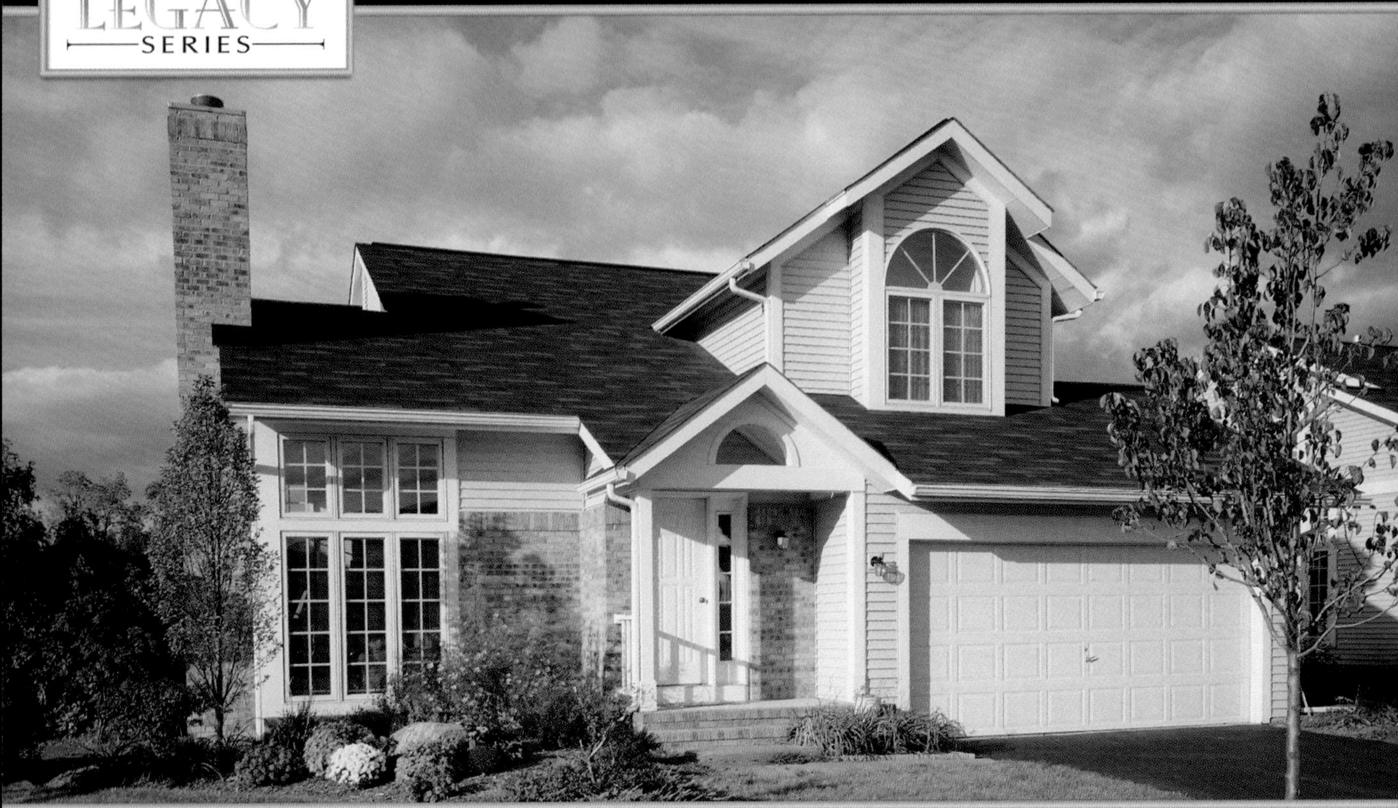

Special Features

- 1,556 total square feet of living area
- A compact home with all the amenities
- Country kitchen combines practicality with access to other areas for eating and entertaining
- Two-way fireplace joins the dining and living areas
- A plant shelf and vaulted ceiling highlight the master bedroom
- 3 bedrooms, 2 1/2 baths, 2-car garage
- Basement foundation

Second Floor
722 sq. ft.

First Floor
834 sq. ft.

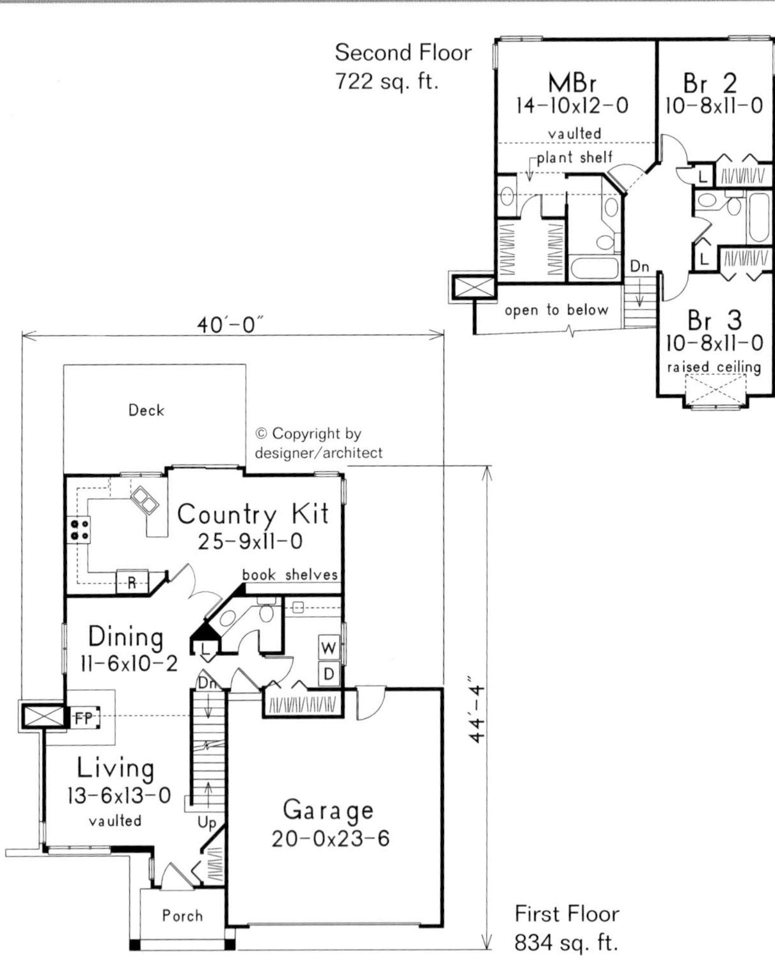

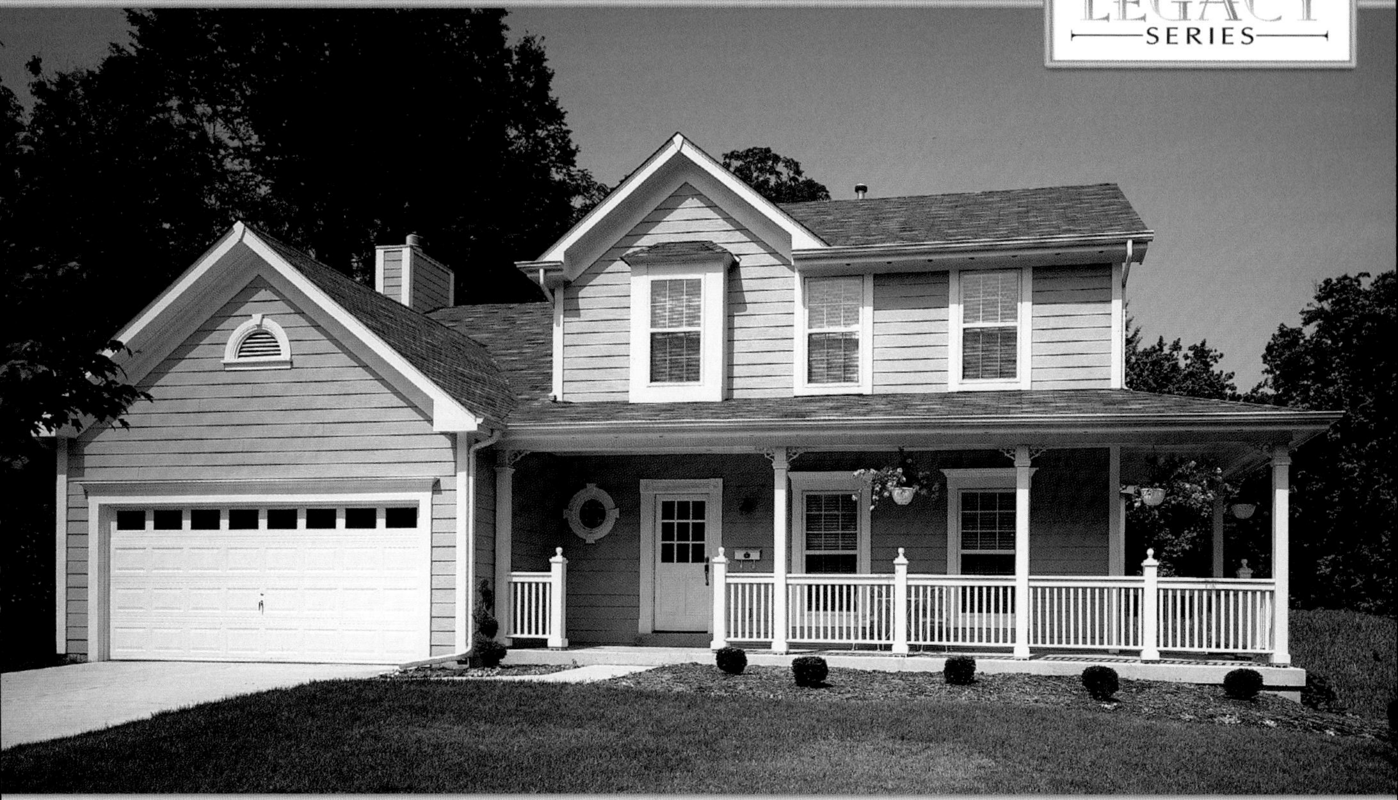

LOWE'S LEGACY SERIES

SPECIAL FEATURES

- 2,135 total square feet of living area
- Family room features extra space, an impressive fireplace and full wall of windows that joins the breakfast room creating a spacious entertainment area
- Washer and dryer are conveniently located on the second floor near the bedrooms
- The kitchen features an island counter and pantry
- 4 bedrooms, 2 1/2 baths, 2-car garage
- Basement foundation

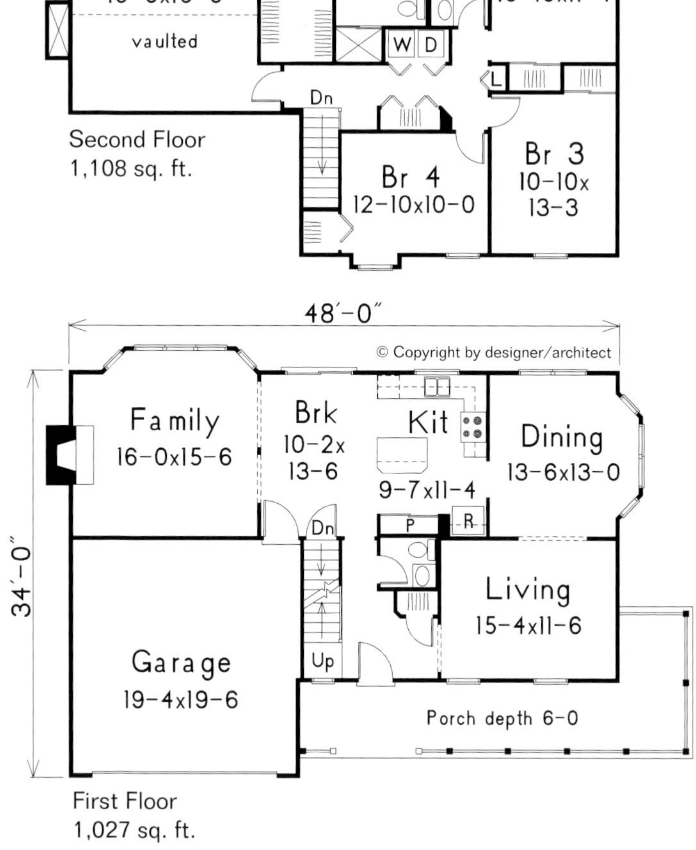

SPECIAL FEATURES

- 1,442 total square feet of living area
- Centrally located living room has a recessed fireplace and 10' ceiling
- Large U-shaped kitchen offers an eating bar and pantry
- Expanded garage provides extra storage and work area
- Spacious master bedroom with sitting area and large walk-in closet
- 3 bedrooms, 2 baths, 2-car garage
- Slab foundation, drawings also include crawl space foundation

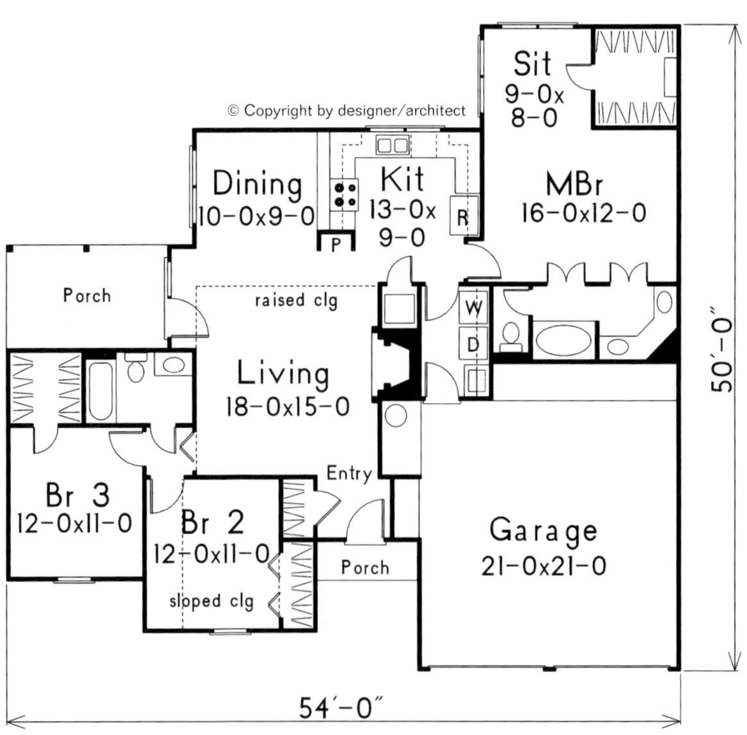

LOWE'S LEGACY SERIES

SPECIAL FEATURES

- 2,333 total square feet of living area
- 9' ceilings on the first floor
- Master bedroom features a large walk-in closet and an inviting double-door entry into a spacious bath
- Convenient laundry room is located near the kitchen
- 4 bedrooms, 3 baths, 2-car side entry garage
- Slab foundation, drawings also include crawl space and partial crawl space/basement foundations

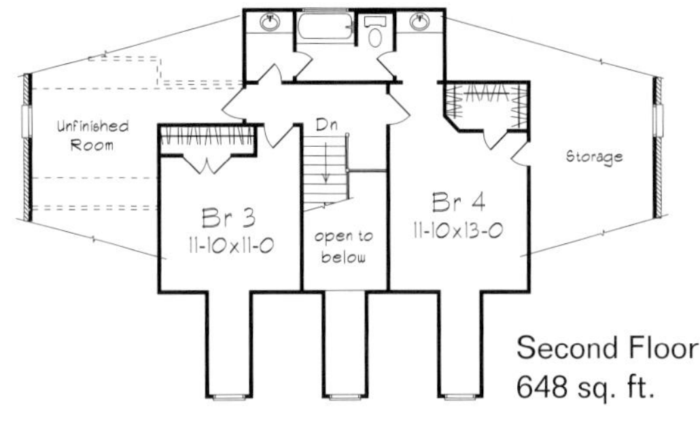

Second Floor
648 sq. ft.

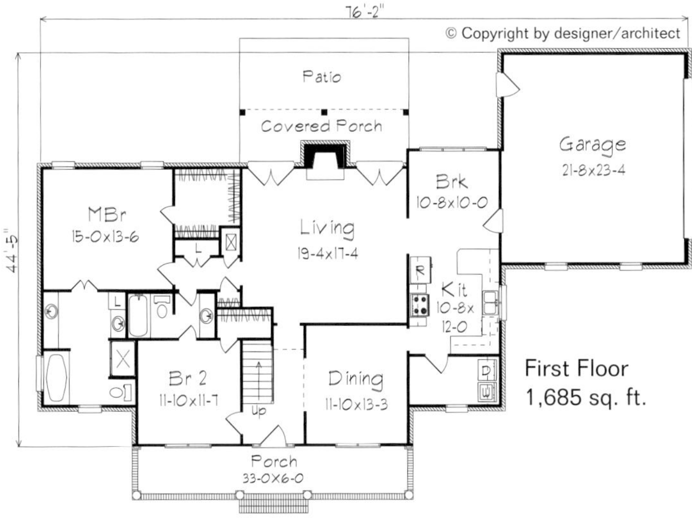

First Floor
1,685 sq. ft.

Special Features

- 2,262 total square feet of living area
- Charming exterior features include large front porch, two patios, front balcony and double bay windows
- Den provides an impressive entry to a sunken family room
- Large master bedroom has a walk-in closet, dressing area and bath
- 2" x 6" exterior walls available, please order plan #537-001D-0117
- 3 bedrooms, 2 1/2 baths, 2-car rear entry garage
- Crawl space foundation, drawings also include basement and slab foundations

Rear View

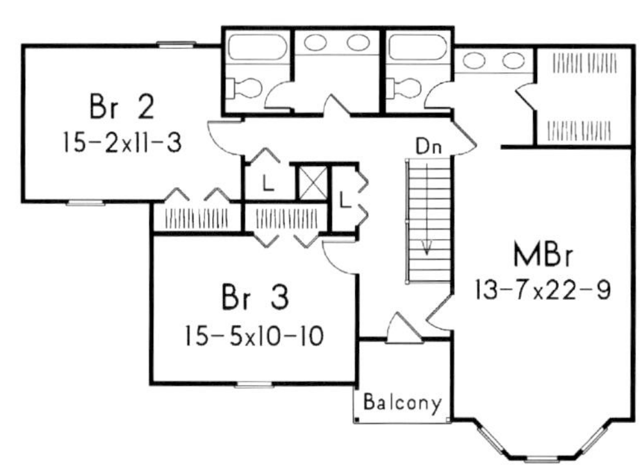

Second Floor
1,135 sq. ft.

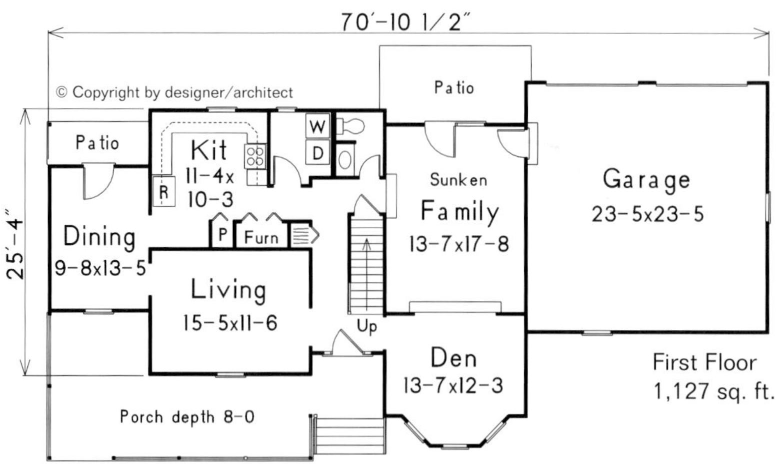

First Floor
1,127 sq. ft.

Plan Number: 537-027D-0003 | Price Code: D

Special Features

- 2,061 total square feet of living area
- Convenient entrance from garage into the home through laundry room
- Master bedroom features a walk-in closet and double-door entrance into the master bath with an oversized tub
- Formal dining room enjoys a tray ceiling
- Kitchen features island cooktop and adjacent breakfast room
- 3 bedrooms, 2 baths, 2-car garage
- Basement foundation

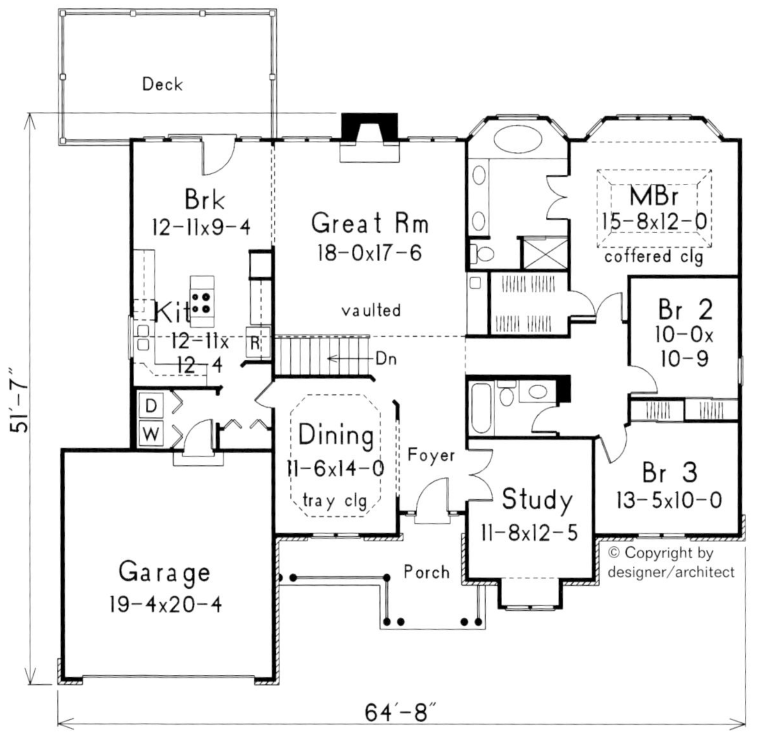

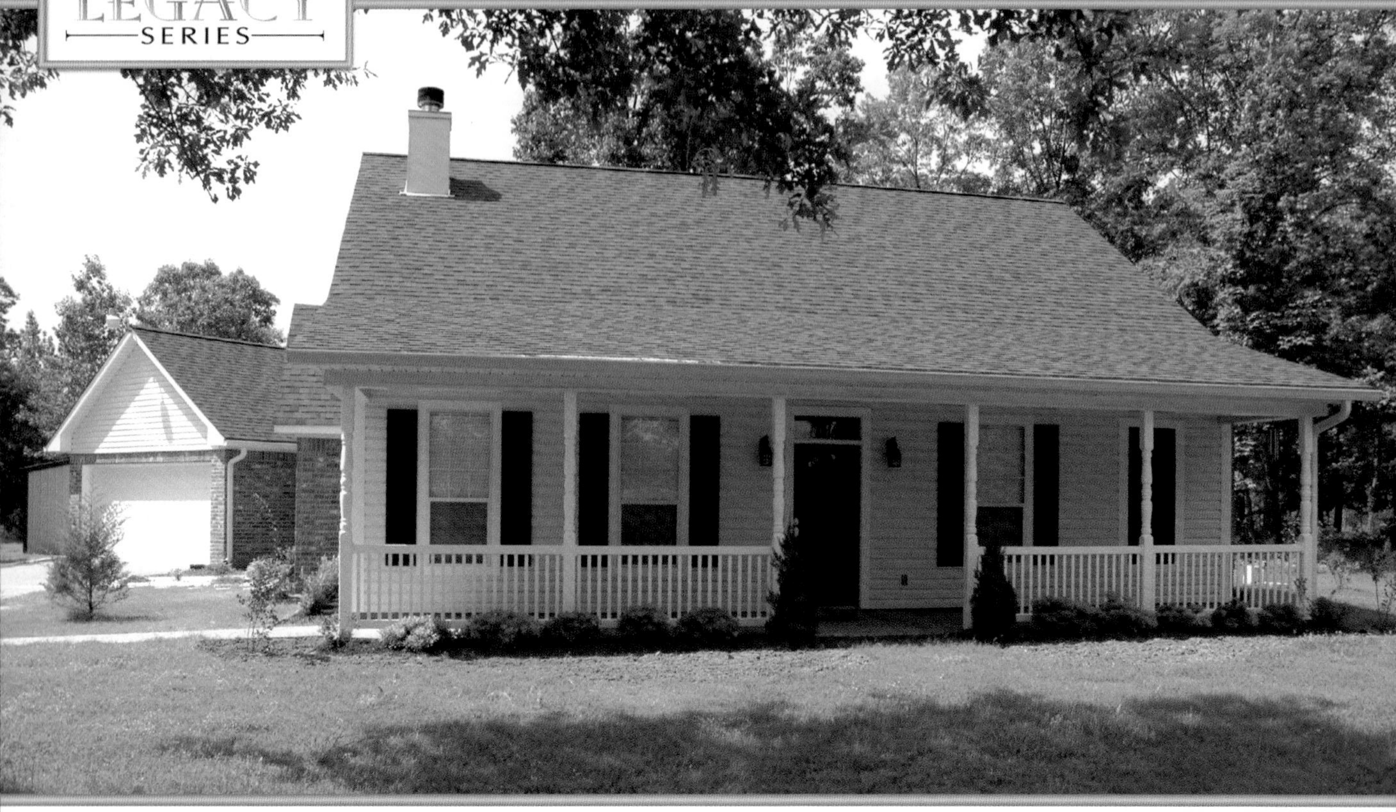

SPECIAL FEATURES

- 1,833 total square feet of living area
- Large master bedroom includes a spacious bath with garden tub, separate shower and large walk-in closet
- The spacious dining area is brightened by large windows and patio access
- Detached two-car garage with walkway leading to house adds charm to this country home
- 3 bedrooms, 2 1/2 baths, 2-car detached side entry garage
- Crawl space foundation, drawings also include slab foundation

Second Floor
545 sq. ft.

First Floor
1,288 sq. ft.

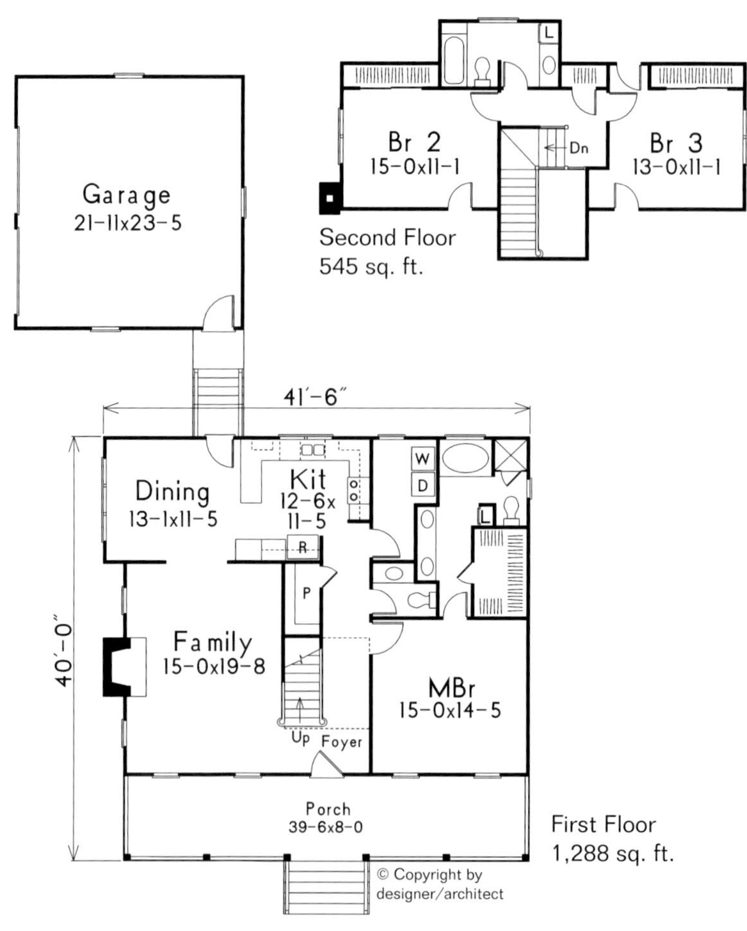

SPECIAL FEATURES

- 2,396 total square feet of living area
- Energy efficient home with 2" x 6" exterior walls
- Generously wide entry welcomes guests
- Central living area with a 12' ceiling and large fireplace serves as a convenient traffic hub
- Kitchen is secluded, yet has easy access to the living, dining and breakfast areas
- Deluxe master bath has a walk-in closet, oversized tub, shower and other amenities
- 4 bedrooms, 2 baths, 2-car garage
- Slab foundation, drawings also include basement and crawl space foundations

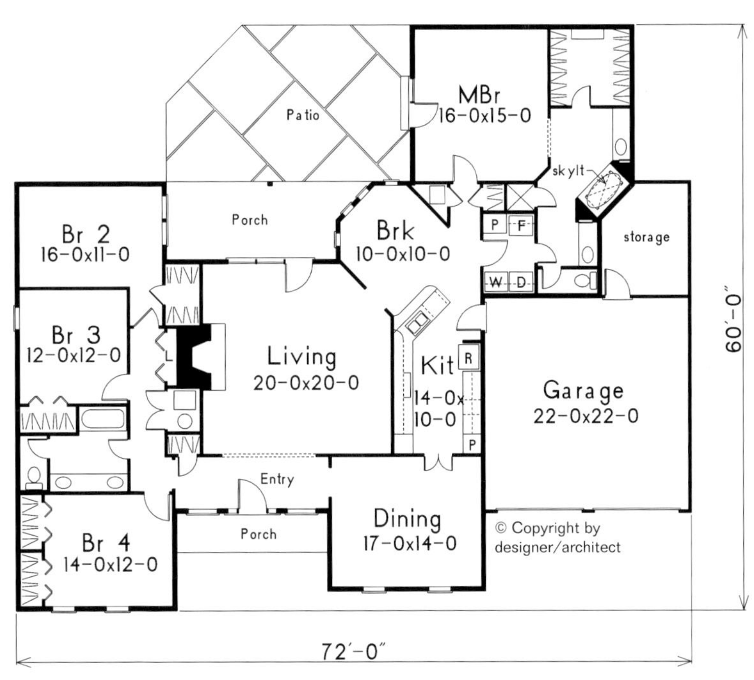

Plan Number: 537-001D-0003 | Price Code: E

Special Features

- 2,286 total square feet of living area
- Fine architectural detail makes this home a showplace with its large windows, intricate brickwork and fine woodwork and trim
- Stunning two-story entry with attractive wood railing and balustrades in the foyer
- Convenient wrap-around kitchen enjoys a window view, planning center and pantry
- Oversized master bedroom includes a walk-in closet and master bath
- 4 bedrooms, 2 1/2 baths, 2-car garage
- Basement foundation, drawings also include crawl space and slab foundations

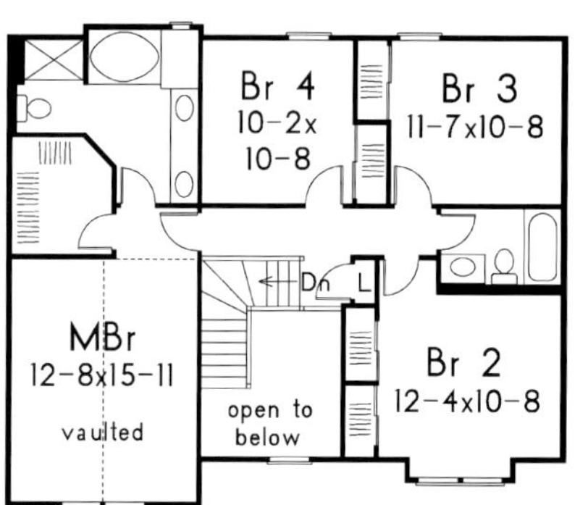

Second Floor
1,003 sq. ft.

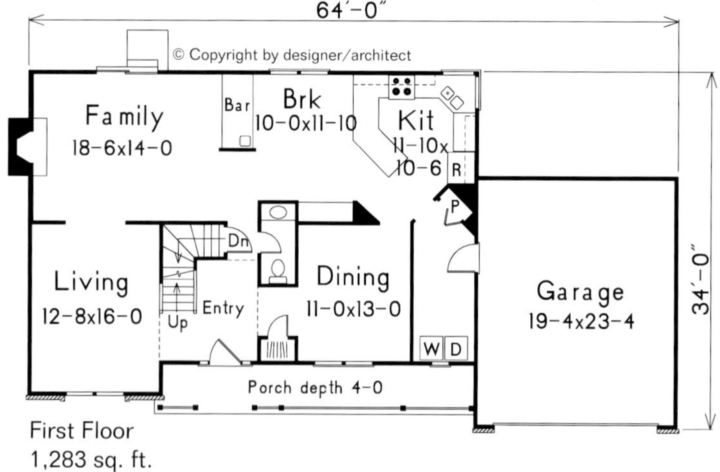

First Floor
1,283 sq. ft.

To Order See Page 288

Plan Number: 537-022D-0026 | Price Code: D

Lowe's Legacy Series

Special Features

- 1,993 total square feet of living area
- Spacious country kitchen boasts a fireplace and plenty of natural light from windows
- Formal dining room features a large bay window and steps down to the sunken living room
- Master bedroom features corner windows, plant shelves and a deluxe private bath
- Entry opens into the vaulted living room with windows flanking the fireplace
- 3 bedrooms, 2 baths, 2-car garage
- Basement foundation

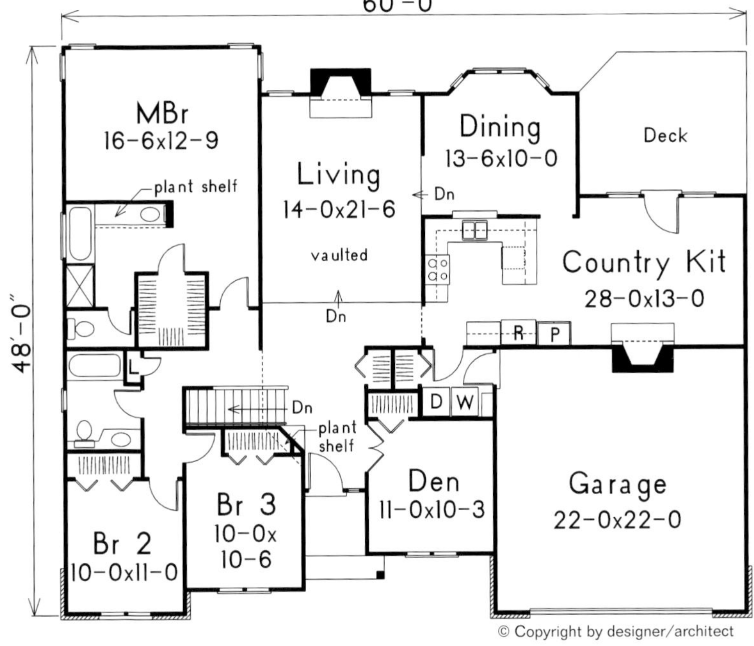

PLAN NUMBER: 537-021D-0011 | PRICE CODE: D

SPECIAL FEATURES

- 1,800 total square feet of living area
- Energy efficient home with 2" x 6" exterior walls
- Covered front and rear porches add outdoor living area
- 12' ceilings in the kitchen, breakfast area, dining and living rooms
- Side entry garage has two storage areas
- Pillared styling with brick and stucco exterior finish
- 3 bedrooms, 2 baths, 2-car side entry garage
- Crawl space foundation, drawings also include slab foundation

Interior View - Living Room

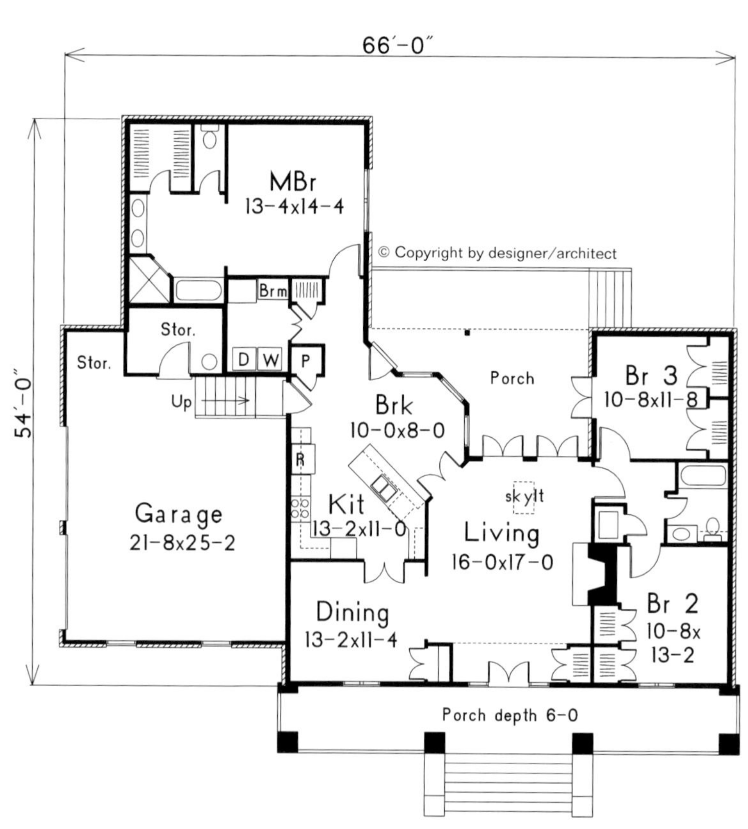

Plan Number: 537-022D-0019 | Price Code: A

Special Features

- 1,283 total square feet of living area
- Vaulted breakfast room has sliding doors that open onto the deck
- Kitchen features a convenient corner sink and pass-through to the dining room
- Open living atmosphere in dining area and great room
- Vaulted great room features a fireplace
- 3 bedrooms, 2 baths, 2-car garage
- Basement foundation

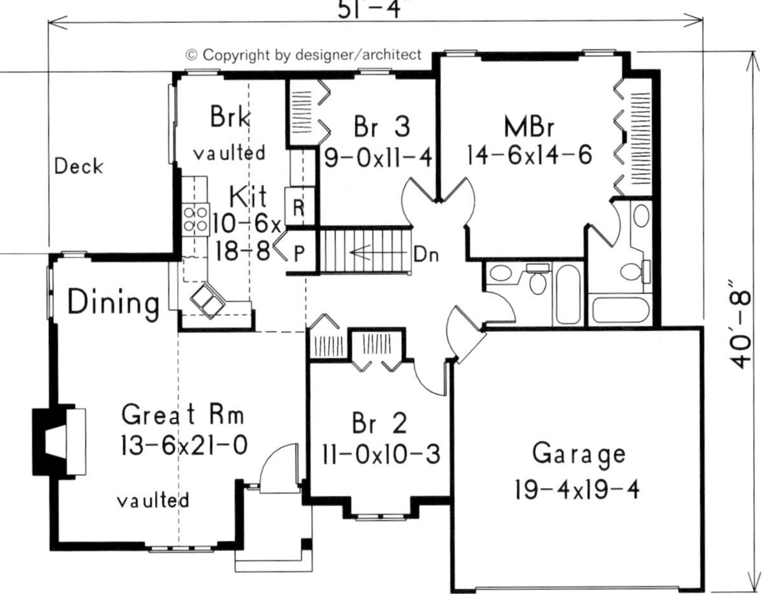

Special Features

- 1,672 total square feet of living area
- Vaulted master bedroom features a walk-in closet and adjoining bath with separate tub and shower
- Energy efficient home with 2" x 6" exterior walls
- Covered front and rear porches
- 12' ceilings in the living room, kitchen and bedroom #2
- Kitchen is complete with a pantry, angled bar and adjacent eating area
- Sloped ceiling in the dining room
- 3 bedrooms, 2 baths, 2-car side entry garage
- Crawl space foundation, drawings also include basement and slab foundations

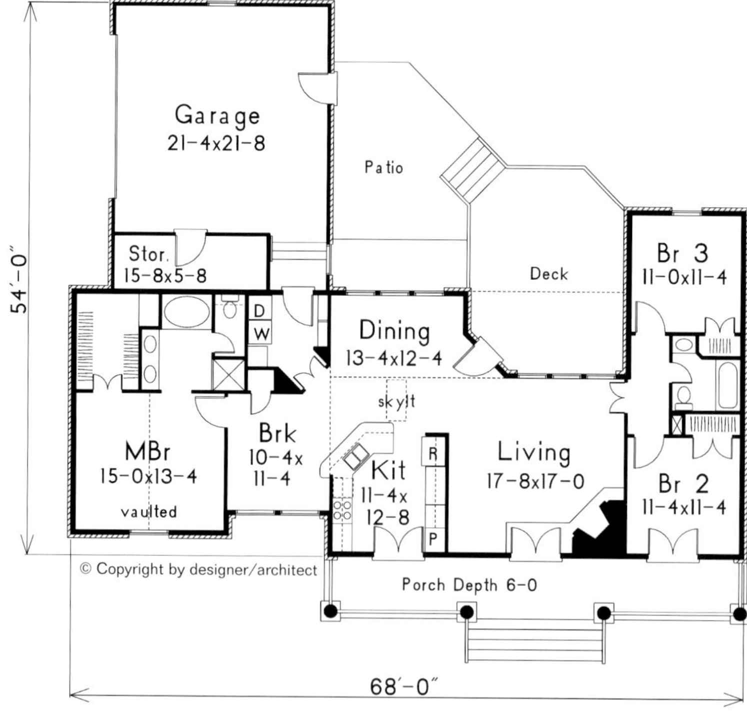

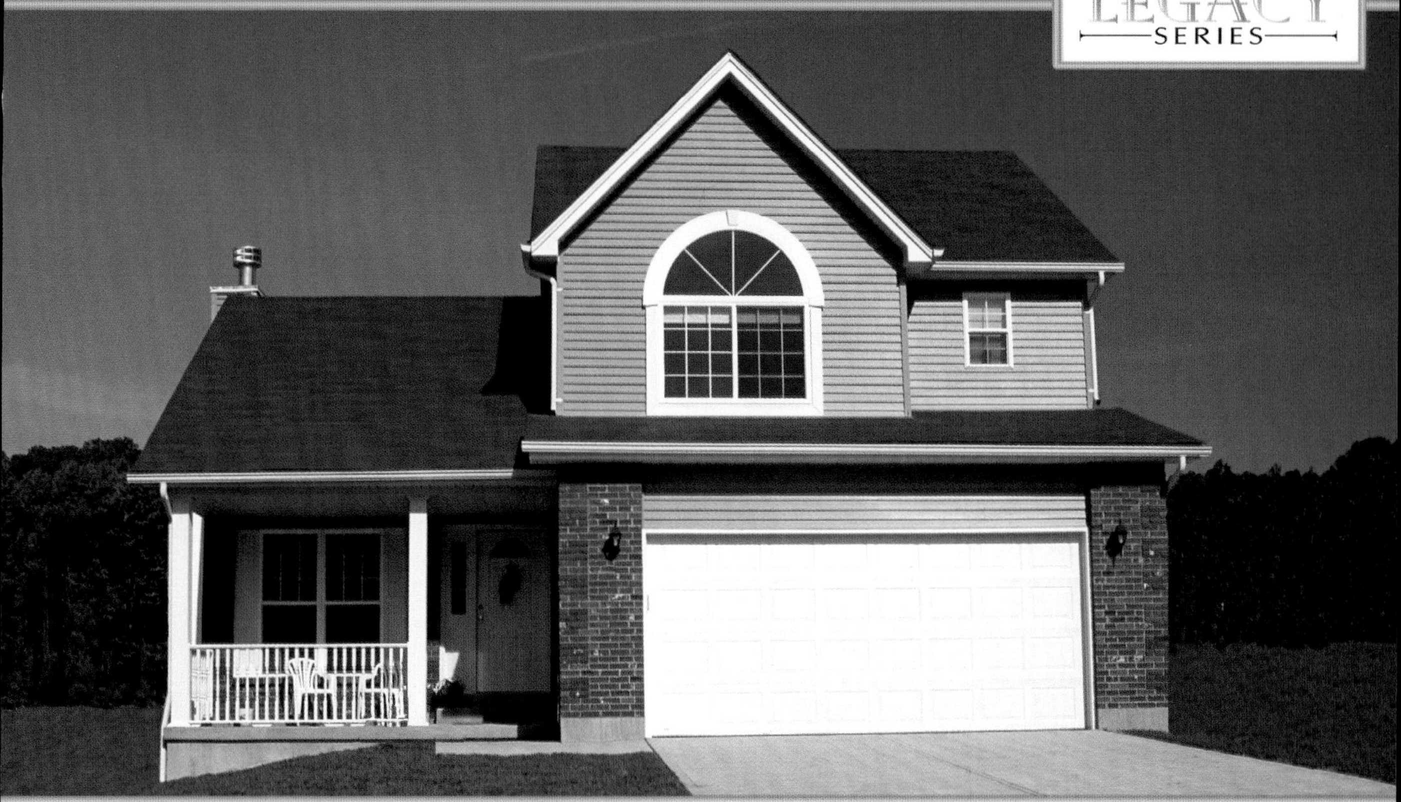

SPECIAL FEATURES

- 1,189 total square feet of living area
- All bedrooms are located on the second floor
- Dining room and kitchen both have views of the patio
- Convenient half bath is located near the kitchen
- Master bedroom has a private bath
- 3 bedrooms, 2 1/2 baths, 2-car garage
- Basement foundation

Second Floor
574 sq. ft.

First Floor
615 sq. ft.

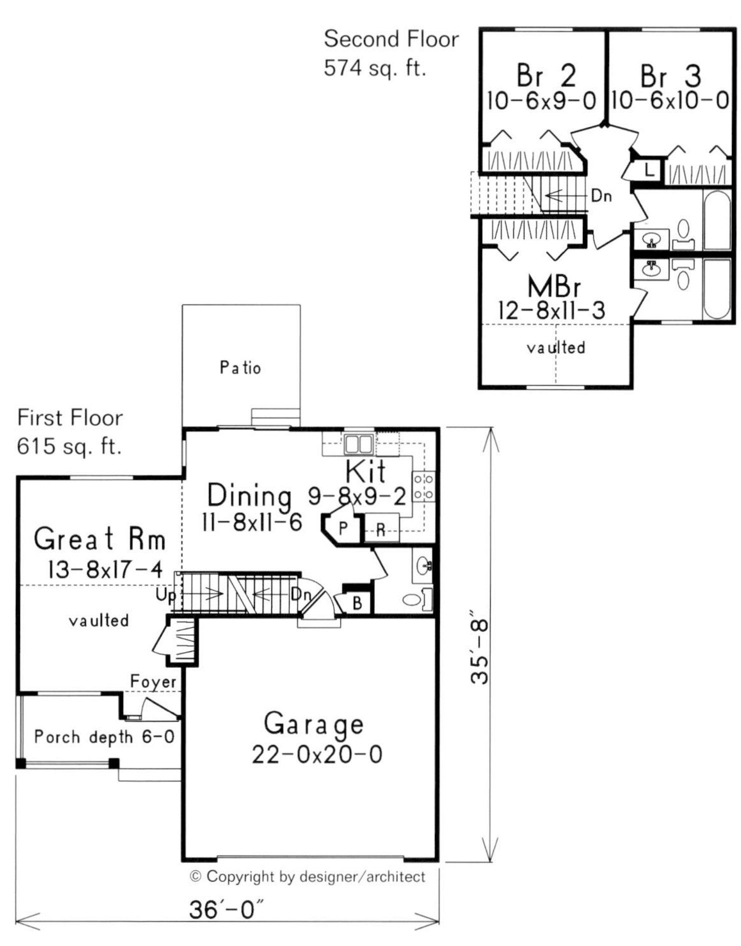

Plan Number: 537-007D-0005 | Price Code: D

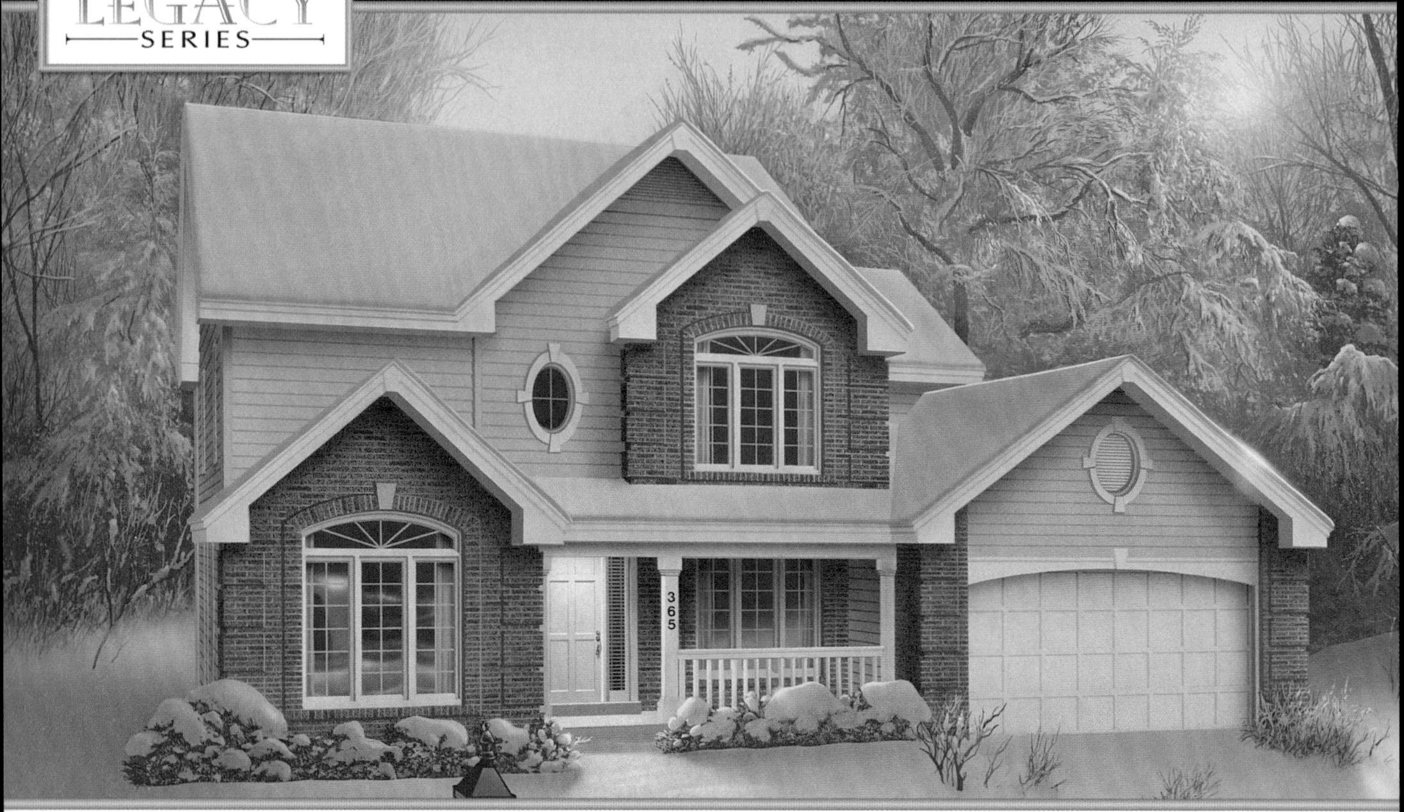

Special Features

- 2,336 total square feet of living area
- Stately sunken living room with partially vaulted ceiling and classic arched transom windows create a pleasant atmosphere
- Family room features plenty of windows and a fireplace with flanking bookshelves
- All bedrooms are located on the second floor for added privacy
- 4 bedrooms, 2 1/2 baths, 2-car garage
- Basement foundation, drawings also include slab and crawl space foundations

Second Floor
1,045 sq. ft.

First Floor
1,291 sq. ft.

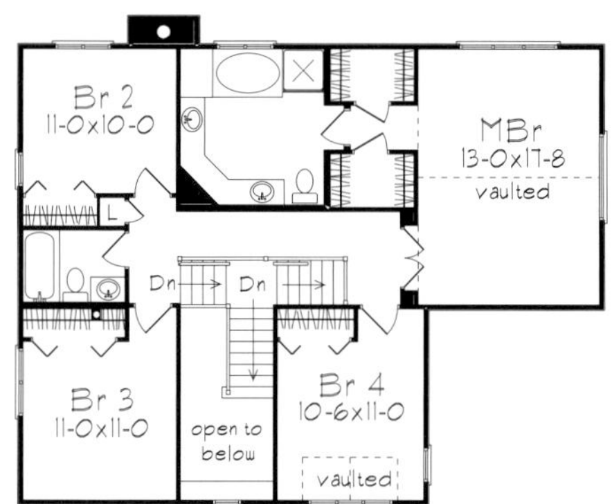

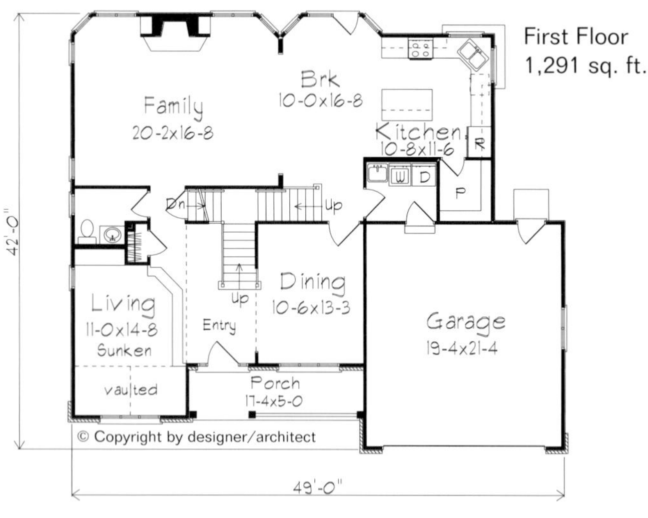

Plan Number: 537-057D-0016 | Price Code: B

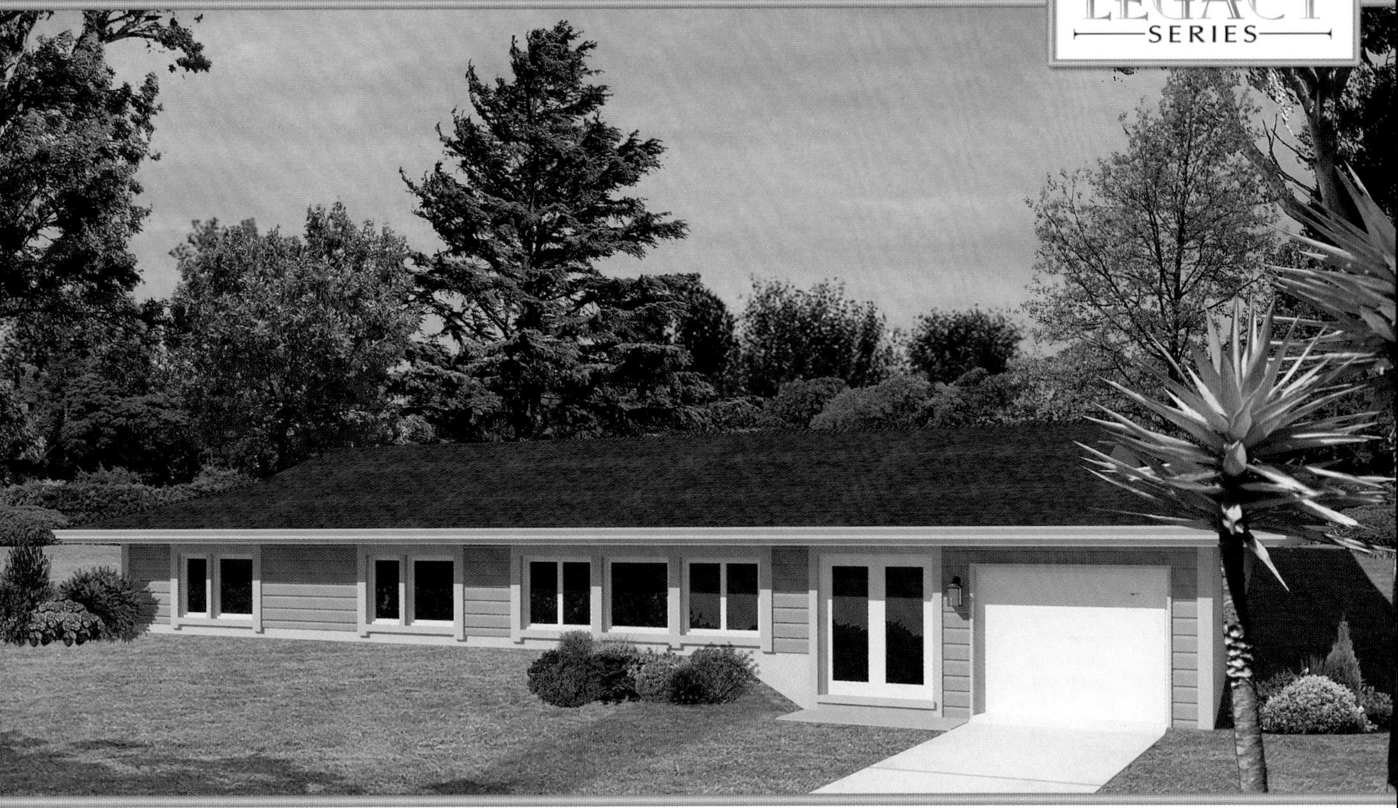

Special Features

- 1,643 total square feet of living area
- Energy efficient home with 2" x 6" exterior walls
- This berm design provides the ultimate in efficiency with windows only on the front walls
- The kitchen, living and dining rooms all combine for a spacious living area in this stylish, economical design
- An office, laundry room and half bath add conveniences for family living
- The massive master bedroom enjoys a deluxe bath with whirlpool tub and two walk-in closets
- 3 bedrooms, 2 1/2 baths, 1-car garage
- Slab foundation

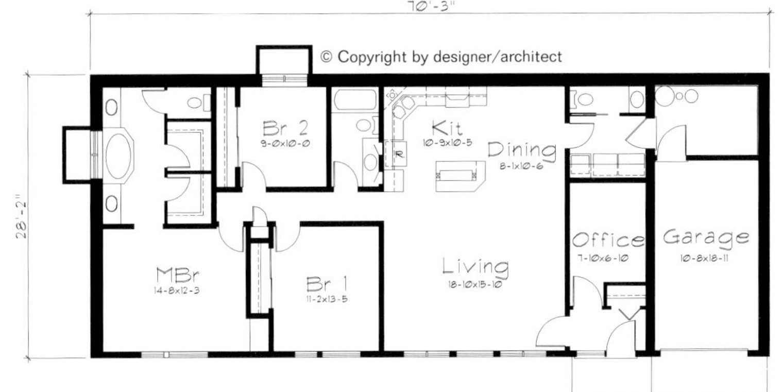

PLAN NUMBER: 537-007D-0180 | PRICE CODE: AA

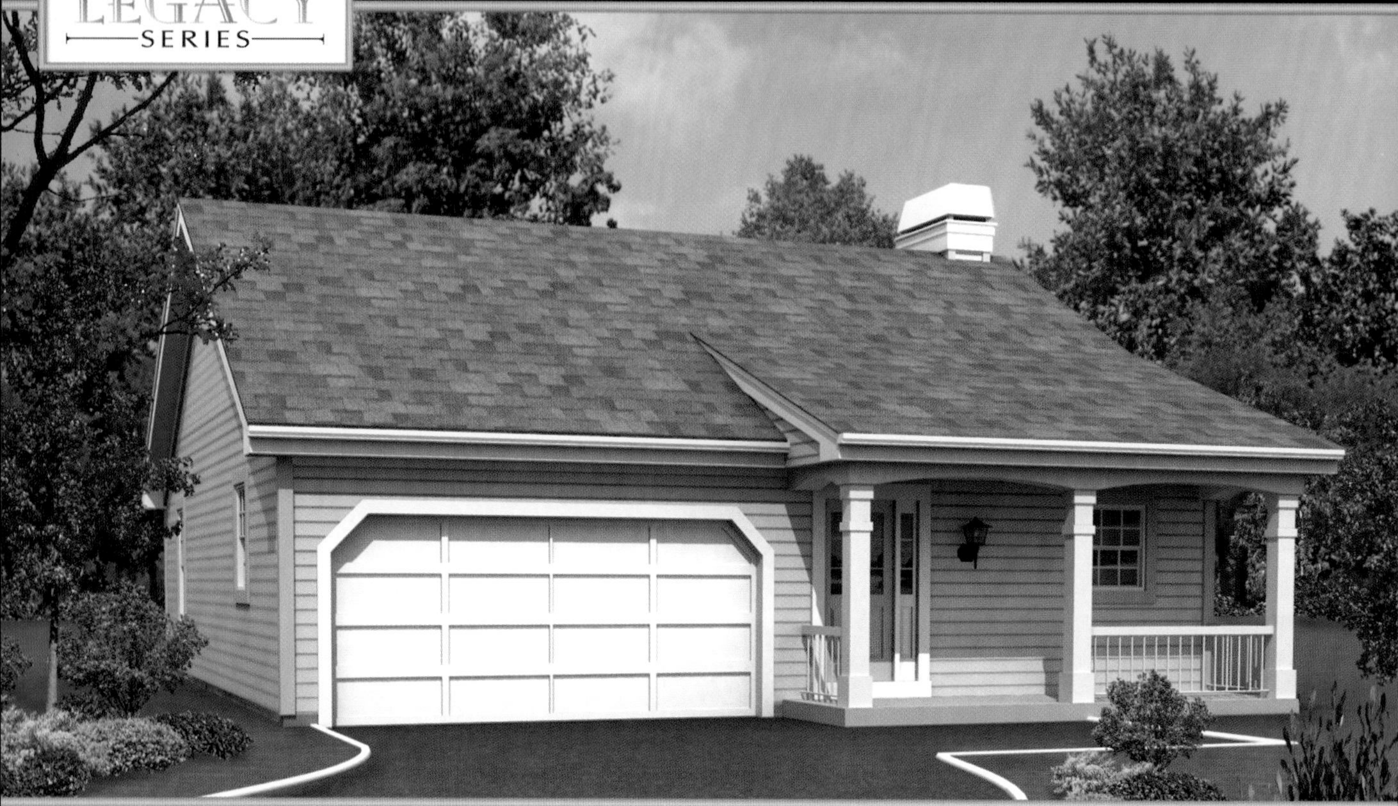

SPECIAL FEATURES

- 1,171 total square feet of living area
- This home is perfect for a starter home, second home on a lake or countryside setting
- The vaulted living room offers many exciting features including a corner fireplace and dining area with sliding doors to the side patio
- A built-in pantry, vaulted ceiling and breakfast bar are just a few amenities of the delightful kitchen
- 3 bedrooms, 2 baths, 2-car garage
- Basement foundation, drawings also include slab and crawl space foundations

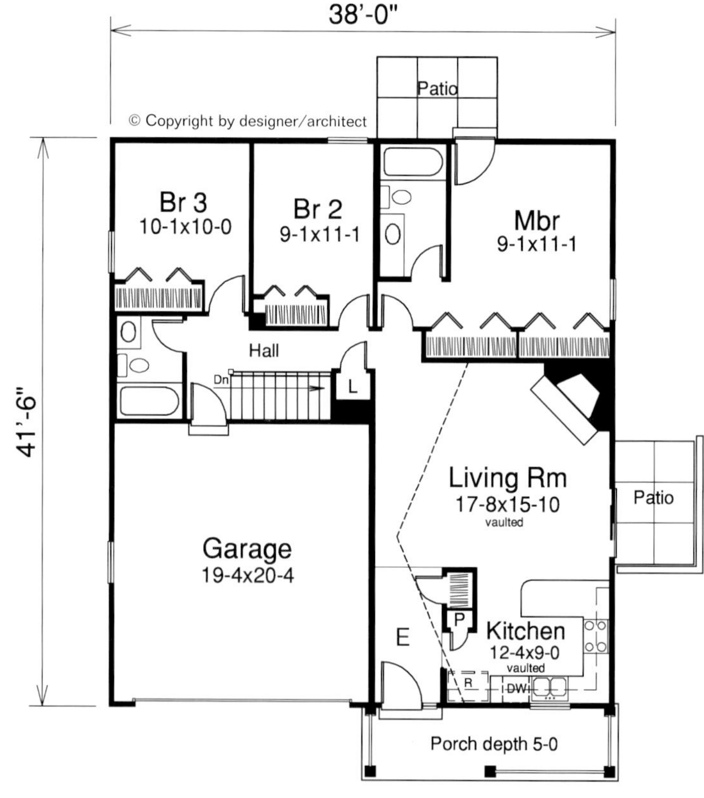

SPECIAL FEATURES

- 1,660 total square feet of living area
- Energy efficient home with 2" x 6" exterior walls
- Convenient gear and equipment room
- Spacious living and dining rooms look even larger with the openness of the foyer and kitchen
- Large wrap-around deck is a great plus for outdoor living
- Broad balcony overlooks living and dining rooms
- 3 bedrooms, 3 baths
- Partial basement/crawl space foundation, drawings also include slab foundation

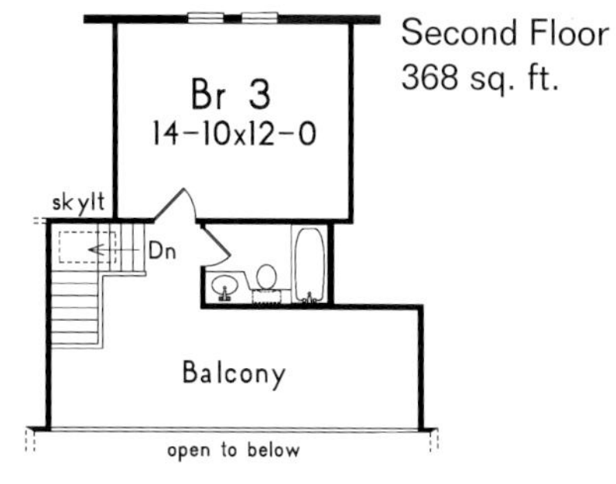

Second Floor
368 sq. ft.

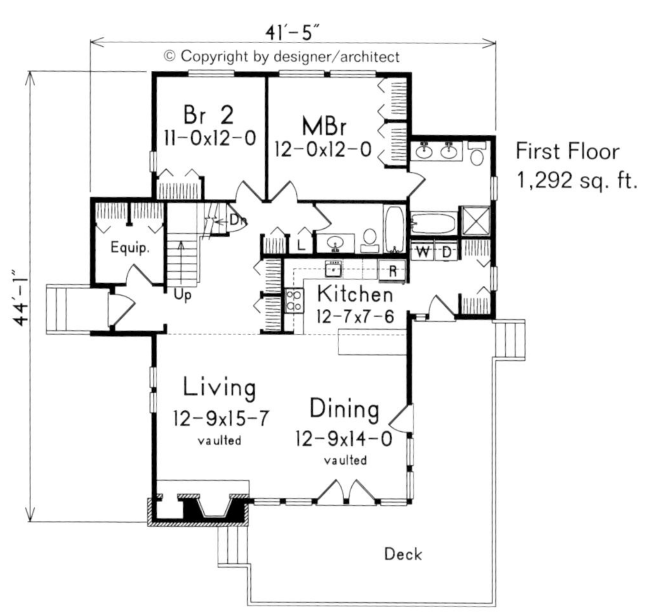

First Floor
1,292 sq. ft.

SPECIAL FEATURES

- 2,058 total square feet of living area
- Handsome two-story foyer with balcony creates a spacious entrance area
- Vaulted master bedroom has a private dressing area and large walk-in closet
- Skylights furnish natural lighting in the hall and master bath
- Laundry closet is conveniently located on the second floor near the bedrooms
- 3 bedrooms, 2 1/2 baths, 2-car garage
- Basement foundation, drawings also include slab and crawl space foundations

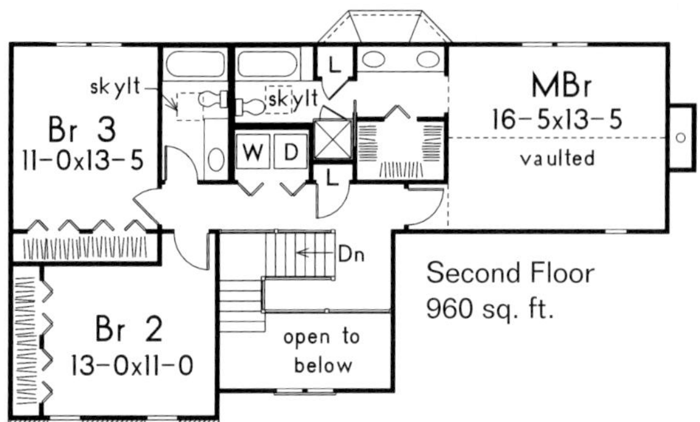

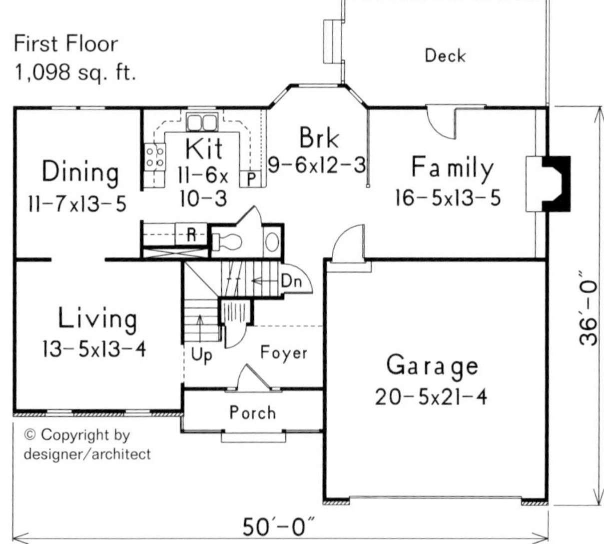

SPECIAL FEATURES

- 1,996 total square feet of living area
- The large covered rear porch enjoys direct access to the master bedroom suite and the living room
- Sculptured entrance has artful plant shelves and a special niche in the foyer
- Master bedroom boasts French doors, a garden tub, desk with bookshelves and generous storage
- Plant shelves and a high ceiling grace the hallway
- 3 bedrooms, 2 baths, 2-car side entry garage
- Slab foundation, drawings also include crawl space foundation

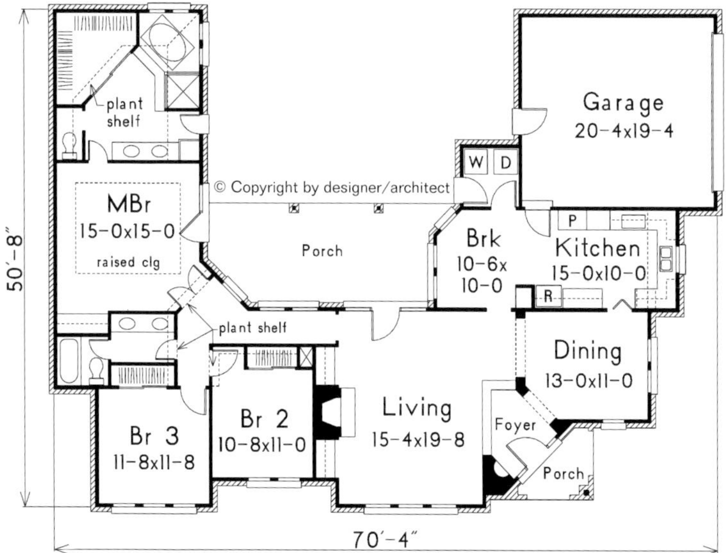

PLAN NUMBER: 537-007D-0011 | PRICE CODE: D

SPECIAL FEATURES

- 2,182 total square feet of living area
- Meandering porch creates an inviting look
- Generous great room has four double-hung windows and sliding doors to the exterior
- Highly functional kitchen features island/breakfast bar, menu desk and convenient pantry
- Each secondary bedroom includes generous closet space and a private bath
- 3 bedrooms, 3 1/2 baths, 2-car side entry garage
- Basement foundation, drawings also include crawl space and slab foundations

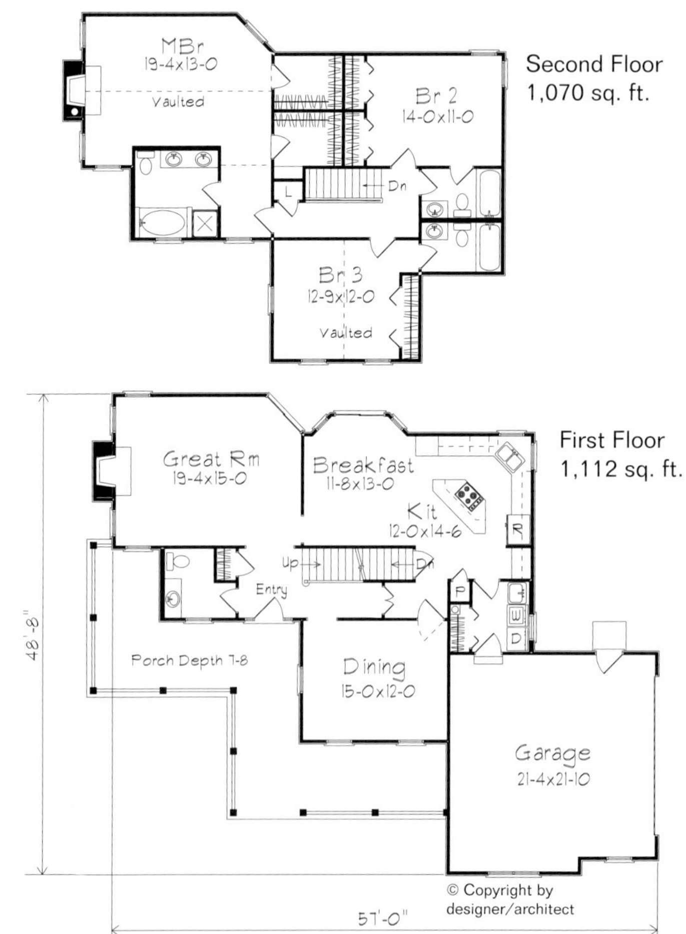

LOWE'S LEGACY SERIES

SPECIAL FEATURES

- 1,202 total square feet of living area
- All the necessary ingredients provided in a simple structure that's affordable to build
- The vaulted living room features a fireplace, dining area and access to the rear patio
- An angled snack bar is the highlight of this well-planned U-shaped kitchen
- 3 bedrooms, 2 baths, 2-car side entry garage
- Basement foundation, drawings also include slab and crawl space foundations

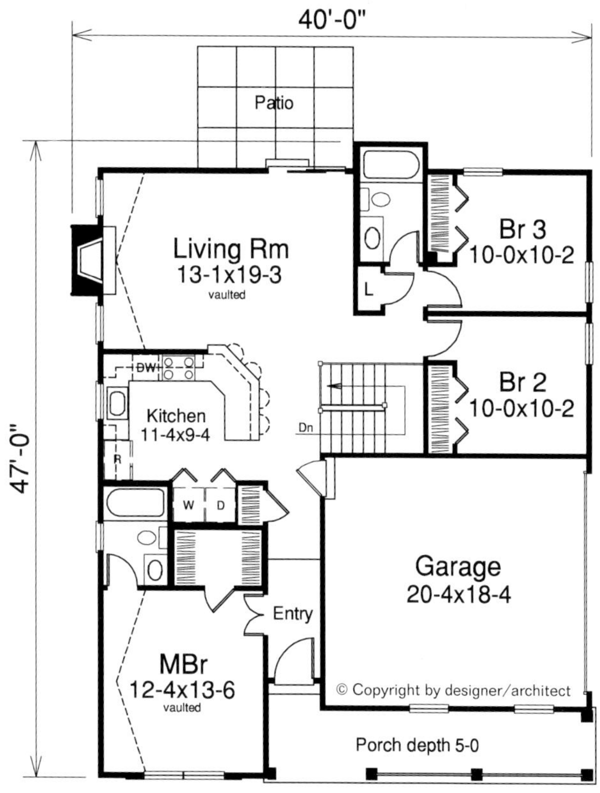

LOWE'S LEGACY SERIES

PLAN NUMBER: 537-001D-0001 | PRICE CODE: B

SPECIAL FEATURES

- 1,605 total square feet of living area
- Vaulted ceilings in the great room, kitchen and breakfast area
- Spacious great room features a large bay window, fireplace, built-in bookshelves and a convenient wet bar
- The formal dining room and breakfast area are perfect for entertaining or everyday living
- Master bedroom has a spacious bath with oval tub and separate shower
- 3 bedrooms, 2 baths, 2-car garage
- Basement foundation, drawings also include slab and crawl space foundations

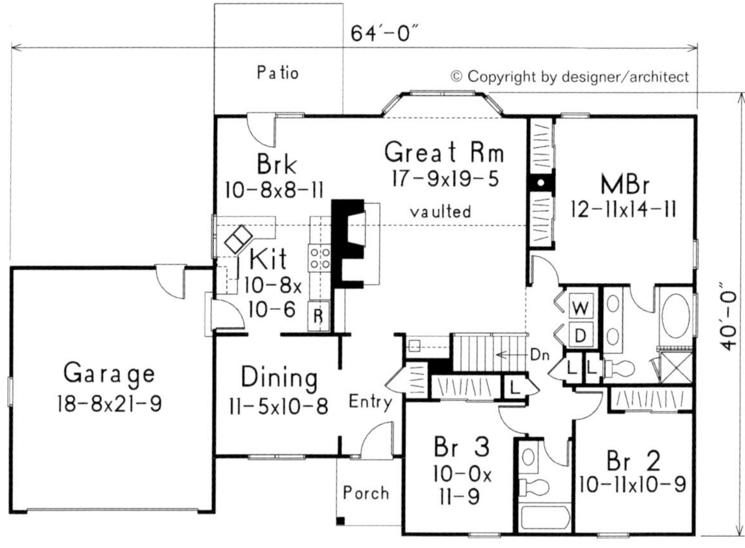

TO ORDER SEE PAGE 288 | CALL TOLL-FREE 1-877-379-3420

LOWE'S LEGACY SERIES

SPECIAL FEATURES

- 882 total square feet of living area
- An inviting porch and entry lure you into this warm and cozy home
- Living room features a vaulted ceiling, bayed dining area and is open to a well-equipped U-shaped kitchen
- The master bedroom has two separate closets and direct access to the rear patio
- 2 bedrooms, 1 bath
- Crawl space foundation, drawings also include slab and basement foundations

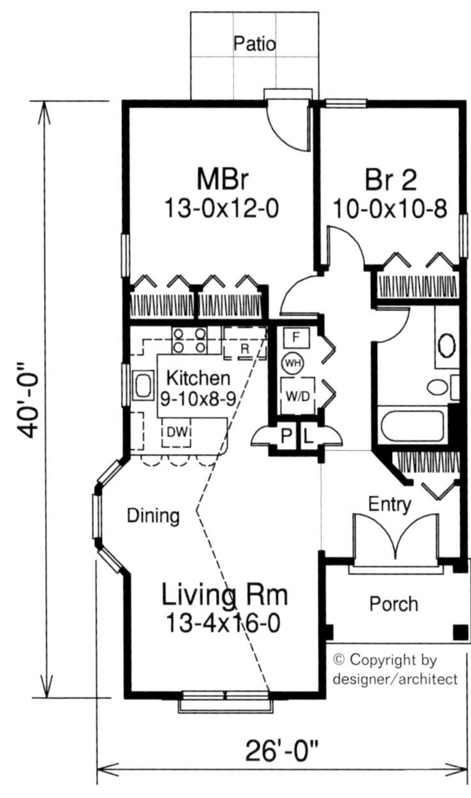

SPECIAL FEATURES

- 1,560 total square feet of living area
- Cozy breakfast room is tucked at the rear of this home and features plenty of windows for natural light
- Large entry has easy access to the secondary bedrooms, utility area, dining and living rooms
- Private master bedroom
- Kitchen overlooks the living room which features a fireplace and patio access
- 3 bedrooms, 2 baths, 2-car garage
- Slab foundation

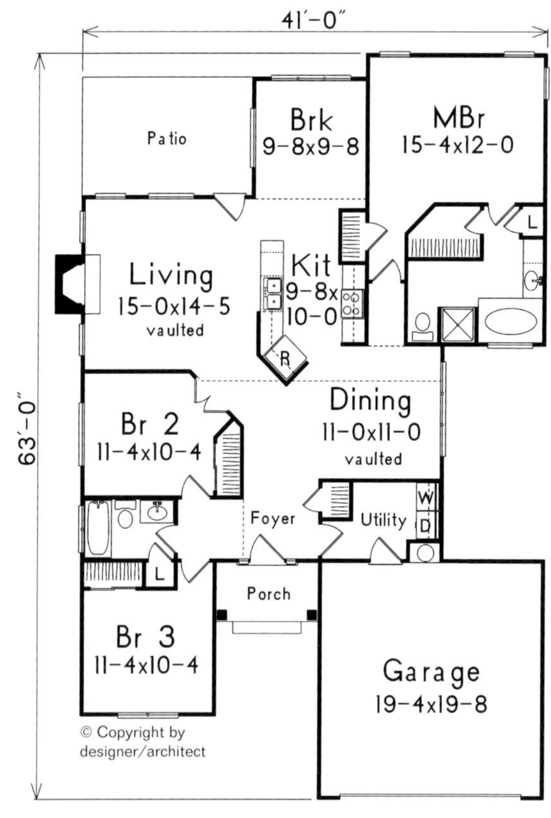

Plan Number: 537-007D-0013 | Price Code: A

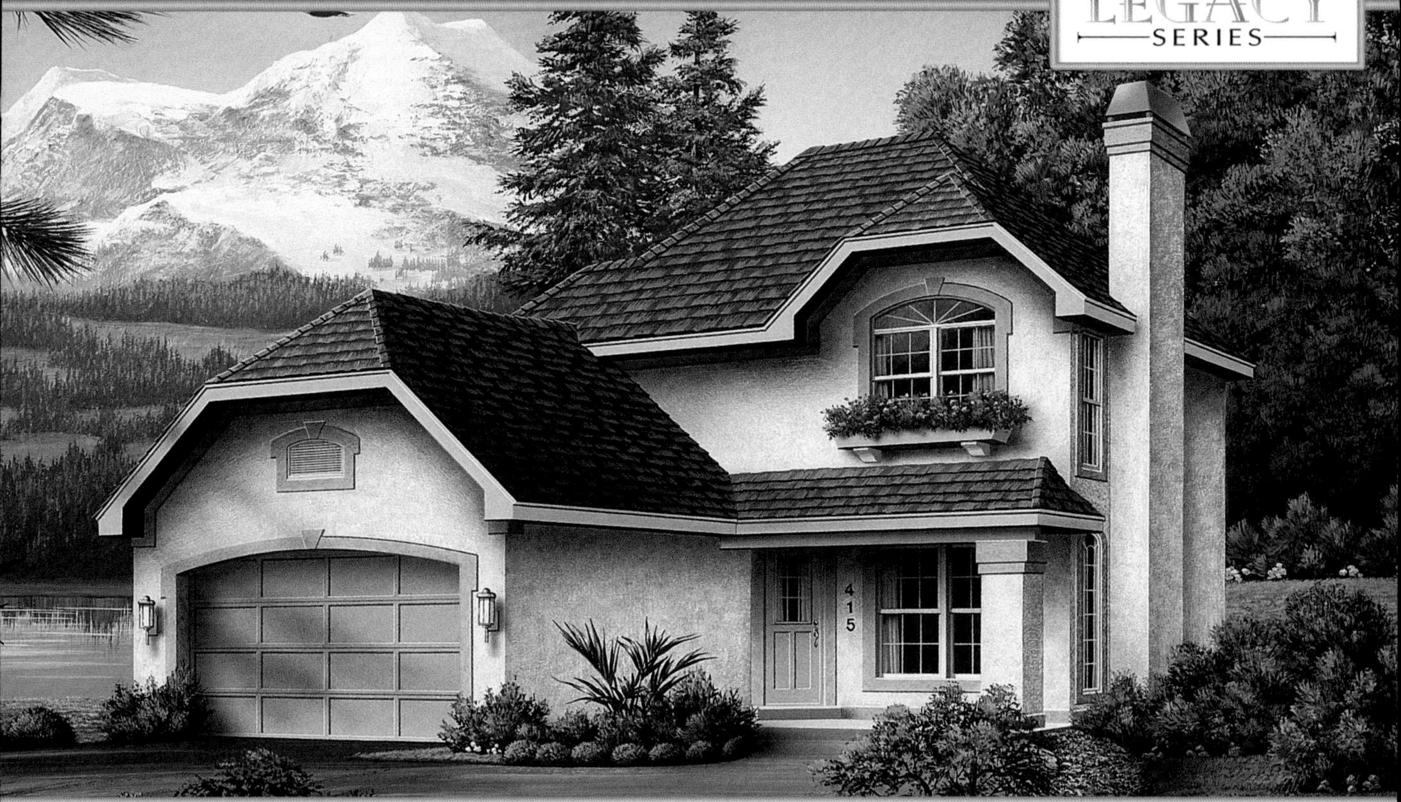

Special Features

- 1,492 total square feet of living area
- Cleverly angled entry spills into the living and dining rooms which share warmth from the fireplace flanked by arched windows
- Master bedroom includes a double-door entry, huge walk-in closet, shower and bath with picture window
- Stucco and dutch-hipped roofs add warmth and charm to the facade
- 3 bedrooms, 2 1/2 baths, 2-car garage
- Basement foundation

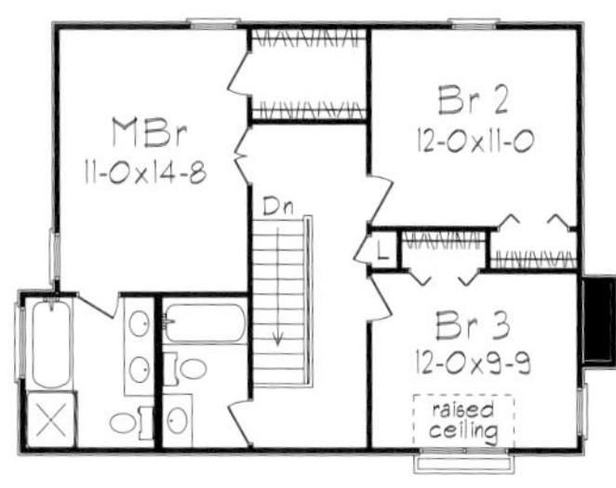

Second Floor
732 sq. ft.

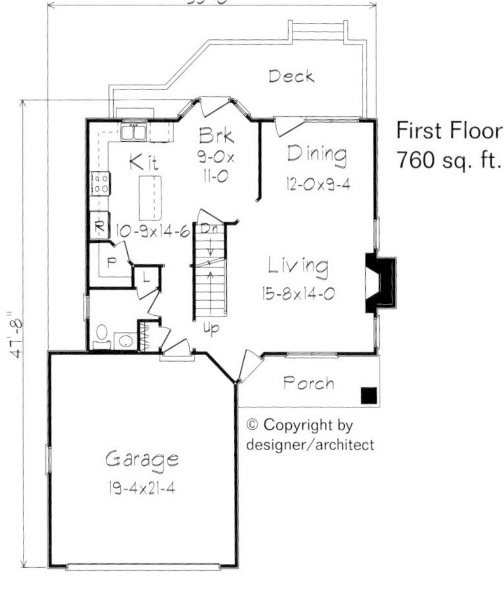

First Floor
760 sq. ft.

SPECIAL FEATURES

- 2,089 total square feet of living area
- Family room features a fireplace, built-in bookshelves and triple sliders opening to the covered patio
- Kitchen overlooks the family room and features a pantry and desk
- Separated from the three secondary bedrooms, the master bedroom becomes a quiet retreat with patio access
- Master bedroom features an oversized bath with walk-in closet and corner tub
- 4 bedrooms, 3 baths, 2-car garage
- Slab foundation

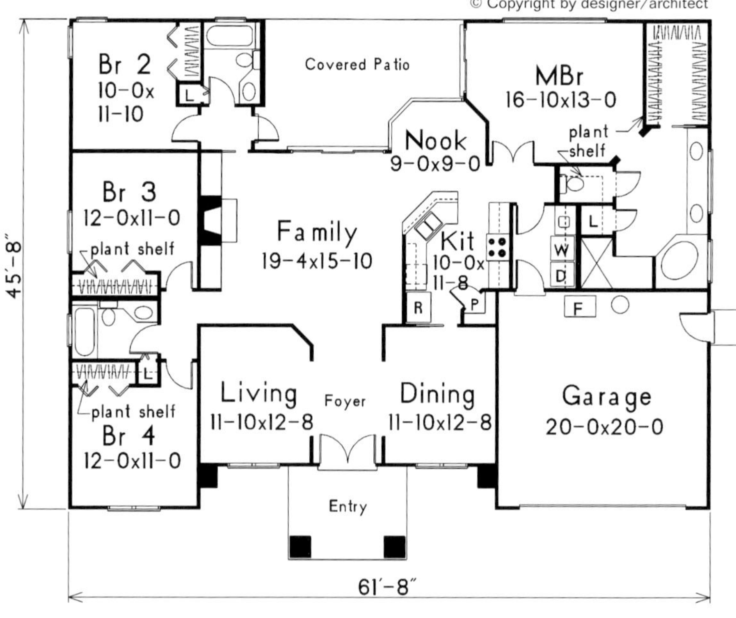

SPECIAL FEATURES

- 1,921 total square feet of living area
- Energy efficient home with 2" x 6" exterior walls
- Sunken family room includes a built-in entertainment center and coffered ceiling
- Sunken formal living room features a coffered ceiling
- Master bedroom dressing area has double sinks, a spa tub, shower and French door to private deck
- Large front porch adds to home's appeal
- 3 bedrooms, 2 1/2 baths, 2-car garage
- Basement foundation

Second Floor
863 sq. ft.

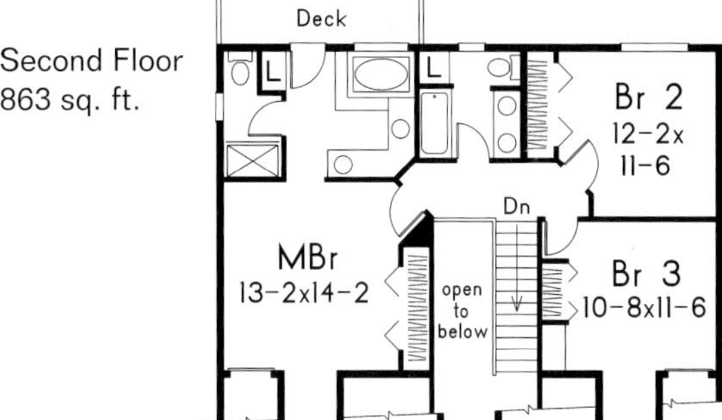

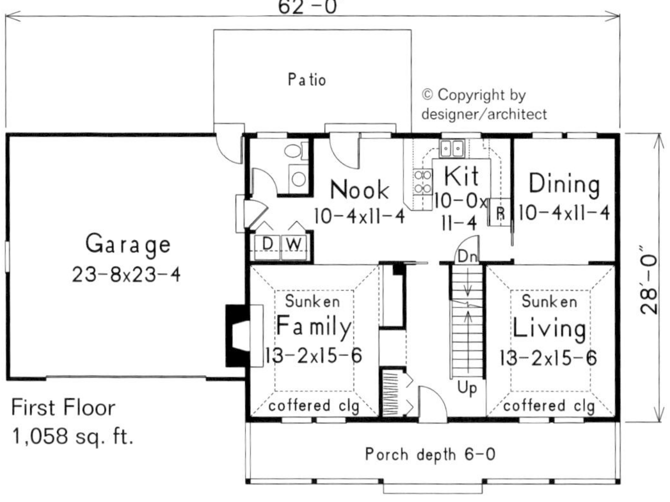

First Floor
1,058 sq. ft.

PLAN NUMBER: 537-007D-0173 | PRICE CODE: C

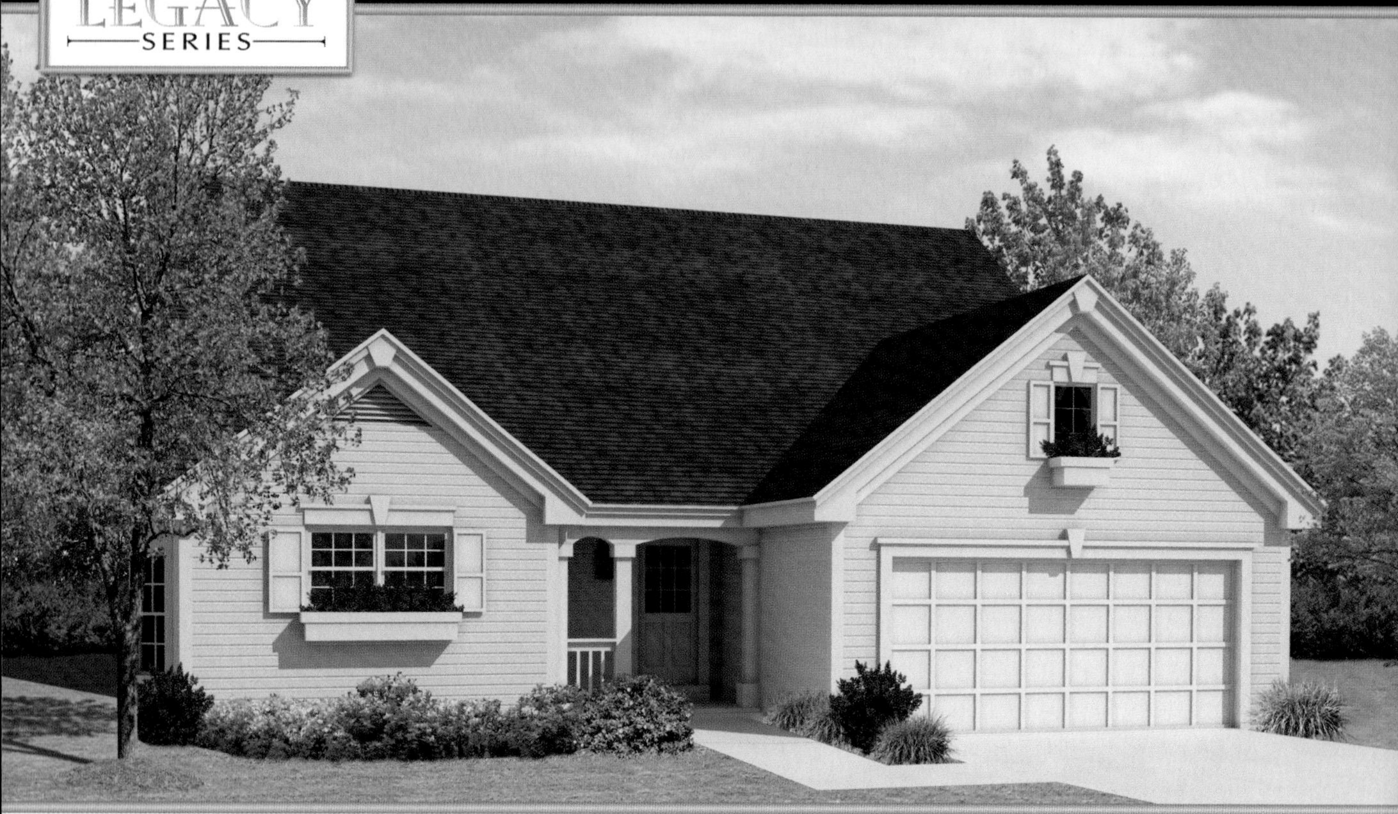

SPECIAL FEATURES

- 2,121 total square feet of living area
- The spacious great room includes a corner fireplace, dining area with bay window and glass sliding doors to the rear patio
- A huge center island with seating for six, built-in pantry and 26' of counterspace are just a few amenities of the awesome kitchen
- Three generously sized bedrooms, two baths and many walk-in closets comprise the second floor
- 4 bedrooms, 3 1/2 baths, 2-car garage
- Basement foundation, drawings also include slab and crawl space foundations

Second Floor
915 sq. ft.

First Floor
1,206 sq. ft.

TO ORDER SEE PAGE 288 | CALL TOLL-FREE 1-877-379-3420

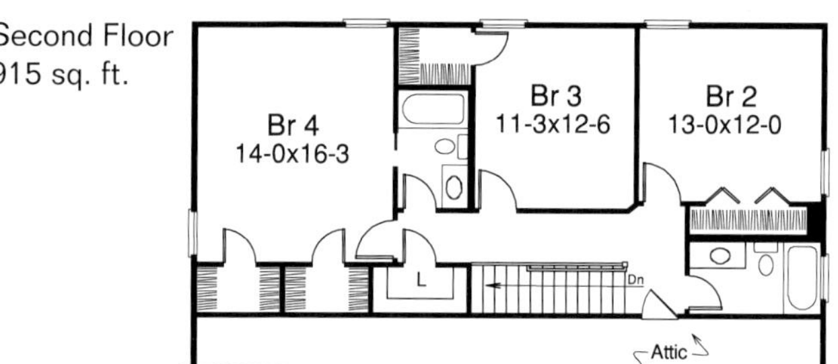

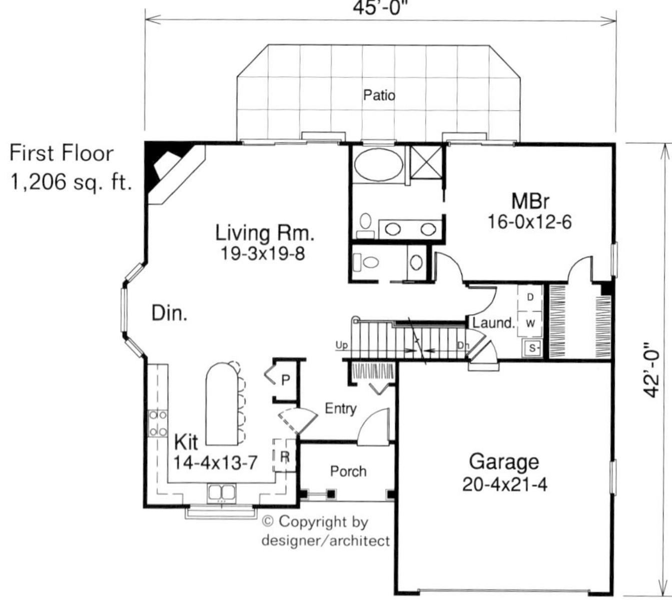

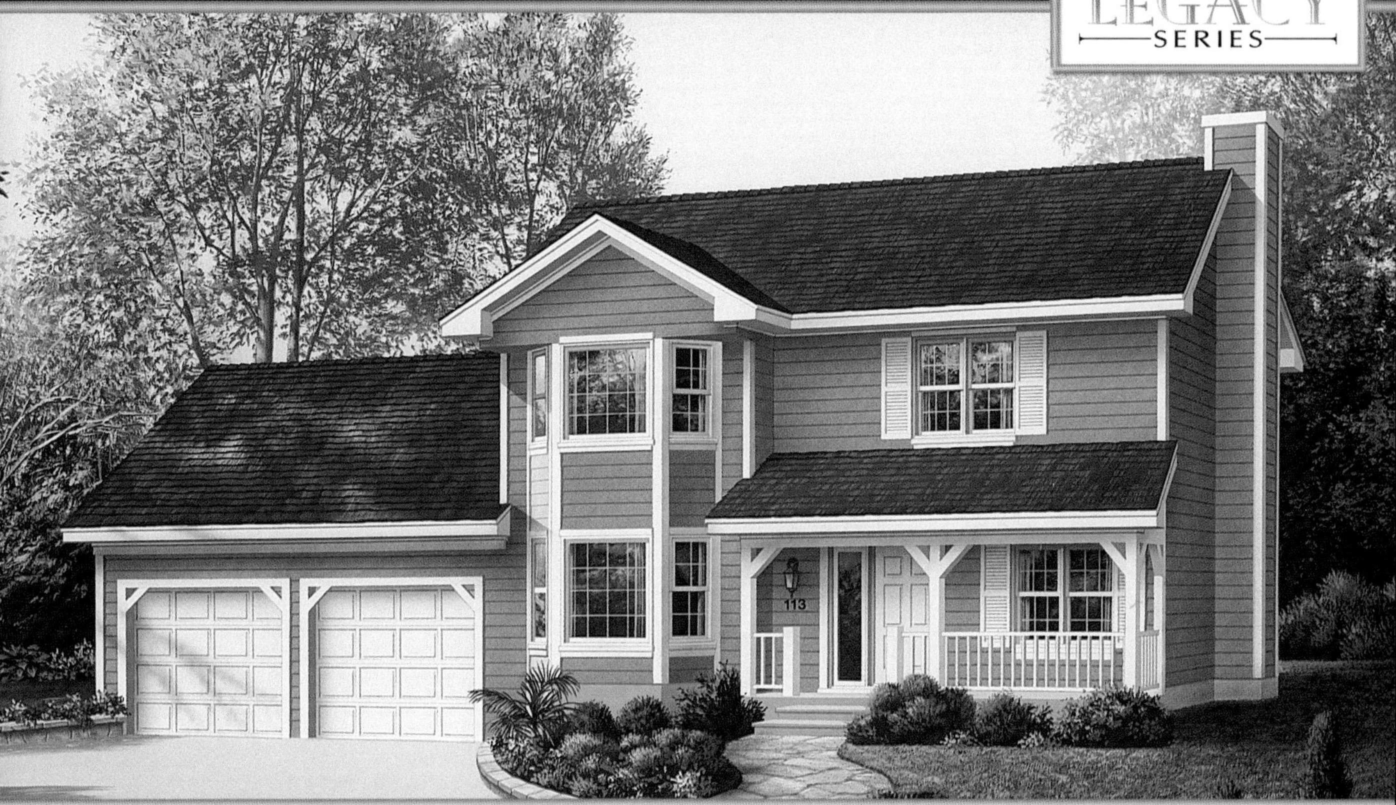

SPECIAL FEATURES

- 1,992 total square feet of living area
- Distinct living, dining and breakfast areas
- Master bedroom boasts a full-end bay window and a cathedral ceiling
- Storage and laundry area are located adjacent to the garage
- Bonus room over the garage for future office or playroom is included in the square footage
- 3 bedrooms, 2 1/2 baths, 2-car garage
- Crawl space foundation, drawings also include basement foundation

Second Floor
1,124 sq. ft.

First Floor
868 sq. ft.

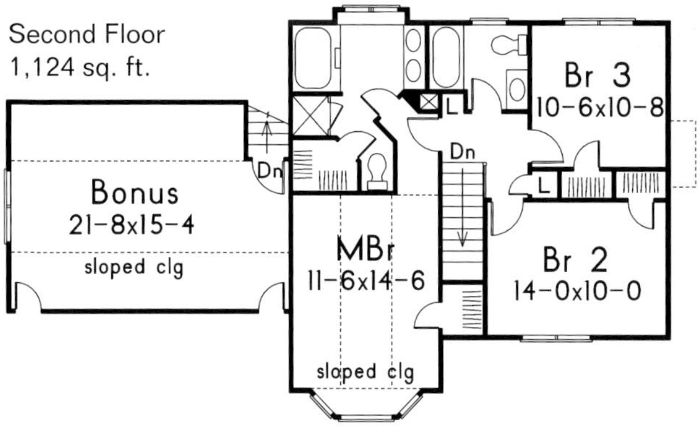

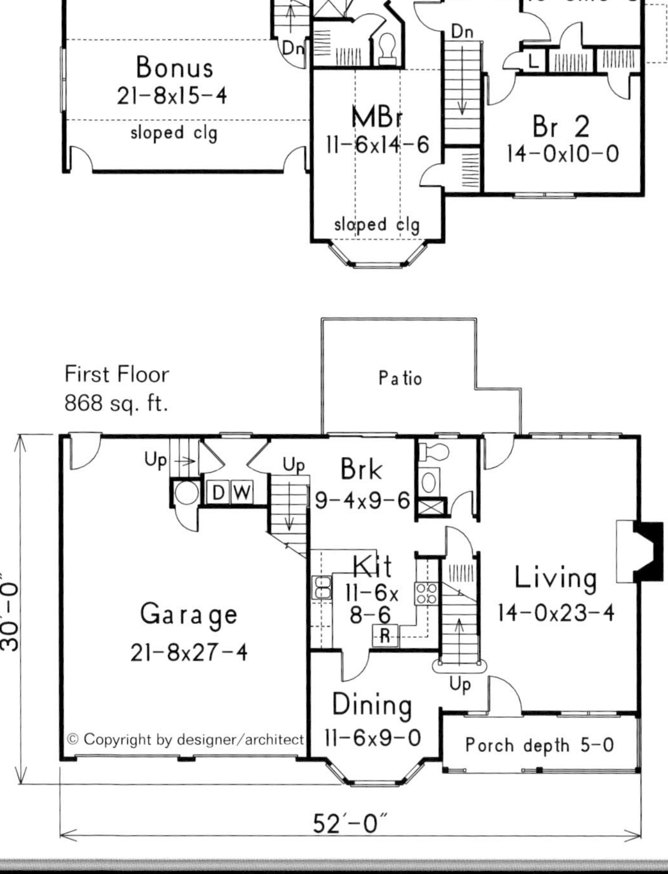

PLAN NUMBER: 537-007D-0014 | PRICE CODE: C

SPECIAL FEATURES

- 1,985 total square feet of living area
- Charming design for a narrow lot
- Dramatic sunken great room features a vaulted ceiling, large double-hung windows and transomed patio doors
- Grand master bedroom includes a double-door entry, large closet, elegant bath and patio access
- 4 bedrooms, 3 1/2 baths, 2-car garage
- Basement foundation

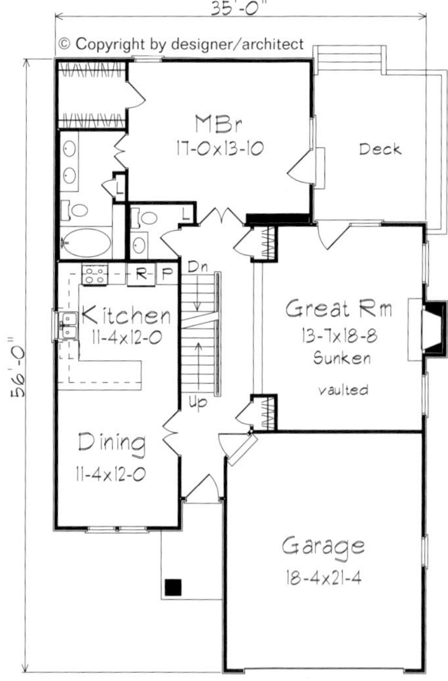

First Floor
1,114 sq. ft.

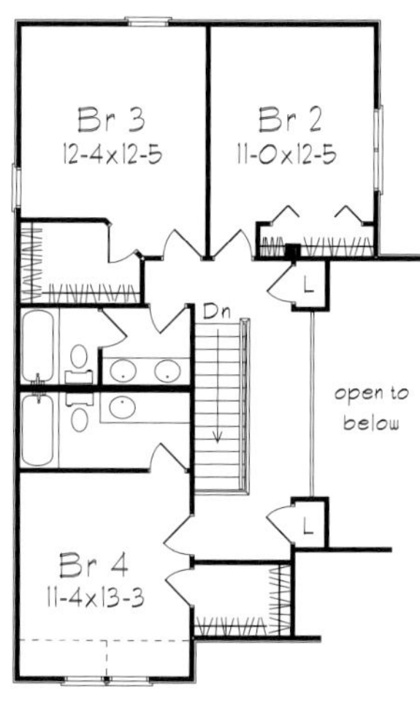

Second Floor
871 sq. ft.

 TO ORDER SEE PAGE 288 | CALL TOLL-FREE 1-877-379-3420

LOWE'S LEGACY SERIES

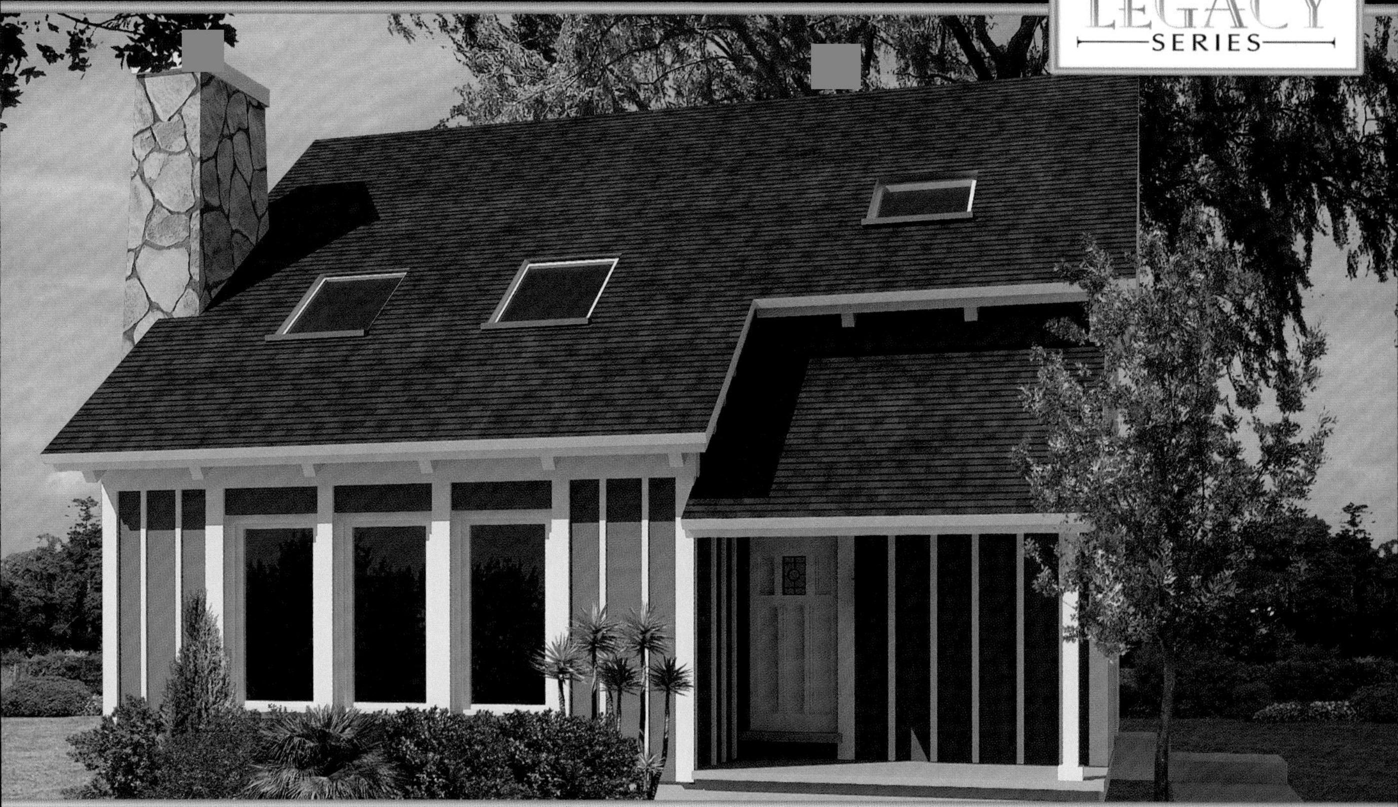

SPECIAL FEATURES

- 1,278 total square feet of living area
- Energy efficient home with 2" x 6" exterior walls
- Enter this home to find a two-story great room topped with skylights that offer a dramatic first impression
- The screened porch extends dining opportunities and provides a lovely space to enjoy the outdoors year round
- The second floor master bedroom includes a private deck for the ultimate in relaxation
- 2 bedrooms, 1 1/2 baths
- Basement foundation

Second Floor
518 sq. ft.

First Floor
760 sq. ft.

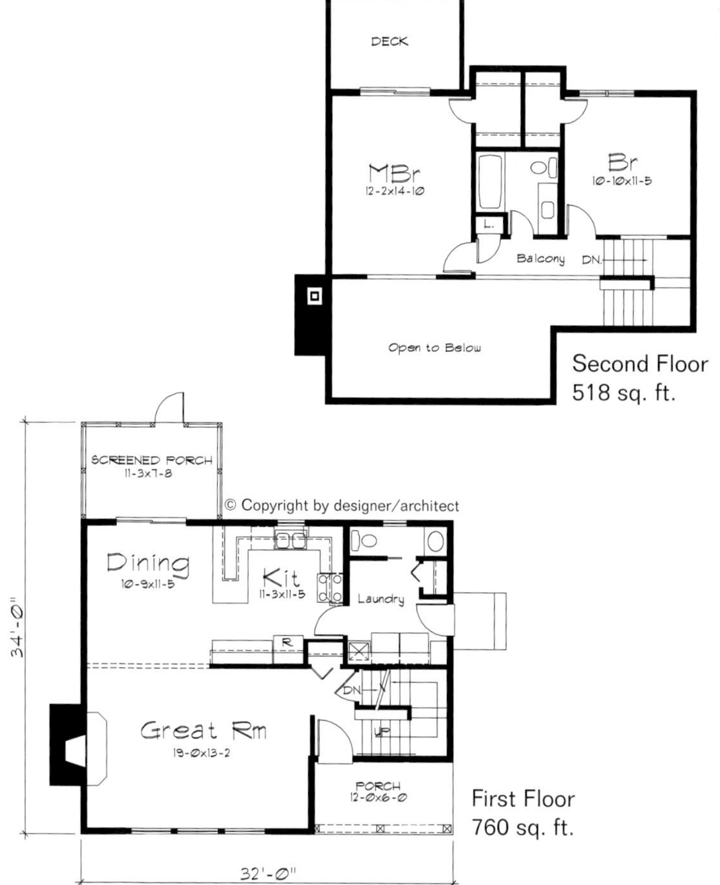

PLAN NUMBER: 537-007D-0168 | PRICE CODE: C

SPECIAL FEATURES

- 1,814 total square feet of living area
- This home enjoys a large country porch for a perfect leisure living area
- The vaulted great room, sunny breakfast room and kitchen with snack bar are all open to one another to create a very open sense of spaciousness
- A sensational lavish bath is the highlight of the master bedroom suite which features double vanities with a make-up counter, a 5' x 5' shower with seat, separate toilet and a step-up whirlpool-in-a-sunroom
- 3 bedrooms, 2 baths, 3-car side entry garage
- Basement foundation

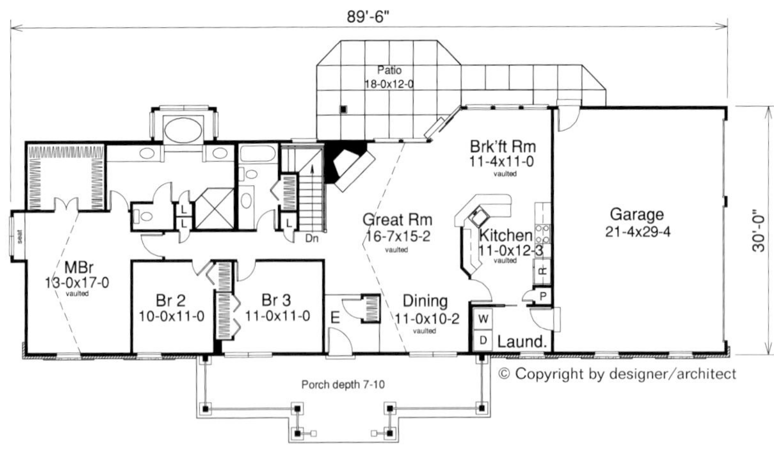

Special Features

- 1,664 total square feet of living area
- L-shaped country kitchen includes pantry and cozy breakfast area
- Bedrooms are located on the second floor for privacy
- Master bedroom includes a walk-in closet, dressing area and bath
- 2" x 6" exterior walls available, please order plan #537-001D-0121
- 3 bedrooms, 2 1/2 baths, 2-car garage
- Crawl space foundation, drawings also include basement and slab foundations

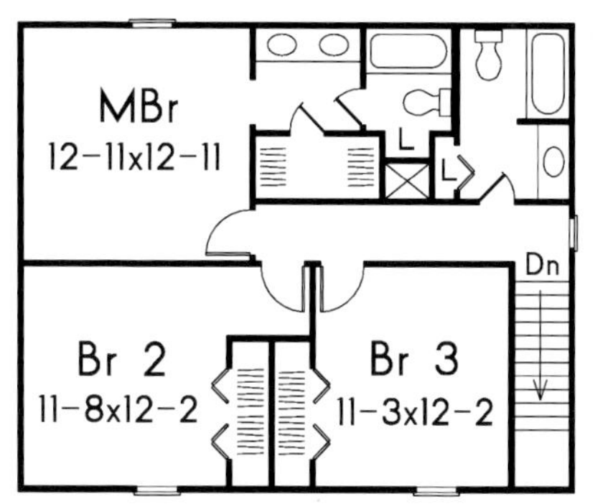

Second Floor
832 sq. ft.

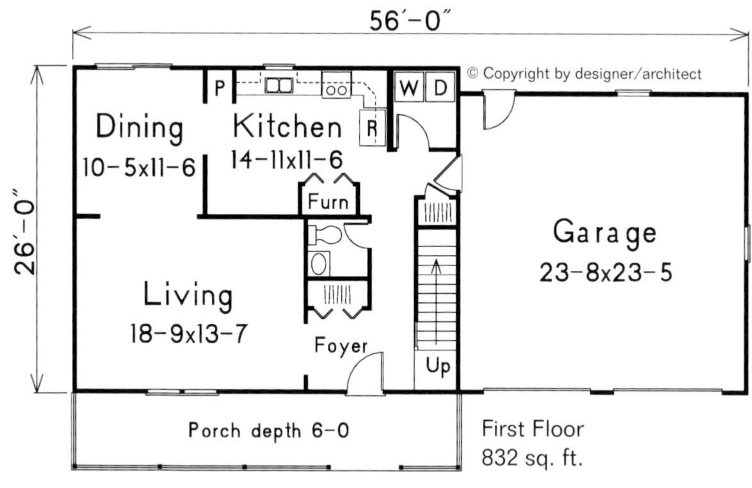

First Floor
832 sq. ft.

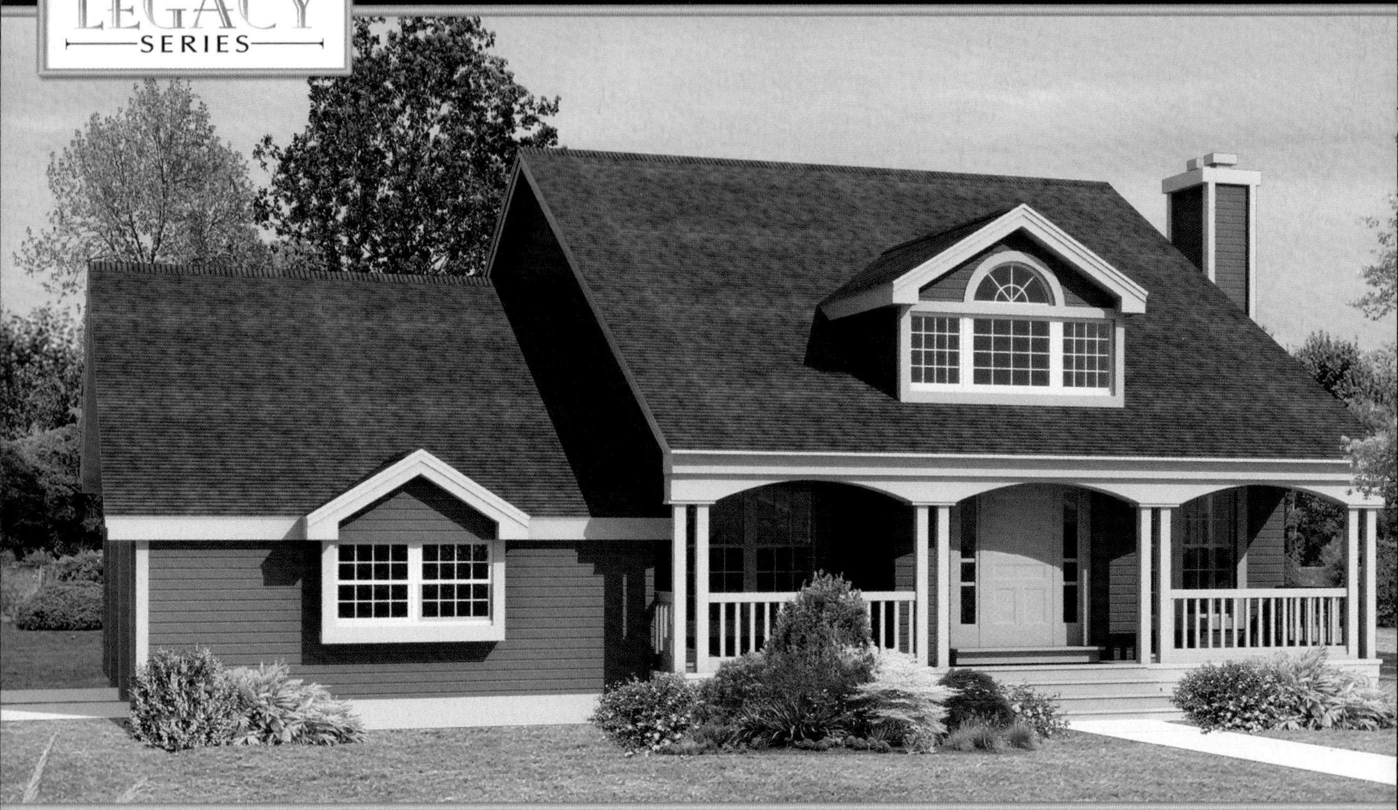

SPECIAL FEATURES

- 2,043 total square feet of living area
- Energy efficient home with 2" x 6" exterior walls
- Two-story central foyer includes two coat closets
- Large combined space is provided by the kitchen, family and breakfast rooms
- Breakfast nook for informal dining looks out to the deck and screened porch
- 3 bedrooms, 2 1/2 baths, 2-car side entry garage
- Basement foundation, drawings also include slab foundation

Second Floor
534 sq. ft.

First Floor
1,509 sq. ft.

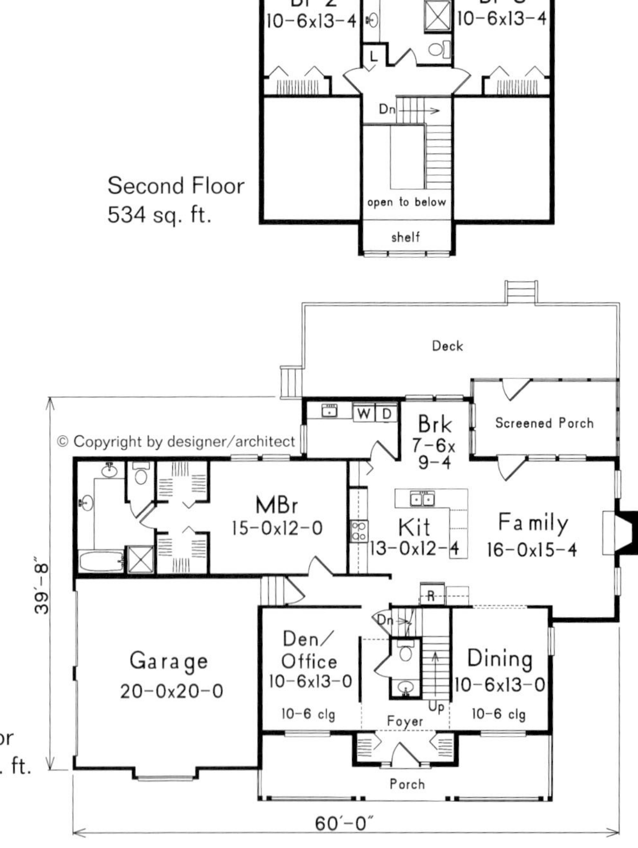

LOWE'S LEGACY SERIES

SPECIAL FEATURES

- 1,747 total square feet of living area
- Entry opens into large family room with coat closet, angled fireplace and attractive plant shelf
- Kitchen and master bedroom access covered patio
- Functional kitchen includes ample workspace
- 4 bedrooms, 2 baths, 2-car garage
- Slab foundation

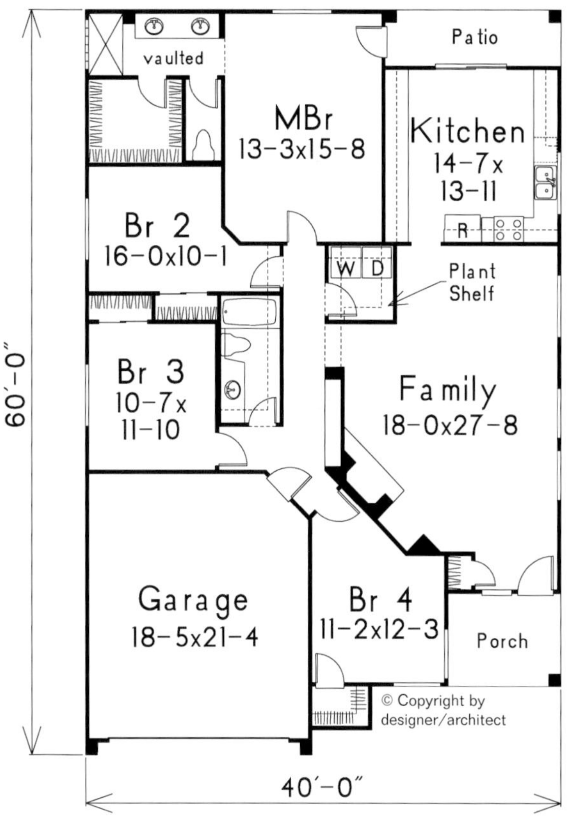

SPECIAL FEATURES

- 1,882 total square feet of living area
- Handsome brick facade
- Spacious great room and dining area combination is brightened by unique corner windows and patio access
- Well-designed kitchen incorporates a breakfast bar peninsula, sweeping casement window above sink and a walk-in pantry island
- Master bedroom features a large walk-in closet and private bath with bay window
- 4 bedrooms, 2 baths, 2-car side entry garage
- Basement foundation

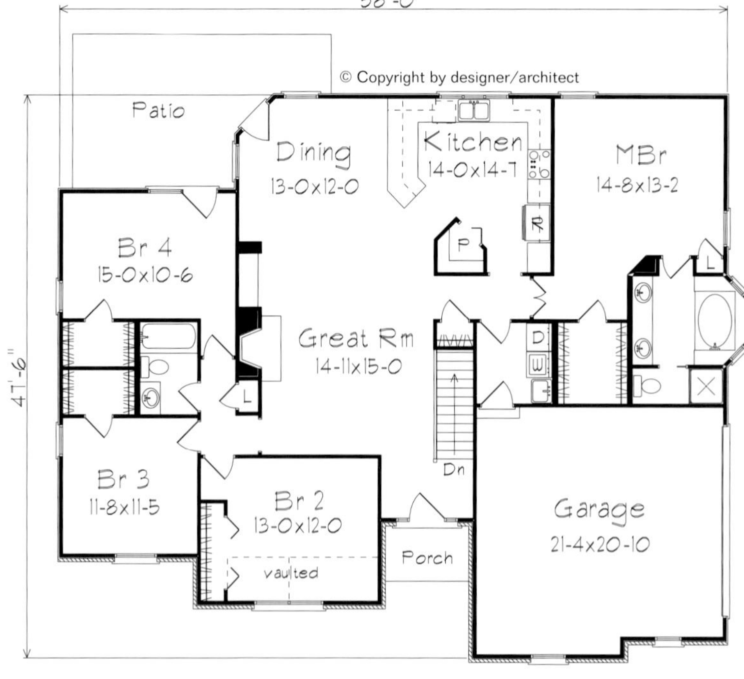

SPECIAL FEATURES

- 1,404 total square feet of living area
- Split-foyer entrance
- Bayed living area features a unique vaulted ceiling and fireplace
- Wrap-around kitchen has corner windows for added sunlight and a bar that overlooks the dining area
- Master bath features a garden tub with separate shower
- Rear deck provides handy access to the dining room and kitchen
- 3 bedrooms, 2 baths, 2-car drive under garage
- Basement foundation, drawings also include partial crawl space foundation

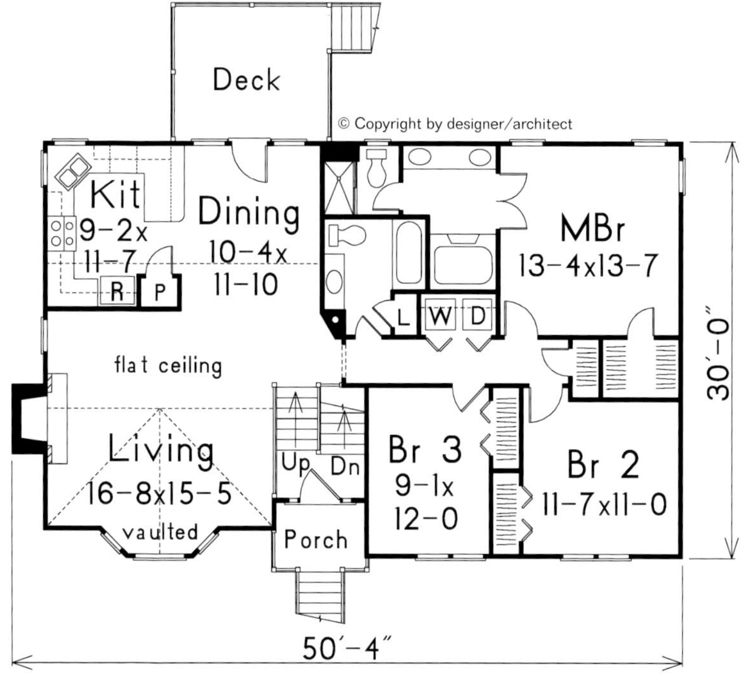

SPECIAL FEATURES

- 1,519 total square feet of living area
- The large living room boasts a vaulted ceiling with plant shelf, fireplace, and opens to the bayed dining area
- The kitchen has an adjoining laundry/ mud room and features a vaulted ceiling, snack counter open to the living and dining areas and a built-in pantry
- Two walk-in closets, a stylish bath and small sitting area accompany the master bedroom
- 4 bedrooms, 2 baths, 2-car garage
- Crawl space foundation, drawings also include slab and basement foundations

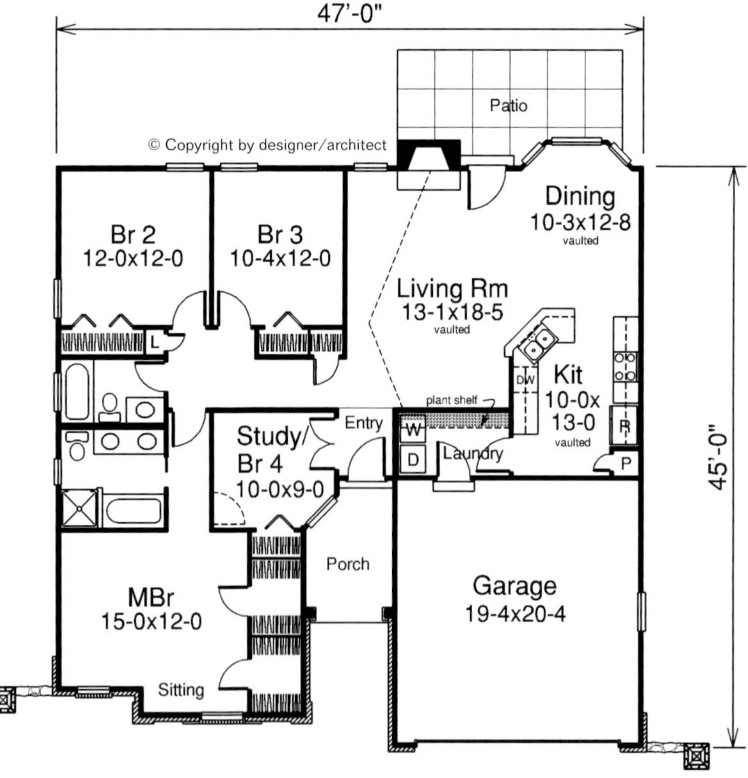

SPECIAL FEATURES

- 988 total square feet of living area
- Pleasant covered porch entry
- The kitchen, living and dining areas are combined to maximize space
- The entry has a convenient coat closet
- Laundry closet is located adjacent to bedrooms
- 3 bedrooms, 1 bath, 1-car garage
- Basement foundation, drawings also include crawl space foundation

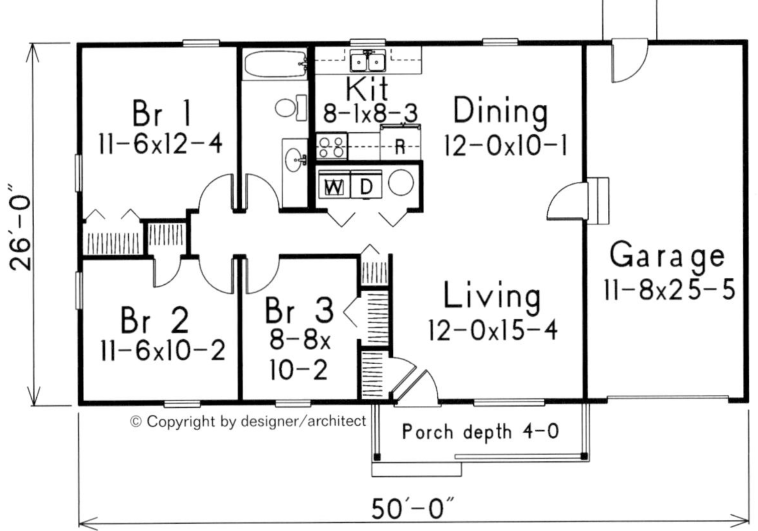

PLAN NUMBER: 537-007D-0018 | PRICE CODE: C

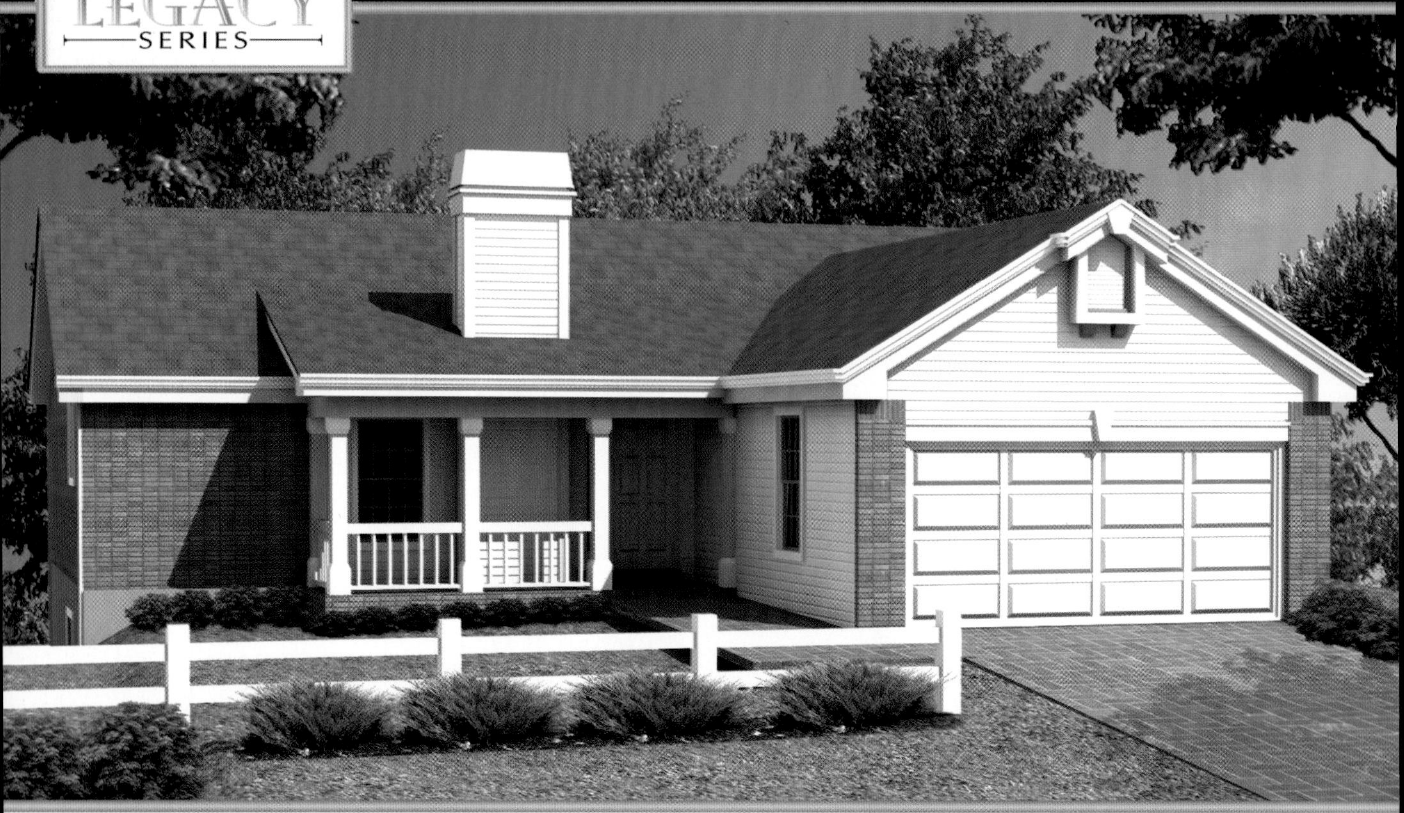

SPECIAL FEATURES

- 1,941 total square feet of living area
- Dramatic, exciting and spacious interior
- Vaulted great room is brightened by a sunken atrium window wall and skylights
- Vaulted U-shaped gourmet kitchen with plant shelf opens to dining room
- First floor half bath features space for a stackable washer and dryer
- 4 bedrooms, 2 1/2 baths, 2-car garage
- Walk-out basement foundation

Lower Level
945 sq. ft.

First Floor
996 sq. ft.

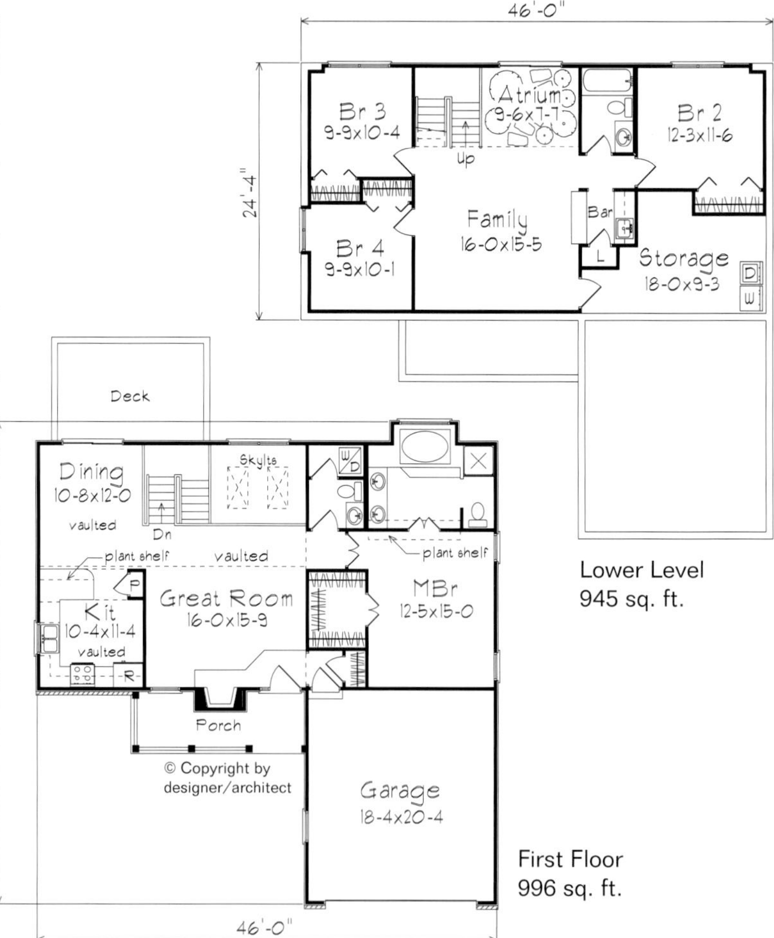

SPECIAL FEATURES

- 1,849 total square feet of living area
- Enormous laundry/mud room has many extras including a storage area and half bath
- Lavish master bath has a corner whirlpool tub, double sinks, separate shower and walk-in closet
- Secondary bedrooms include walk-in closets
- Kitchen has a wrap-around eating counter and is positioned between the formal dining area and breakfast room for convenience
- 3 bedrooms, 2 1/2 baths, 2-car side entry garage
- Slab foundation, drawings also include crawl space foundation

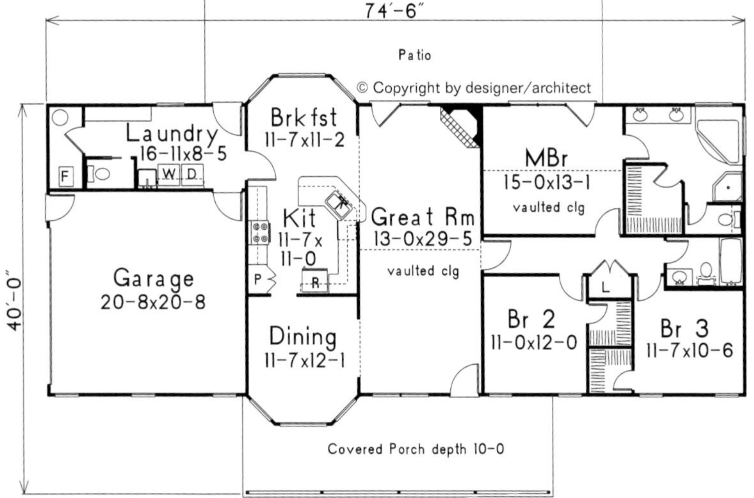

PLAN NUMBER: 537-037D-0006 | PRICE CODE: C

SPECIAL FEATURES

- 1,772 total square feet of living area
- Extended porches in front and rear provide a charming touch
- Large bay windows lend distinction to the dining room and bedroom #3
- Efficient U-shaped kitchen
- Master bedroom includes two walk-in closets
- Full corner fireplace in family room
- 3 bedrooms, 2 baths, 2-car detached garage
- Slab foundation, drawings also include crawl space foundation

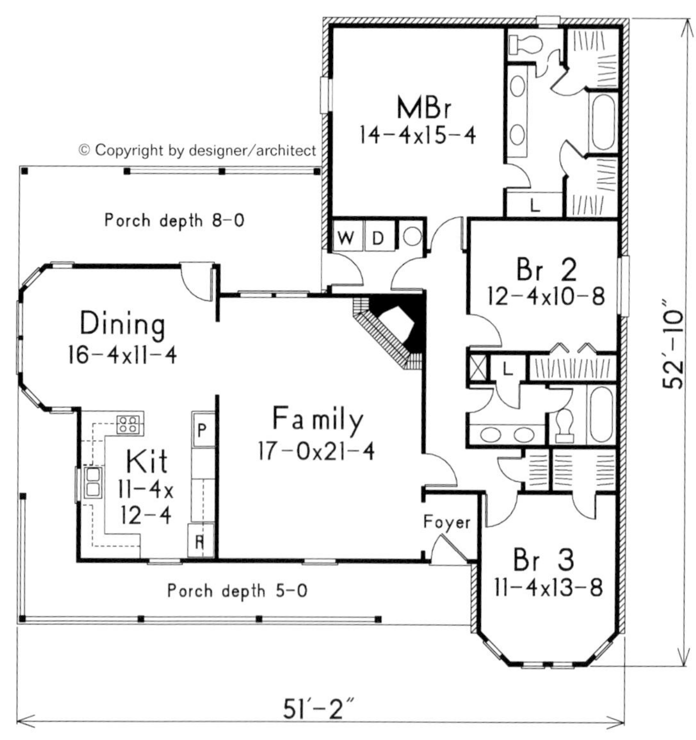

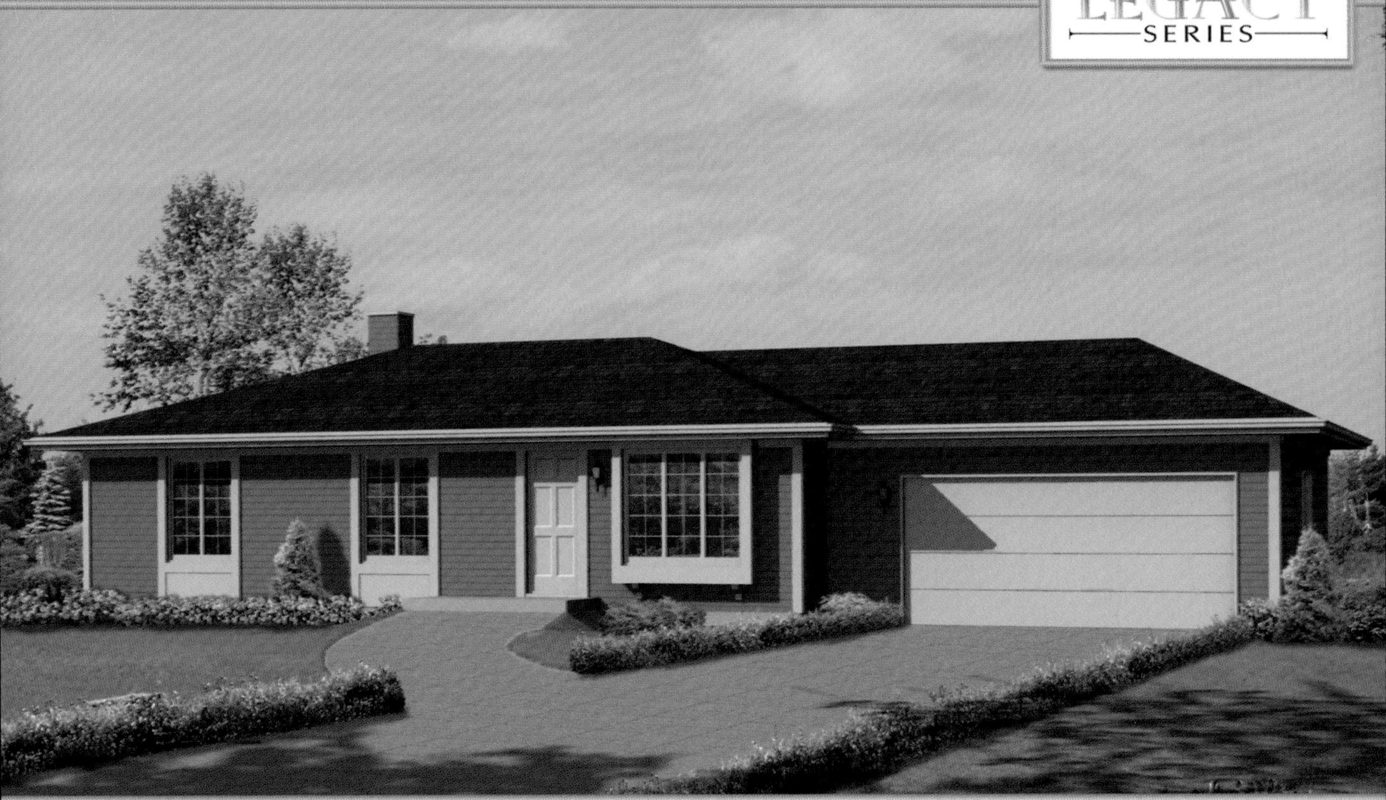

SPECIAL FEATURES

- 1,176 total square feet of living area
- The living room features an entry area with large coat closet and box-bay window
- The kitchen has an eating area and adjoins a very spacious family area
- Master bedroom has a huge walk-in closet and shares a compartmented bath with two secondary bedrooms
- 3 bedrooms, 1 1/2 baths, optional 2-car garage
- Basement foundation, drawings also include crawl space and slab foundations

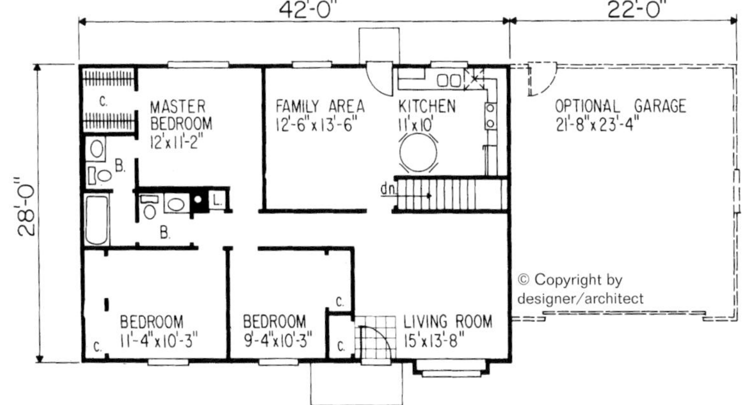

Plan Number: 537-007D-0161 | Price Code: A

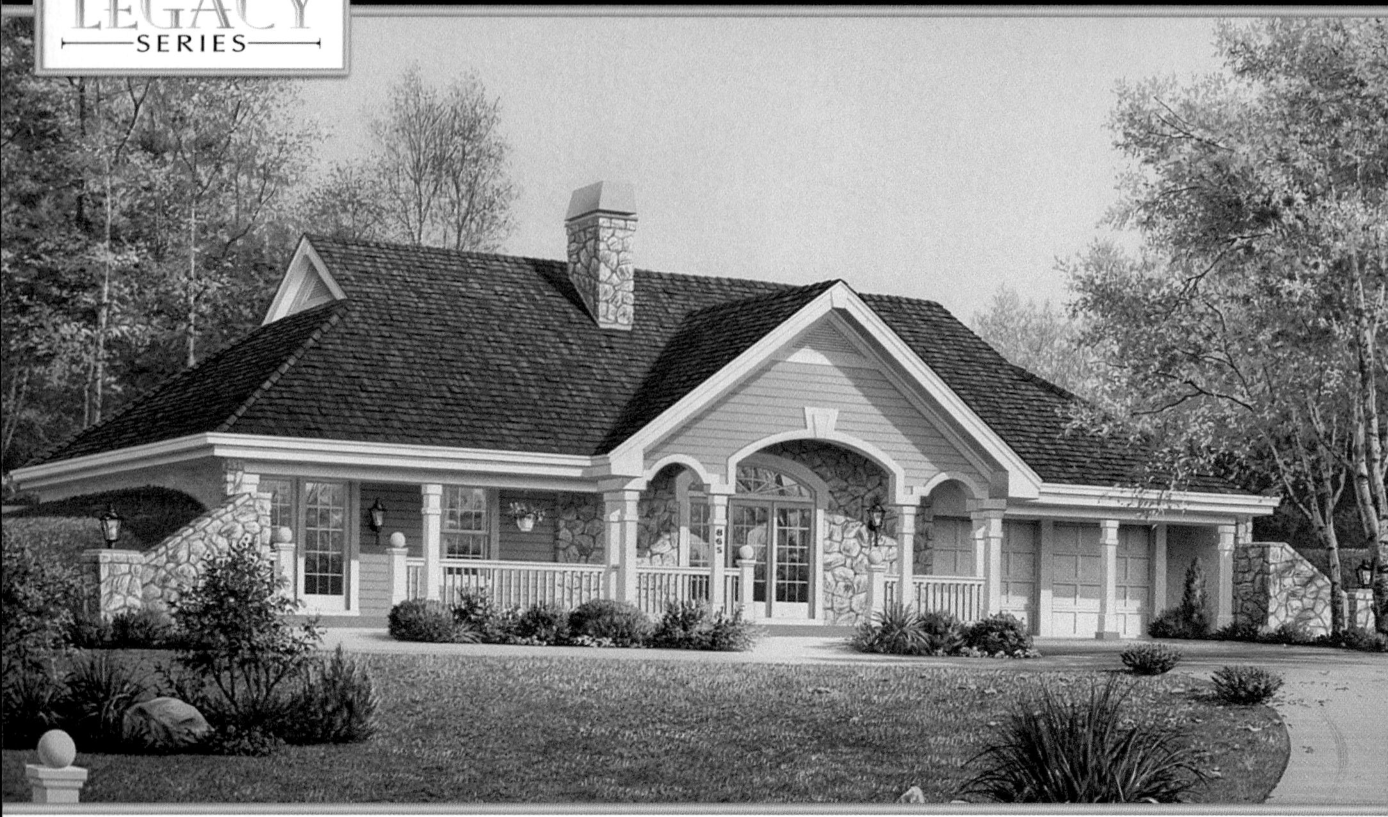

Special Features

- 1,480 total square feet of living area
- Home has great looks and lots of space
- Nestled in a hillside with only one exposed exterior wall, this home offers efficiency, protection and affordability
- Triple patio doors with an arched transom bathe the living room with sunlight
- The kitchen features a snack bar open to the living room, large built-in pantry and adjoins a spacious dining area
- 2 bedrooms, 2 baths, 2-car garage
- Slab foundation

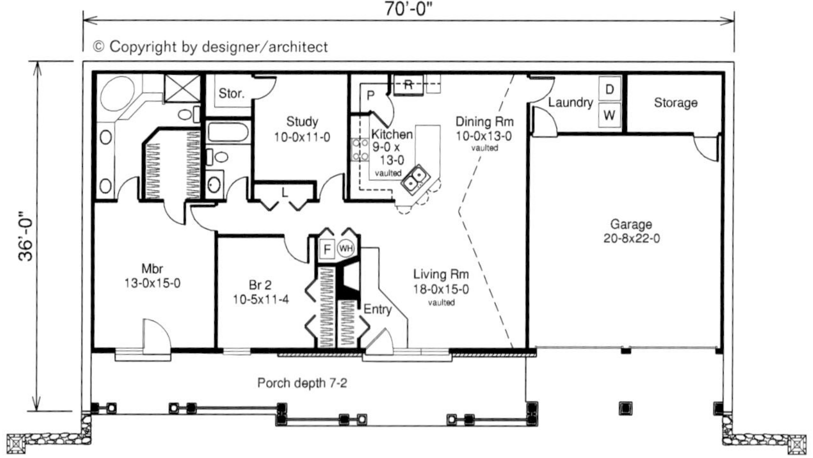

LOWE'S LEGACY SERIES

SPECIAL FEATURES

- 1,865 total square feet of living area
- The large foyer opens into an expansive dining area and great room
- Home features vaulted ceilings throughout
- Master bedroom features an angled entry, vaulted ceiling, plant shelf and bath with double vanity, tub and shower
- 4 bedrooms, 2 baths, 2-car garage
- Slab foundation, drawings also include crawl space foundation

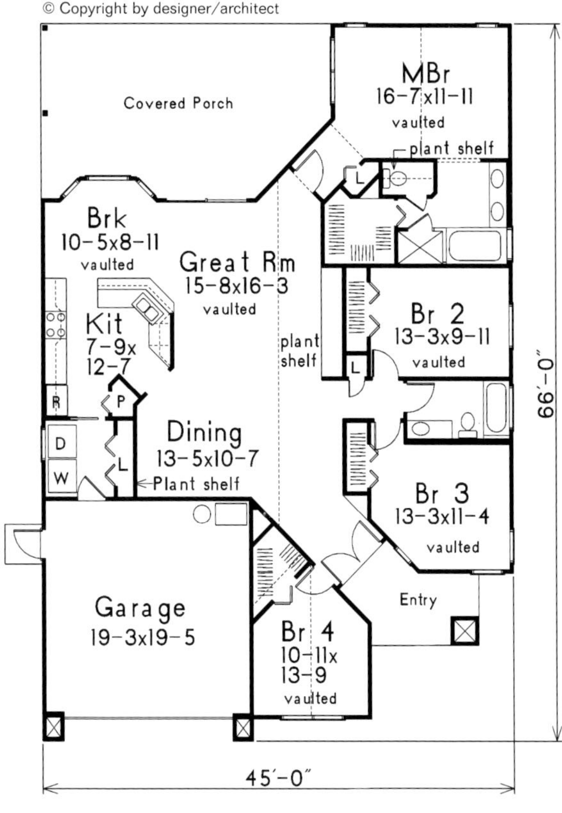

LOWE'S LEGACY SERIES

PLAN NUMBER: 537-007D-0029 | **PRICE CODE:** AAA

SPECIAL FEATURES

- 576 total square feet of living area
- Perfect country retreat features vaulted living room and entry with skylights and a plant shelf above
- A double-door entry leads to the vaulted bedroom with bath access
- Kitchen offers generous storage and a pass-through breakfast bar
- 1 bedroom, 1 bath
- Crawl space foundation

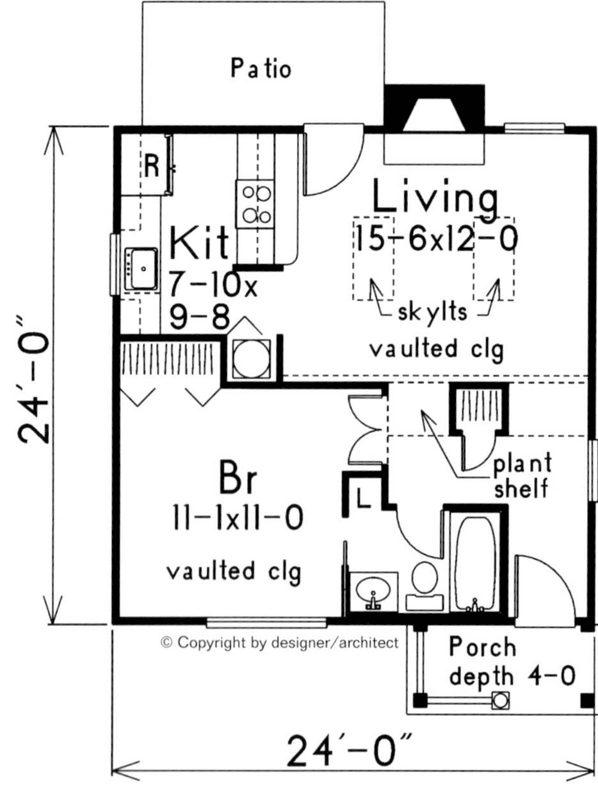

Special Features

- 1,127 total square feet of living area
- Plant shelf joins kitchen and dining room
- Vaulted master bedroom has double walk-in closets, deck access and a private bath
- Great room features a vaulted ceiling, fireplace and sliding doors to the covered deck
- Ideal home for a narrow lot
- 2 bedrooms, 2 baths, 2-car garage
- Basement foundation

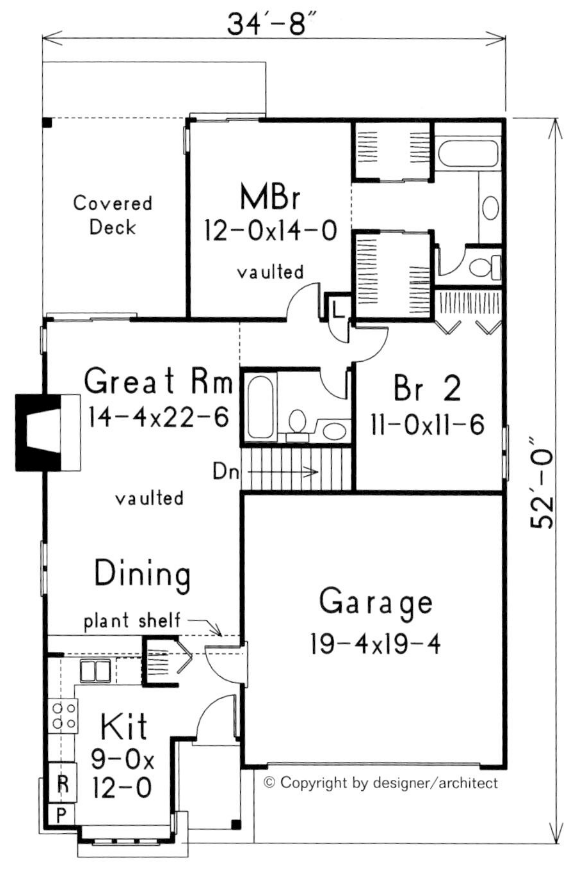

SPECIAL FEATURES

- 1,344 total square feet of living area
- Kitchen has side entry, laundry area, pantry and joins the family/dining area
- Master bedroom includes a private bath
- Linen and storage closets in hall
- Covered porch opens to the spacious living room with a handy coat closet
- 3 bedrooms, 2 baths
- Crawl space foundation, drawings also include basement and slab foundations

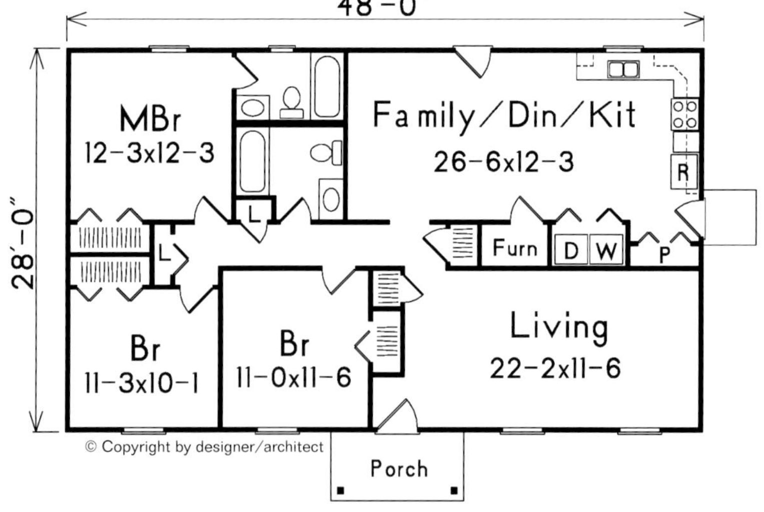

SPECIAL FEATURES

- 615 total square feet of living area
- The handsome exterior includes a front porch and upper gabled box windows
- The first floor features an oversized two-car garage with built-in storage shelves and a large mechanical room
- A large living room with fireplace, entertainment alcove and kitchen open to an eating area are just a few of the many features of the second floor
- 1 bedroom, 1 bath, 2-car garage
- Slab foundation

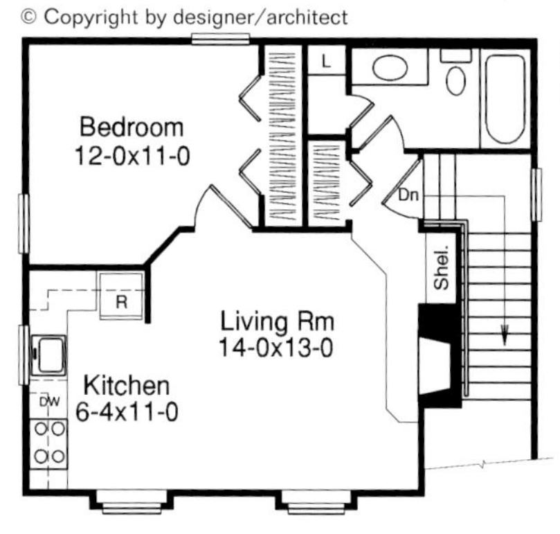

Second Floor
615 sq. ft.

27'-0"

26'-0"

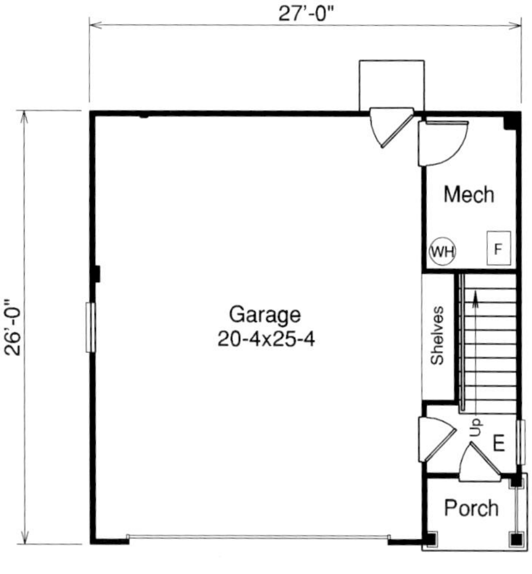

First Floor

Mech

WH

F

Garage
20-4x25-4

Shelves

Up

E

Porch

Special Features

- 2,365 total square feet of living area
- 9' ceilings throughout the home
- Expansive central living room is complemented by a corner fireplace
- Breakfast bay overlooks the rear porch
- Master bedroom features a bath with two walk-in closets and vanities, a separate tub and shower and handy linen closet
- Peninsula keeps kitchen private
- 4 bedrooms, 2 baths, 2-car carport
- Slab foundation

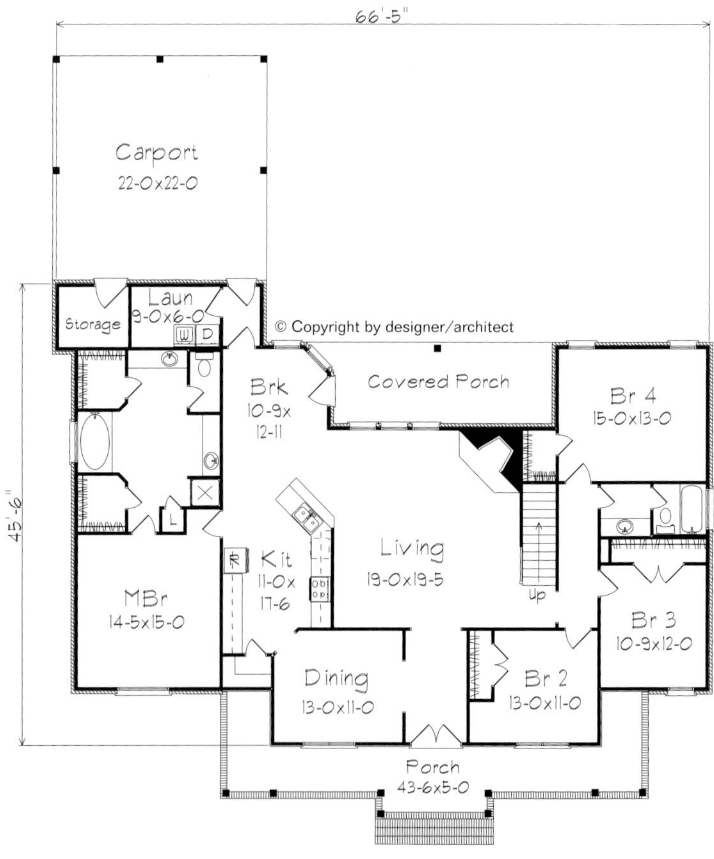

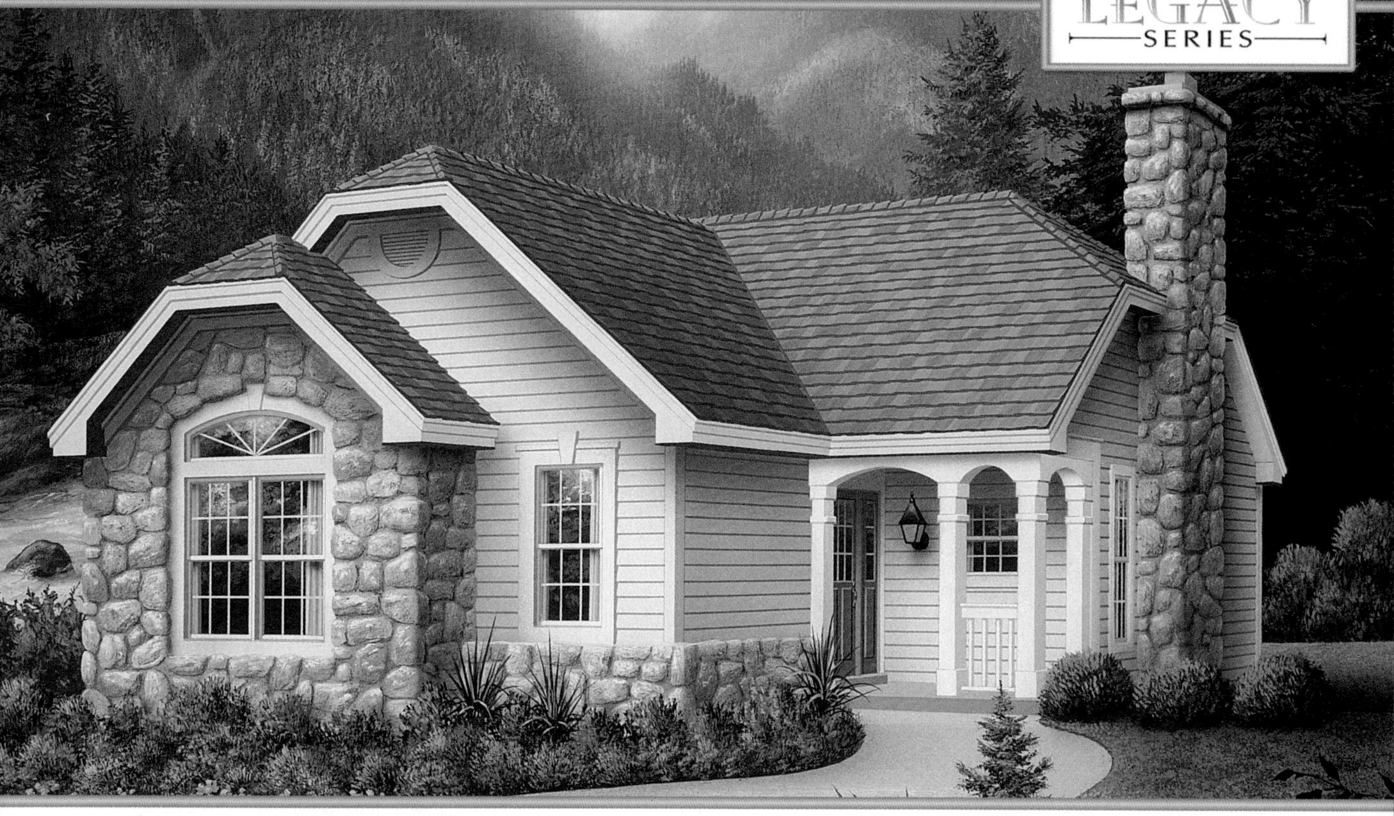

SPECIAL FEATURES

- 1,231 total square feet of living area
- Dutch gables and stone accents provide an enchanting appearance
- The spacious living room offers a masonry fireplace, atrium with window wall and is open to a dining area with bay window
- Kitchen has a breakfast counter, lots of cabinet space and glass sliding doors to a balcony
- 380 square feet of optional living area on the lower level
- 2 bedrooms, 2 baths, 1-car drive under garage
- Walk-out basement foundation

First Floor
1,231 sq. ft.

Optional
Lower Level

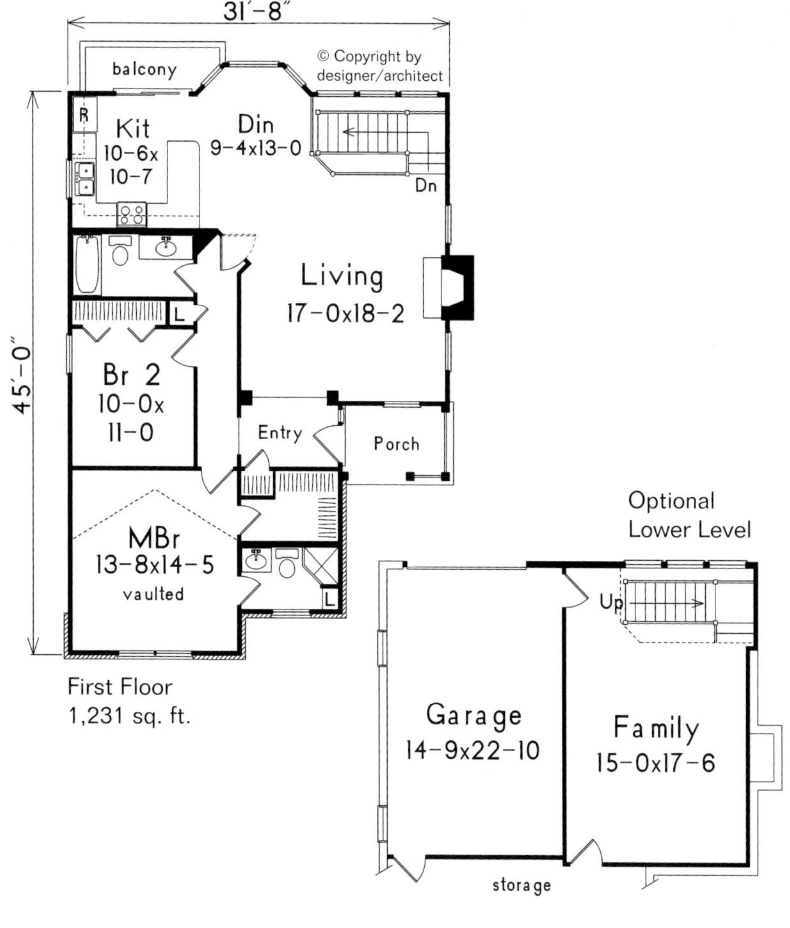

PLAN NUMBER: 537-018D-0006 | PRICE CODE: B

SPECIAL FEATURES

- 1,742 total square feet of living area
- Efficient kitchen combines with the breakfast area and great room creating a spacious living area
- Master bedroom includes a private bath with huge walk-in closet, shower and corner tub
- Great room boasts a fireplace and access outdoors
- Laundry room is conveniently located near the kitchen and garage
- 3 bedrooms, 2 baths, 2-car garage
- Slab foundation, drawings also include crawl space foundation

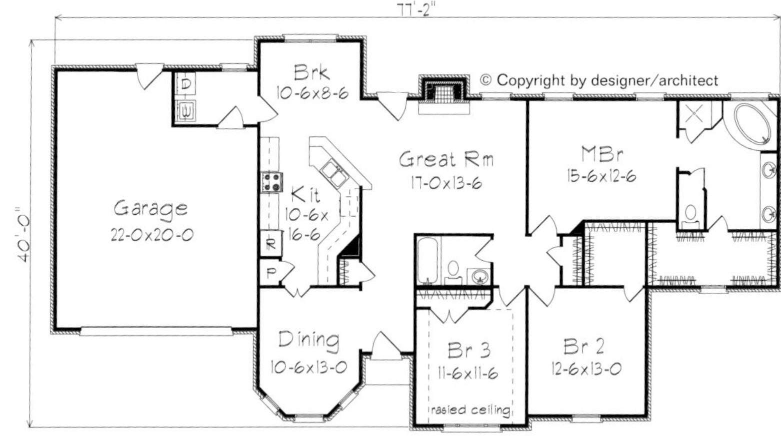

LOWE'S LEGACY SERIES

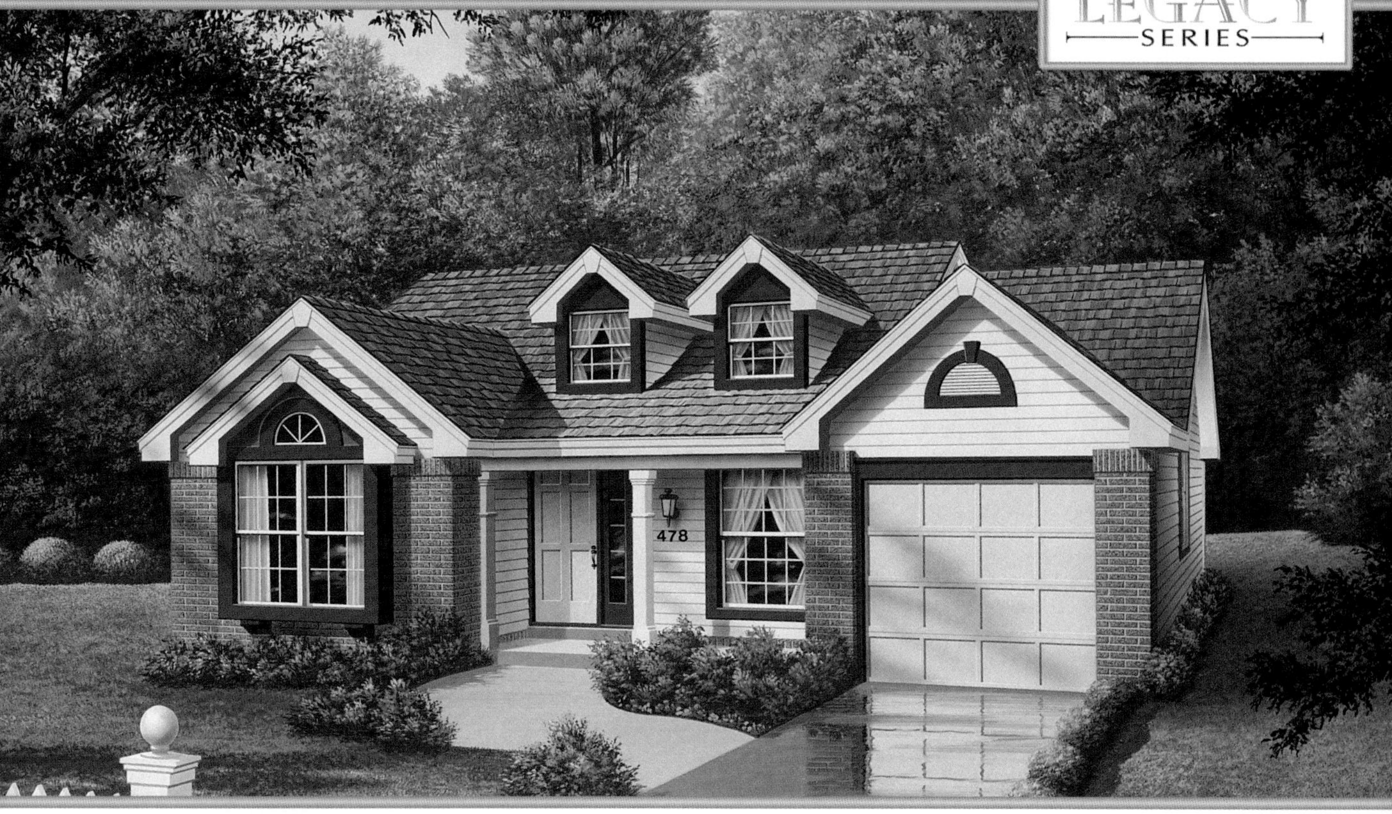

SPECIAL FEATURES

- 1,092 total square feet of living area
- A box window and inviting porch with dormers create a charming facade
- Eat-in kitchen offers a pass-through breakfast bar, corner window wall to patio, pantry and convenient laundry room with half bath
- Master bedroom features a double-door entry and walk-in closet
- 3 bedrooms, 1 1/2 baths, 1-car garage
- Basement foundation

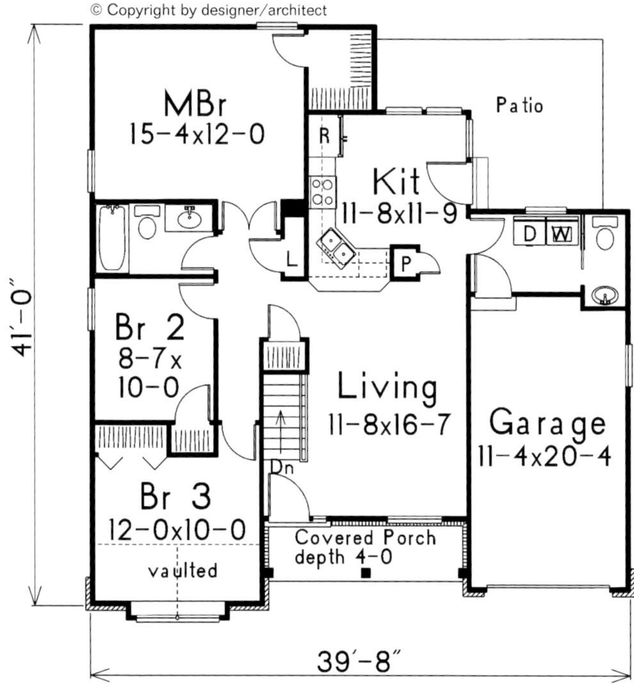

PLAN NUMBER: 537-007D-0156 | PRICE CODE: AAA

SPECIAL FEATURES

- 809 total square feet of living area
- This attractive earth berm home is perfectly designed for a vacation retreat
- Nestled in a hillside with only one exposed exterior wall, this home offers efficiency, protection and affordability
- A large porch creates an ideal space for lazy afternoons and quiet evenings
- All rooms are very spacious and three closets plus the laundry room provide abundant storage
- 1 bedroom, 1 bath
- Slab foundation

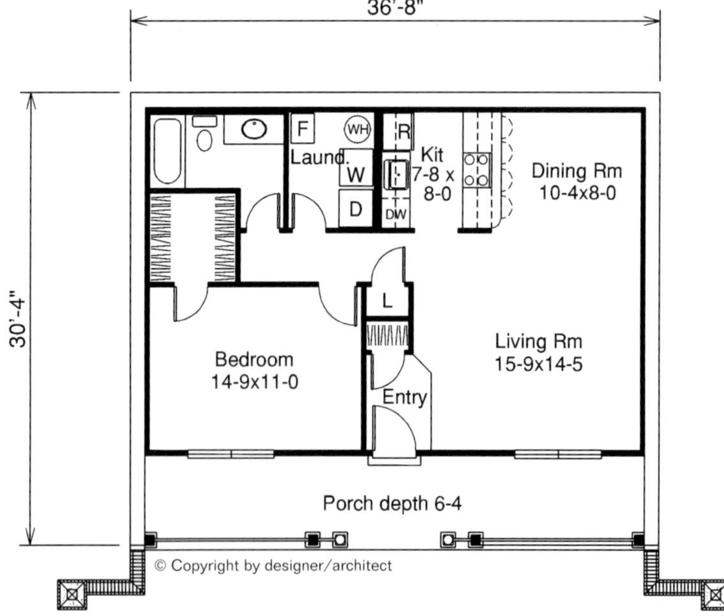

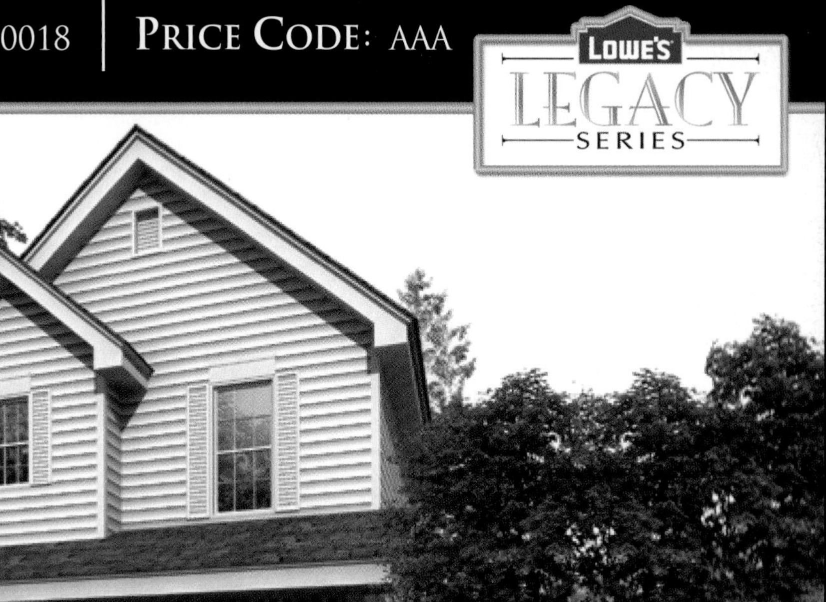

SPECIAL FEATURES

- 858 total square feet of living area
- Stackable washer/dryer is located in the kitchen
- Large covered porch graces this exterior
- Both bedrooms have walk-in closets
- 2 bedrooms, 1 bath
- Crawl space foundation

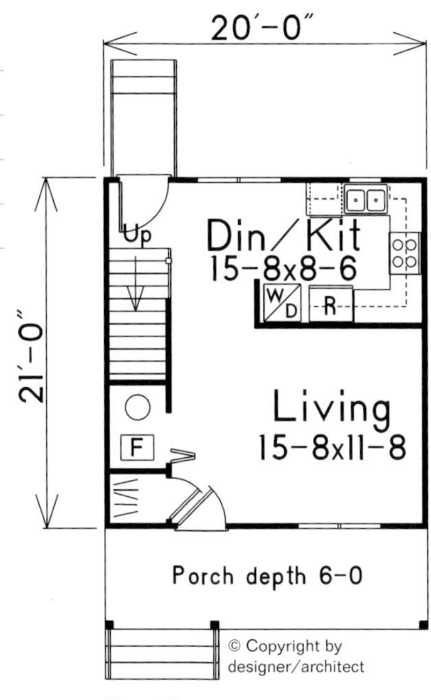

© Copyright by designer/architect

First Floor
420 sq. ft.

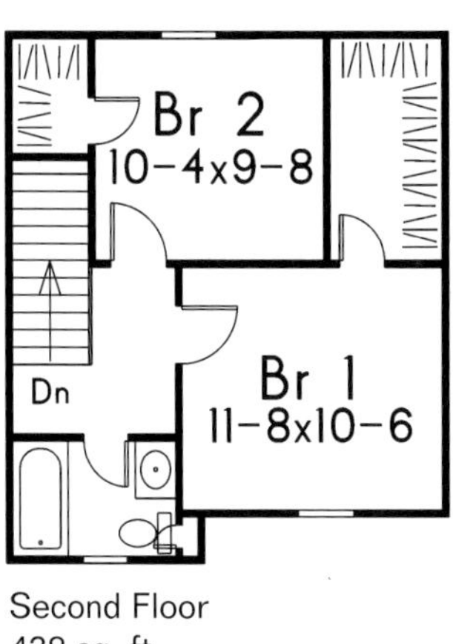

Second Floor
438 sq. ft.

SPECIAL FEATURES

- 1,294 total square feet of living area
- Great room features a fireplace and large bay with windows and patio doors
- Enjoy a laundry room immersed in light with large windows, an arched transom and attractive planter box
- Vaulted master bedroom features a bay window and two walk-in closets
- Bedroom #2 boasts a vaulted ceiling, plant shelf and half bath, perfect for a studio
- 2 bedrooms, 1 full bath, 2 half baths, 1-car rear entry garage
- Basement foundation

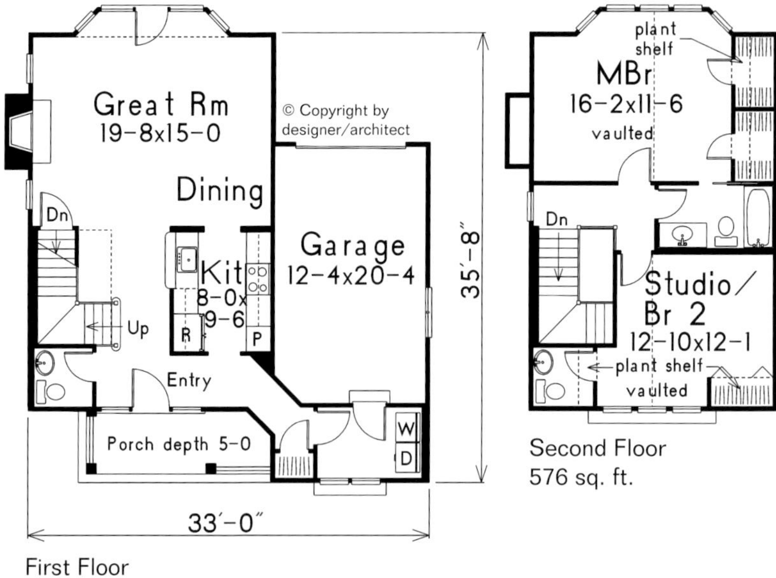

First Floor
718 sq. ft.

Second Floor
576 sq. ft.

LOWE'S LEGACY SERIES

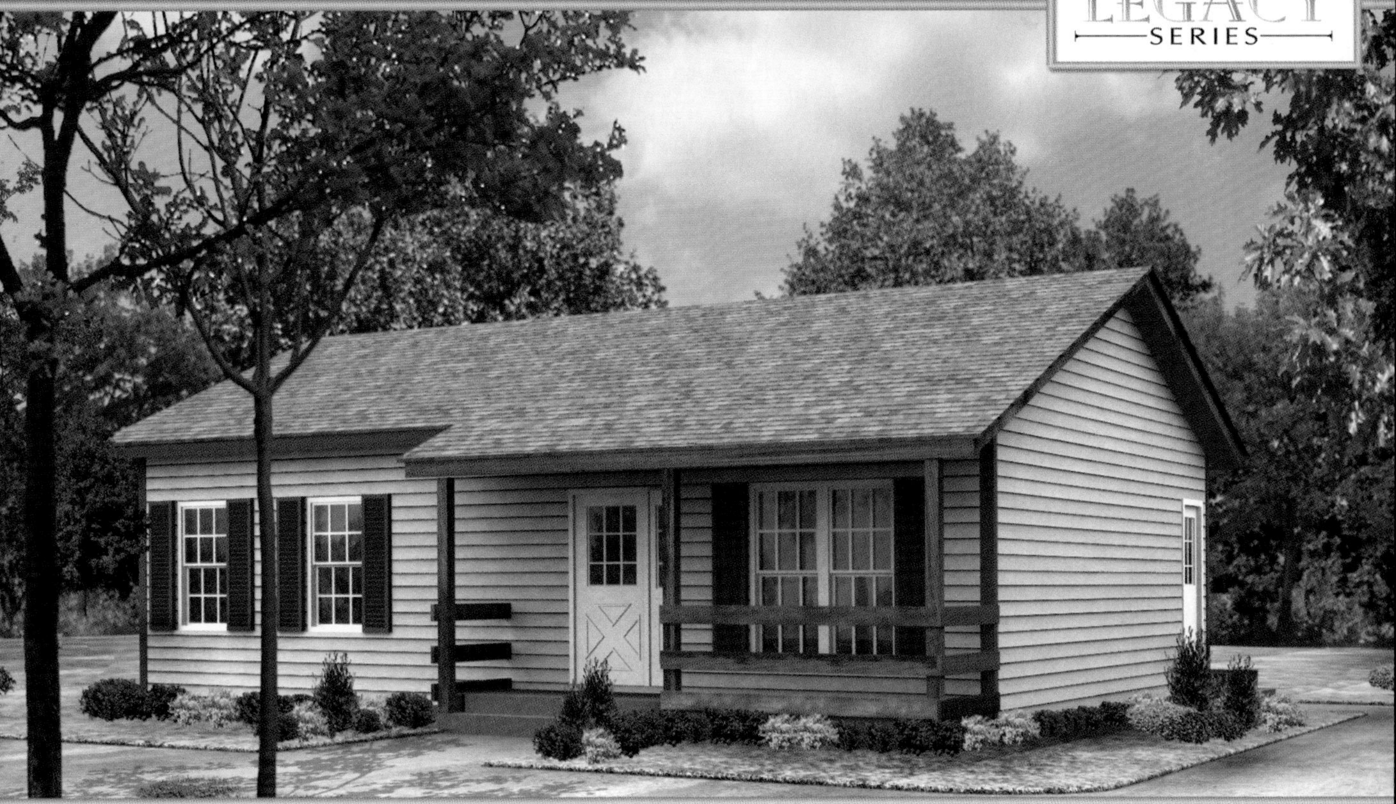

SPECIAL FEATURES

- 864 total square feet of living area
- L-shaped kitchen with convenient pantry is adjacent to the dining area
- Easy access to laundry area, linen closet and storage closet
- Both bedrooms include ample closet space
- 2 bedrooms, 1 bath
- Crawl space foundation, drawings also include basement and slab foundations

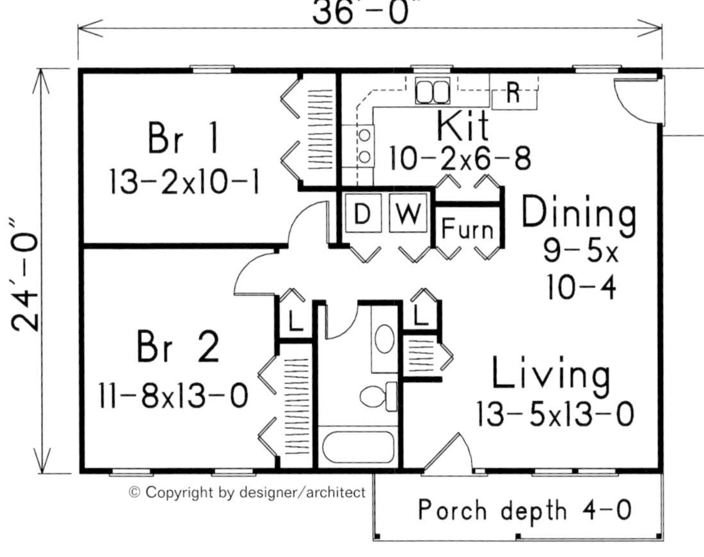

Plan Number: 537-007D-0105 | Price Code: AA

Special Features

- 1,084 total square feet of living area
- Delightful country porch for quiet evenings
- The living room offers a front feature window which invites the sun and includes a fireplace and dining area with private patio
- The U-shaped kitchen features lots of cabinets and a bayed breakfast room with built-in pantry
- Both bedrooms have walk-in closets and access to their own bath
- 2 bedrooms, 2 baths
- Basement foundation

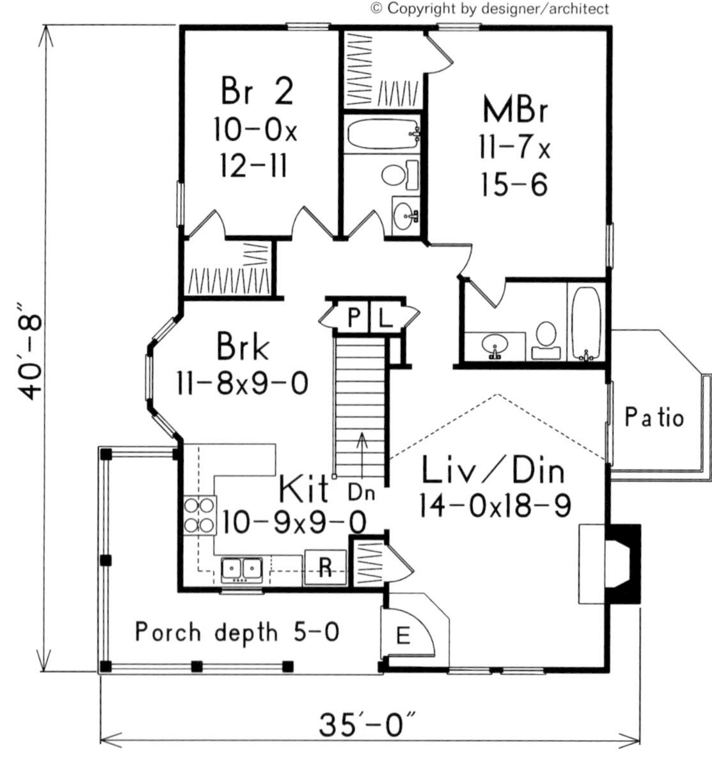

To Order See Page 288 | Call Toll-Free 1-877-379-3420

LOWE'S LEGACY SERIES

SPECIAL FEATURES

- 1,314 total square feet of living area
- Energy efficient home with 2" x 6" exterior walls
- Covered porch adds immediate appeal and welcoming charm
- Open floor plan combined with a vaulted ceiling offers spacious living
- Functional kitchen is complete with a pantry and eating bar
- Cozy fireplace in the living room
- Private master bedroom features a large walk-in closet and bath
- 3 bedrooms, 2 baths, 2-car garage
- Basement foundation

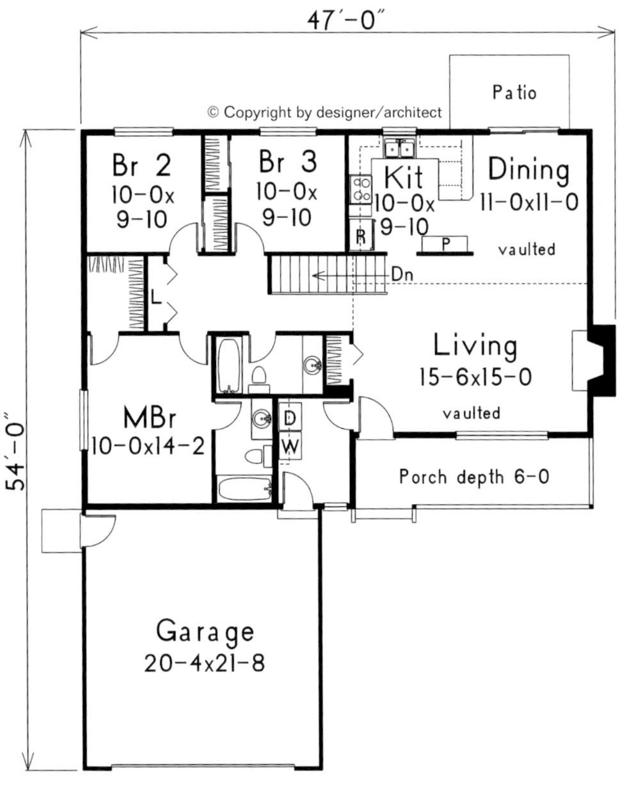

Special Features

- 1,242 total square feet of living area
- Energy efficient home with 2" x 6" exterior walls
- The wide foyer opens to the living room for a spacious atmosphere and grand first impression
- The centrally located kitchen easily serves the large dining and living rooms
- The split-bedroom design allows privacy for the homeowners who will love spending time in their master bedroom retreat
- 3 bedrooms, 2 baths, 2-car garage
- Basement foundation

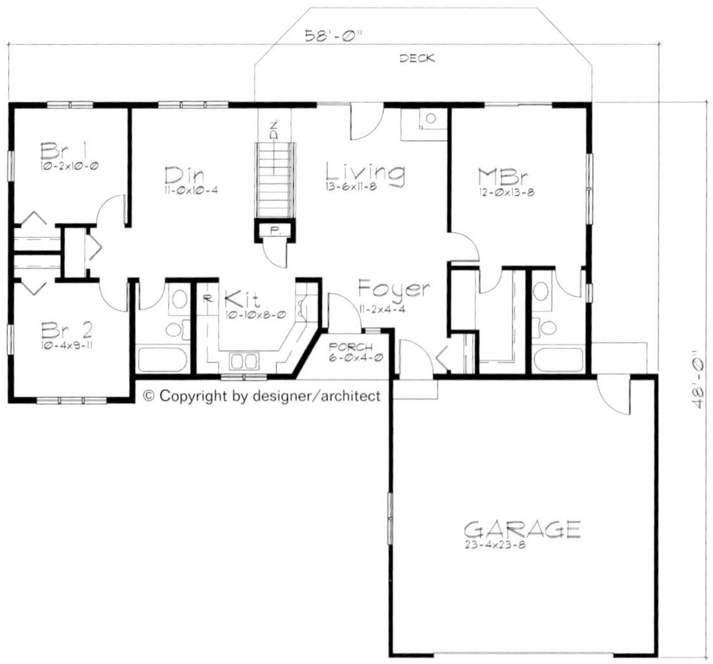

SPECIAL FEATURES

- 1,196 total square feet of living area
- Home includes an extra-deep porch for evening relaxation
- The large living room enjoys a corner fireplace, dining area featuring a wide bay window with sliding doors to the rear patio, and a snack bar open to the kitchen
- The master bedroom has a nice walk-in closet, its own linen closet and a roomy bath with a double-bowl vanity and garden tub
- 3 bedrooms, 2 baths, 1-car side entry garage
- Crawl space foundation, drawings also include slab foundation

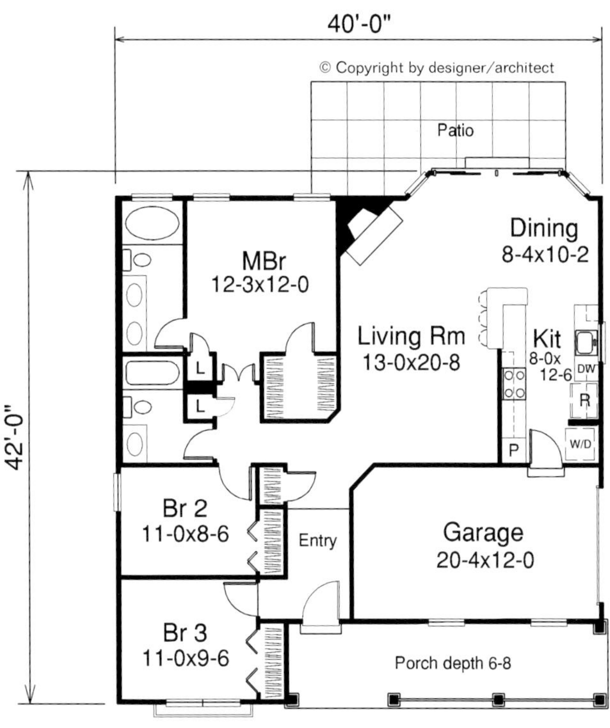

Plan Number: 537-037D-0008 | Price Code: C

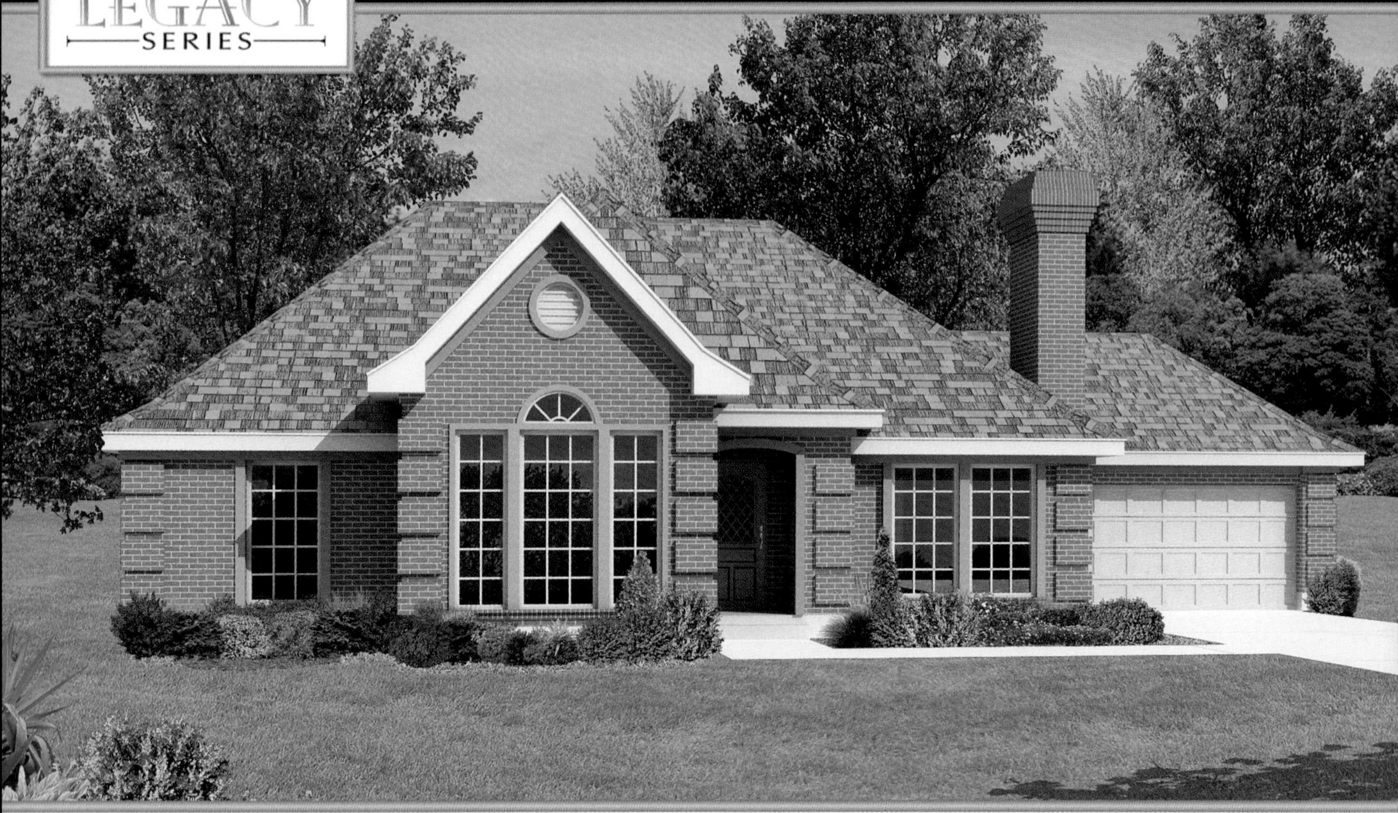

Special Features

- 1,707 total square feet of living area
- The formal living room off the entry hall has a high sloping ceiling and prominent fireplace
- Kitchen and breakfast area allow access to an oversized garage and rear porch
- Master bedroom has an impressive vaulted ceiling, luxurious bath, large walk-in closet and separate tub and shower
- Utility room is conveniently located near the bedrooms
- 3 bedrooms, 2 baths, 2-car garage
- Slab foundation

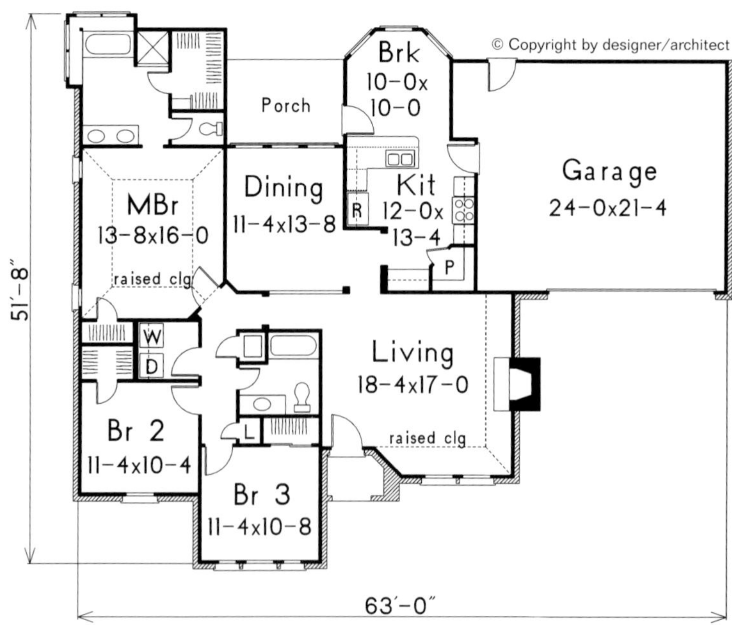

LOWE'S LEGACY SERIES

SPECIAL FEATURES

- 1,403 total square feet of living area
- Impressive living areas for a modest-sized home
- Special master/hall bath has linen storage, step-up tub and lots of window light
- Spacious closets everywhere you look
- 3 bedrooms, 2 baths, 2-car drive under garage
- Basement foundation

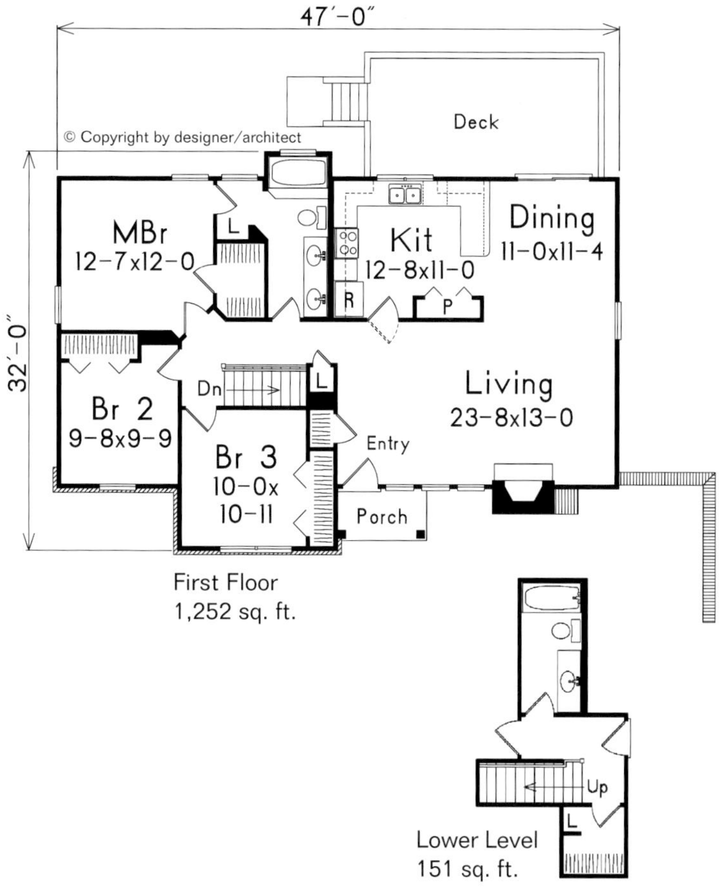

First Floor
1,252 sq. ft.

Lower Level
151 sq. ft.

Plan Number: 537-022D-0011 | Price Code: B

Special Features

- 1,630 total square feet of living area
- Crisp facade and full windows front and back offer open viewing
- Wrap-around rear deck is accessible from the breakfast room, dining room and master bedroom
- Vaulted ceilings top the living room and master bedroom
- Sitting area and large walk-in closet complement the master bedroom
- 3 bedrooms, 2 baths, 2-car garage
- Basement foundation

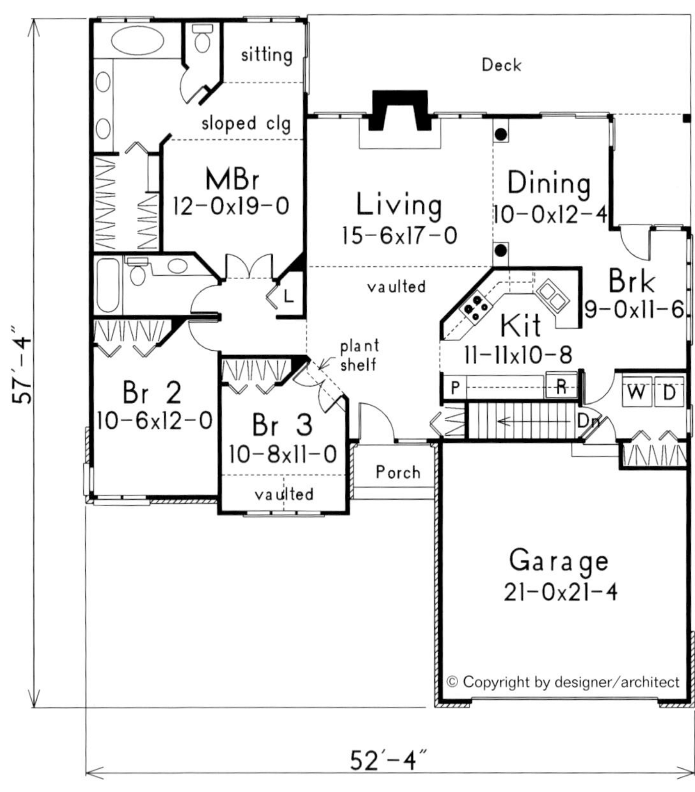

LOWE'S LEGACY SERIES

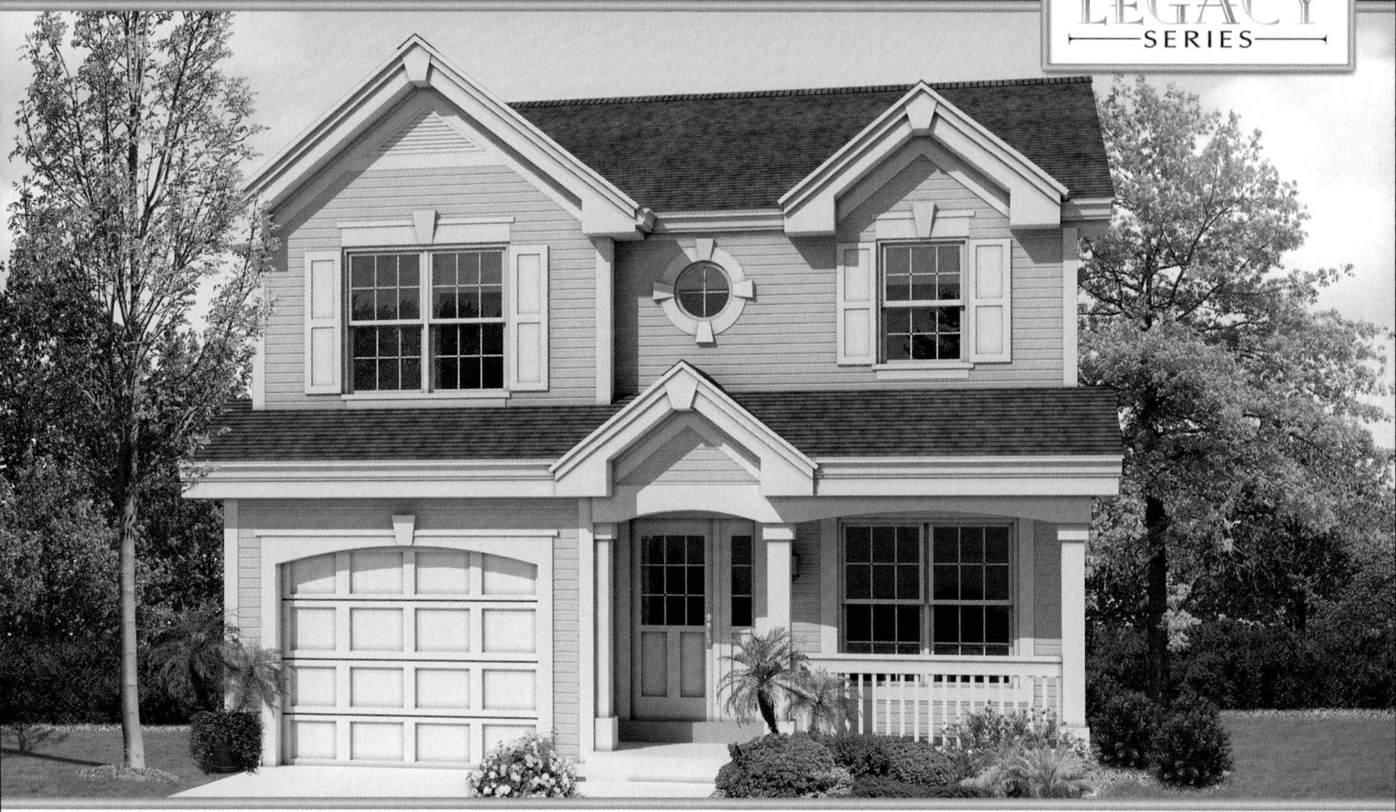

SPECIAL FEATURES

- 1,167 total square feet of living area
- Attractive exterior is enhanced with multiple gables
- Sizable living room features a separate entry foyer and view to front porch
- Functional kitchen has a breakfast room with bay window, built-in pantry and laundry room with half bath
- The master bedroom offers three closets and a luxury bath
- 2 bedrooms, 2 1/2 baths, 1-car garage
- Basement foundation

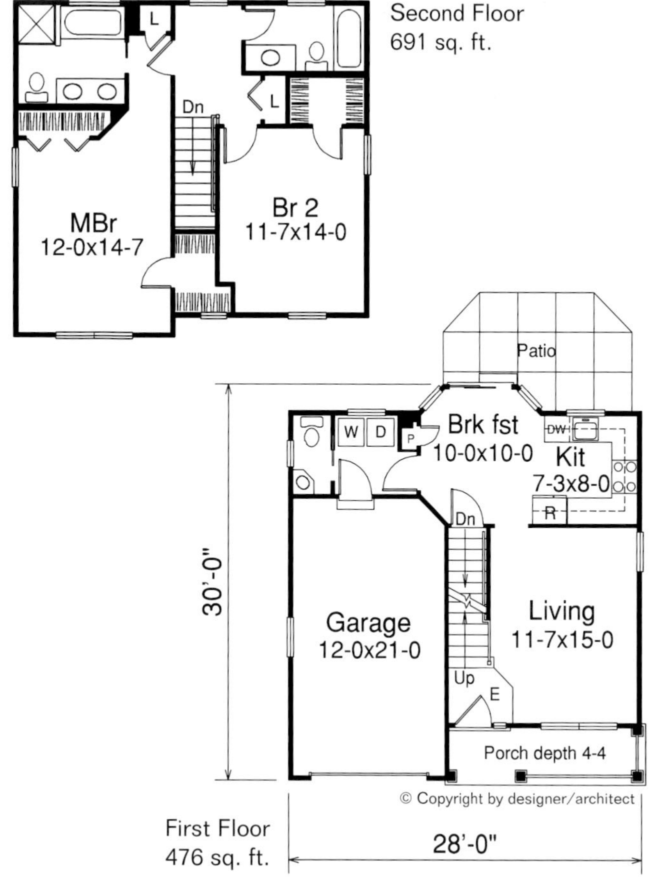

PLAN NUMBER: 537-006D-0001 | PRICE CODE: B

SPECIAL FEATURES

- 1,643 total square feet of living area
- Family room has a vaulted ceiling, open staircase and arched windows allowing for plenty of light
- Kitchen captures full use of space, with a pantry, storage, ample counterspace and work island
- Large closets and storage areas throughout
- Roomy master bath has a skylight for natural lighting plus a separate tub and shower
- Rear of house provides ideal location for future screened-in porch
- 3 bedrooms, 2 baths, 2-car side entry garage
- Basement foundation, drawings also include slab and crawl space foundations

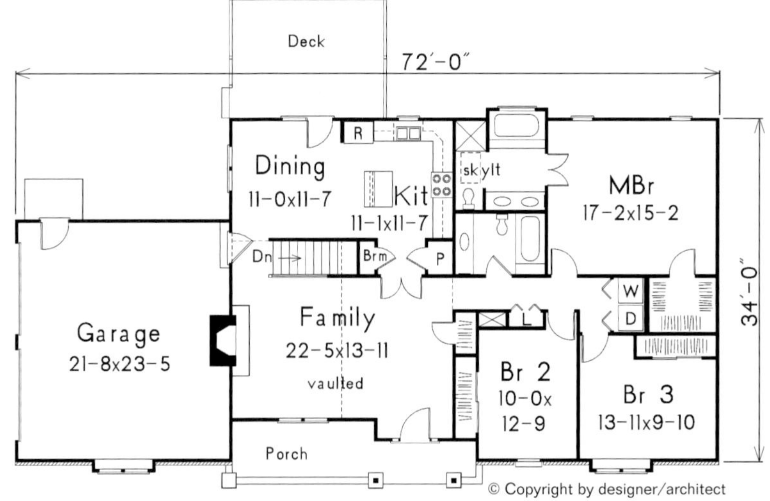

TO ORDER SEE PAGE 288 | CALL TOLL-FREE 1-877-379-3420

SPECIAL FEATURES

- 1,195 total square feet of living area
- Dining room opens onto the patio
- Master bedroom features a vaulted ceiling, private bath and walk-in closet
- Coat closets are located by both the entrances
- Convenient secondary entrance is located at the back of the garage
- 3 bedrooms, 2 baths, 2-car garage
- Basement foundation

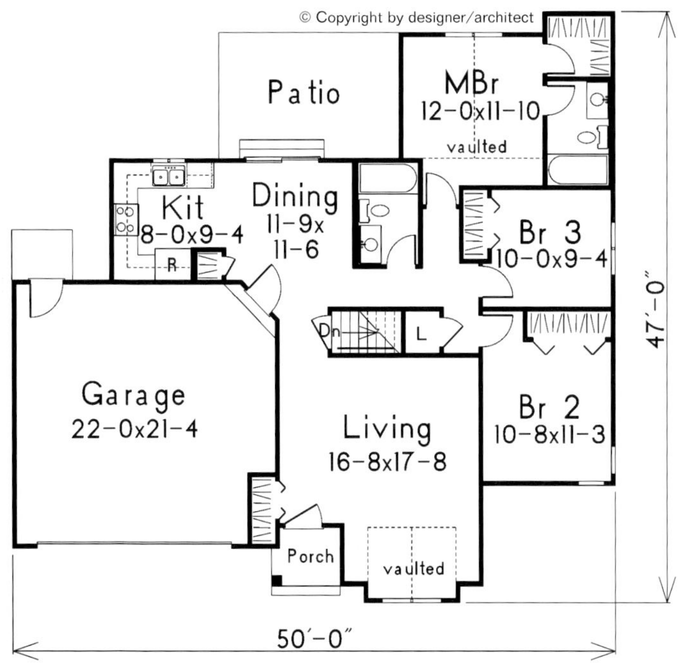

Plan Number: 537-007D-0039 | Price Code: B

Special Features

- 1,563 total square feet of living area
- Enjoyable wrap-around porch and lower sundeck
- Vaulted entry is adorned with a palladian window, plant shelves, stone floor and fireplace
- Huge vaulted great room has a magnificent view through a two-story atrium window wall
- 2 bedrooms, 1 1/2 baths
- Walk-out basement foundation

Rear View

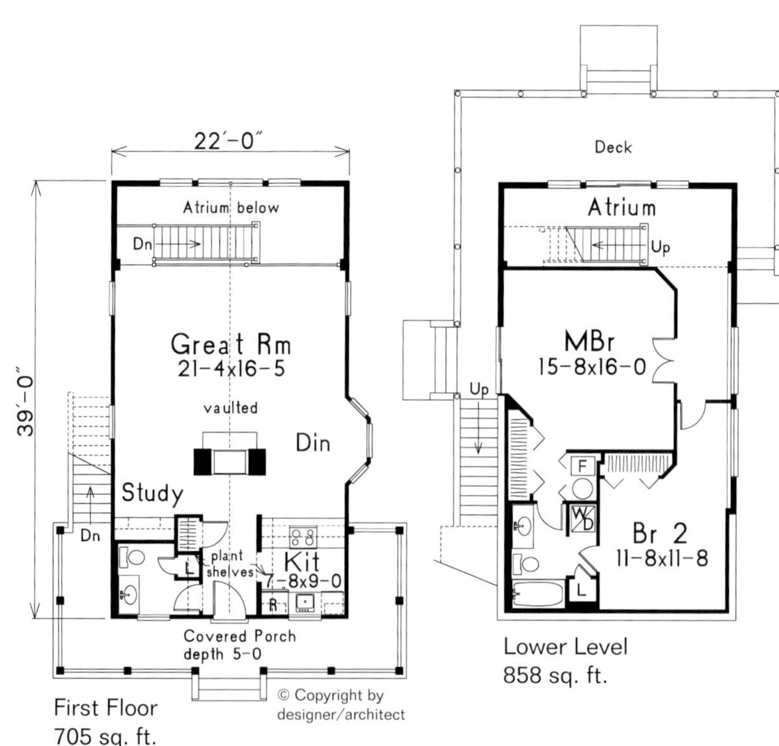

First Floor
705 sq. ft.

Lower Level
858 sq. ft.

LOWE'S LEGACY SERIES

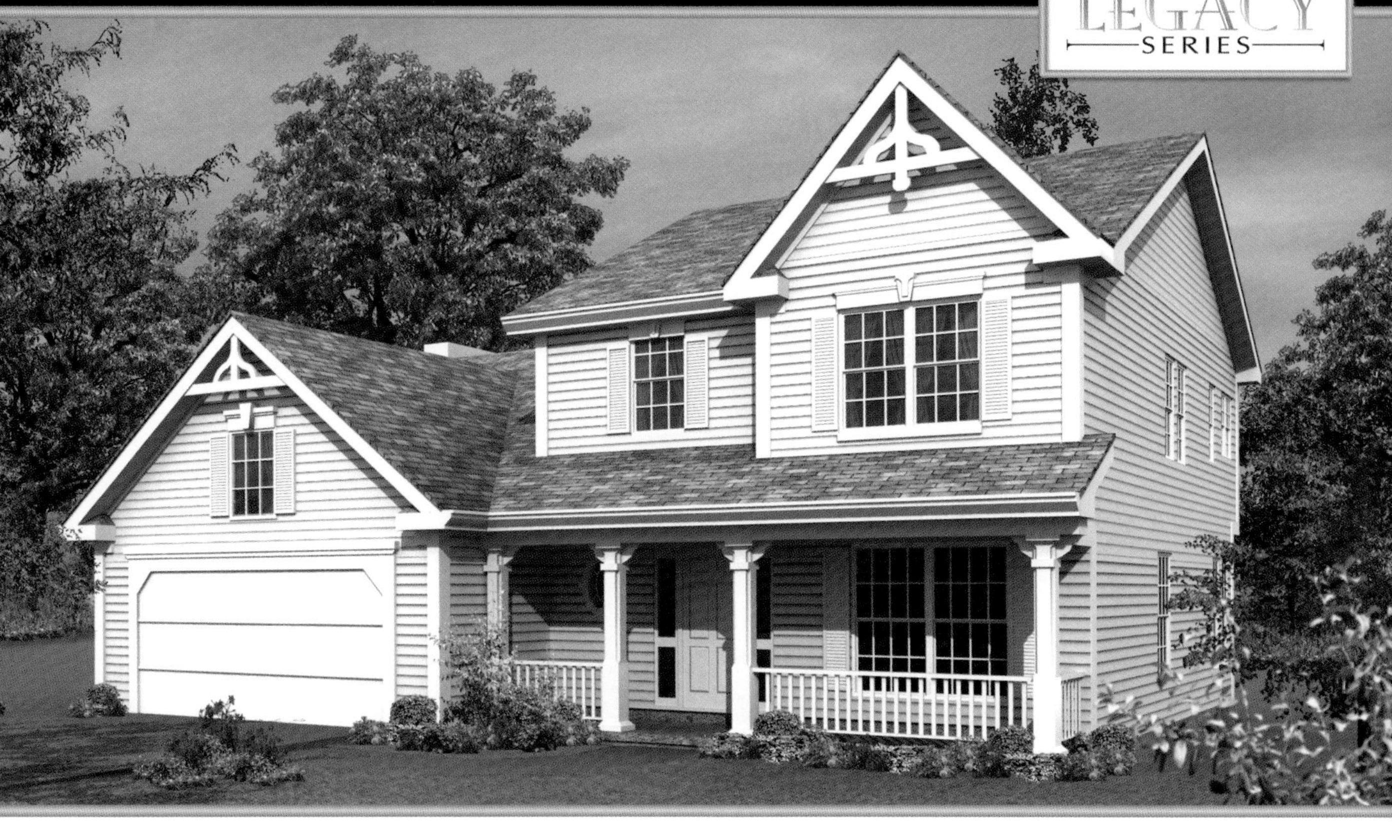

SPECIAL FEATURES

- 2,180 total square feet of living area
- Energy efficient home with 2" x 6" exterior walls
- Informal dinette and formal dining area flank the kitchen
- The grand fireplace is the focal point in the vaulted family room
- Master bedroom includes a bath with a walk-in closet, shower and corner garden tub
- 3 bedrooms, 2 1/2 baths, 2-car garage
- Basement foundation

Second Floor
952 sq. ft.

© Copyright by designer/architect

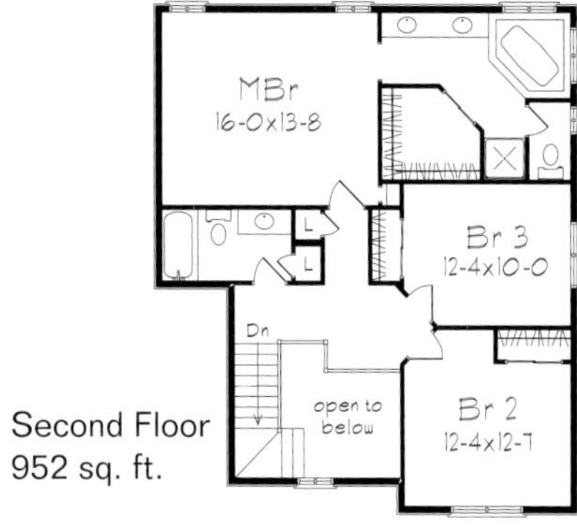

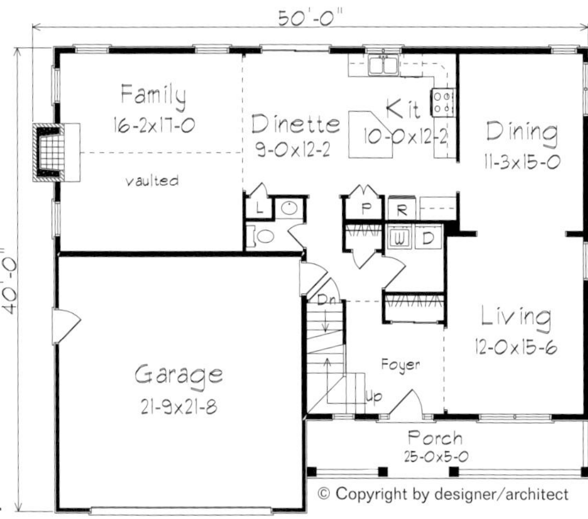

First Floor
1,228 sq. ft.

Special Features

- 1,343 total square feet of living area
- Separate and convenient family, living and dining areas
- Nice-sized master bedroom enjoys a large closet and private bath
- Foyer with convenient coat closet opens into combined living and dining rooms
- Family room has access to the outdoors through sliding glass doors
- 3 bedrooms, 2 baths, 2-car garage
- Crawl space foundation, drawings also include basement foundation

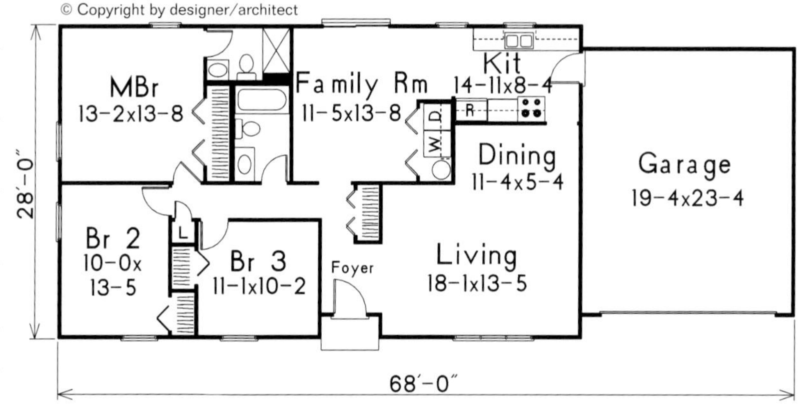

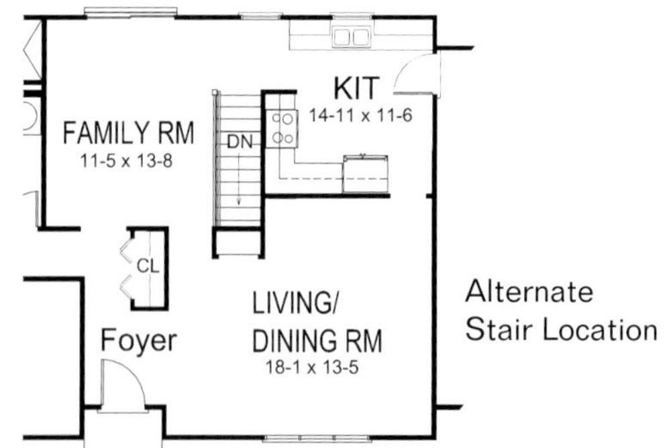

Alternate Stair Location

LOWE'S LEGACY SERIES

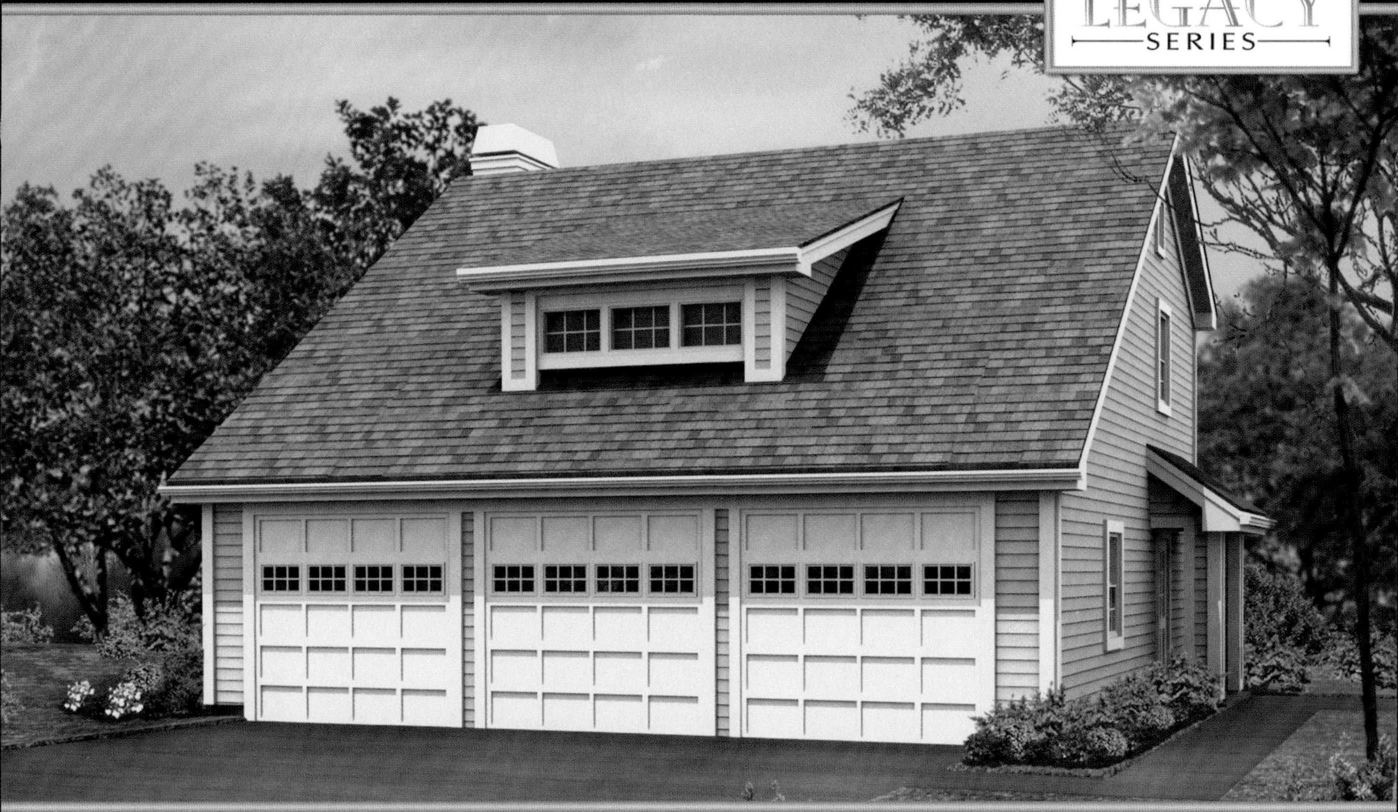

SPECIAL FEATURES

- 1,005 total square feet of living area
- Two-story apartment is disguised with a one-story facade featuring triple garage doors and a roof dormer
- Side porch leads to an entry hall which accesses the living room, U-shaped kitchen, powder room and stairs to the second floor
- The large living room has a fireplace, sliding doors to the rear patio, dining area with bay window and opens to the kitchen with breakfast bar
- The second floor is comprised of two bedrooms and a bath
- 2 bedrooms, 1 1/2 baths, 3-car garage
- Slab foundation

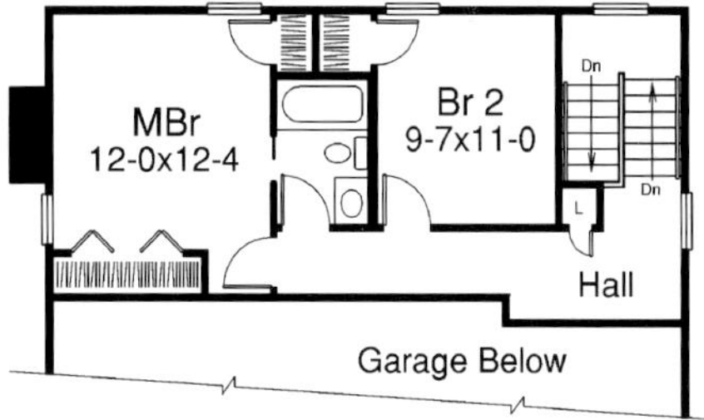

Second Floor
492 sq. ft.

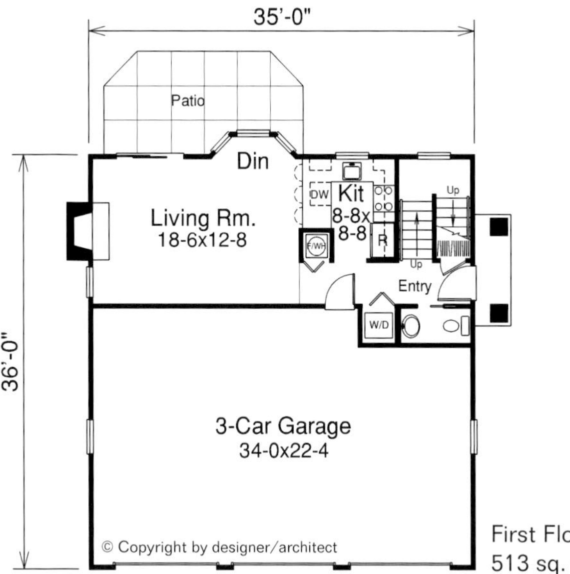

First Floor
513 sq. ft.

SPECIAL FEATURES

632 total square feet of living area

Porch leads to a vaulted entry and stair with feature window, coat closet and access to garage/laundry

Cozy living room offers a vaulted ceiling, fireplace, large palladian window and pass-through to kitchen

A garden tub with arched window is part of a very roomy bath

1 bedroom, 1 bath, 2-car garage

Slab foundation

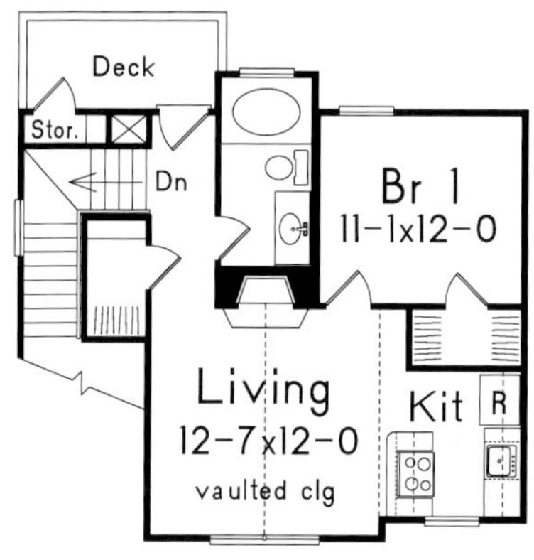

Second Floor
512 sq. ft.

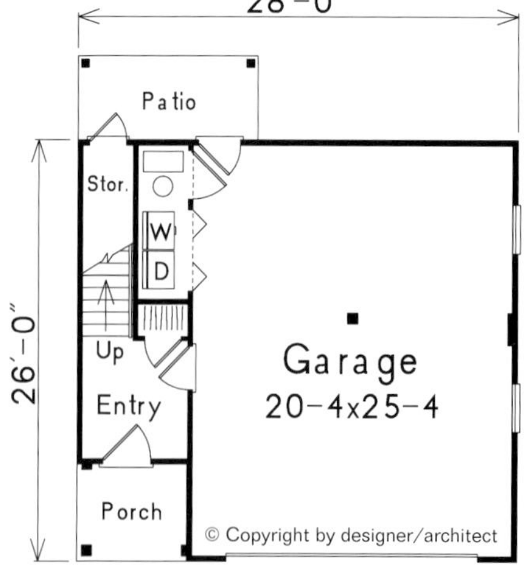

First Floor
120 sq. ft.

SPECIAL FEATURES

- 1,617 total square feet of living area
- Kitchen and breakfast area overlook the great room with fireplace
- Formal dining room features a vaulted ceiling and an elegant circle-top window
- All bedrooms are located on the second floor for privacy
- 3 bedrooms, 2 1/2 baths, 2-car garage
- Partial crawl space/slab foundation

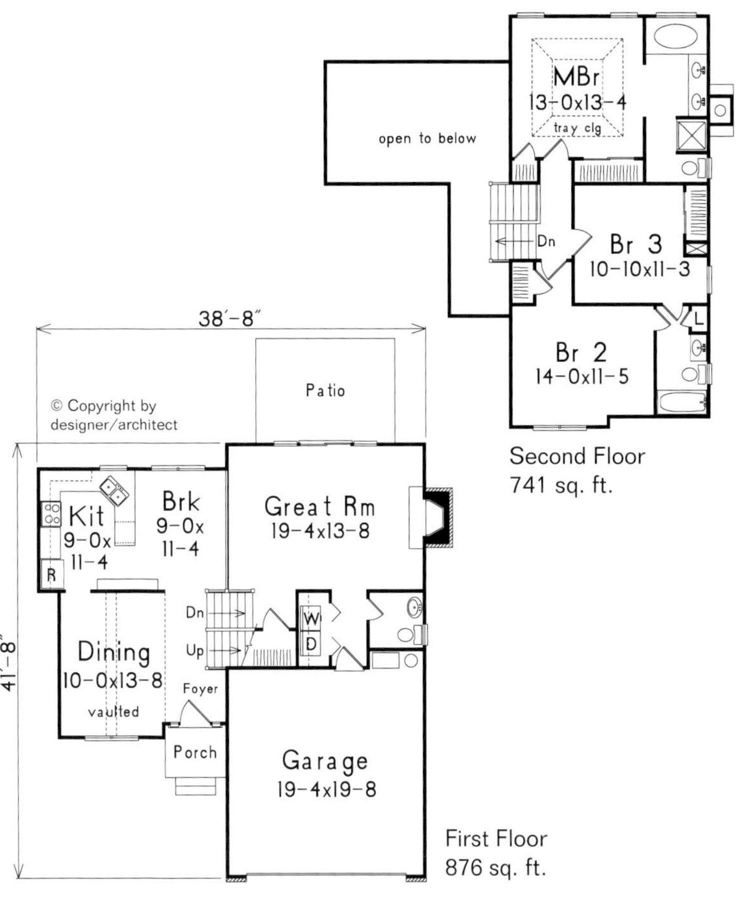

Second Floor
741 sq. ft.

First Floor
876 sq. ft.

Plan Number: 537-017D-0008 | Price Code: B

Special Features

- 1,466 total square feet of living area
- Energy efficient home with 2" x 6" exterior walls
- Foyer separates the living room from the dining room and contains a generous coat closet
- Large living room features a corner fireplace, bay window and pass-through to the kitchen
- Informal breakfast area opens to a large terrace through sliding glass doors which brighten the area
- Master bedroom has a large walk-in closet and private bath
- 3 bedrooms, 2 baths, 2-car garage
- Basement foundation, drawings also include slab foundation

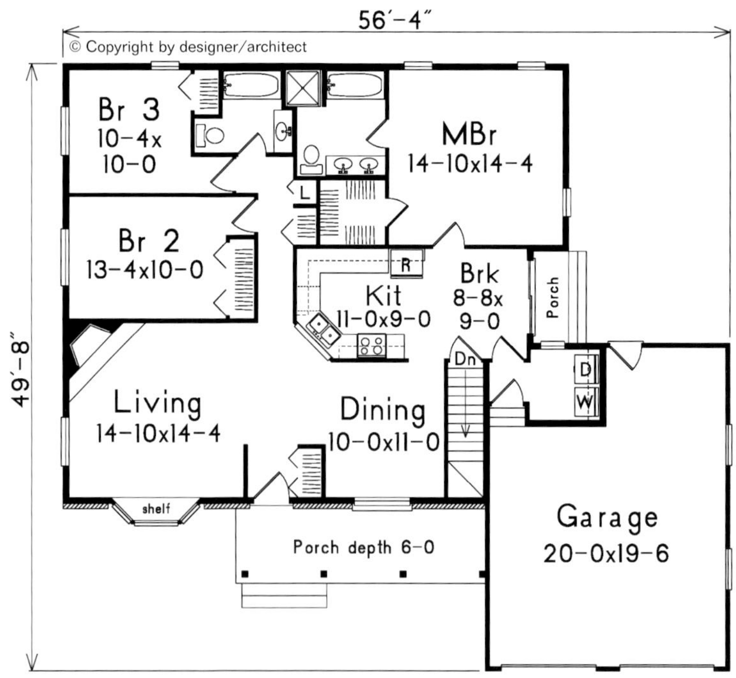

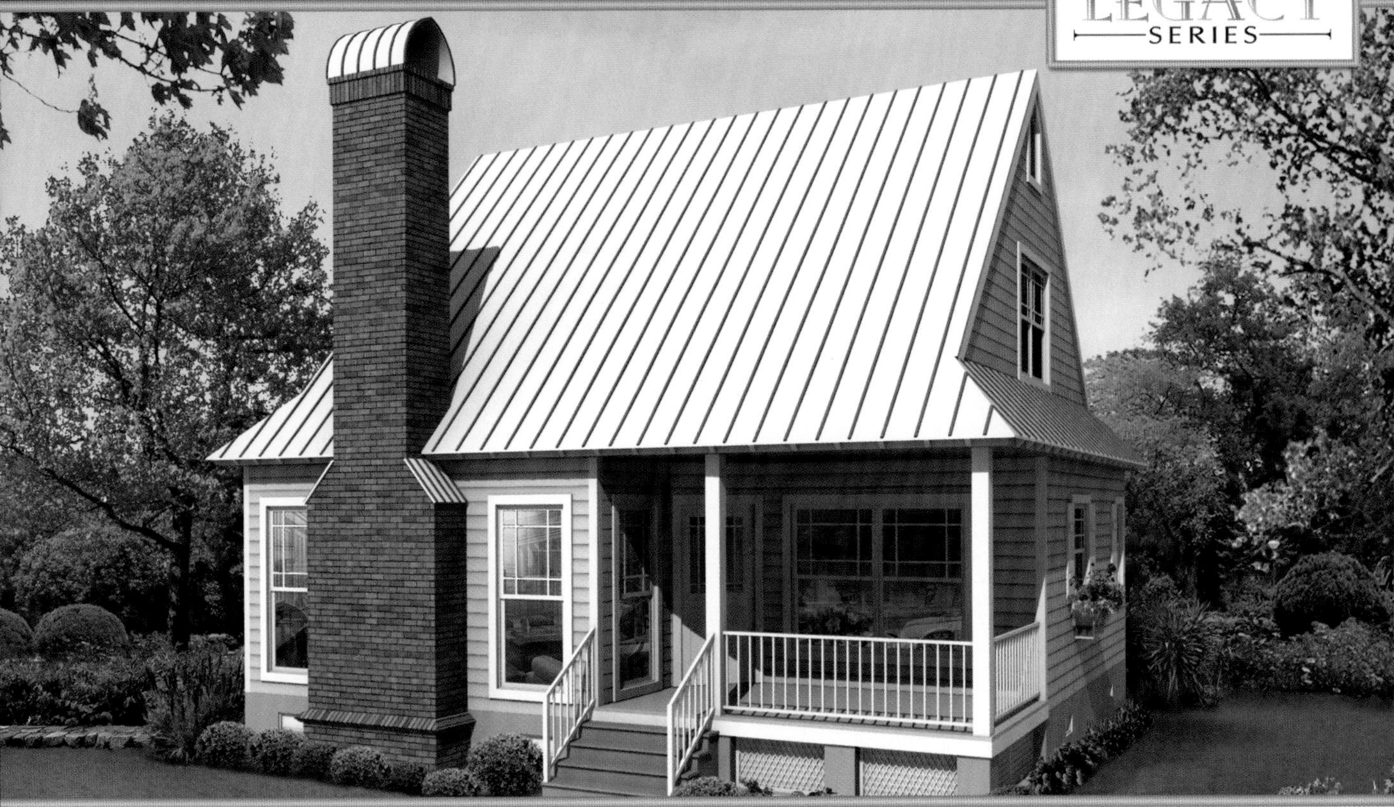

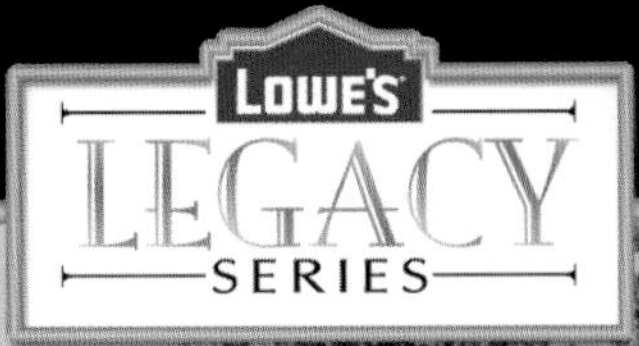

SPECIAL FEATURES

- 1,028 total square feet of living area
- Well-designed bath contains laundry facilities
- L-shaped kitchen has a handy pantry
- Tall windows flank the family room fireplace
- Cozy covered porch provides unique angled entry into home
- 3 bedrooms, 1 bath
- Crawl space foundation

Second Floor
300 sq. ft.

First Floor
728 sq. ft.

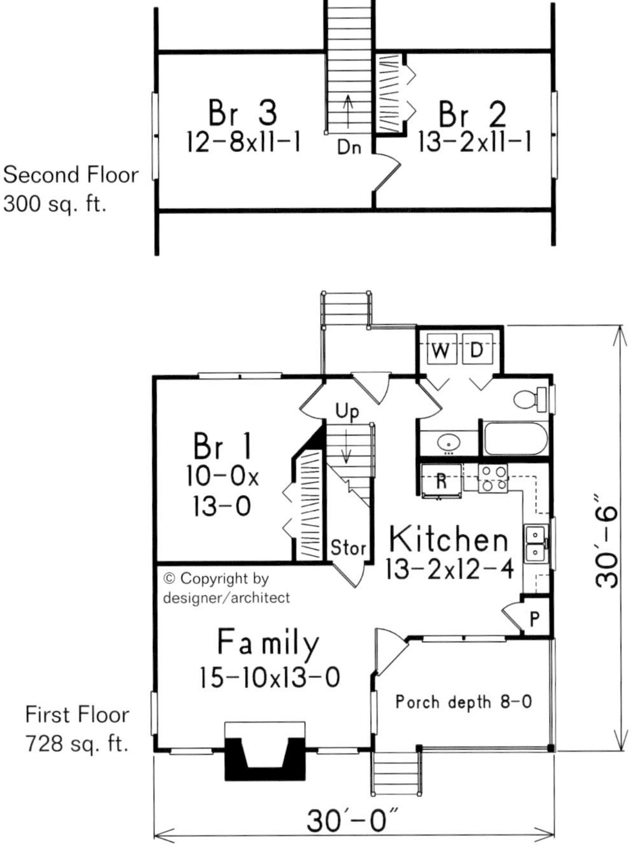

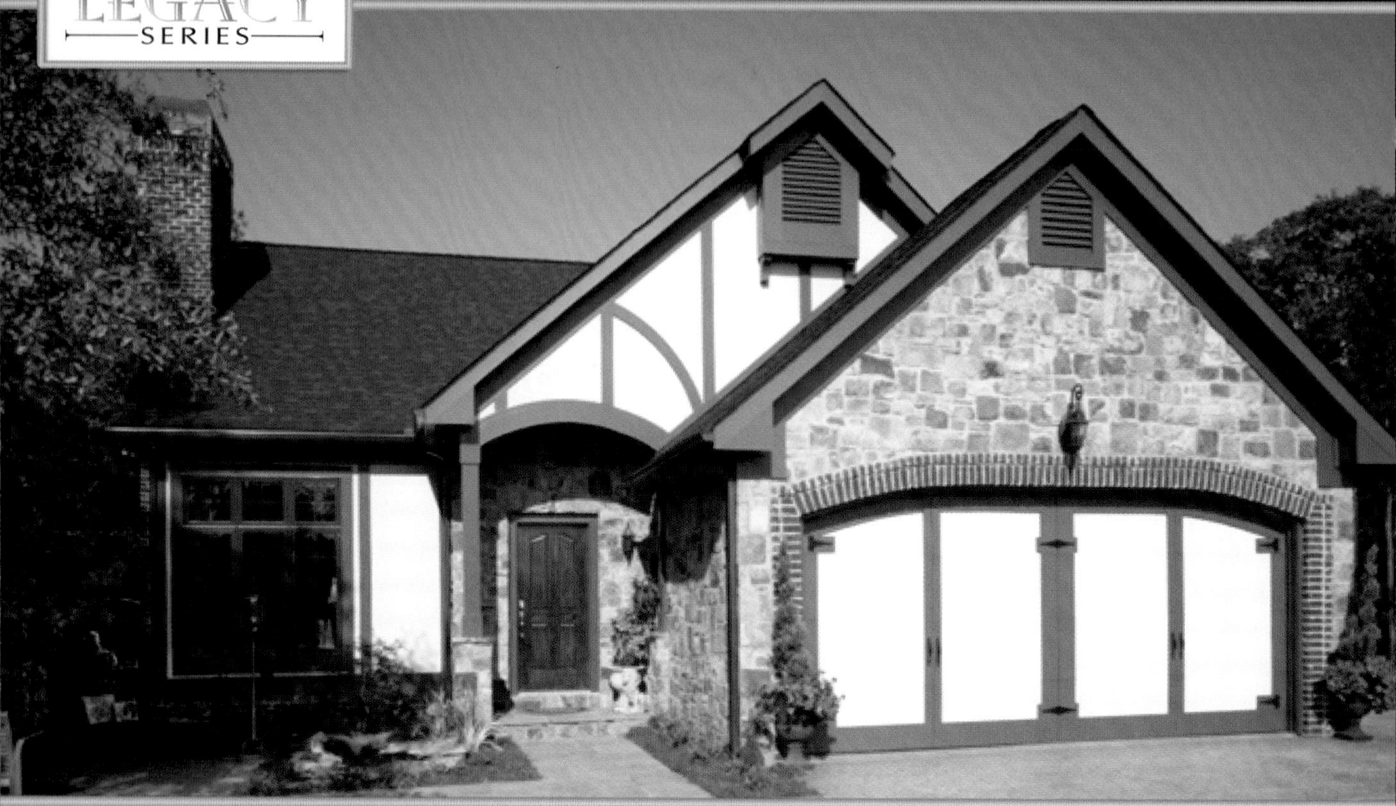

Special Features

- 1,767 total square feet of living area
- Vaulted dining room has a view onto the patio
- Master suite is vaulted with a private bath and walk-in closet
- An arched entry leads to the vaulted living room featuring tall windows and a fireplace
- 3 bedrooms, 2 1/2 baths, 2-car garage
- Basement foundation

Second Floor
500 sq. ft.

First Floor
1,267 sq. ft.

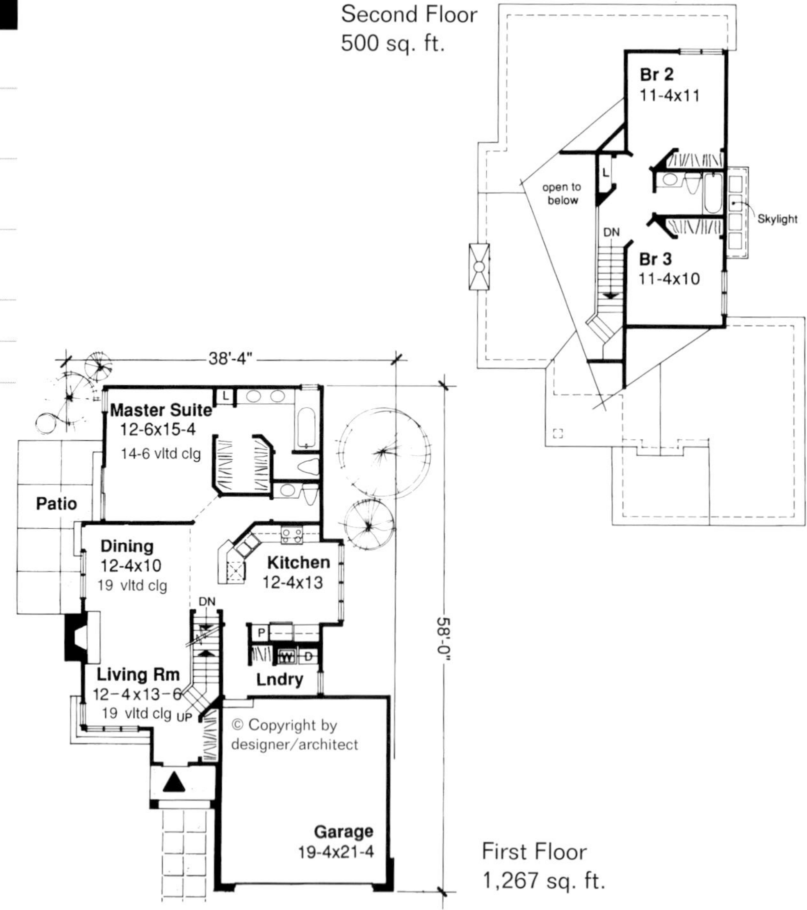

LOWE'S LEGACY SERIES

SPECIAL FEATURES

- 480 total square feet of living area
- Inviting wrap-around porch and rear covered patio are perfect for summer evenings
- Living room features a fireplace, separate entry foyer with coat closet and sliding doors to the rear patio
- The compact but complete kitchen includes a dining area with bay window and window at sink for patio views
- 1 bedroom, 1 bath, 1-car garage
- Slab foundation

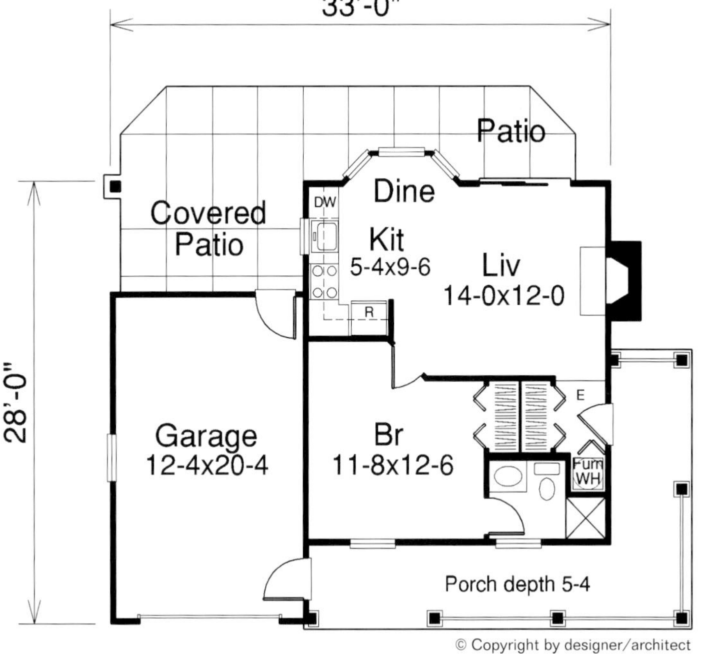

SPECIAL FEATURES

- 1,700 total square feet of living area
- Two-story entry with T-stair is illuminated with a decorative oval window
- Skillfully designed U-shaped kitchen has a built-in pantry
- All bedrooms have generous closet storage and are common to a spacious hall with a walk-in cedar closet
- 4 bedrooms, 2 1/2 baths, 2-car side entry garage
- Basement foundation

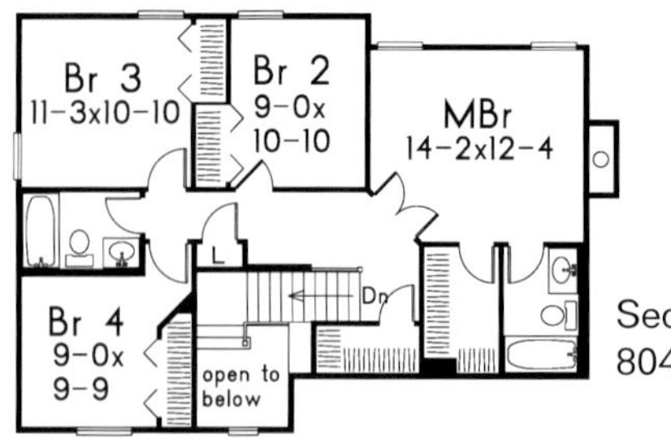

Second Floor
804 sq. ft.

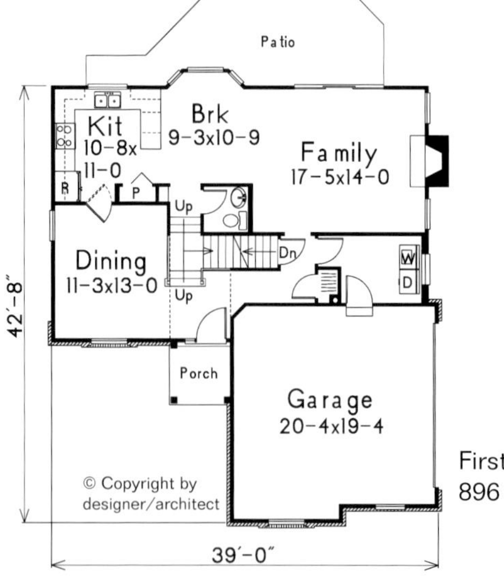

First Floor
896 sq. ft.

SPECIAL FEATURES

- 829 total square feet of living area
- U-shaped kitchen opens into living area by a 42" high counter
- Oversized bay window and French door accent dining room
- Gathering space is created by the large living room
- Convenient utility room and linen closet
- 1 bedroom, 1 bath
- Slab foundation

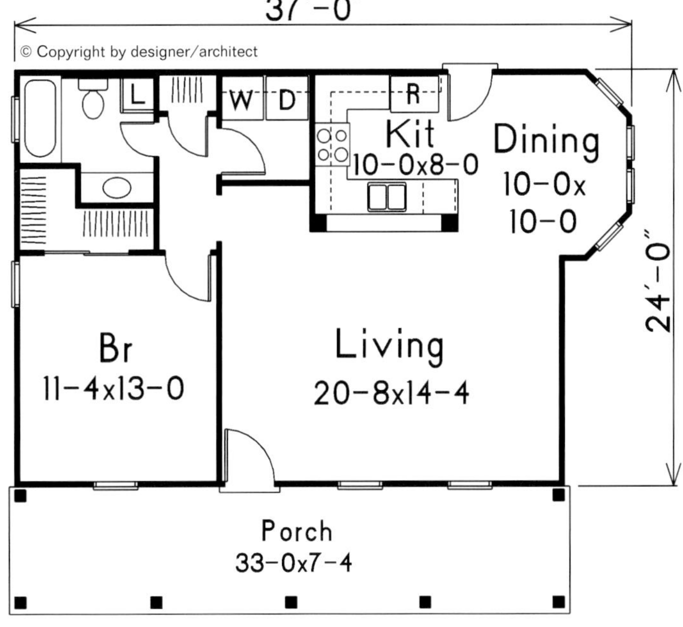

SPECIAL FEATURES

- 1,000 total square feet of living area
- Bath includes convenient closeted laundry area
- Master bedroom includes double closets and private access to the bath
- The foyer features a handy coat closet
- L-shaped kitchen provides easy access outdoors
- 3 bedrooms, 1 bath
- Crawl space foundation, drawings also include basement and slab foundations

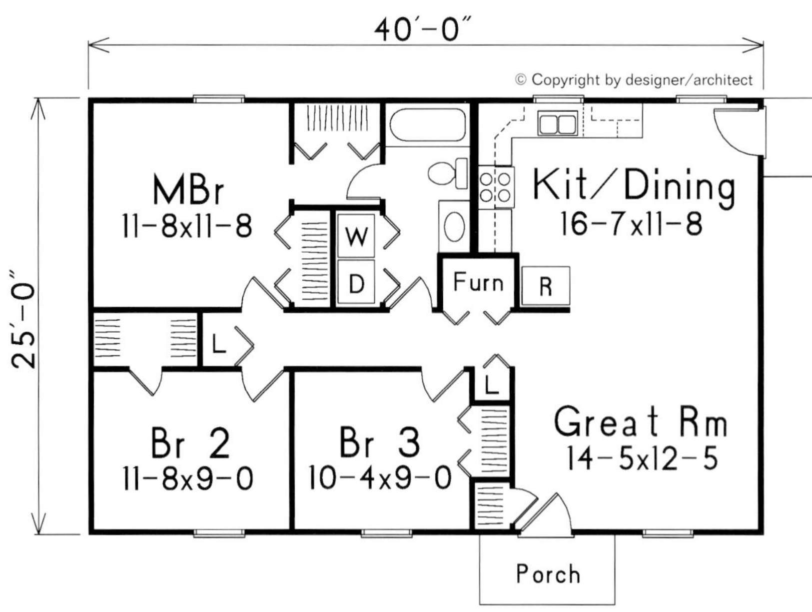

SPECIAL FEATURES

801 total square feet of living area

A wrap-around porch, roof dormer and fancy stonework all contribute to a delightful and charming exterior

The living room enjoys a separate entry, a stone fireplace, vaulted ceiling and lots of windows

The well-equipped kitchen has a snack bar and dining area with bay which offers access to the rear patio

An oversized two-car garage features a large vaulted room ideal for a shop, studio, hobby room or office with built-in cabinets and access to the porch

2 bedrooms, 1 bath, 2-car side entry garage

Slab foundation

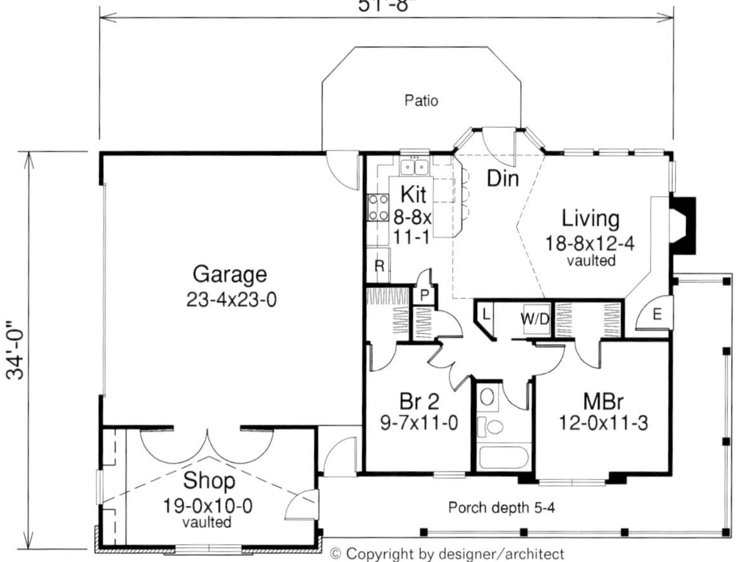

Special Features

- 1,823 total square feet of living area
- Vaulted living room is spacious and easily accesses the dining area
- The master bedroom boasts a tray ceiling, large walk-in closet and a private bath with a corner whirlpool tub
- Cheerful dining area is convenient to the U-shaped kitchen and also enjoys patio access
- Centrally located laundry room connects the garage to the living areas
- 3 bedrooms, 2 baths, 2-car garage
- Basement foundation

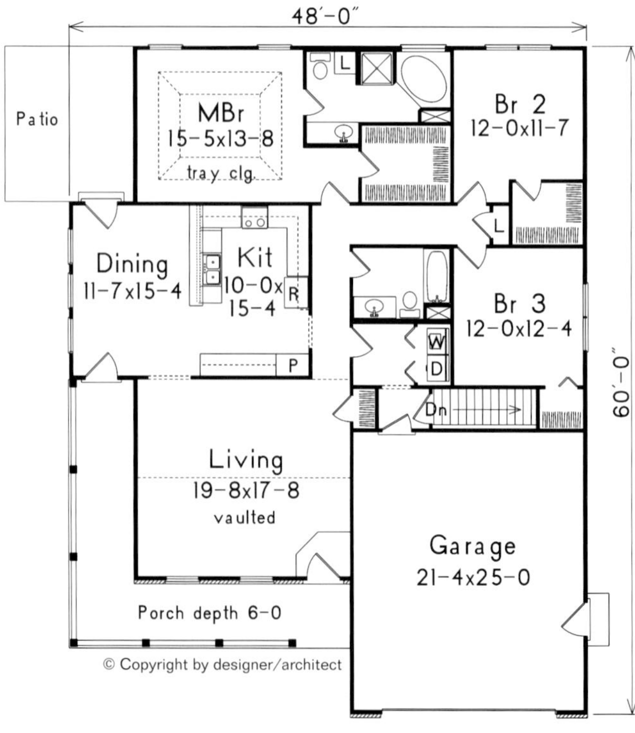

LOWE'S LEGACY SERIES

SPECIAL FEATURES

- 1,320 total square feet of living area
- Functional U-shaped kitchen features a pantry
- Large living and dining areas join to create an open atmosphere
- Secluded master bedroom includes a private full bath
- Covered front porch opens into a large living area with a convenient coat closet
- Utility/laundry room is located near the kitchen
- 3 bedrooms, 2 baths
- Crawl space foundation

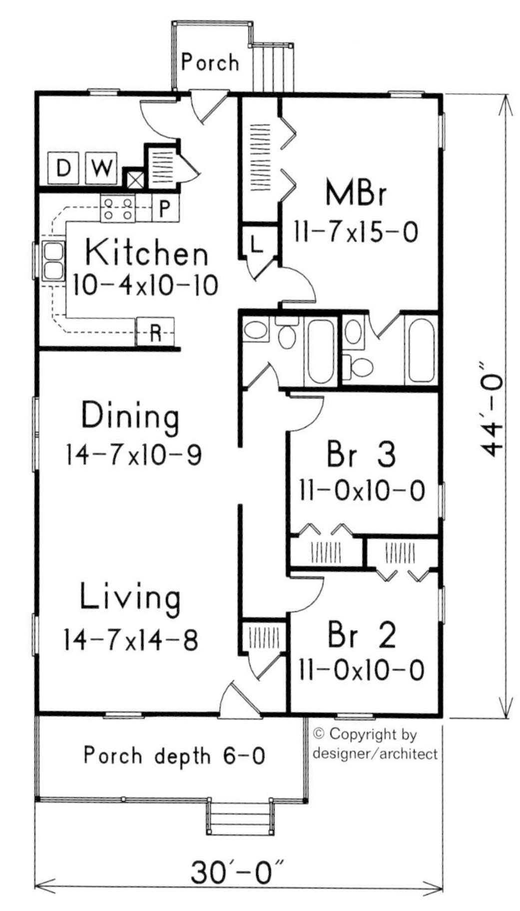

Special Features

- 1,609 total square feet of living area
- Kitchen captures full use of space with pantry, ample cabinets and workspace
- Master bedroom is well secluded with a walk-in closet and private bath
- Large utility room includes a sink and extra storage
- Attractive bay window in the dining area provides light
- 3 bedrooms, 2 1/2 baths, 2-car garage
- Slab foundation

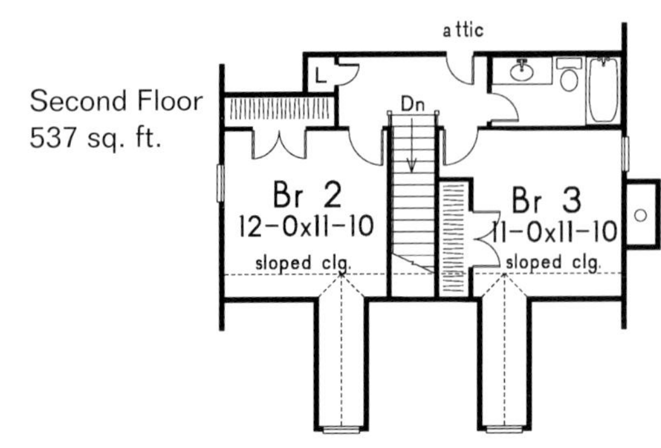

Second Floor
537 sq. ft.

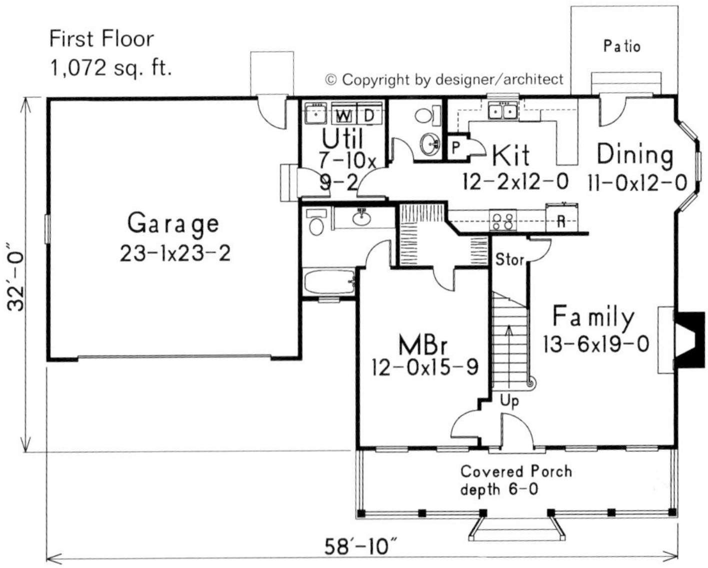

First Floor
1,072 sq. ft.

To Order See Page 288 |

LOWE'S LEGACY SERIES

SPECIAL FEATURES

- 914 total square feet of living area
- Large porch for leisure evenings
- Dining area with bay window, open stair and pass-through kitchen create openness
- Basement includes generous garage space, storage area, finished laundry and mechanical room
- 2 bedrooms, 1 bath, 2-car drive under rear entry garage
- Basement foundation

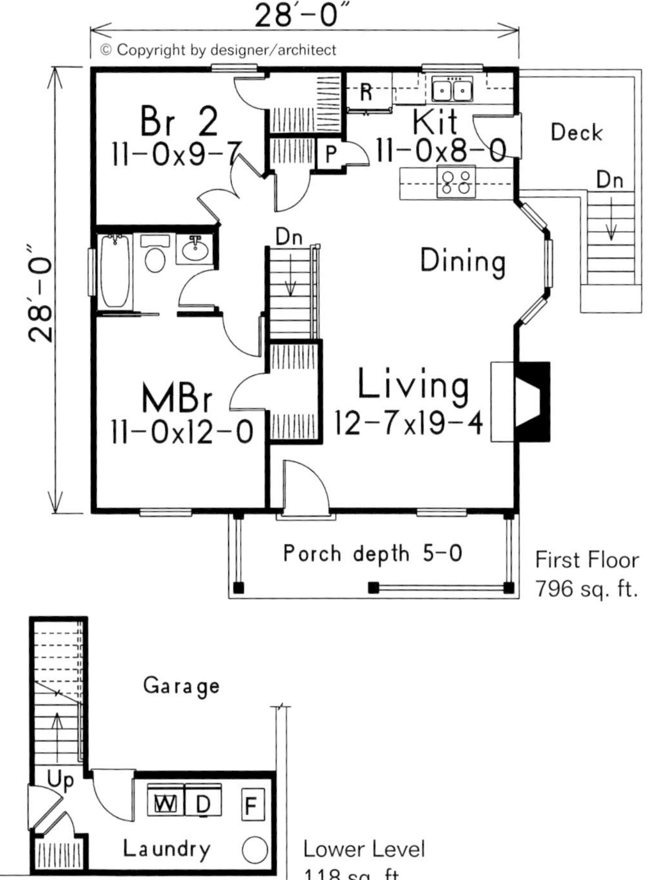

Plan Number: 537-007D-0134 | Price Code: A

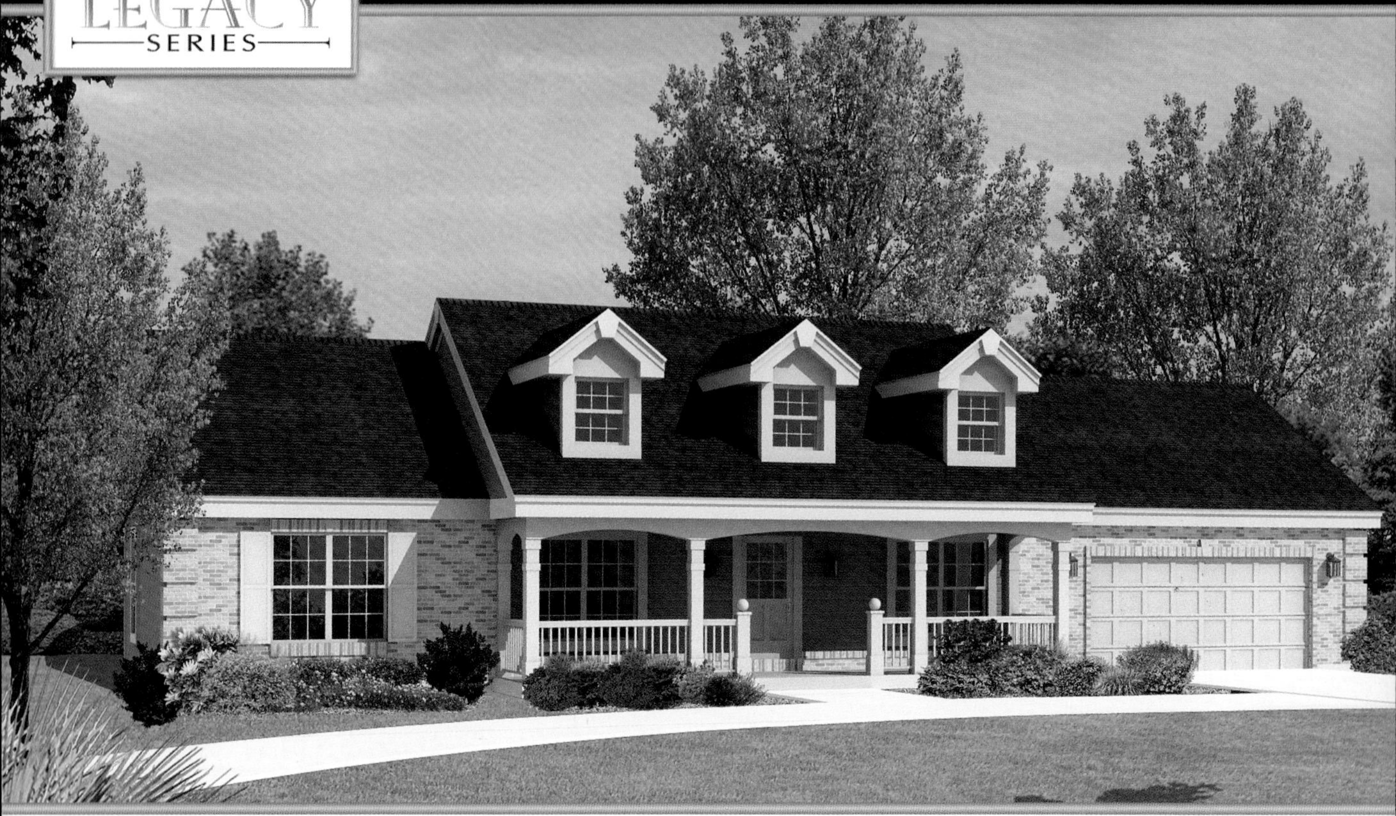

Special Features

- 1,310 total square feet of living area
- The combination of brick quoins, roof dormers and an elegant porch creates a classic look
- Open-space floor plan has vaulted kitchen, living and dining rooms
- The master bedroom is vaulted and enjoys privacy from other bedrooms
- A spacious laundry room is convenient to the kitchen and master bedroom with access to an oversized garage
- 3 bedrooms, 2 baths, 2-car garage
- Basement foundation, drawings also include crawl space and slab foundations

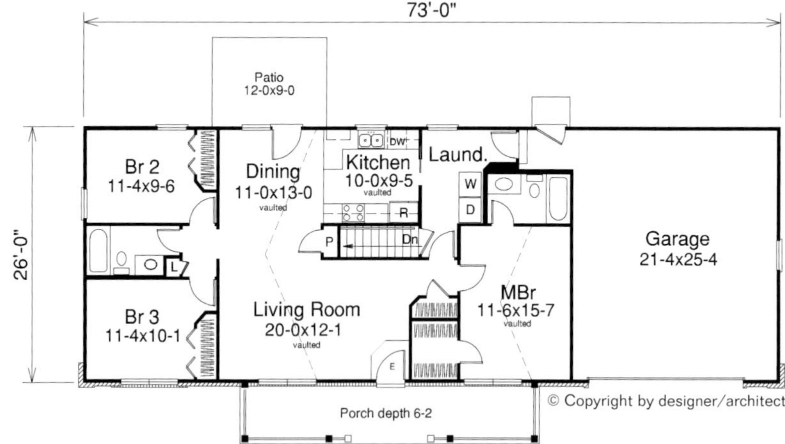

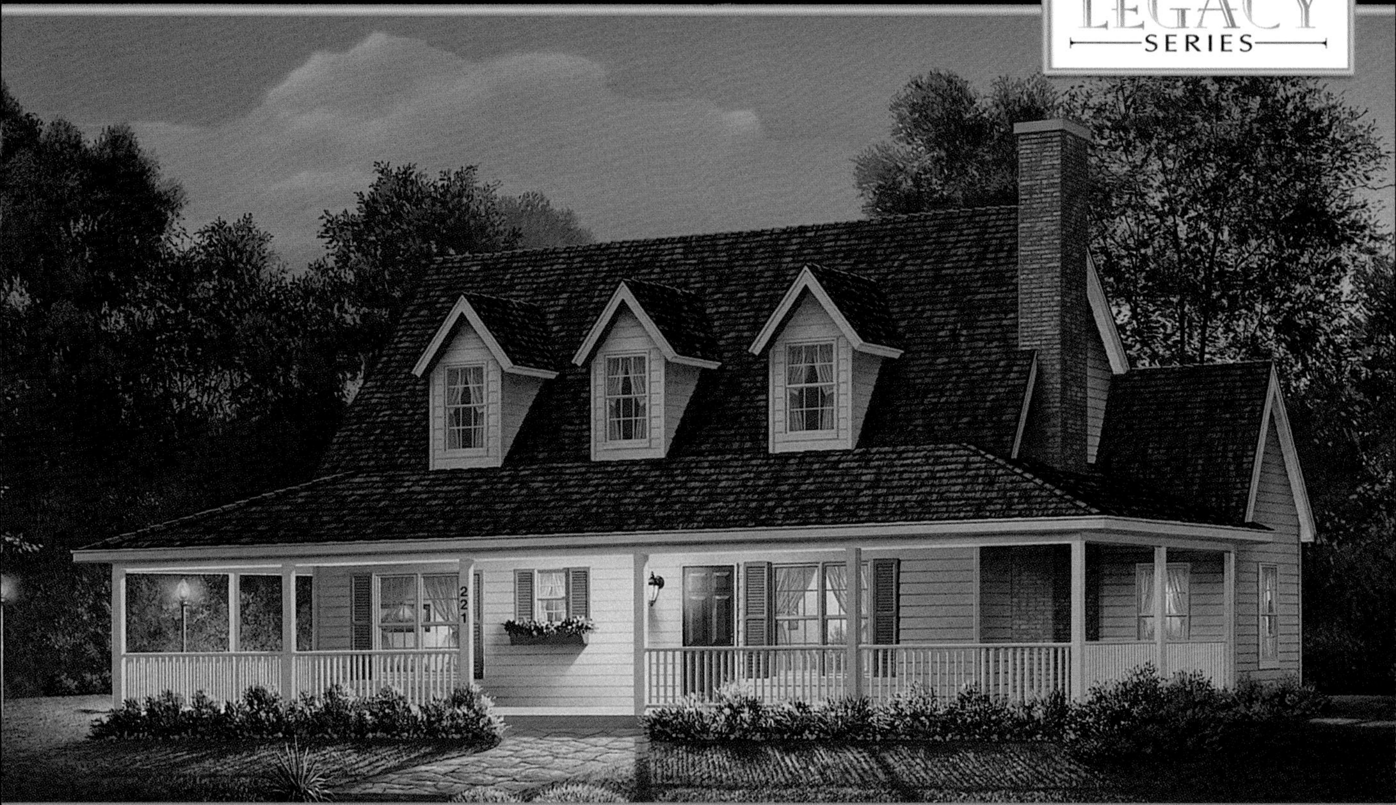

SPECIAL FEATURES

- 1,619 total square feet of living area
- Private second floor bedroom and bath
- Kitchen features a snack bar and adjacent dining area
- Master bedroom has a private bath
- Centrally located washer and dryer
- 3 bedrooms, 3 baths
- Basement foundation, drawings also include crawl space and slab foundations

Second Floor
360 sq. ft.

First Floor
1,259 sq. ft.

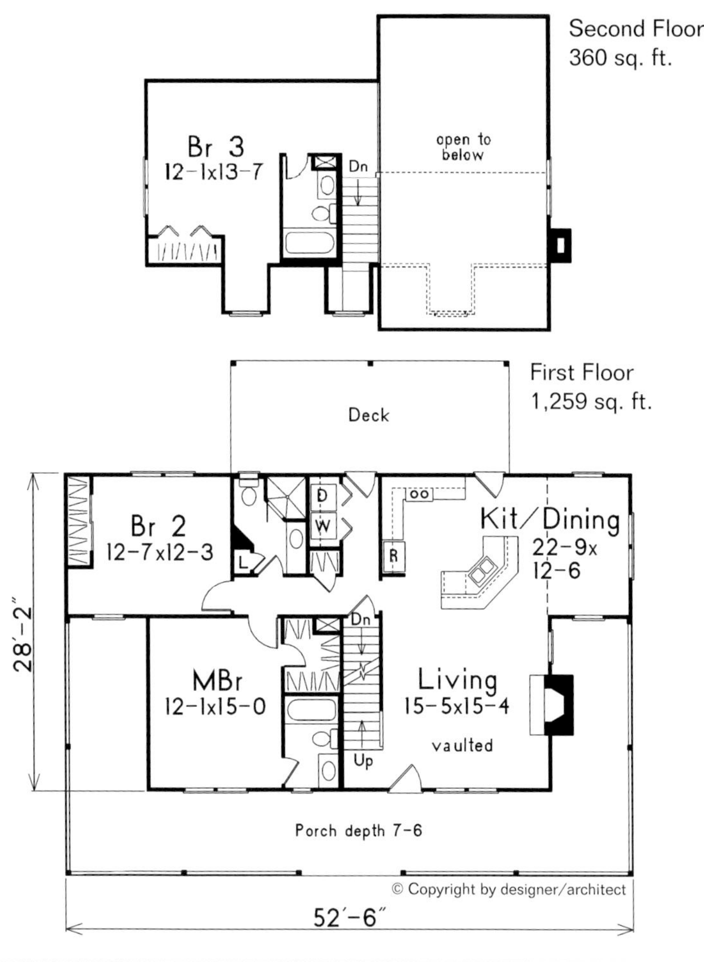

SPECIAL FEATURES

- 647 total square feet of living area
- Large vaulted room for living/sleeping has plant shelves on each end, stone fireplace and wide glass doors for views
- Roomy kitchen is vaulted and has a bayed dining area and fireplace
- Step down into a sunken and vaulted bath featuring a 6'-0" whirlpool tub-in-a-bay with shelves at each end for storage
- A large palladian window adorns each end of the cottage giving a cheery atmosphere throughout
- 1 living/sleeping room, 1 bath
- Crawl space foundation

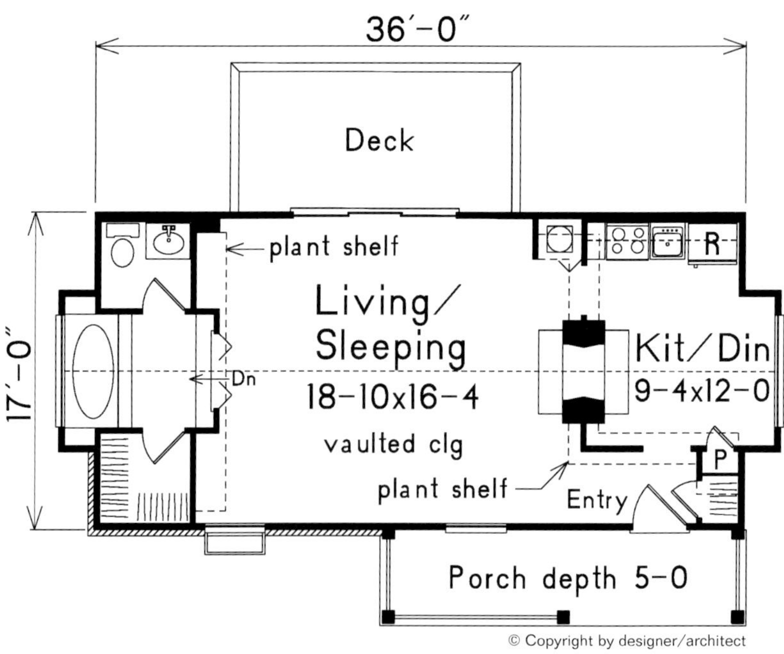

SPECIAL FEATURES

- 1,800 total square feet of living area
- Energy efficient home with 2" x 6" exterior walls
- The stylish kitchen and breakfast area feature large windows that allow a great view outdoors
- Covered front and rear porches provide an added dimension to this home's living space
- Generous storage areas and a large utility room
- Large separate master bedroom with adjoining bath has a large tub and corner shower
- 3 bedrooms, 2 baths, 2-car garage
- Crawl space foundation, drawings also include slab foundation

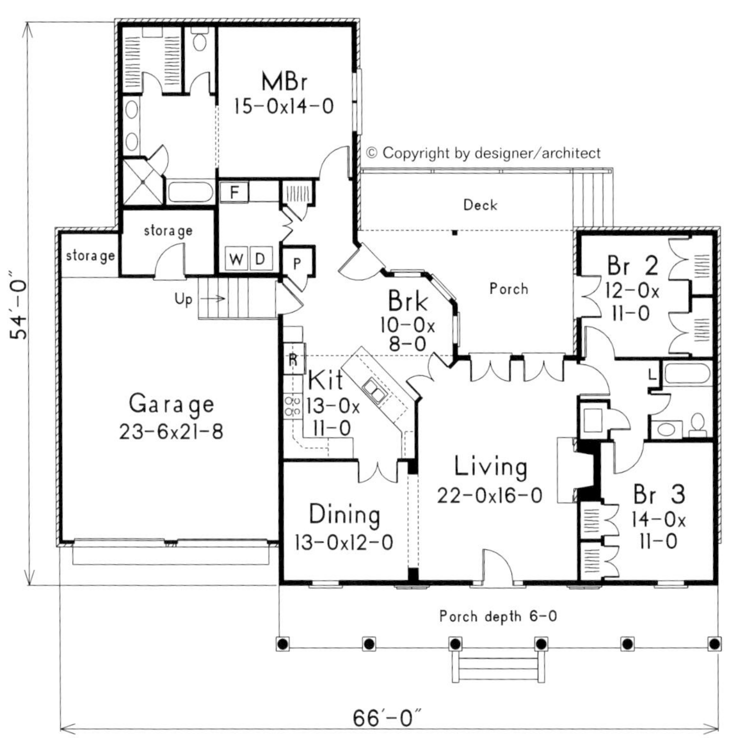

Plan Number: 537-001D-0002 | Price Code: C

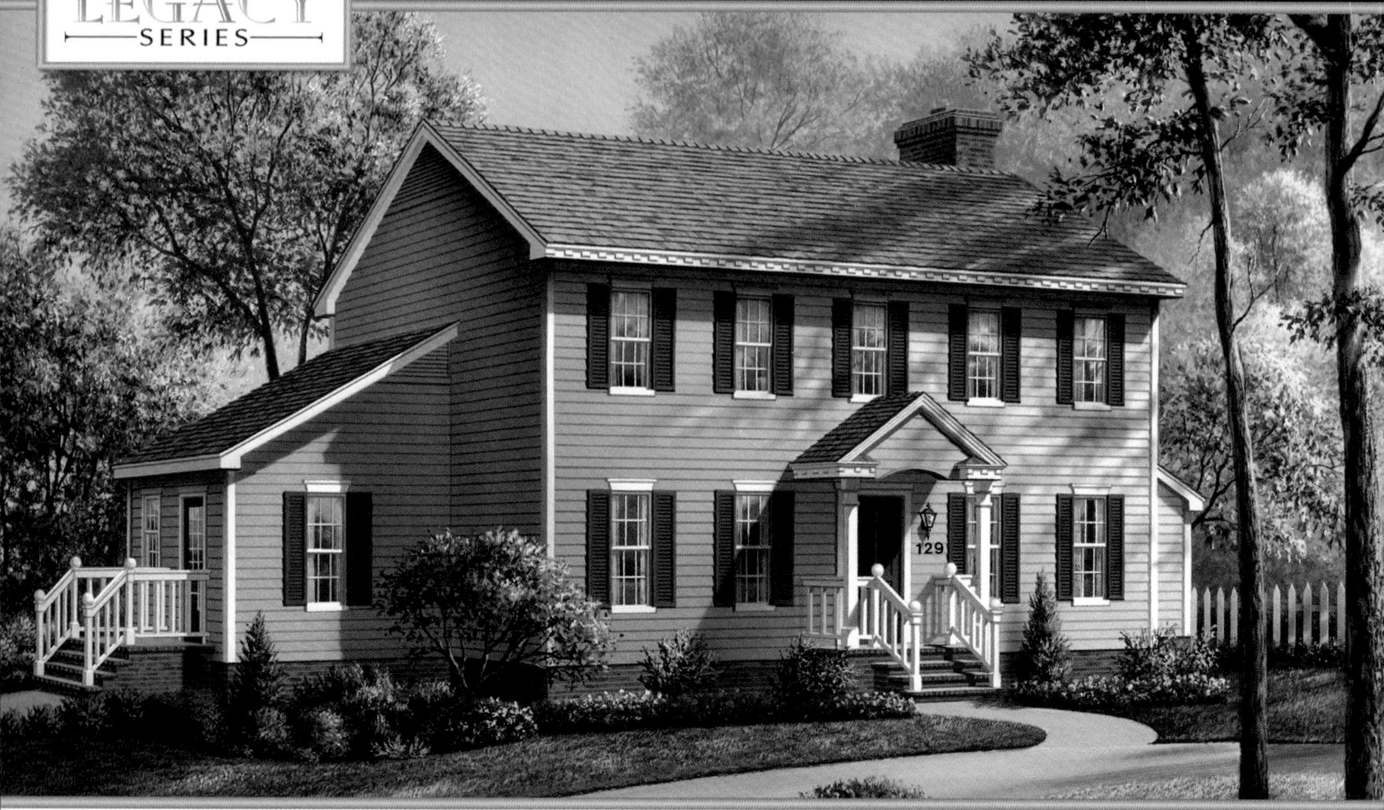

Special Features

- 2,032 total square feet of living area
- Definite separation of living, dining and family rooms permits varied activities without disturbances
- Convenient side entrance leads directly to the laundry area and kitchen
- Breakfast room enjoys a charming bay window
- Handy outdoor storage room
- 4 bedrooms, 2 1/2 baths
- Crawl space foundation

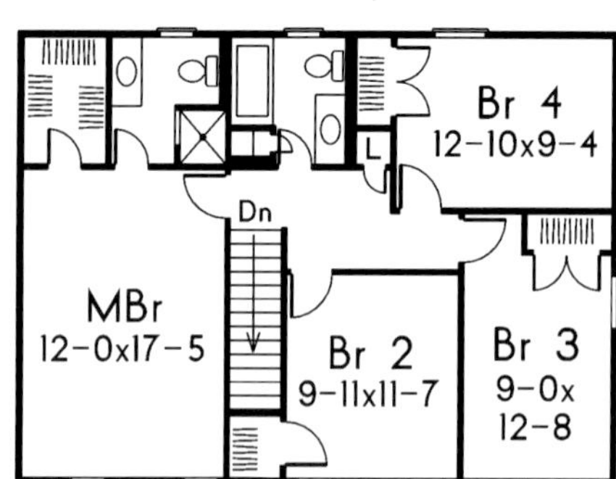

Second Floor
936 sq. ft.

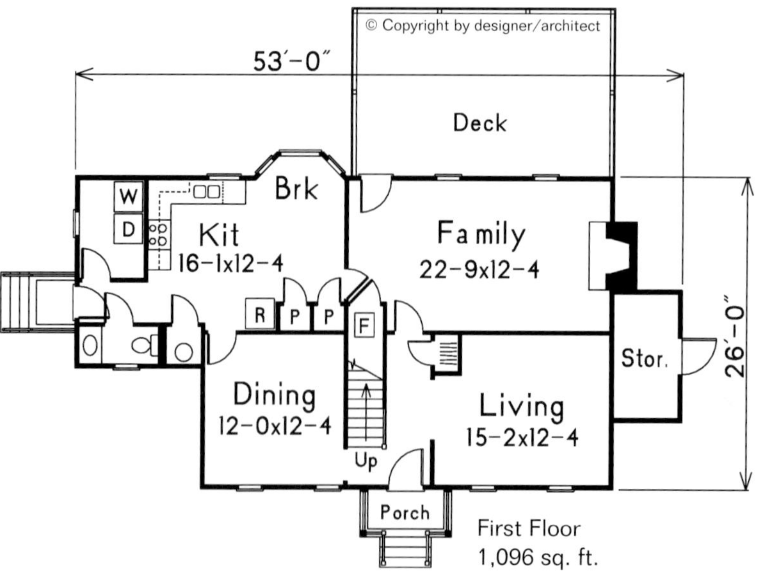

First Floor
1,096 sq. ft.

LOWE'S LEGACY SERIES

SPECIAL FEATURES

- 969 total square feet of living area
- Eye-pleasing facade enjoys stone accents with country porch for quiet evenings
- A bayed dining area, cozy fireplace and atrium with sunny two-story windows are the many features of the living room
- Step-saver kitchen includes a pass-through snack bar
- 325 square feet of optional living area on the lower level
- 2 bedrooms, 1 bath, 1-car rear entry drive under garage
- Walk-out basement foundation

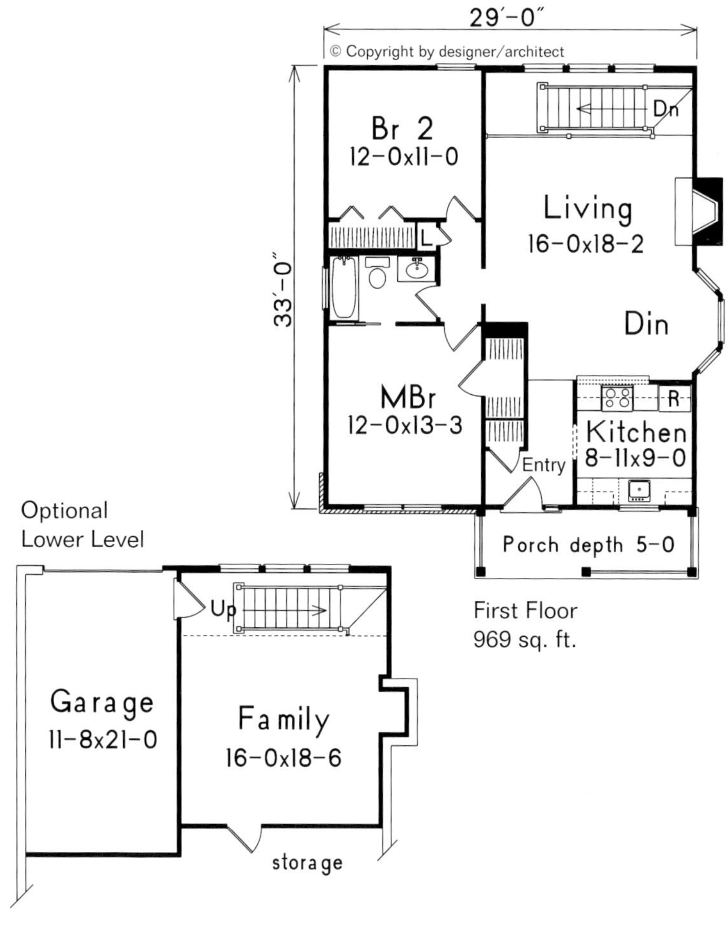

First Floor
969 sq. ft.

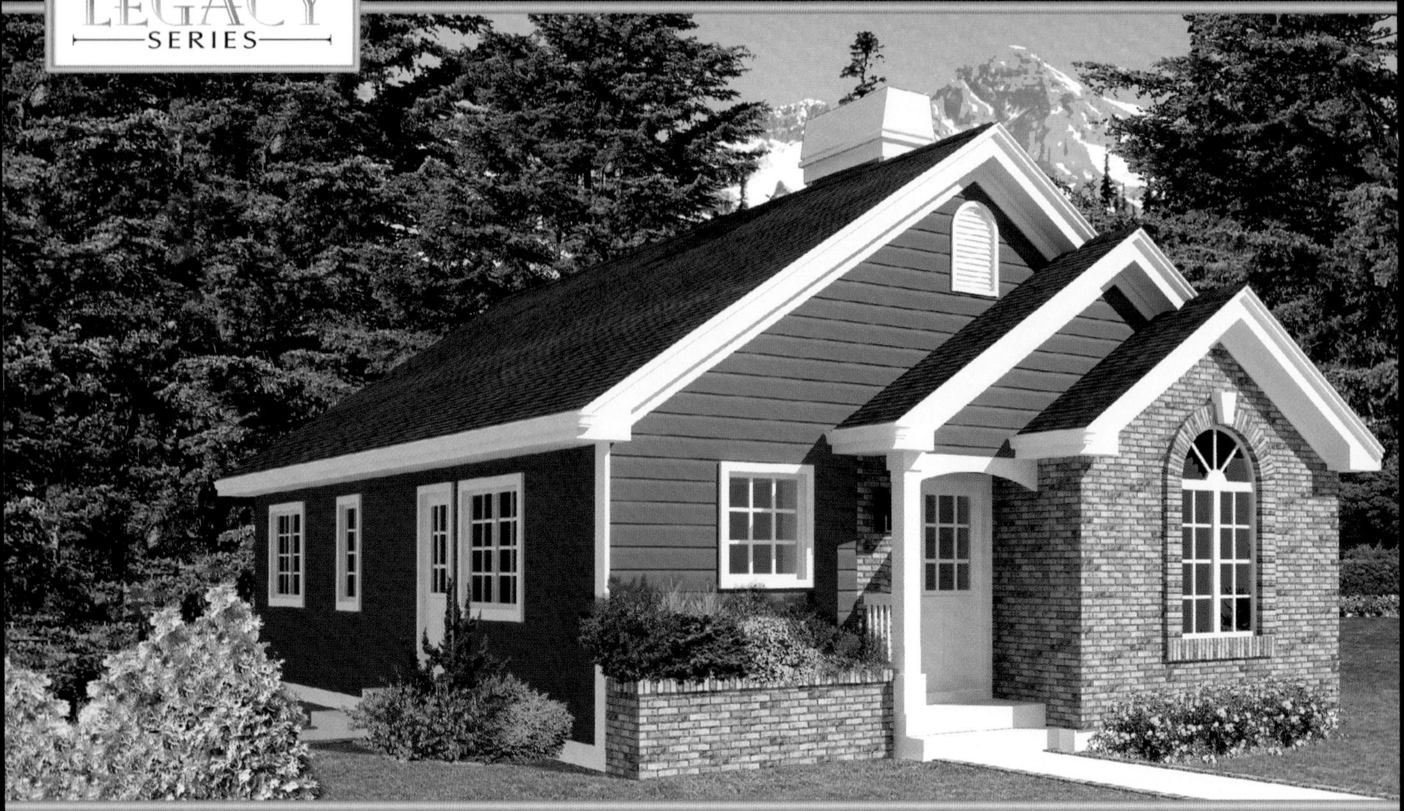

SPECIAL FEATURES

- 1,112 total square feet of living area
- Energy efficient home with 2" x 6" exterior walls
- Brick, an arched window and planter box decorate the facade of this lovely ranch home
- The eat-in kitchen offers an abundance of counterspace and enjoys access to the outdoors
- Three bedrooms are situated together for easy family living
- 3 bedrooms, 1 bath
- Basement foundation

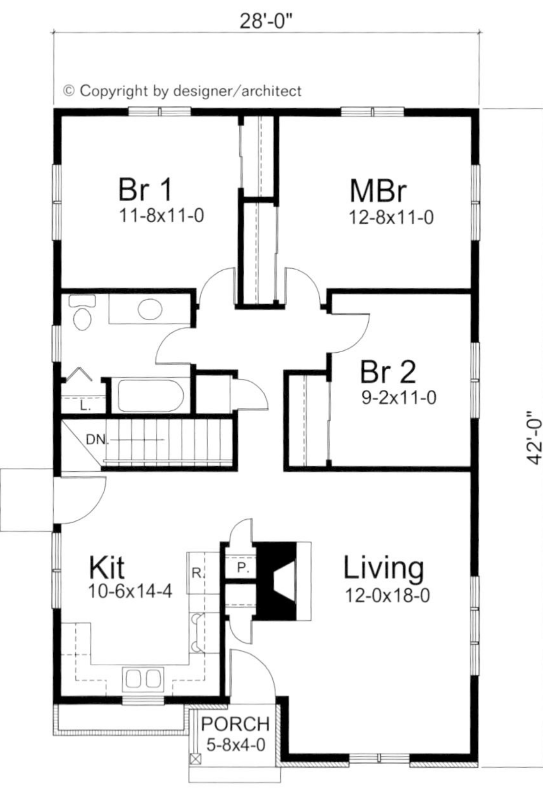

SPECIAL FEATURES

- 1,316 total square feet of living area
- Porches are accessible from entry, dining room and study/bedroom #2
- The living room enjoys a vaulted ceiling, corner fireplace and twin windows with an arched transom above
- A kitchen is provided with corner windows, an outdoor plant shelf, a snack bar, a built-in pantry and opens to a large dining room
- Bedrooms are very roomy, feature walk-in closets and have easy access to oversized baths
- 2 bedrooms, 2 baths, 2-car side entry garage
- Basement foundation, drawings also include crawl space and slab foundations

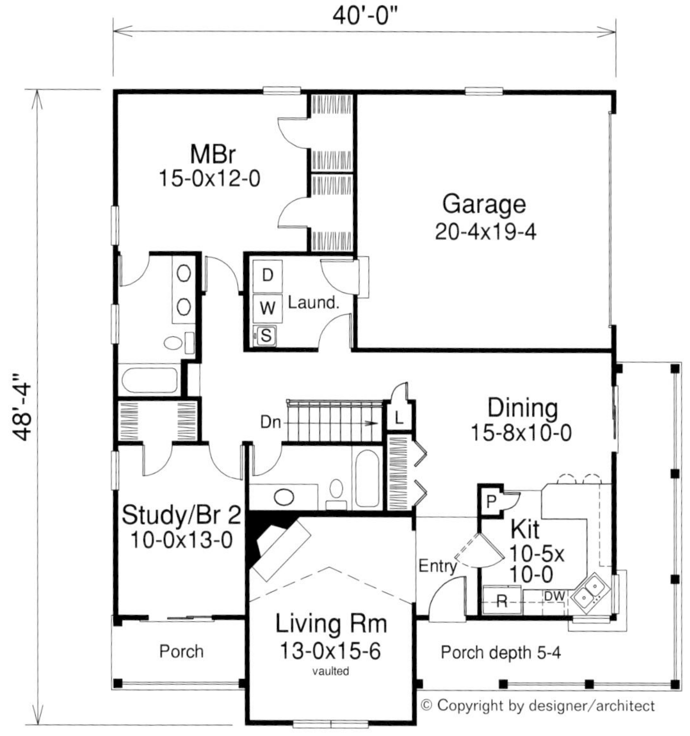

SPECIAL FEATURES

- 1,516 total square feet of living area
- Spacious great room is open to dining area with a bay and unique stair location
- Attractive and well-planned kitchen offers breakfast bar and built-in pantry
- Smartly designed master bedroom enjoys patio view
- 3 bedrooms, 2 baths, 2-car garage
- Basement foundation

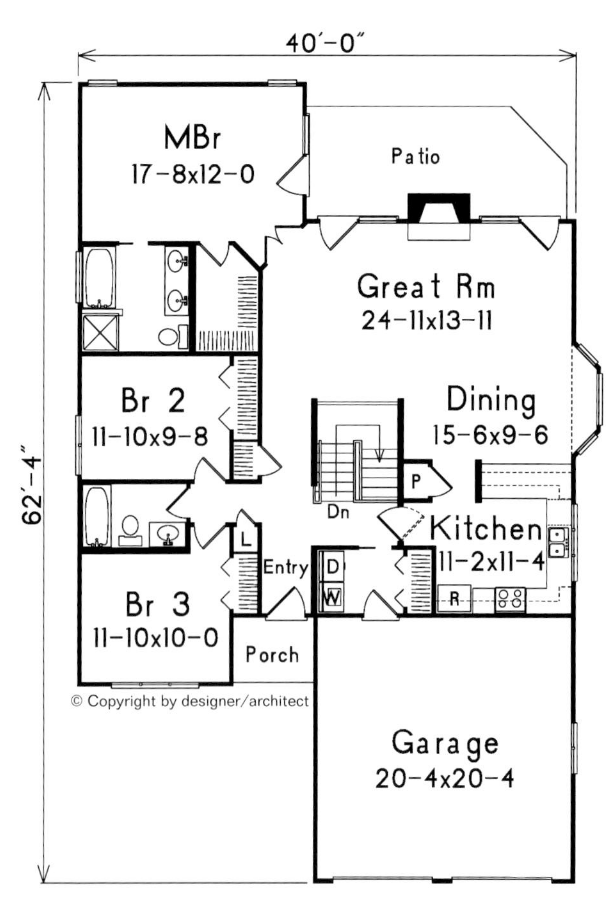

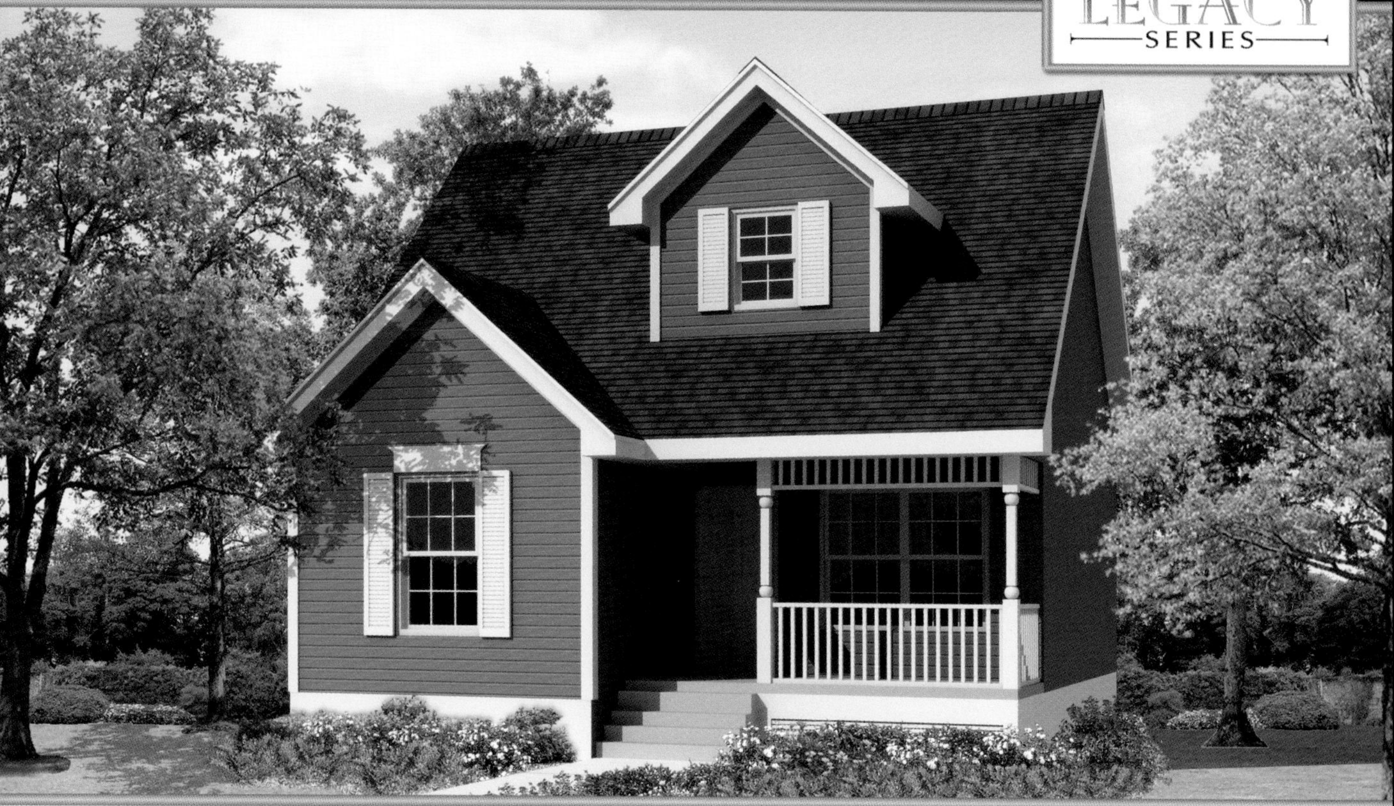

LOWE'S LEGACY SERIES

SPECIAL FEATURES

- 954 total square feet of living area
- Kitchen has a cozy bayed eating area
- Master bedroom has a walk-in closet and private bath
- Large great room has access to the back porch
- Convenient coat closet is near the front entry
- 3 bedrooms, 2 baths
- Basement foundation

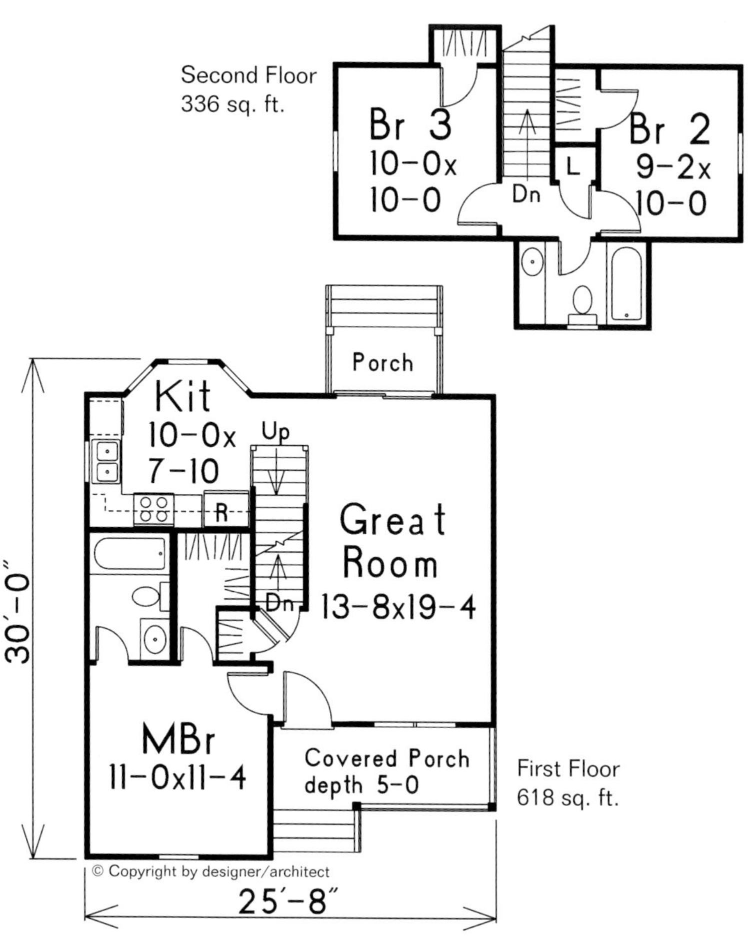

Plan Number: 537-037D-0031 | Price Code: C

Special Features

- 1,923 total square feet of living area
- The foyer opens into a spacious living room with fireplace and splendid view of the covered porch
- Kitchen has a walk-in pantry adjacent to the laundry area and breakfast room
- All bedrooms feature walk-in closets
- Secluded master bedroom includes unique angled bath with spacious walk-in closet
- 3 bedrooms, 2 baths, 2-car garage
- Slab foundation

Rear View

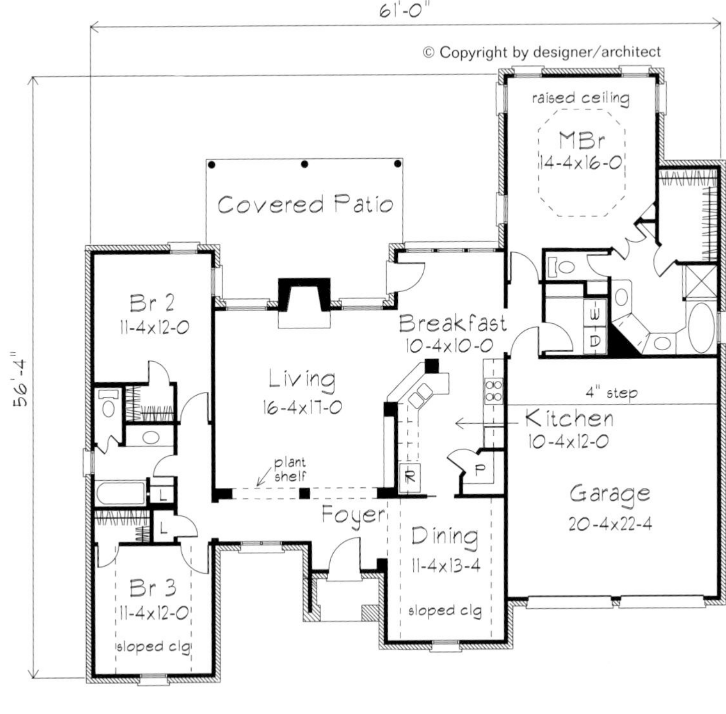

PLAN NUMBER: 537-007D-0131 | PRICE CODE: C

SPECIAL FEATURES

- 2,050 total square feet of living area
- Large living room with fireplace enjoys a view to the front porch and access to the rear screened porch
- L-shaped kitchen has a built-in pantry, island snack bar and breakfast area with bay window
- Master bedroom is vaulted and has a luxury bath and abundant closet space
- The spacious secondary bedrooms each have a walk-in closet
- 3 bedrooms, 2 1/2 baths, 2-car detached garage
- Basement foundation, drawings also include slab and crawl space foundations

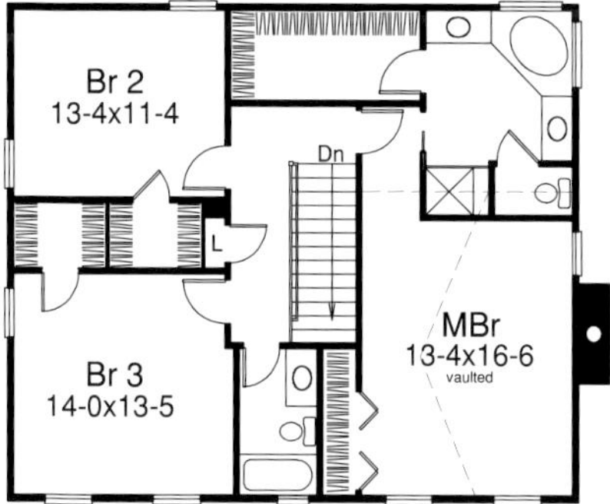

Second Floor
1,080 sq. ft.

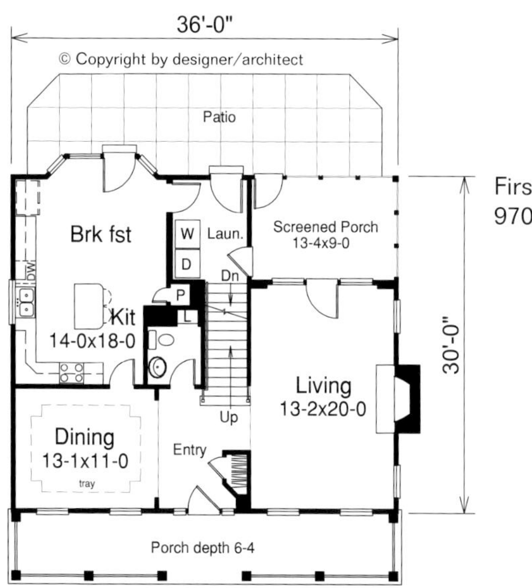

First Floor
970 sq. ft.

Plan Number: 537-007D-0107 | Price Code: AA

Special Features

- 1,161 total square feet of living area
- Brickwork and feature window add elegance to this home for a narrow lot
- Living room enjoys a vaulted ceiling, fireplace and opens to the kitchen
- U-shaped kitchen offers a breakfast area with bay window, snack bar and built-in pantry
- 3 bedrooms, 2 baths
- Basement foundation

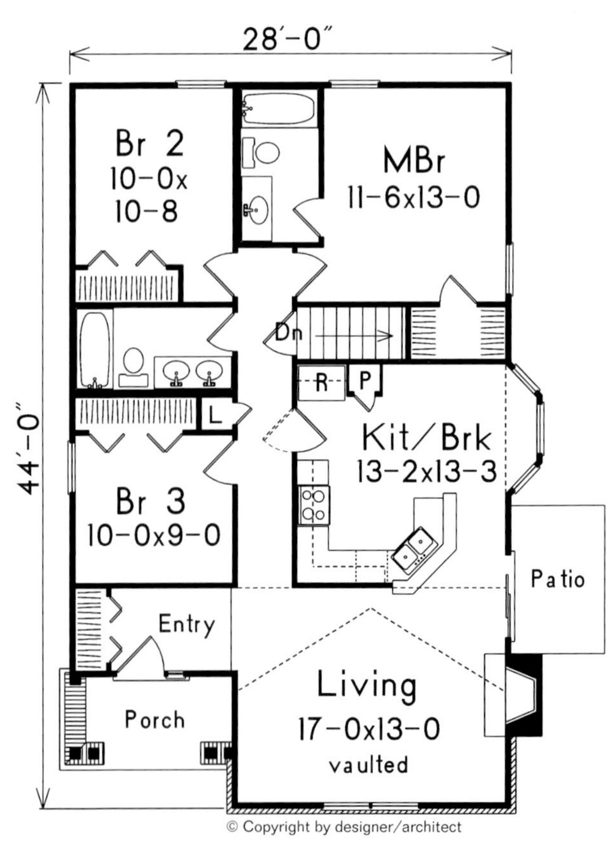

LOWE'S LEGACY SERIES

SPECIAL FEATURES

- 1,170 total square feet of living area
- Master bedroom enjoys privacy at the rear of this home
- Kitchen has an angled bar that overlooks the great room and breakfast area
- Living areas combine to create a greater sense of spaciousness
- Great room has a cozy fireplace
- 3 bedrooms, 2 baths, 2-car garage
- Slab foundation

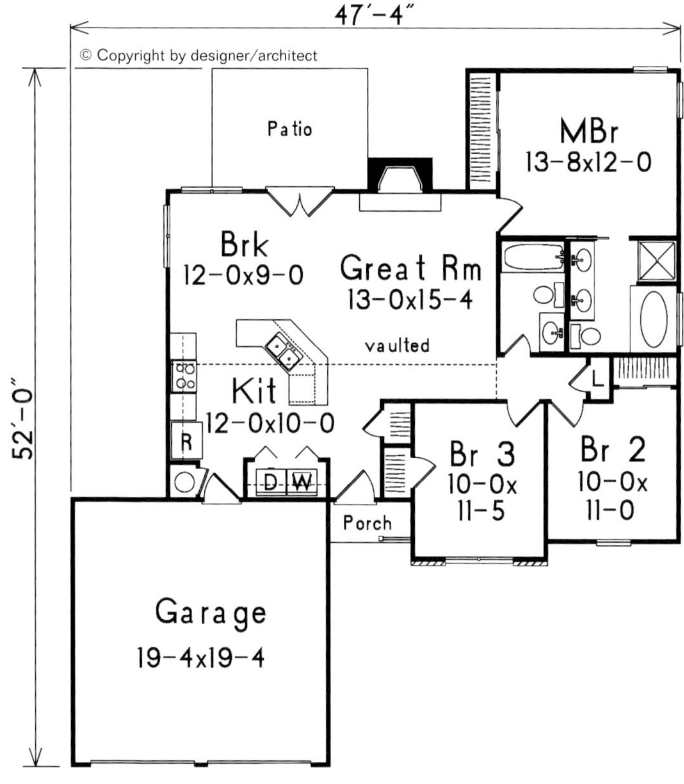

SPECIAL FEATURES

- 1,367 total square feet of living area
- Energy efficient home with 2" x 6" exterior walls
- Neat front porch shelters the entrance
- Dining room has a full wall of windows and convenient storage area
- Breakfast area leads to the rear terrace through sliding doors
- The large living room features a high ceiling, skylight and fireplace
- 3 bedrooms, 2 baths, 2-car garage
- Basement foundation, drawings also include slab foundation

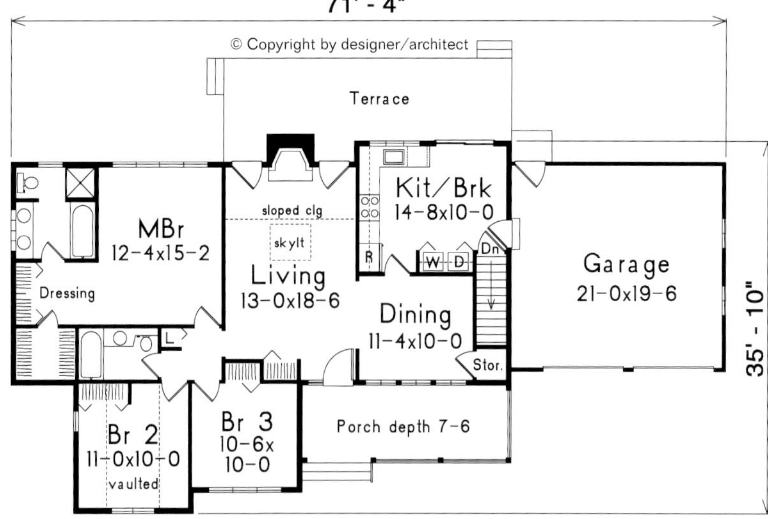

SPECIAL FEATURES

- 1,321 total square feet of living area
- Rear entry garage and elongated brick wall add to the appealing facade
- Dramatic vaulted living room includes corner fireplace and towering feature windows
- Breakfast room is immersed in light from two large windows and glass sliding doors
- 3 bedrooms, 2 baths, 1-car rear entry garage
- Basement foundation

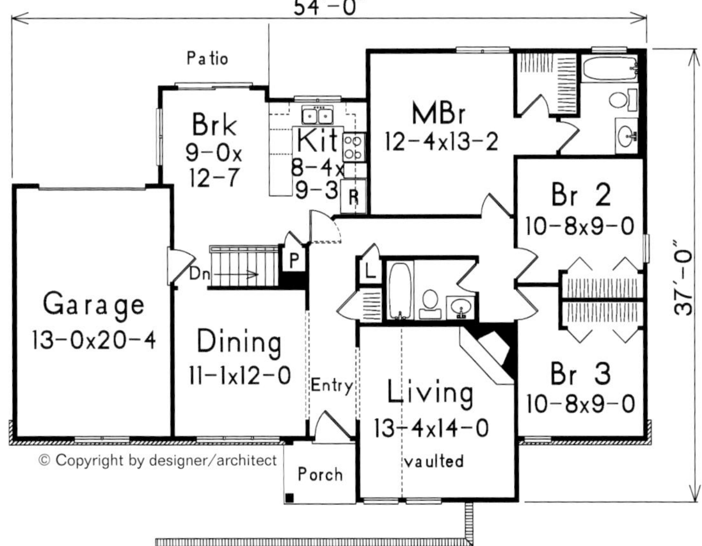

SPECIAL FEATURES

- 1,365 total square feet of living area
- Home is easily adaptable for physical accessibility featuring no stairs and extra-wide hall baths, laundry and garage
- Living room has separate entry and opens to a spacious dining room with view of rear patio
- L-shaped kitchen is well equipped and includes a built-in pantry
- All bedrooms are spaciously sized and offer generous closet storage
- 3 bedrooms, 2 baths, 1-car garage
- Slab foundation

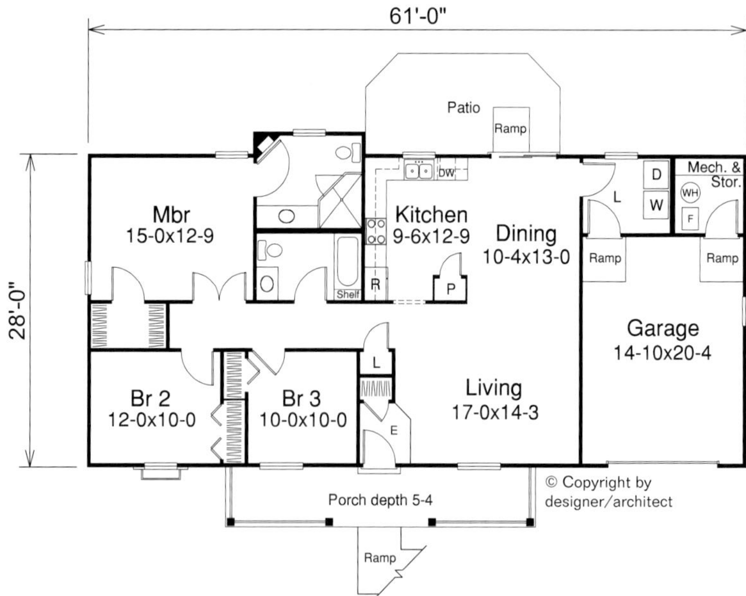

SPECIAL FEATURES

- 720 total square feet of living area
- Abundant windows in living and dining rooms provide generous sunlight
- Secluded laundry area has a handy storage closet
- U-shaped kitchen with large breakfast bar opens into living area
- Large covered deck offers plenty of outdoor living space
- 2 bedrooms, 1 bath
- Crawl space foundation, drawings also include slab foundation

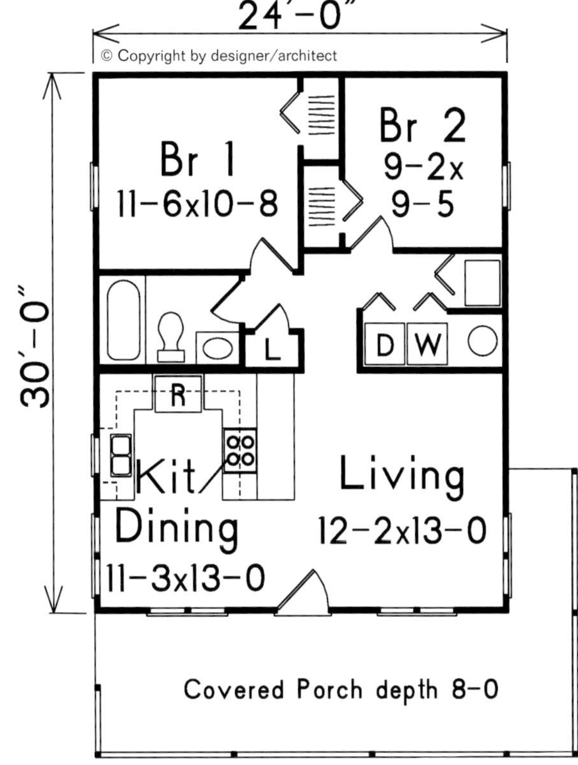

SPECIAL FEATURES

- 1,712 total square feet of living area
- Stylish stucco exterior enhances curb appeal
- Sunken great room offers corner fireplace flanked by 9' wide patio doors
- Well-designed kitchen features ideal view of the great room and fireplace through breakfast bar opening
- 3 bedrooms, 2 1/2 baths, 2-car garage
- Crawl space foundation

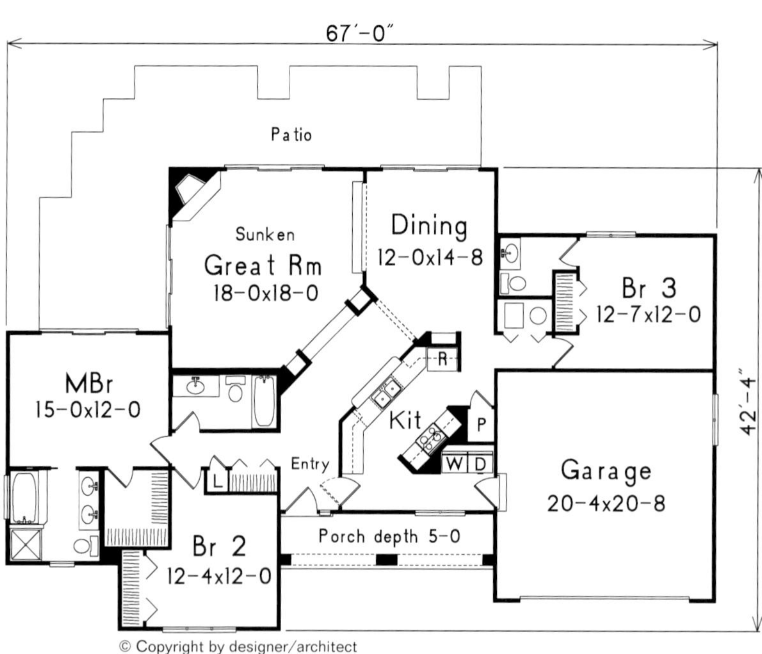

SPECIAL FEATURES

- 1,854 total square feet of living area
- Front entrance is enhanced by arched transom windows and rustic stone
- Isolated master bedroom includes a dressing area and walk-in closet
- Family room features a high sloped ceiling and large fireplace
- Breakfast area accesses the covered rear porch
- 3 bedrooms, 2 1/2 baths, 2-car side entry garage
- Basement foundation

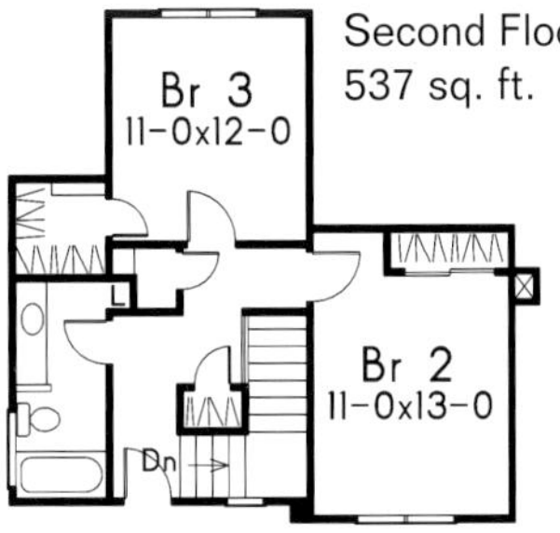

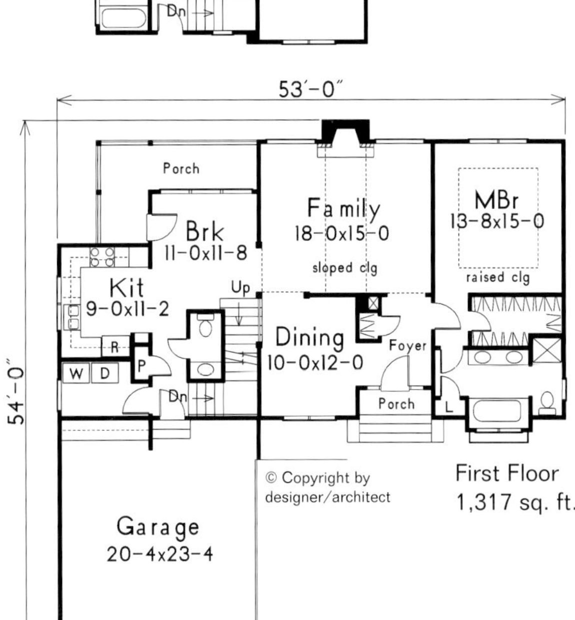

PLAN NUMBER: 537-007D-0102 | PRICE CODE: A

SPECIAL FEATURES

- 1,452 total square feet of living area
- Large living room features a cozy corner fireplace, bayed dining area and access from the entry with guest closet
- Forward master bedroom enjoys having its own bath and linen closet
- Three additional bedrooms share a bath with a double-bowl vanity
- 4 bedrooms, 2 baths
- Basement foundation

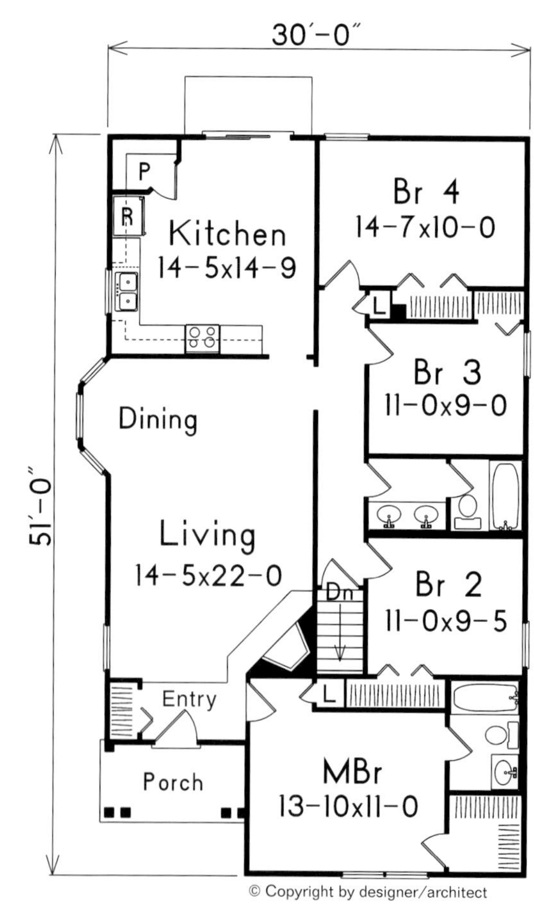

SPECIAL FEATURES

- 1,846 total square feet of living area
- Enormous living area combines with the dining and breakfast rooms that are both complemented by extensive windows and high ceilings
- Master bedroom has a walk-in closet, display niche and deluxe bath
- Secondary bedrooms share a bath and feature large closet space and a corner window
- Oversized two-car garage has plenty of storage and workspace with handy access to the kitchen through the utility area
- Breakfast nook has wrap-around windows adding to eating enjoyment
- 3 bedrooms, 2 baths, 2-car garage
- Slab foundation

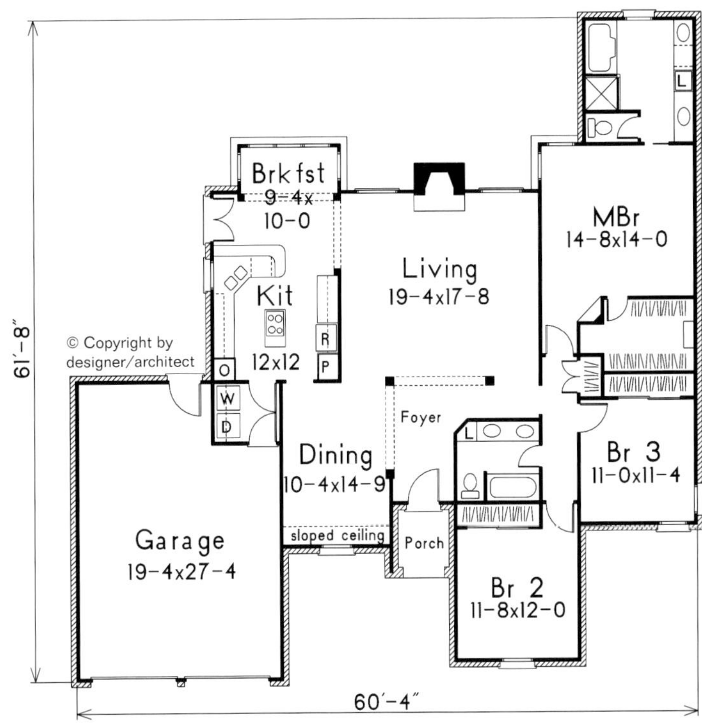

SPECIAL FEATURES

- 1,302 total square feet of living area
- Triple gables, decorative porch and brickwork create a handsome exterior
- The U-shaped kitchen features a snack bar, built-in pantry, open woodcrafted stairs to the basement and adjacent laundry/mud room
- Sliding doors to the patio and a fireplace with flanking windows adorn the large vaulted family room
- The master bedroom accesses the patio through glass sliding doors and includes a private bath and walk-in closet
- 3 bedrooms, 2 baths, 2-car garage
- Basement foundation

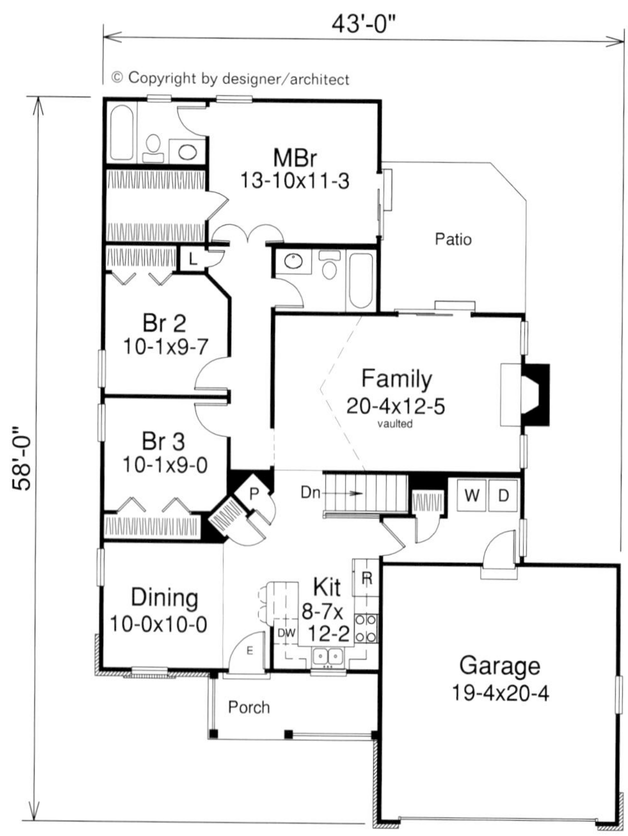

LOWE'S LEGACY SERIES

SPECIAL FEATURES

- 1,344 total square feet of living area
- Family/dining room has sliding glass doors to the outdoors
- Master bedroom features a private bath
- Hall bath includes a double-bowl vanity for added convenience
- U-shaped kitchen features a large pantry and laundry area
- 2" x 6" exterior walls available, please order plan #537-001D-0108
- 3 bedrooms, 2 baths, 2-car garage
- Crawl space foundation, drawings also include basement and slab foundations

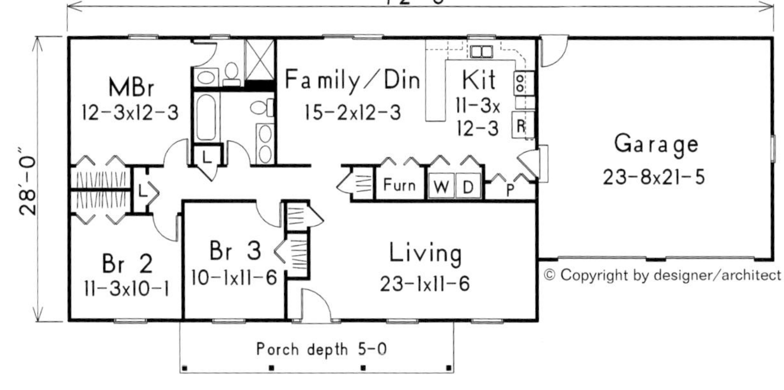

PLAN NUMBER: 537-007D-0053 | PRICE CODE: D

SPECIAL FEATURES

- 2,334 total square feet of living area
- Roomy front porch gives home a country flavor
- Vaulted great room boasts a fireplace, TV alcove, pass-through snack bar to kitchen and atrium featuring bayed window wall and a descending stair to the family room
- Oversized master bedroom features a vaulted ceiling, double-door entry and large walk-in closet
- 3 bedrooms, 2 baths, 2-car garage
- Walk-out basement foundation

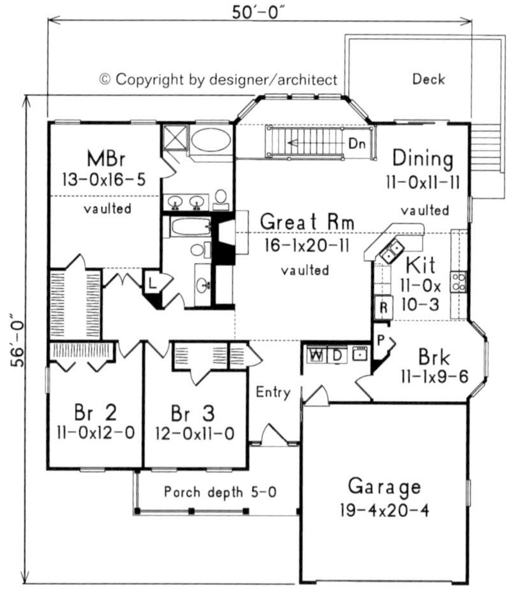

First Floor
1,777 sq. ft.

Rear View

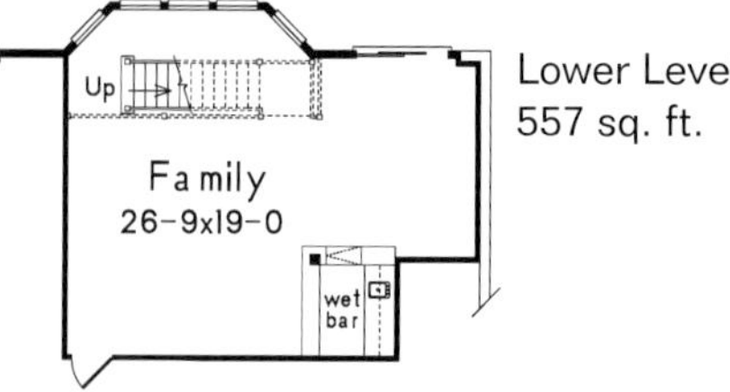

Lower Level
557 sq. ft.

TO ORDER SEE PAGE 288

LOWE'S LEGACY SERIES

SPECIAL FEATURES

- 1,948 total square feet of living area
- Family room offers warmth with an oversized fireplace and rustic beamed ceiling
- Fully-appointed kitchen extends into the family room
- Practical mud room is adjacent to the kitchen
- 3 bedrooms, 3 baths
- Basement foundation, drawings also include crawl space foundation

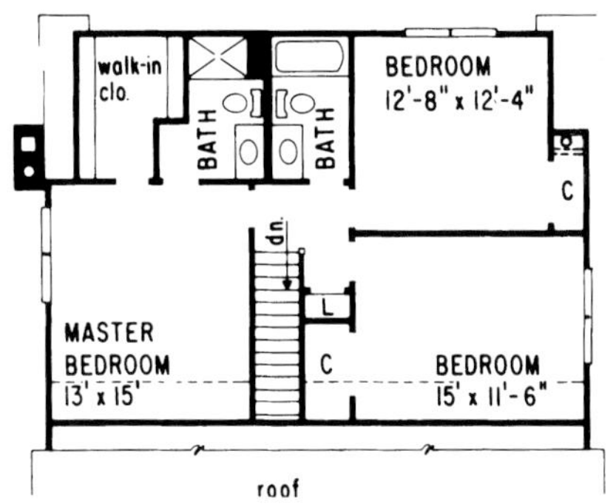

Second Floor
868 sq. ft.

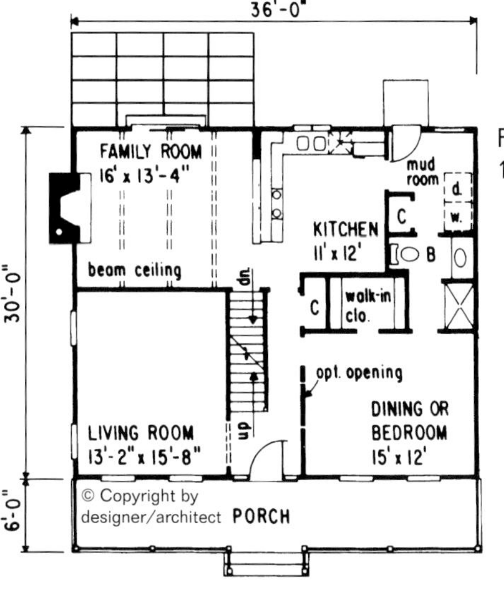

First Floor
1,080 sq. ft.

PLAN NUMBER: 537-065L-0170 | PRICE CODE: B

SPECIAL FEATURES

- 1,537 total square feet of living area
- A corner fireplace in the great room is visible from the foyer offering a dramatic first impression
- The kitchen island connects to the dining area that features a sloped ceiling and access to the rear porch
- The private master bedroom enjoys its own bath, walk-in closet and access to the rear porch
- 3 bedrooms, 2 baths, 2-car garage
- Basement foundation

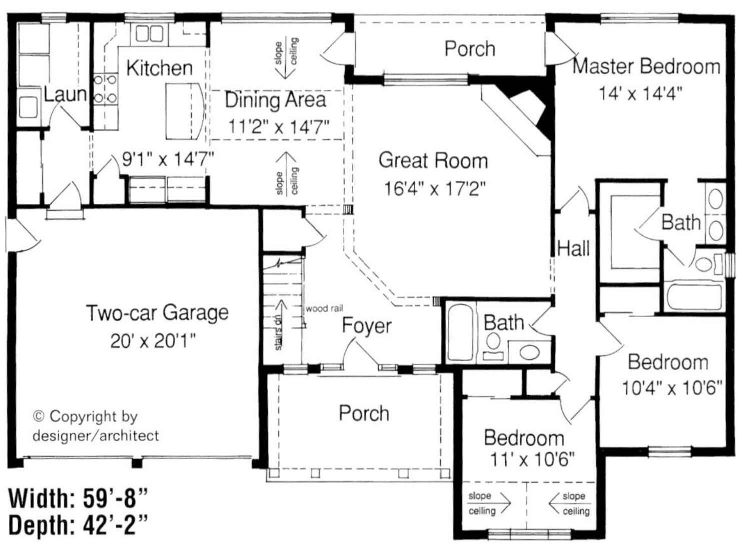

Plan Number: 537-007D-0124 | Price Code: C

Lowe's Legacy Series

Special Features

- 1,944 total square feet of living area
- Spacious surrounding porch, covered patio and stone fireplace create an expansive ponderosa appearance
- The large entry leads to a grand-sized great room featuring a vaulted ceiling, fireplace, wet bar and access to the porch through three patio doors
- The U-shaped kitchen is open to the hearth room and enjoys a snack bar, fireplace and patio access
- A luxury bath, walk-in closet and doors to the porch are a few of the amenities of the master bedroom
- 3 bedrooms, 2 baths, 3-car detached garage
- Basement foundation

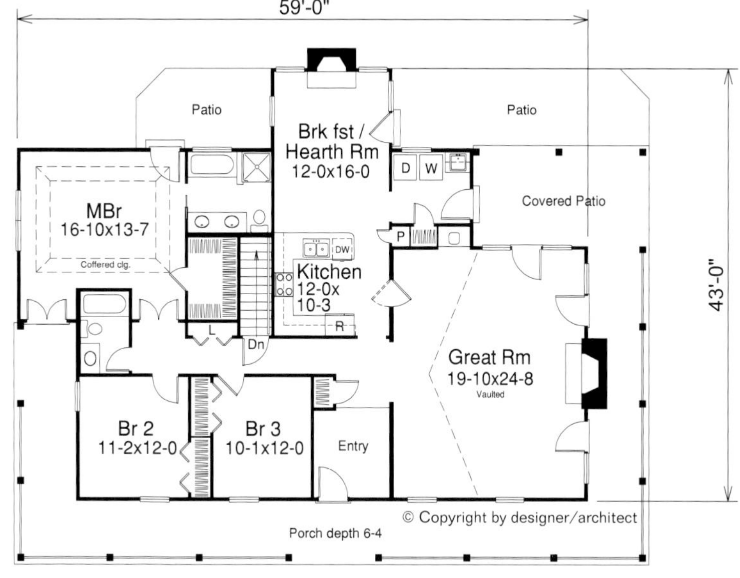

Plan Number: 537-022D-0002 | Price Code: A

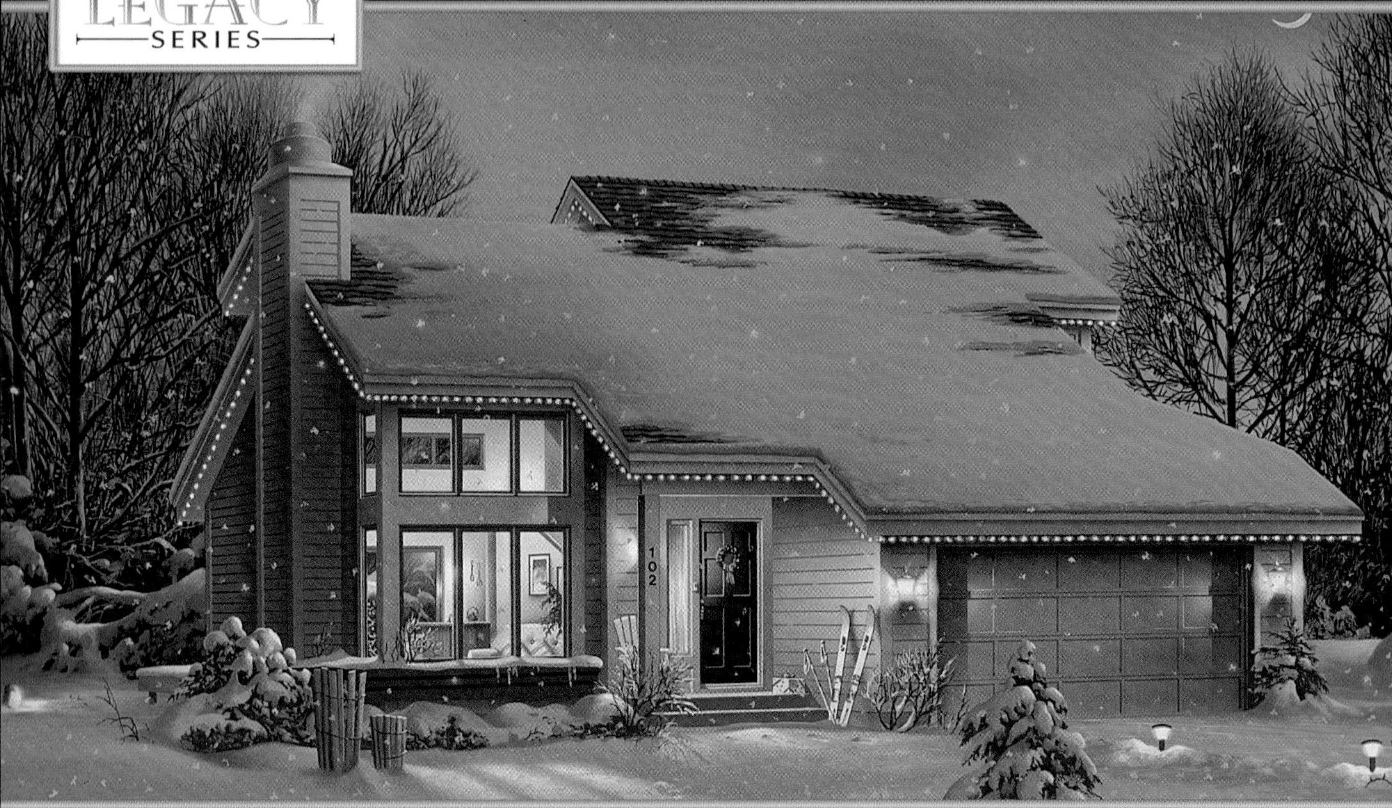

Special Features

- 1,246 total square feet of living area
- Corner living room window adds openness and light
- Out-of-the-way kitchen with dining area accesses the outdoors
- Private first floor master bedroom has a corner window
- Large walk-in closet is located in bedroom #3
- Easily built perimeter allows economical construction
- 3 bedrooms, 2 baths, 2-car garage
- Basement foundation

First Floor
846 sq. ft.

Second Floor
400 sq. ft.

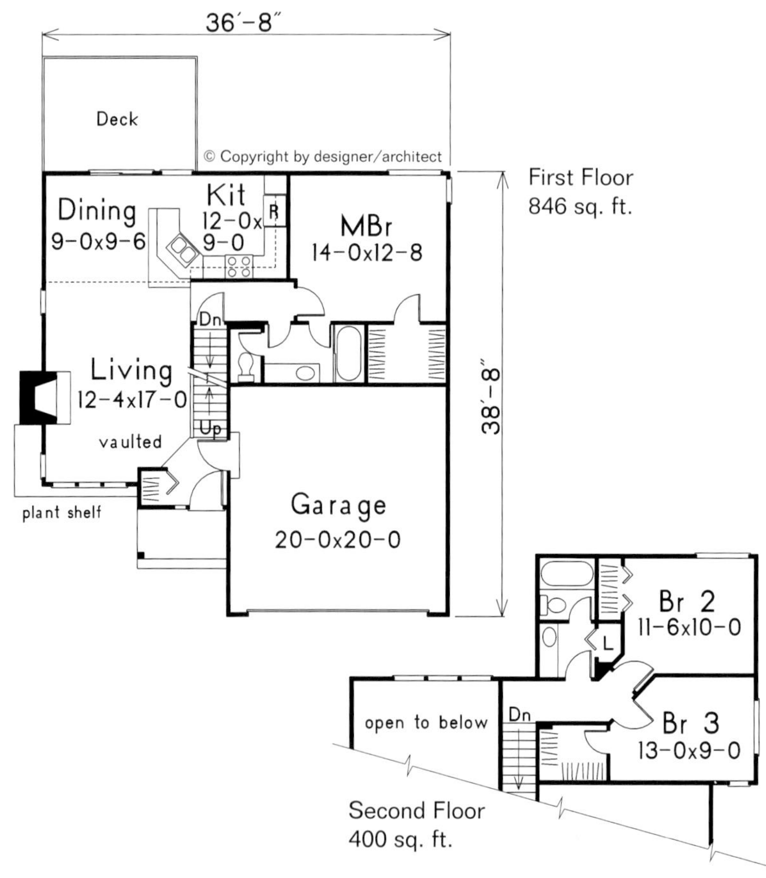

Plan Number: 537-001D-0030 | Price Code: A

Special Features

- 1,416 total square feet of living area
- Family room includes fireplace, elevated plant shelf and vaulted ceiling
- Patio is accessible from the dining area and garage
- Centrally located laundry area
- Oversized walk-in pantry in the kitchen
- 3 bedrooms, 2 baths, 2-car garage
- Basement foundation, drawings also include crawl space and slab foundations

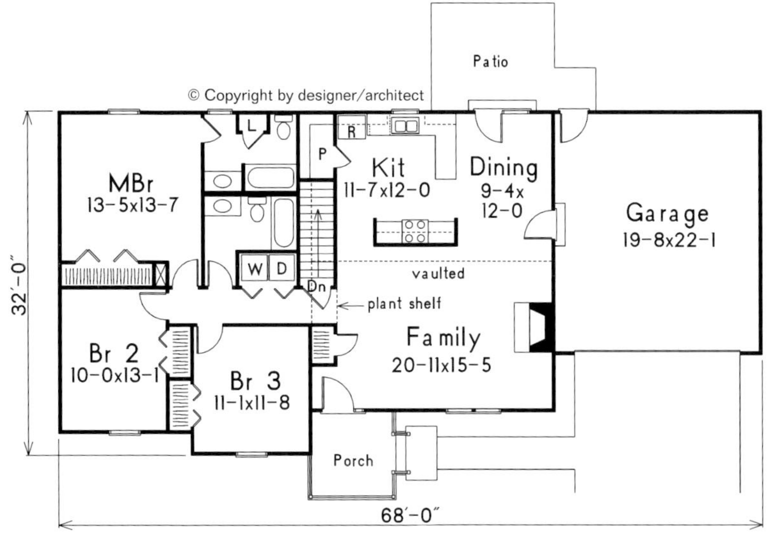

PLAN NUMBER: 537-003D-0002 | PRICE CODE: B

SPECIAL FEATURES

- 1,676 total square feet of living area
- The living area skylights and large breakfast room with bay window provide plenty of sunlight
- The master bedroom has a walk-in closet and both the secondary bedrooms have large closets
- Vaulted ceilings, plant shelving and a fireplace provide a quality living area
- 3 bedrooms, 2 baths, 2-car garage
- Basement foundation, drawings also include crawl space and slab foundations

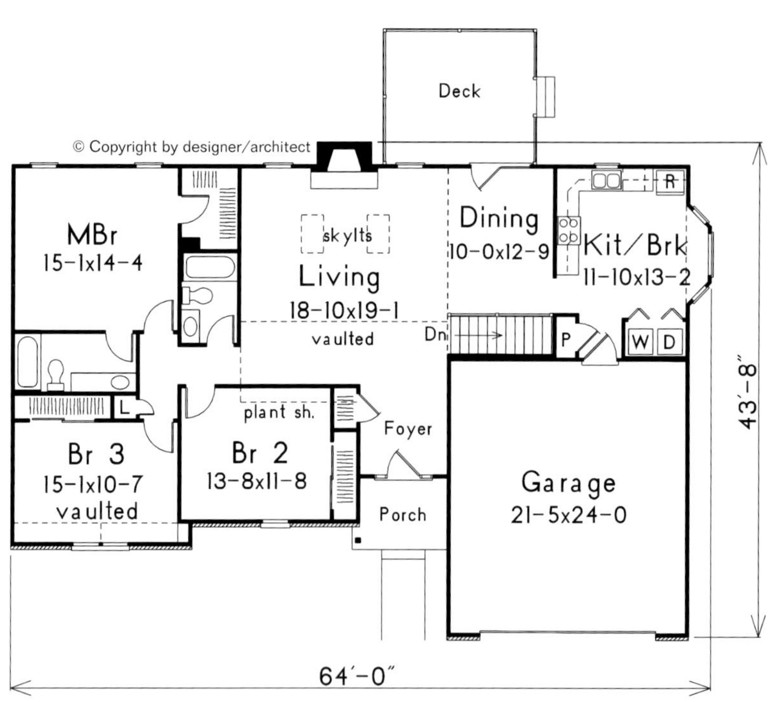

SPECIAL FEATURES

- 1,340 total square feet of living area
- Grand-sized vaulted living and dining rooms offer fireplace, wet bar and breakfast counter open to a spacious kitchen
- Vaulted master bedroom features a double-door entry, walk-in closet and an elegant bath
- Basement includes a huge two-car garage and space for a bedroom/bath expansion
- 3 bedrooms, 2 baths, 2-car drive under garage with storage area
- Basement foundation

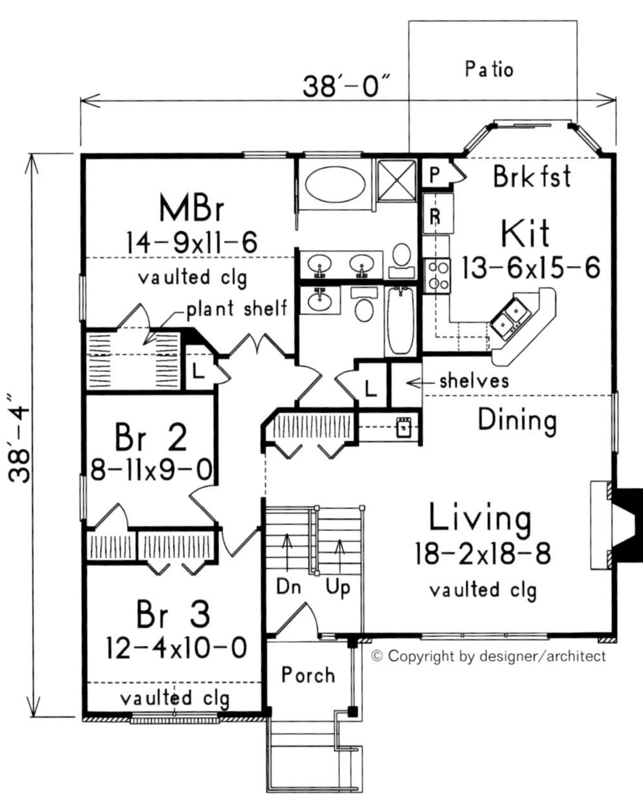

Plan Number: 537-027D-0001 | Price Code: C

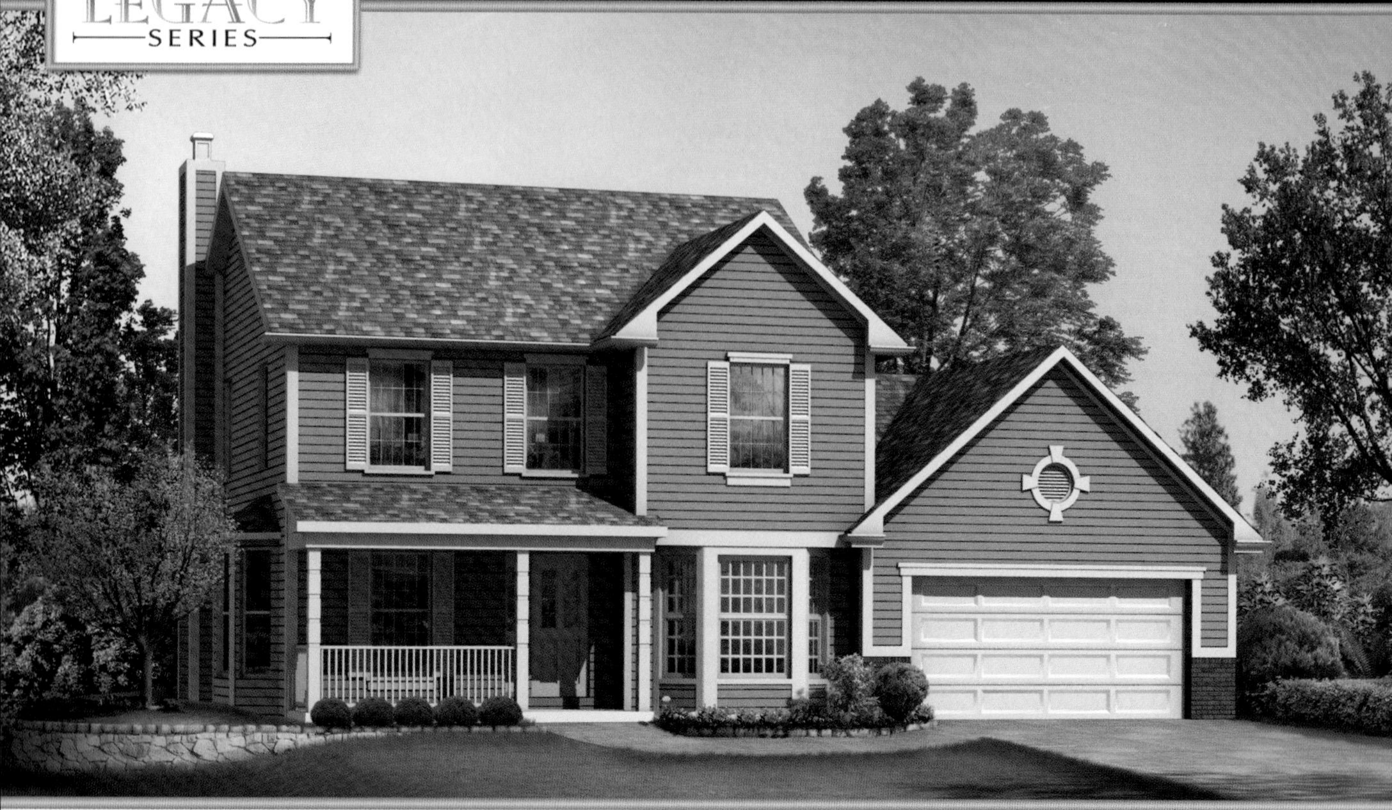

Special Features

- 2,147 total square feet of living area
- Living and dining rooms are adjacent to the entry foyer for easy access
- The kitchen is conveniently located next to the sunny breakfast nook
- Master bedroom includes a large walk-in closet and luxurious bath
- The breakfast area offers easy access to the deck
- 4 bedrooms, 2 1/2 baths, 2-car garage
- Basement foundation

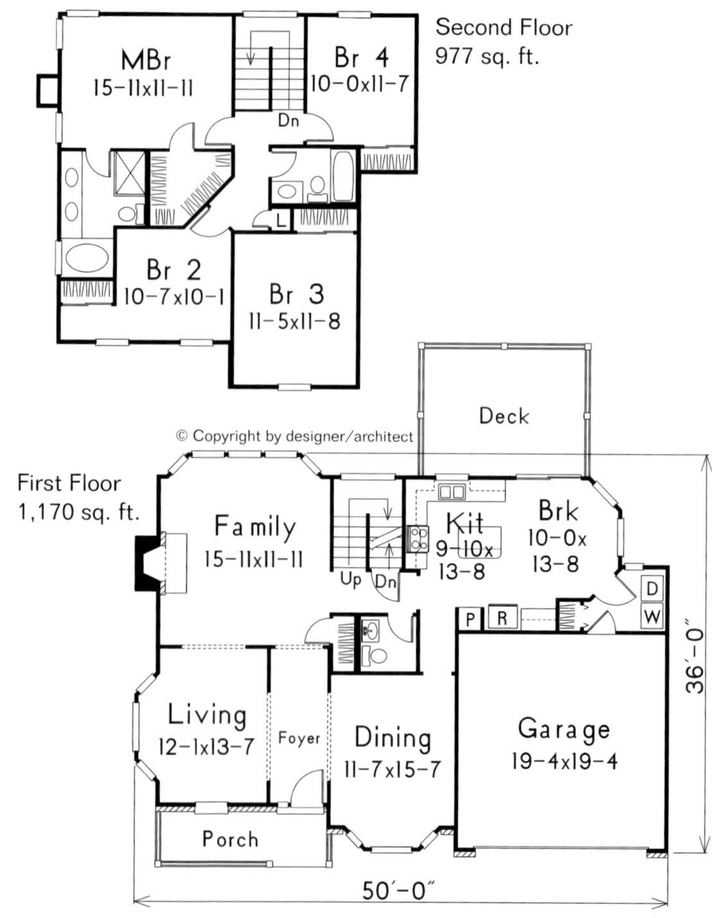

SPECIAL FEATURES

- 1,308 total square feet of living area
- Multi-gabled facade and elongated porch create a pleasing country appeal
- Large dining room with bay window and view to rear patio opens to a full-functional kitchen with snack bar
- An attractive U-shaped stair with hall overlook leads to the second floor
- 3 bedrooms, 1 full bath, 2 half baths, 2-car garage
- Basement foundation

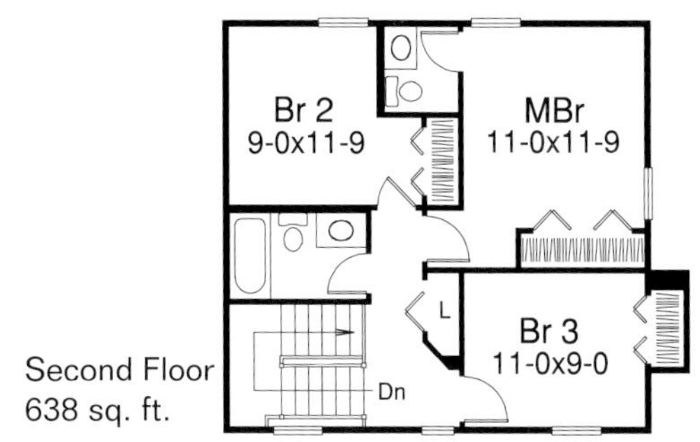

Second Floor
638 sq. ft.

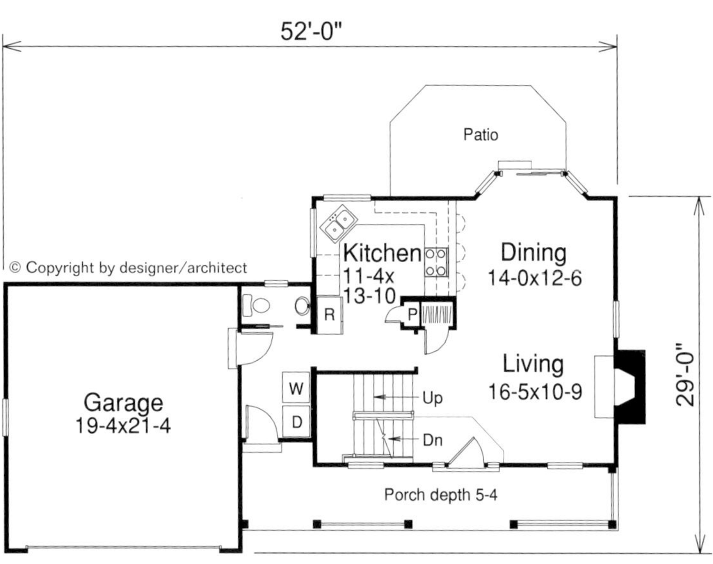

First Floor
670 sq. ft.

SPECIAL FEATURES

- 2,218 total square feet of living area
- Vaulted great room has an arched colonnade entry, bay windowed atrium with staircase and a fireplace
- Vaulted kitchen enjoys bay doors to deck, pass-through breakfast bar and walk-in pantry
- Breakfast room offers a bay window and snack bar open to the kitchen with a large laundry room nearby
- Atrium opens to 1,217 square feet of optional living area below
- 4 bedrooms, 2 baths, 2-car garage
- Walk-out basement foundation

Rear View

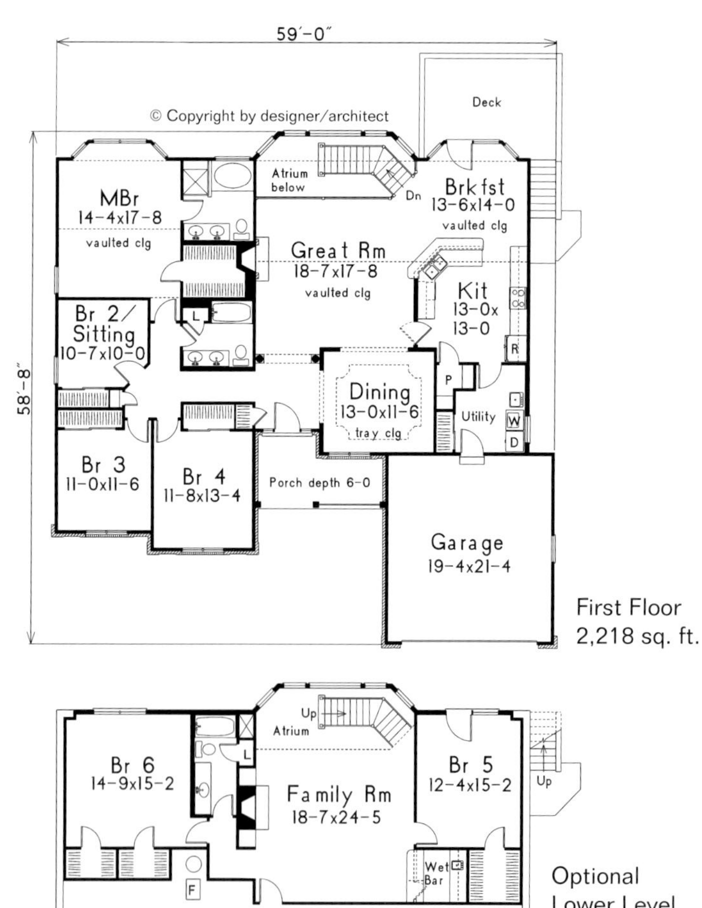

TO ORDER SEE PAGE 288 | CALL TOLL-FREE 1-877-379-3420

Plan Number: 537-008D-0094 | Price Code: A

Special Features

- 1,364 total square feet of living area
- Master bedroom features a spacious walk-in closet and private bath
- Living room is highlighted with several windows
- Kitchen with snack bar is adjacent to the dining area
- Plenty of storage space throughout
- 3 bedrooms, 2 baths, optional 2-car garage
- Basement foundation, drawings also include crawl space foundation

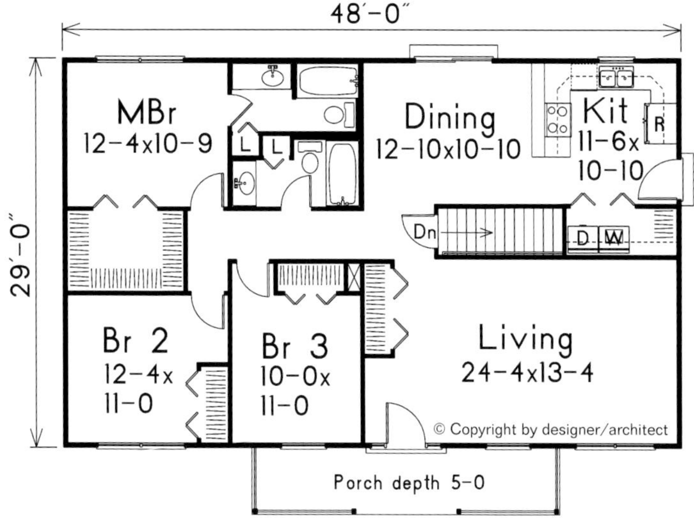

Special Features

- 1,154 total square feet of living area
- U-shaped kitchen features a large breakfast bar and handy laundry area
- Private second floor bedrooms share a half bath
- Large living/dining area opens to deck
- 3 bedrooms, 1 1/2 baths
- Crawl space foundation, drawings also include slab foundation

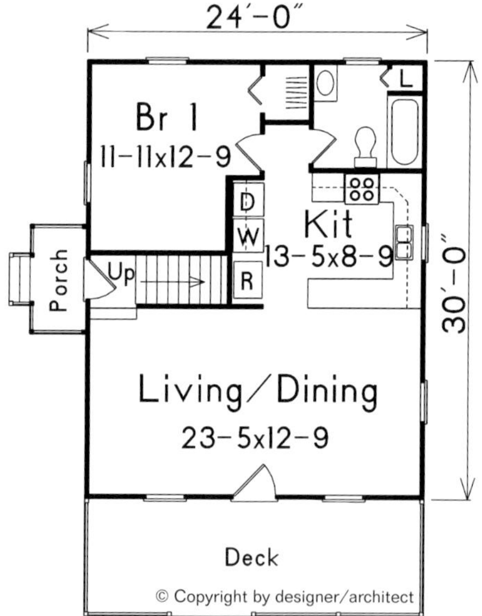

First Floor
720 sq. ft.

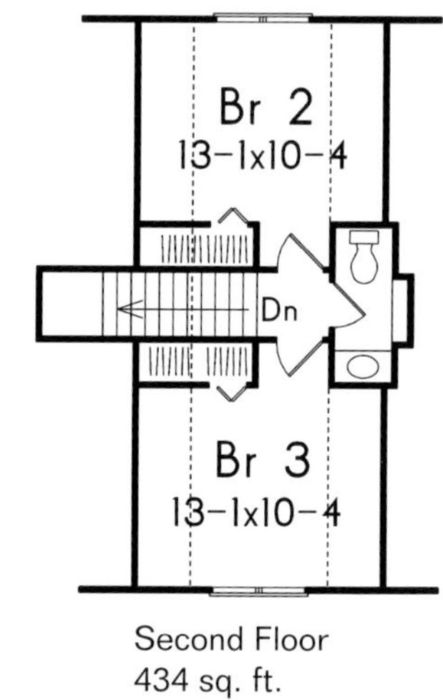

Second Floor
434 sq. ft.

SPECIAL FEATURES

- 1,994 total square feet of living area
- Convenient entrance from the garage into the main living area through the utility room
- Bedroom #2 features a 12' vaulted ceiling and the dining room boasts a 10' ceiling
- Master bedroom offers a full bath with an oversized tub, separate shower and walk-in closet
- Entry leads to the formal dining room and attractive living room with double French doors and fireplace
- 3 bedrooms, 2 baths, 2-car garage
- Slab foundation

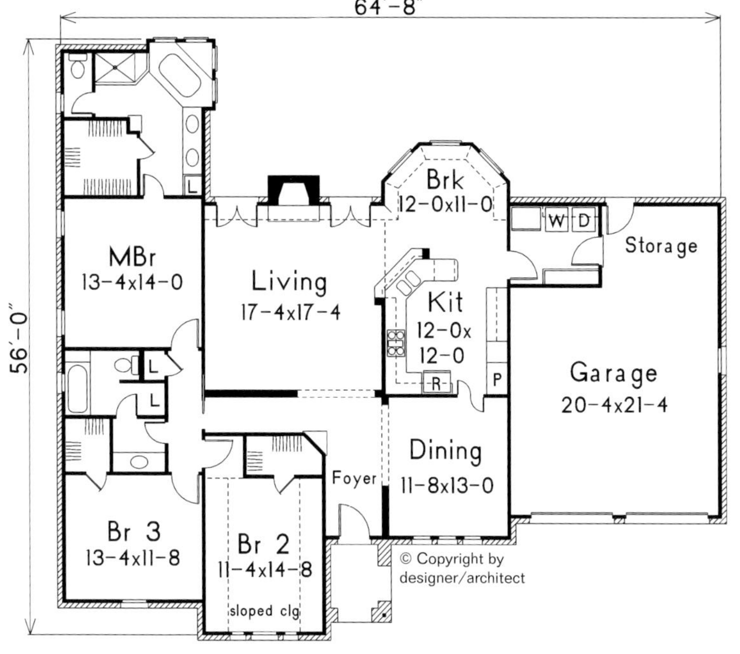

SPECIAL FEATURES

- 1,559 total square feet of living area
- A cozy country appeal is provided by a spacious porch, masonry fireplace, roof dormers and a perfect balance of stonework and siding
- Large living room enjoys a fireplace, bayed dining area and separate entry
- A U-shaped kitchen is adjoined by a breakfast room with bay window and large pantry
- 3 bedrooms, 2 1/2 baths, 2-car drive under side entry garage
- Basement foundation

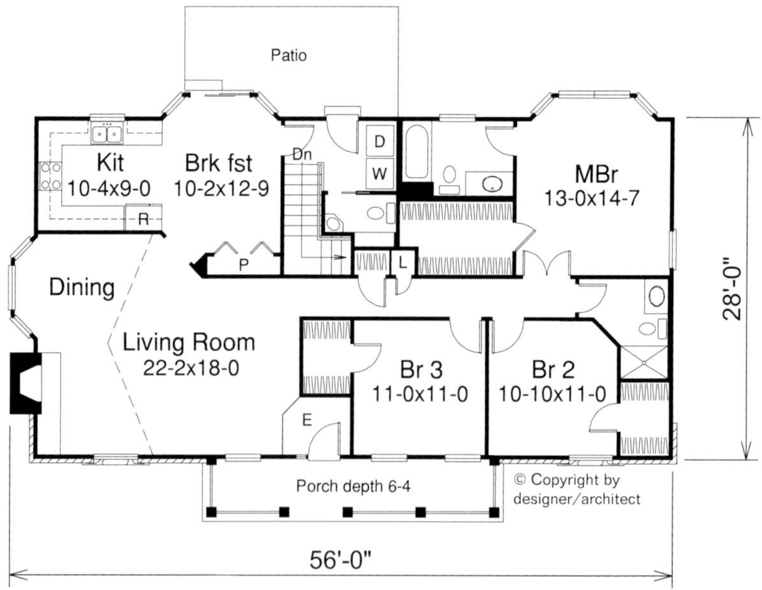

PLAN NUMBER: 537-008D-0169 | PRICE CODE: AA

SPECIAL FEATURES

- 1,042 total square feet of living area
- Living room is brightened by several windows
- Spacious kitchen includes a laundry closet and space for dining
- Front entry has a handy coat closet
- Plenty of extra storage space is located in the garage
- 2 bedrooms, 1 bath, 2-car garage
- Basement foundation, drawings also include crawl space and slab foundations

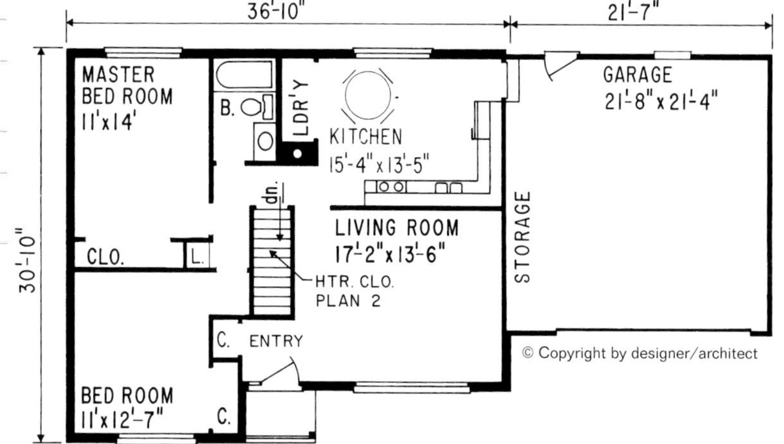

LOWE'S LEGACY SERIES

PLAN NUMBER: 537-007D-0070 | PRICE CODE: AA

SPECIAL FEATURES

- 929 total square feet of living area
- Spacious living room with dining area has access to the 8' x 12' deck through glass sliding doors
- Splendid U-shaped kitchen features a breakfast bar, oval window above sink and impressive cabinet storage
- Master bedroom enjoys a walk-in closet and large elliptical feature window
- Laundry, storage closet and mechanical space are located off the first floor garage
- 2 bedrooms, 1 bath, 3-car side entry garage
- Slab foundation

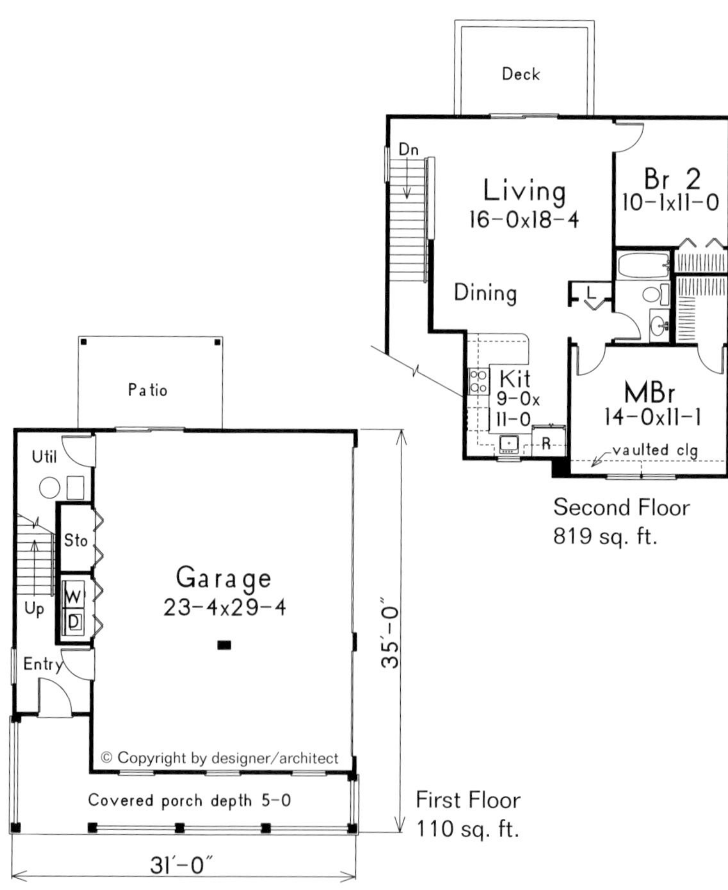

SPECIAL FEATURES

- 1,839 total square feet of living area
- Energy efficient home with 2" x 6" exterior walls
- An abundance of front-facing windows help to keep this berm home bright and cheerful
- The centrally located kitchen easily serves the more formal living and dining rooms as well as the casual family room
- The master bedroom enjoys private access to the bath
- 3 bedrooms, 1 bath
- Slab foundation

SPECIAL FEATURES

- 1,914 total square feet of living area
- Great room features a vaulted ceiling, dining area, entry foyer, corner fireplace and 9' wide sliding doors to the rear patio
- The secluded secondary bedrooms offer walk-in closets and share a Jack and Jill bath
- A multi-purpose room has a laundry alcove and can easily be used as a hobby room, sewing room or small office
- Bedroom #4 can be open to the master bedroom suite and utilized as a private study or nursery
- 4 bedrooms, 3 baths, 2-car garage
- Basement foundation

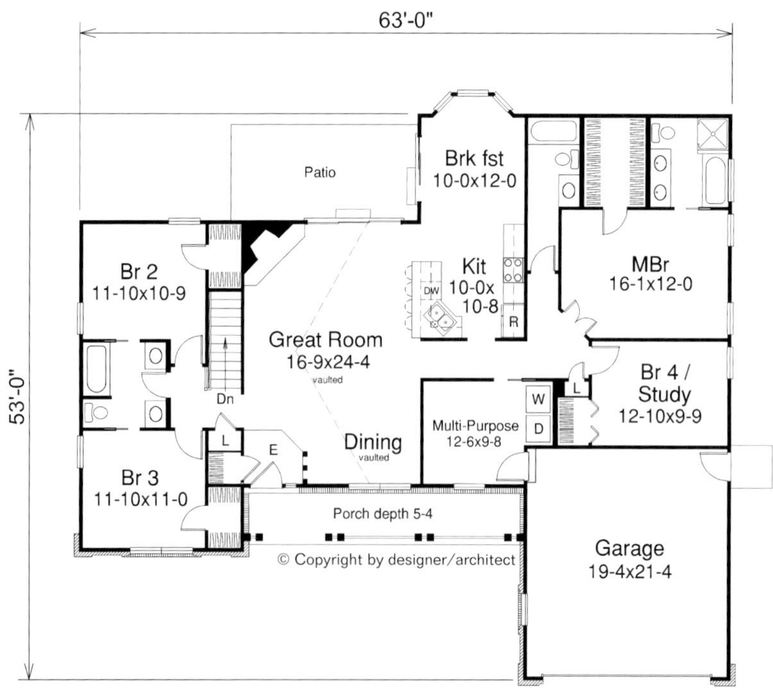

LOWE'S LEGACY SERIES

SPECIAL FEATURES

- 1,399 total square feet of living area
- Living room overlooks the dining area through arched columns
- Laundry room contains a handy half bath
- Spacious master bedroom includes a sitting area, walk-in closet and plenty of sunlight
- 3 bedrooms, 1 1/2 baths, 1-car garage
- Basement foundation, drawings also include crawl space and slab foundations

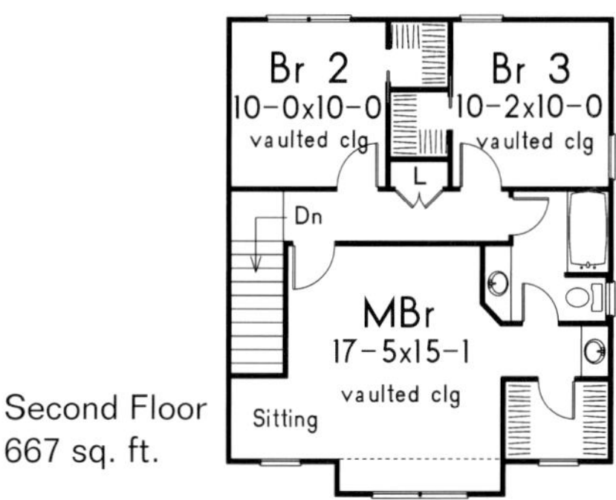

Second Floor
667 sq. ft.

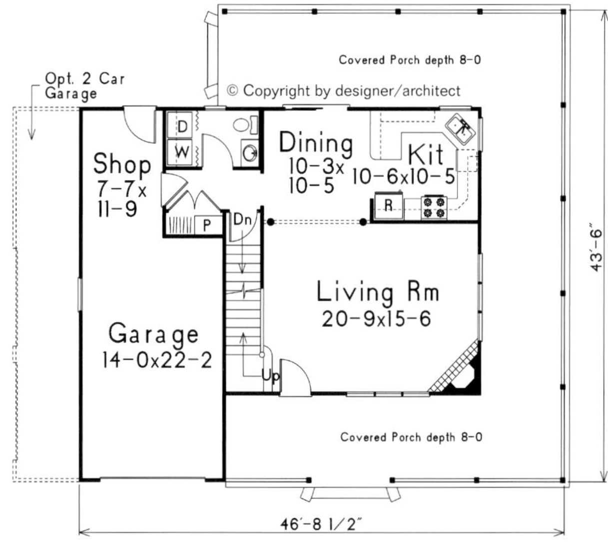

First Floor
732 sq. ft.

SPECIAL FEATURES

- 1,453 total square feet of living area
- Energy efficient home with 2" x 6" exterior walls
- Decorative vents, window trim, shutters and brick blend to create dramatic curb appeal
- Kitchen opens to the living area and includes a salad sink in the island as well as a pantry and handy laundry room
- Exquisite master bedroom is highlighted by a vaulted ceiling, dressing area with walk-in closet, private bath and spa tub/shower
- 3 bedrooms, 2 baths, 2-car garage
- Basement foundation, drawings also include crawl space foundation

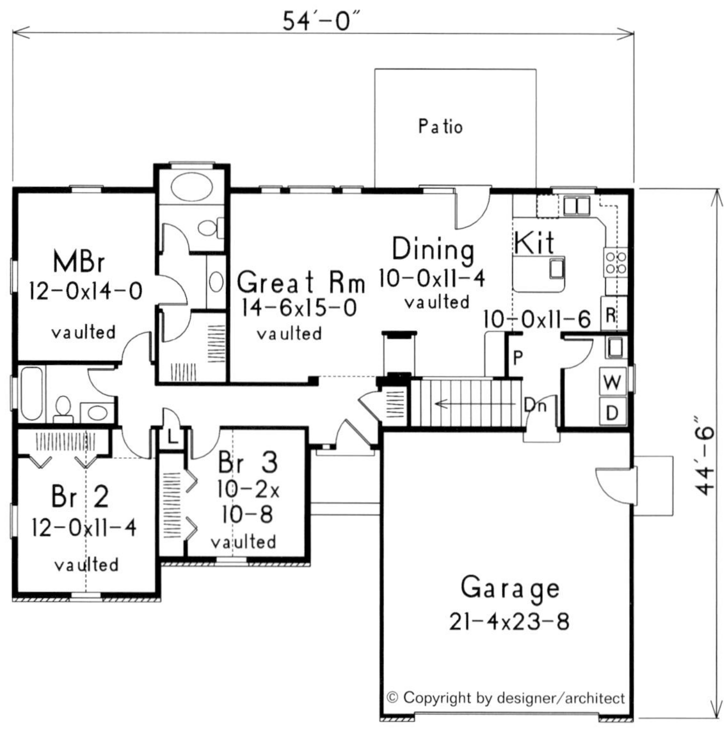

LOWE'S LEGACY SERIES

SPECIAL FEATURES

- 1,711 total square feet of living area
- U-shaped kitchen joins the breakfast and family rooms for an open living atmosphere
- Master bedroom has a secluded covered porch and private bath
- Balcony overlooks the family room that features a fireplace and accesses the deck
- 3 bedrooms, 2 1/2 baths, 2-car garage
- Basement foundation

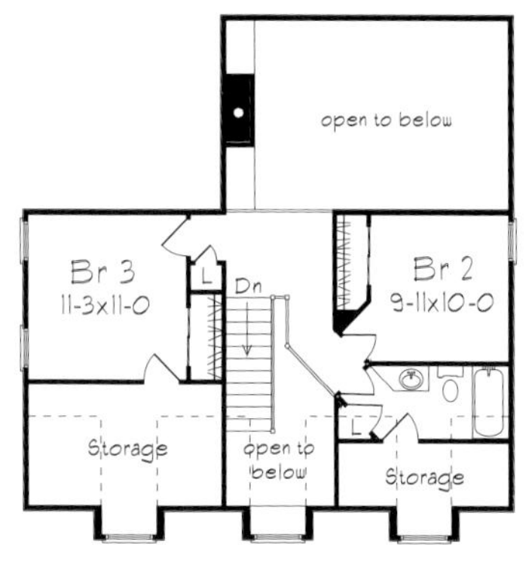

Second Floor
483 sq. ft.

First Floor
1,228 sq. ft.

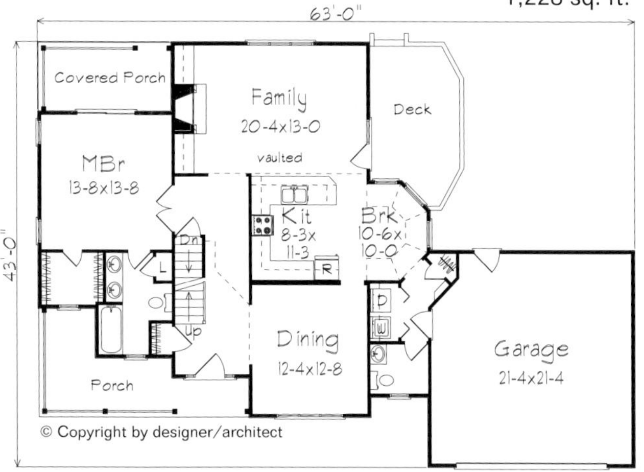

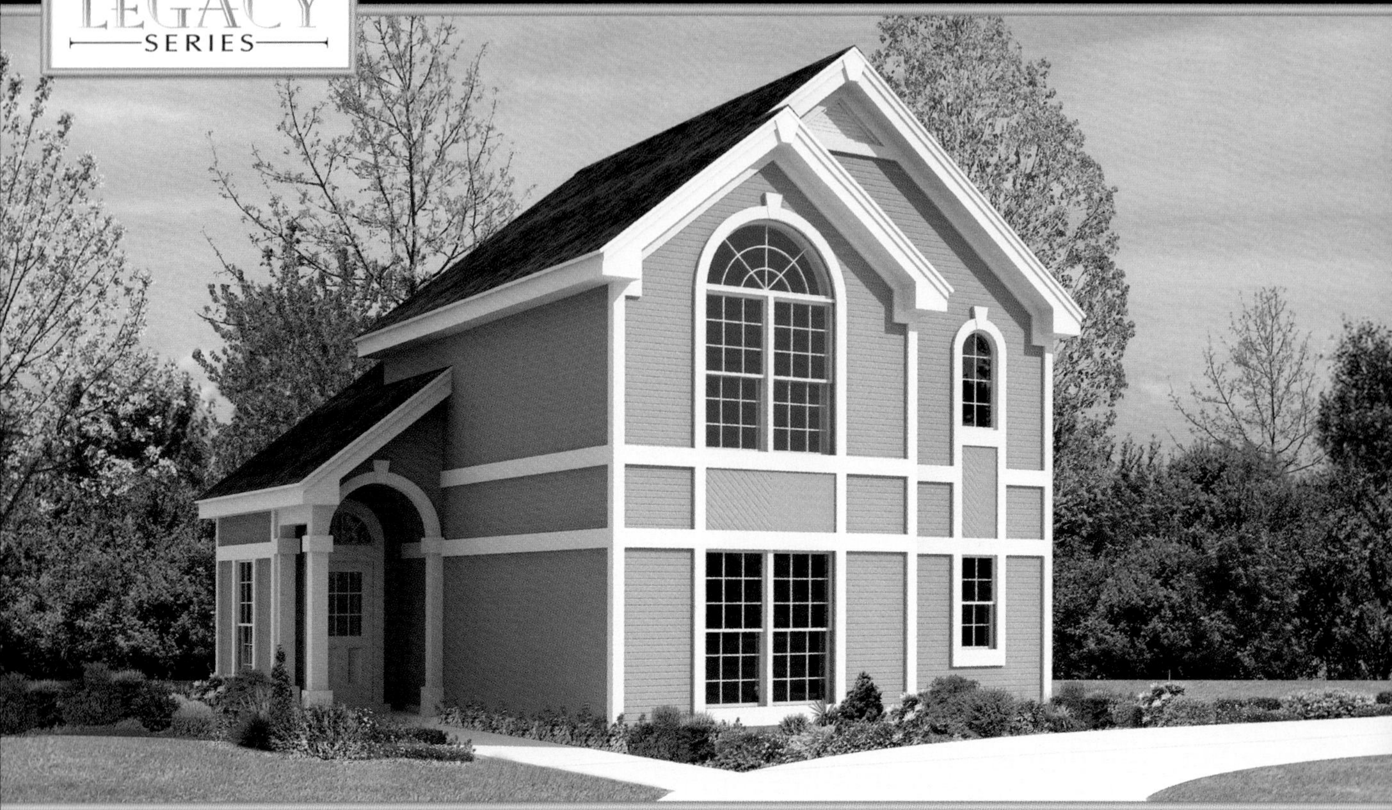

SPECIAL FEATURES

- 902 total square feet of living area
- Vaulted entry with laundry room leads to a spacious second floor apartment
- The large living room features an entry coat closet, L-shaped kitchen with pantry and dining area/balcony overlooking atrium window wall
- Roomy bedroom with walk-in closet is convenient to hall bath
- 1 bedroom, 1 bath, 2-car side entry garage
- Slab foundation

Second Floor
664 sq. ft.

First Floor
238 sq. ft.

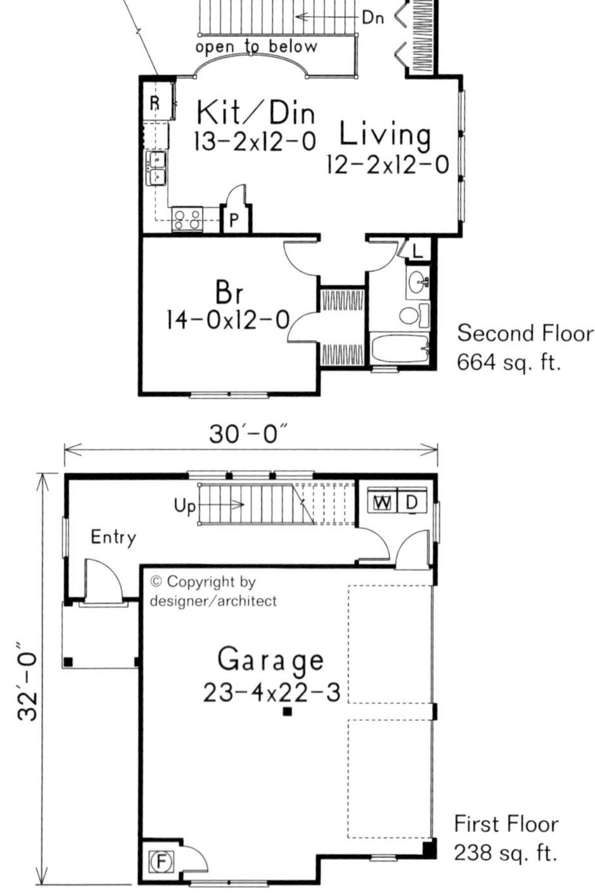

SPECIAL FEATURES

- 2,137 total square feet of living area
- Spacious porch for plants, chairs and family gatherings
- Huge living room includes front and rear views
- U-shaped kitchen features abundant storage
- Laundry room with large closet has its own porch
- 4 bedrooms, 2 1/2 baths, 2-car garage
- Partial basement/crawl space foundation

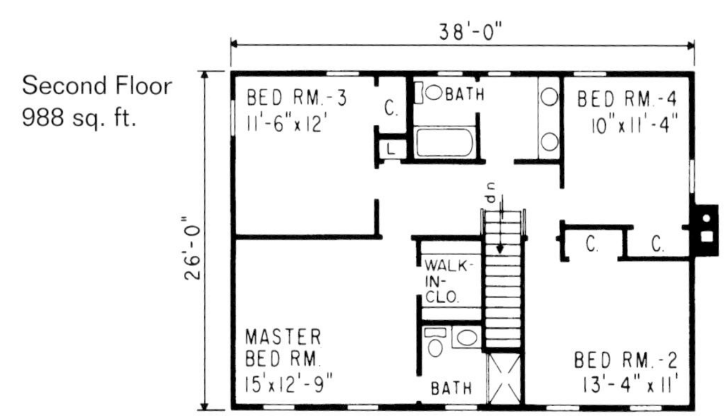

Second Floor
988 sq. ft.

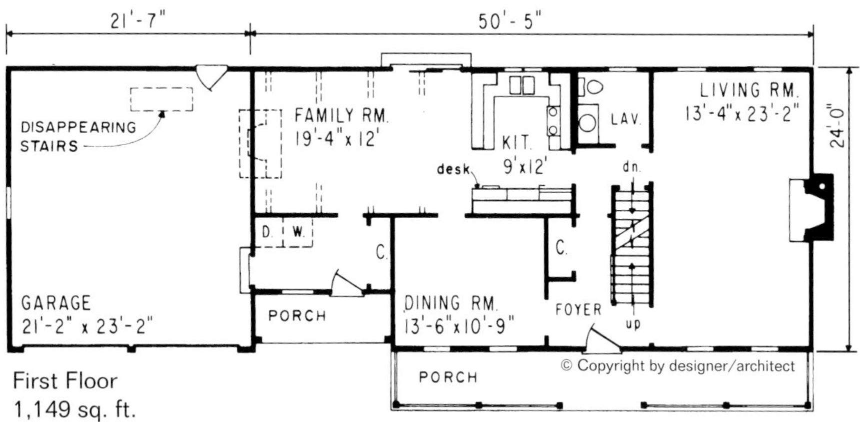

First Floor
1,149 sq. ft.

SPECIAL FEATURES

- 1,621 total square feet of living area
- The front exterior includes an attractive gable-end arched window and extra-deep porch
- A grand-scale great room enjoys a coffered ceiling, fireplace, access to the wrap-around deck and is brightly lit with numerous French doors and windows
- The master bedroom suite has a sitting area, double walk-in closets and a luxury bath
- 223 square feet of optional finished space on the lower level
- 3 bedrooms, 2 baths, 2-car drive under side entry garage
- Basement foundation

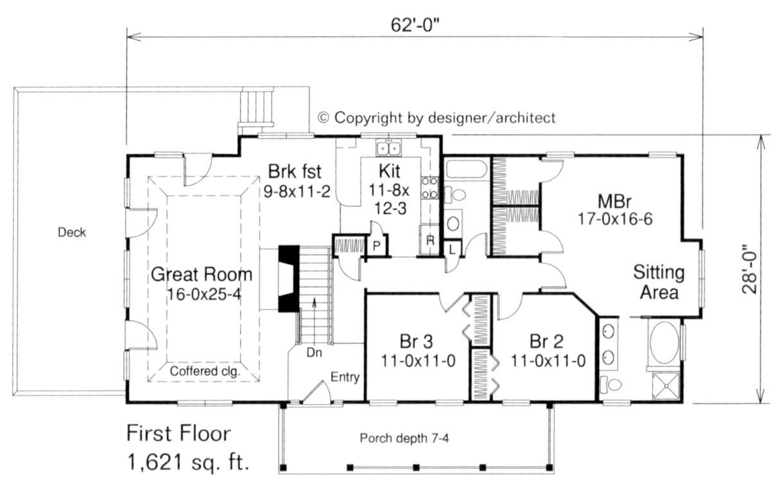

First Floor
1,621 sq. ft.

Lower Level With
Optional Laundry Area

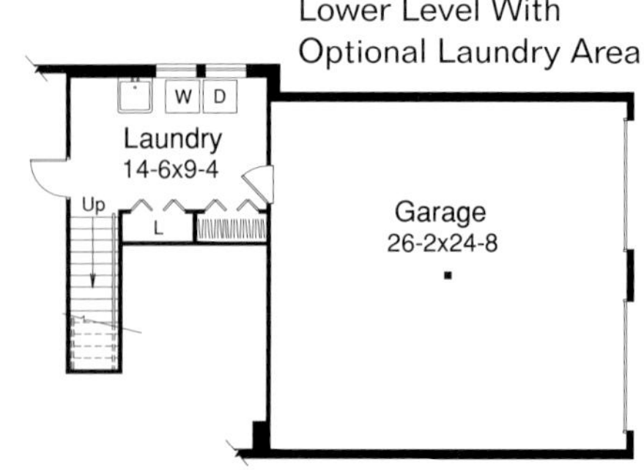

Plan Number: 537-033D-0013 | Price Code: D

Lowe's Legacy Series

Special Features

- 1,813 total square feet of living area
- Bedrooms are located on the second floor for privacy
- Living room with large bay window joins the dining room for expansive formal entertaining
- The family room, dinette and kitchen combine for an impressive living area
- Two-story foyer and L-shaped stairs create a dramatic entry
- Inviting covered porch
- 3 bedrooms, 2 1/2 baths, 2-car garage
- Basement foundation

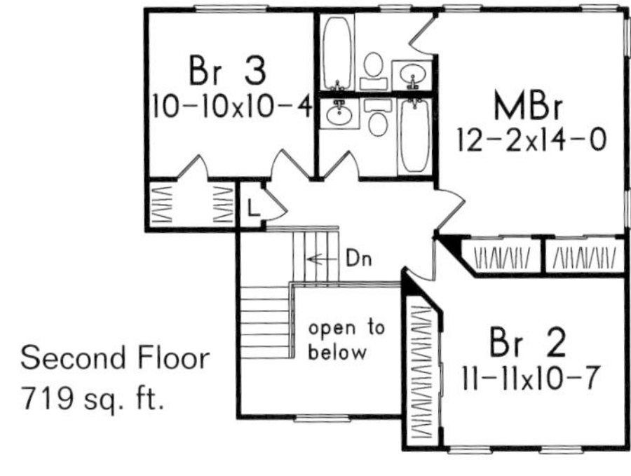

Second Floor
719 sq. ft.

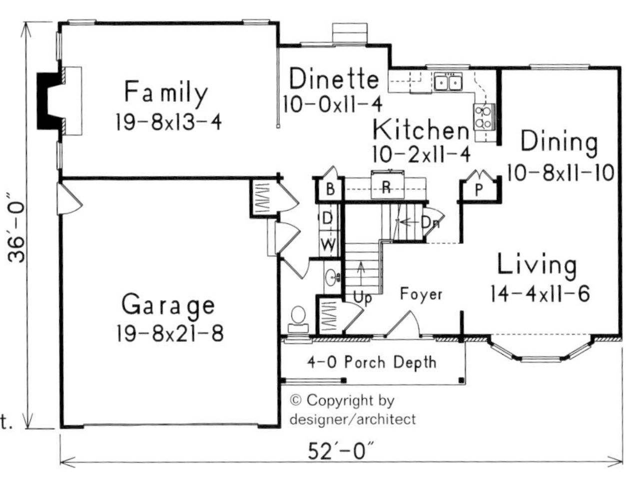

First Floor
1,094 sq. ft.

SPECIAL FEATURES

- 1,998 total square feet of living area
- Large family room features a fireplace and access to the kitchen and dining area
- Skylights add daylight to the second floor baths
- Utility room is conveniently located near the garage and kitchen
- Kitchen/breakfast area includes a pantry, island workspace and easy access to the patio
- 3 bedrooms, 2 1/2 baths, 2-car side entry garage
- Basement foundation, drawings also include crawl space and slab foundations

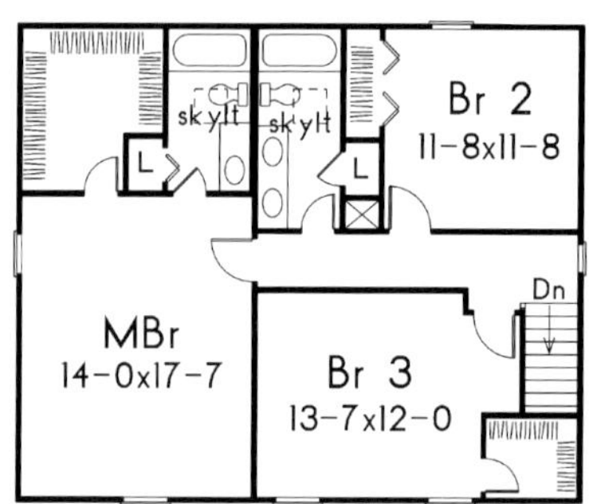

Second Floor
938 sq. ft.

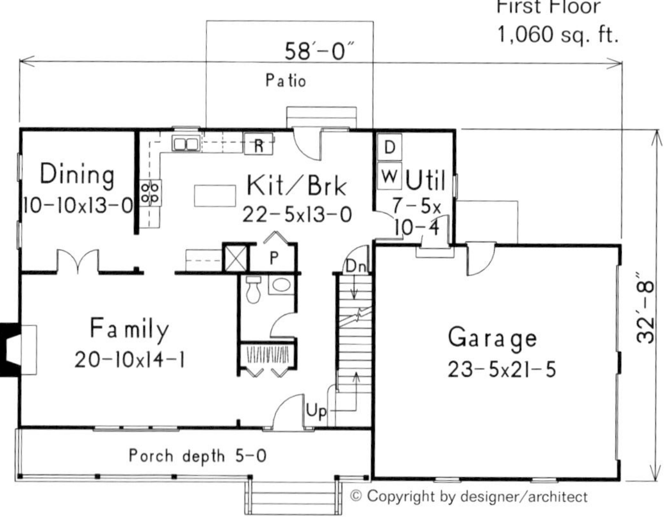

First Floor
1,060 sq. ft.

SPECIAL FEATURES

- 1,278 total square feet of living area
- Excellent U-shaped kitchen with garden window opens to an enormous great room with vaulted ceiling, fireplace and two skylights
- Vaulted master bedroom offers a double-door entry, access to a deck and bath and two walk-in closets
- The bath has a double-bowl vanity and dramatic step-up garden tub with a lean-to greenhouse window
- 805 square feet of optional living area on the lower level with family room, bedroom #4 and bath
- 3 bedrooms, 1 bath, 2-car garage
- Walk-out basement foundation

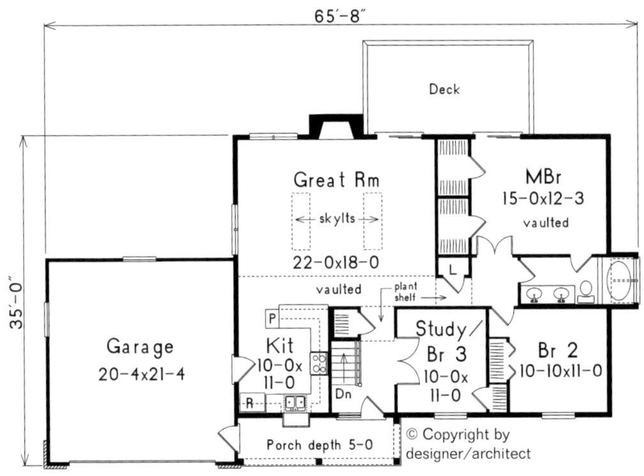

First Floor
1,278 sq. ft.

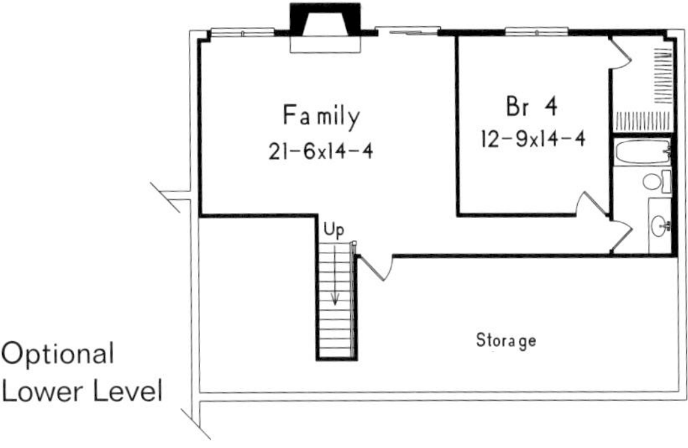

Optional
Lower Level

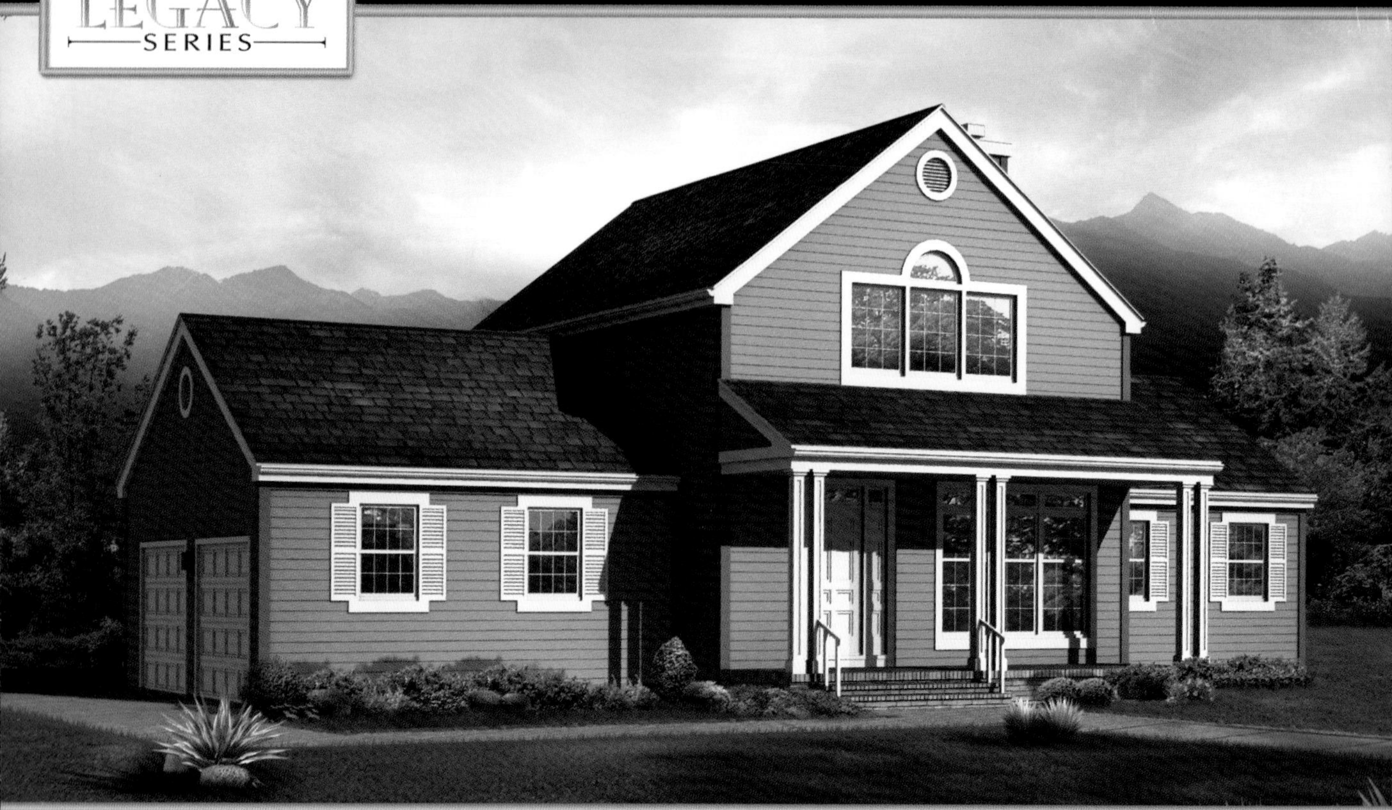

SPECIAL FEATURES

- 1,805 total square feet of living area
- Energy efficient home with 2" x 6" exterior walls
- Master bedroom forms its own wing
- Second floor bedrooms share a hall bath
- Large great room with fireplace blends into the formal dining room
- 3 bedrooms, 2 1/2 baths, 2-car side entry garage
- Basement foundation, drawings also include slab foundation

Second Floor
560 sq. ft.

First Floor
1,245 sq. ft.

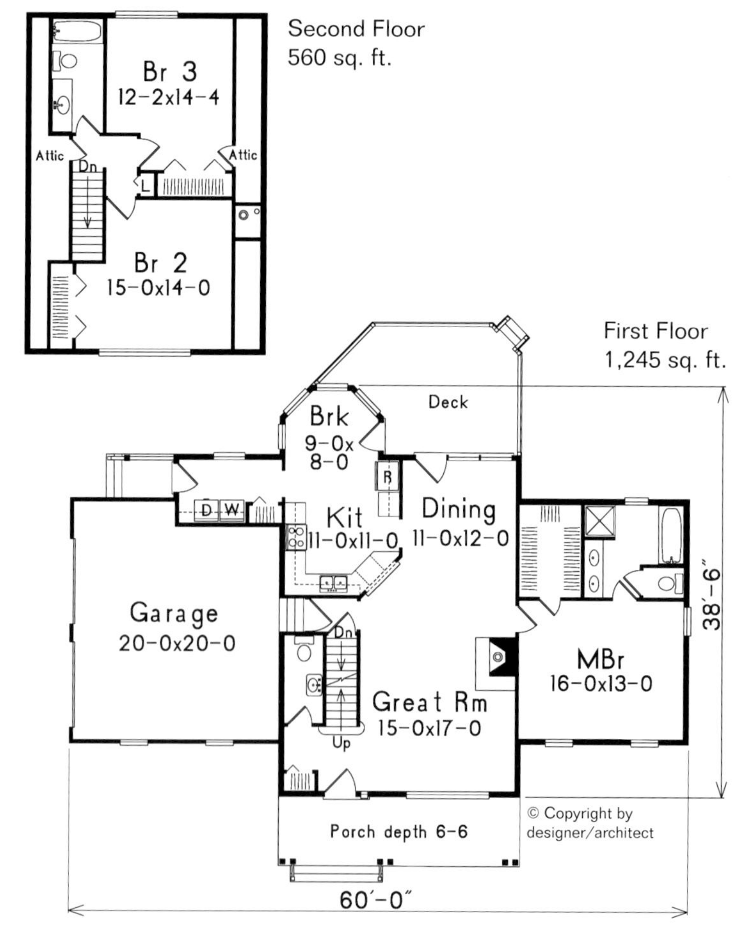

SPECIAL FEATURES

- 1,609 total square feet of living area
- Efficient kitchen includes a corner pantry and adjacent laundry room
- Breakfast room boasts plenty of windows and opens onto a rear deck
- Master bedroom features a tray ceiling and private deluxe bath
- Entry opens into large living area with fireplace
- 4 bedrooms, 2 baths, 2-car garage
- Basement foundation

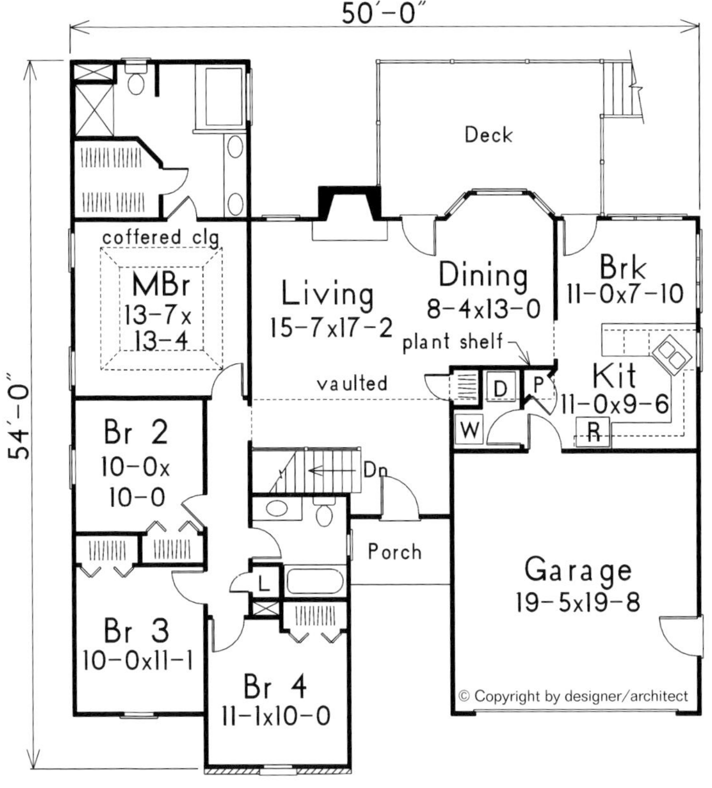

PLAN NUMBER: 537-007D-0115 | PRICE CODE: AAA

SPECIAL FEATURES

- 588 total square feet of living area
- May be built as a duplex, 4-car garage or apartment garage/vacation cabin as shown
- Very livable plan in a small footprint
- Living room features a functional entry, bayed dining area, corner fireplace and opens to kitchen with breakfast bar
- 1 bedroom, 1 bath, 2-car side entry garage
- Slab foundation
- 1,176 square feet of living area when built as a duplex

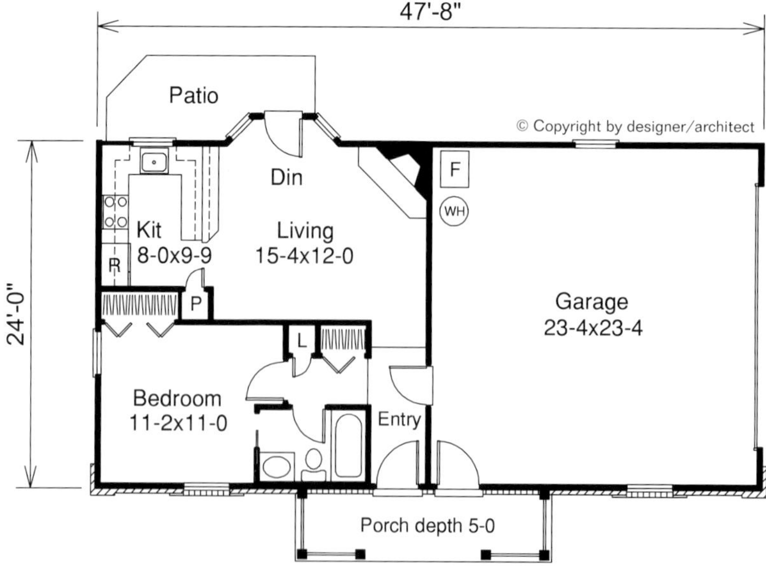

TO ORDER SEE PAGE 288 | CALL TOLL-FREE 1-877-379-3420

SPECIAL FEATURES

- 2,059 total square feet of living area
- Octagon-shaped breakfast room offers plenty of windows and creates a view to the veranda
- First floor master bedroom has a large walk-in closet and deluxe bath
- 9' ceilings throughout the home
- Secondary bedrooms and bath feature dormers and are adjacent to the cozy sitting area
- 3 bedrooms, 2 1/2 baths, 2-car detached garage
- Slab foundation, drawings also include basement and crawl space foundations

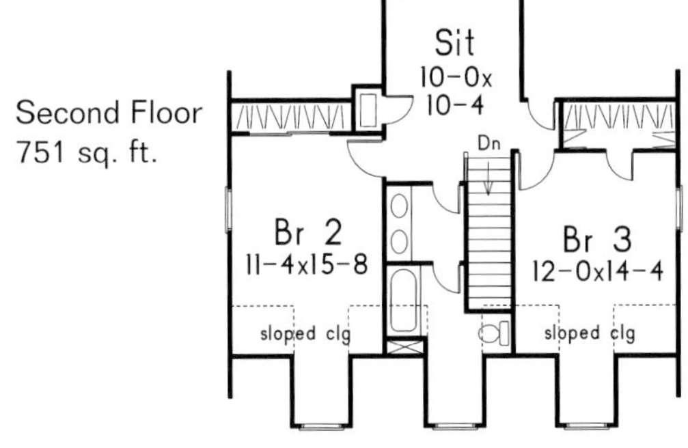

Second Floor
751 sq. ft.

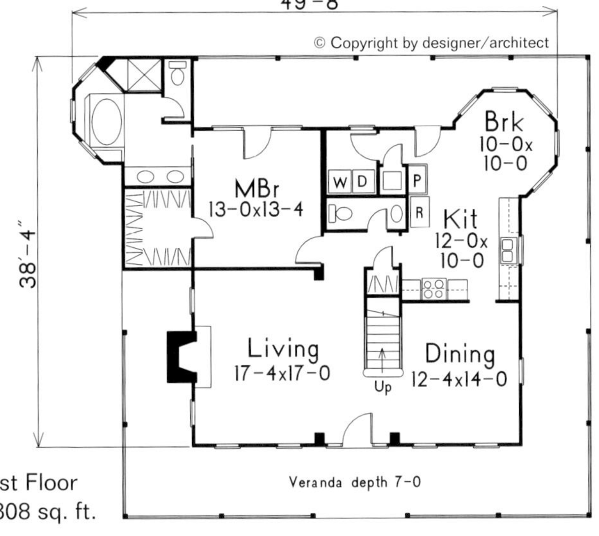

First Floor
1,308 sq. ft.

PRICE CODE: B

LOWE'S LEGACY SERIES

SPECIAL FEATURES

- 1,787 total square feet of living area
- Large great room with fireplace and vaulted ceiling features three large skylights and windows galore
- Cooking is sure to be a pleasure in this L-shaped well-appointed kitchen which includes a bayed breakfast area with access to the rear deck
- Every bedroom offers a spacious walk-in closet with a convenient laundry room just steps away
- 415 square feet of optional living area available on the lower level
- 3 bedrooms, 2 baths, 2-car drive under garage
- Walk-out basement foundation

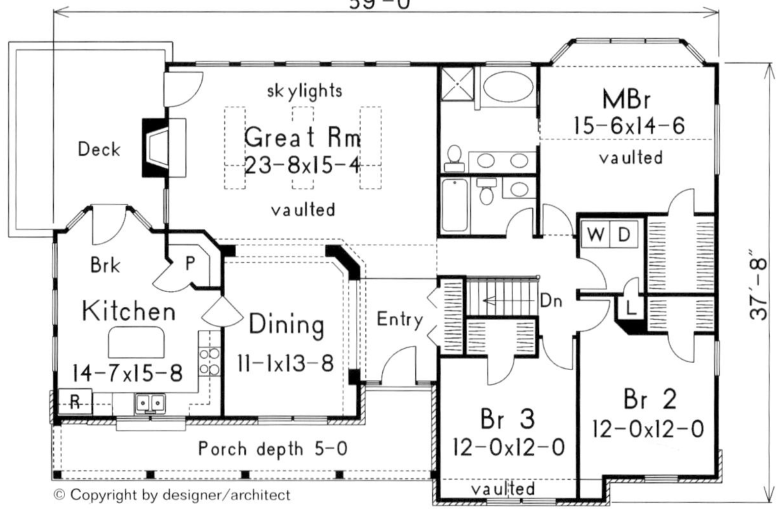

SPECIAL FEATURES

- 1,818 total square feet of living area
- Breakfast room is tucked behind the kitchen and has a laundry closet and deck access
- Living and dining areas share a vaulted ceiling and fireplace
- Master bedroom has two closets, a large double-bowl vanity and a separate tub and shower
- Large front porch wraps around the home
- 4 bedrooms, 2 1/2 baths, 2-car drive under garage
- Basement foundation

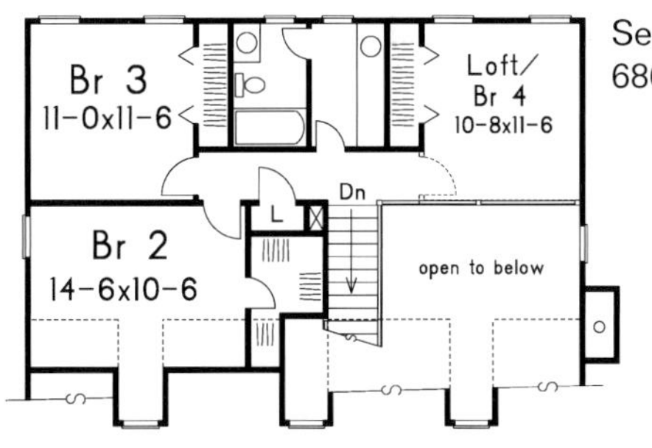

Second Floor
686 sq. ft.

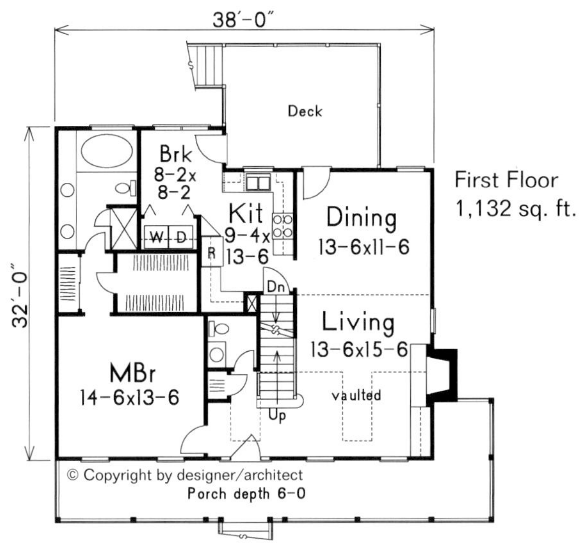

First Floor
1,132 sq. ft.

SPECIAL FEATURES

- 1,104 total square feet of living area
- Master bedroom includes a private bath
- Convenient side entrance to the dining area/kitchen
- Laundry area is located near the kitchen
- Large living area creates a comfortable atmosphere
- 3 bedrooms, 2 baths
- Crawl space foundation, drawings also include basement and slab foundations

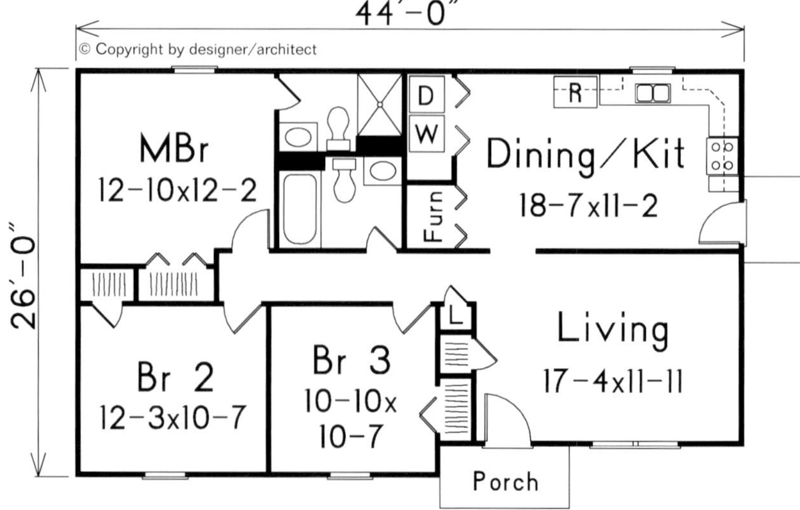

Plan Number: 537-007D-0114 | Price Code: B

Lowe's Legacy Series

Special Features

- 1,671 total square feet of living area
- Triple gables and stone facade create great curb appeal
- Two-story entry with hallway leads to a spacious family room, dining area with bay window and U-shaped kitchen
- Second floor features a large master bedroom with luxury bath, huge walk-in closet, overlook to entry and two secondary bedrooms with hall bath
- 3 bedrooms, 2 1/2 baths, 2-car garage
- Basement foundation

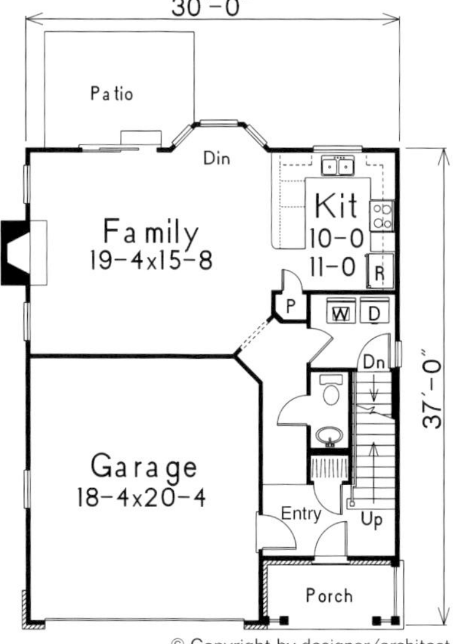

First Floor
680 sq. ft.

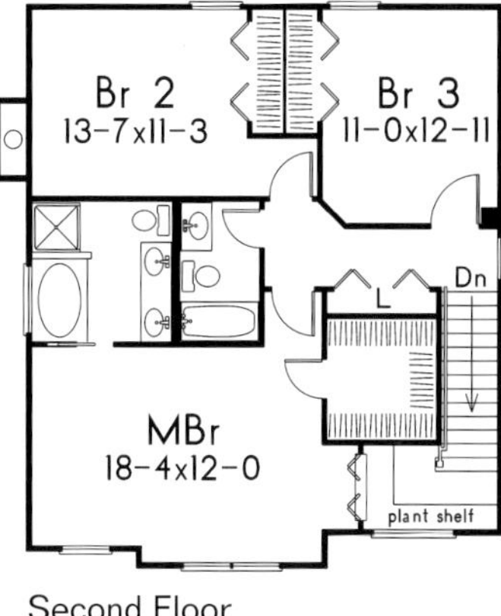

Second Floor
991 sq. ft.

PLAN NUMBER: 537-045D-0009 | PRICE CODE: B

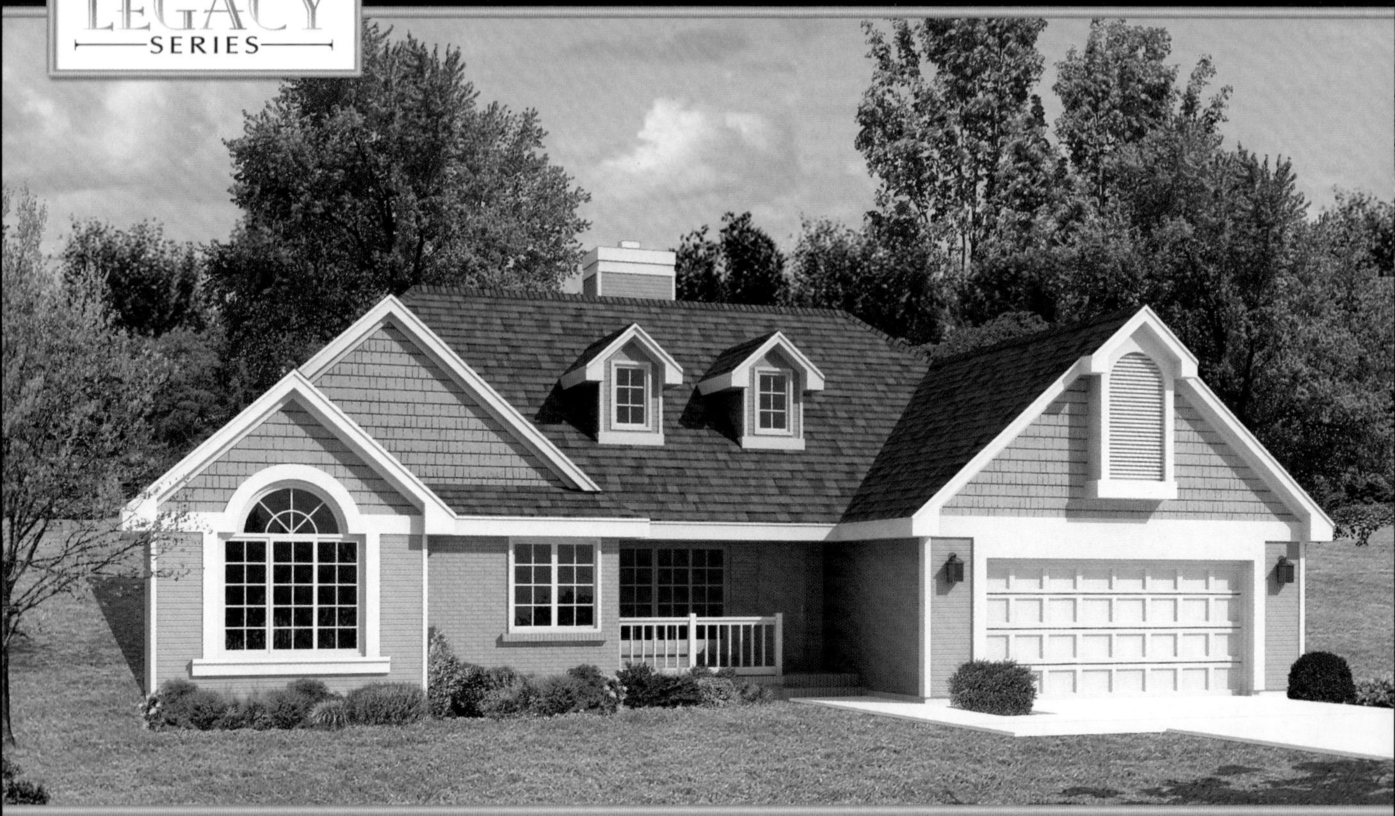

SPECIAL FEATURES

- 1,684 total square feet of living area
- The bayed dining area boasts convenient double-door access onto the large deck
- The family room features several large windows for brightness
- Bedrooms are separate from living areas for privacy
- Master bedroom offers a bath with walk-in closet, double-bowl vanity and both a shower and a whirlpool tub
- 3 bedrooms, 2 1/2 baths, 2-car garage
- Basement foundation

 TO ORDER SEE PAGE 288

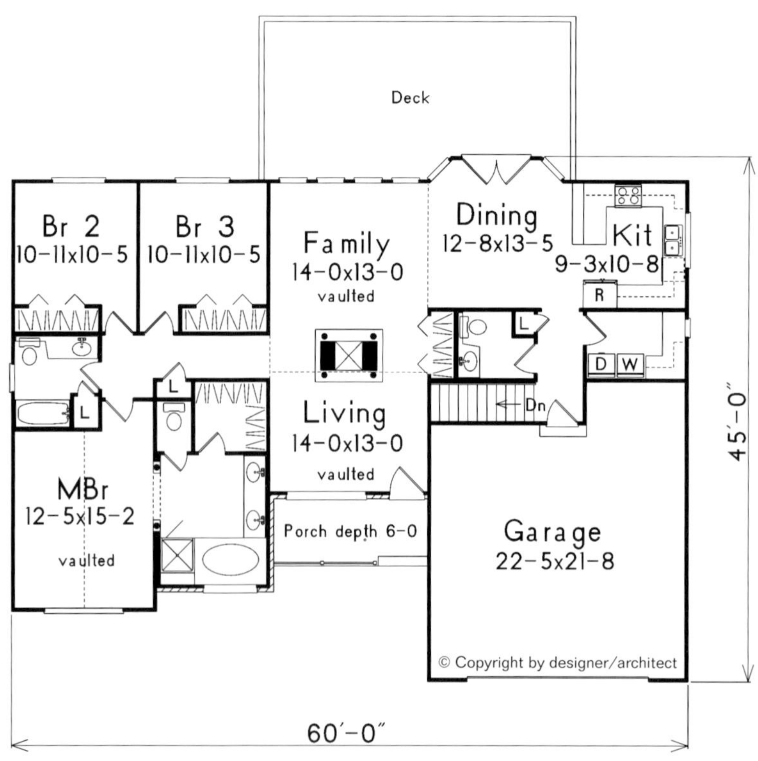

Plan Number: 537-006D-0004 | Price Code: C

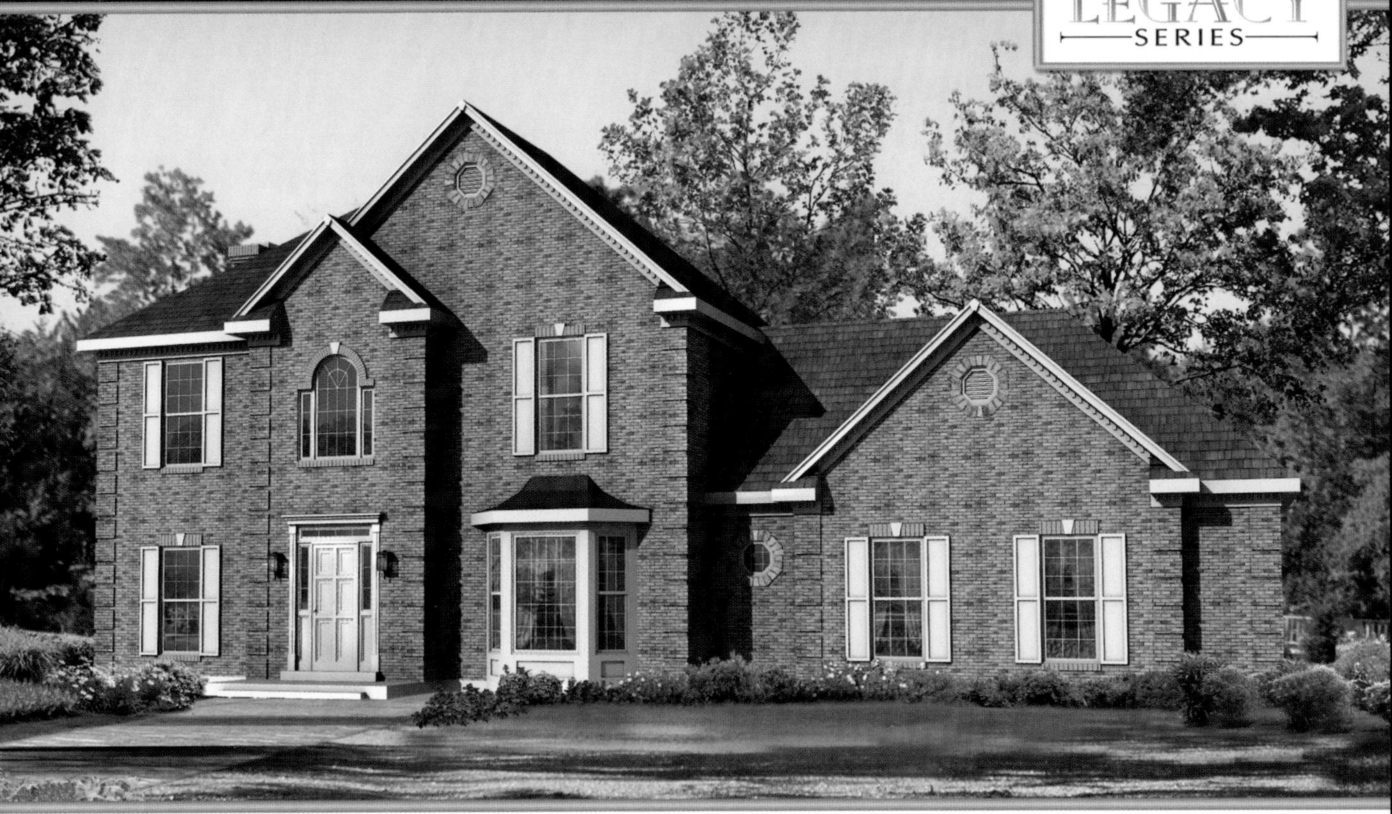

Special Features

- 1,996 total square feet of living area
- Dining area features an octagon-shaped coffered ceiling and built-in china cabinet
- Both the master bath and second floor bath have cheerful skylights
- Family room includes a wet bar and fireplace flanked by attractive quarter round windows
- 9' ceilings throughout the first floor with plant shelving in foyer and dining area
- 3 bedrooms, 2 1/2 baths, 2-car side entry garage
- Basement foundation, drawings also include crawl space and slab foundations

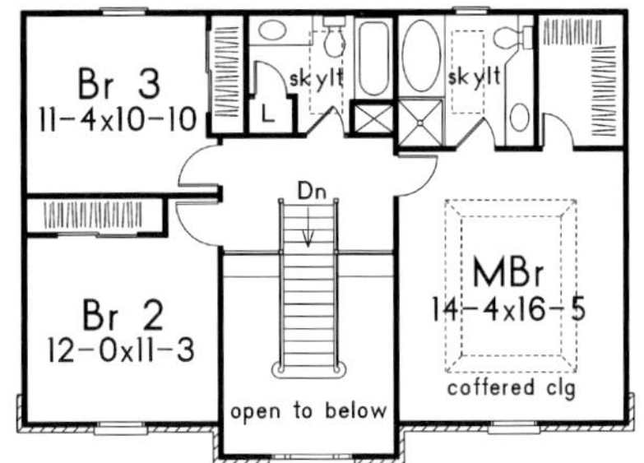

Second Floor
859 sq. ft.

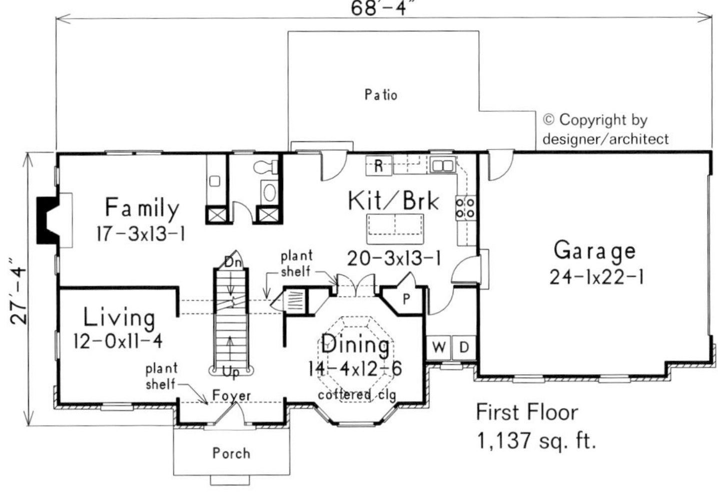

First Floor
1,137 sq. ft.

SPECIAL FEATURES

- 1,427 total square feet of living area
- Practical storage space is situated in the garage
- Convenient laundry closet is located on the lower level
- Kitchen and dining area both have sliding doors that access the deck
- Large expansive space is created by vaulted living and dining rooms
- 3 bedrooms, 2 baths, 2-car drive under garage
- Basement foundation

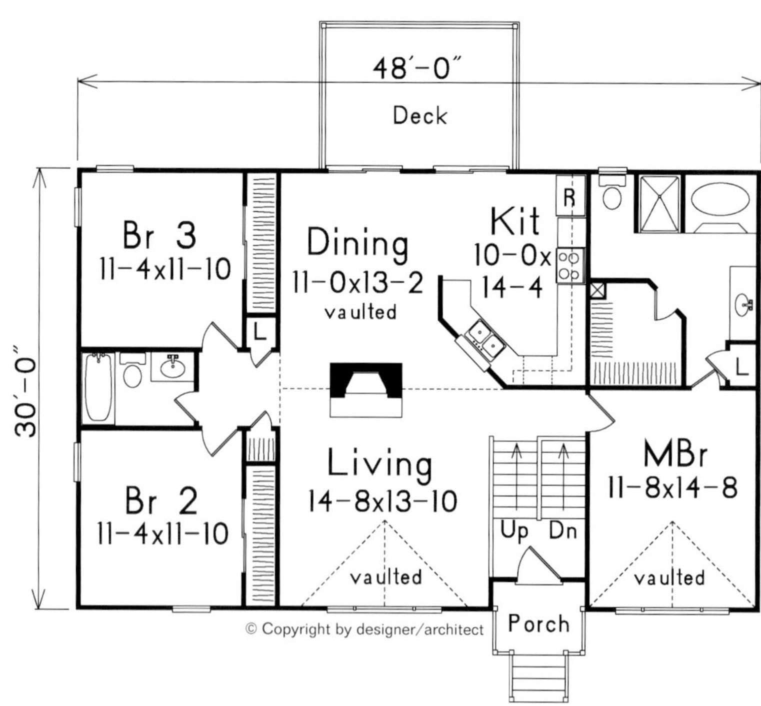

Plan Number: 537-007D-0087 | Price Code: A

Lowe's LEGACY SERIES

Special Features

- 1,332 total square feet of living area
- Home offers both basement and first floor entry locations
- A dramatic living room features a vaulted ceiling, fireplace, exterior balcony and dining area
- An L-shaped kitchen offers spacious cabinetry, breakfast area with bay window and access to the rear patio
- 3 bedrooms, 2 baths, 4-car tandem garage
- Walk-out basement foundation

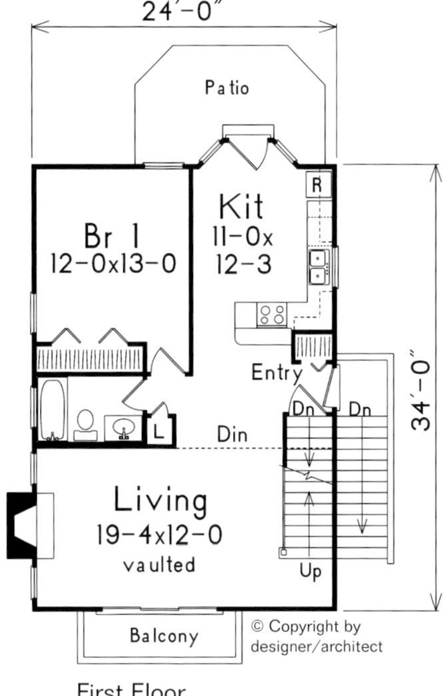

First Floor
828 sq. ft.

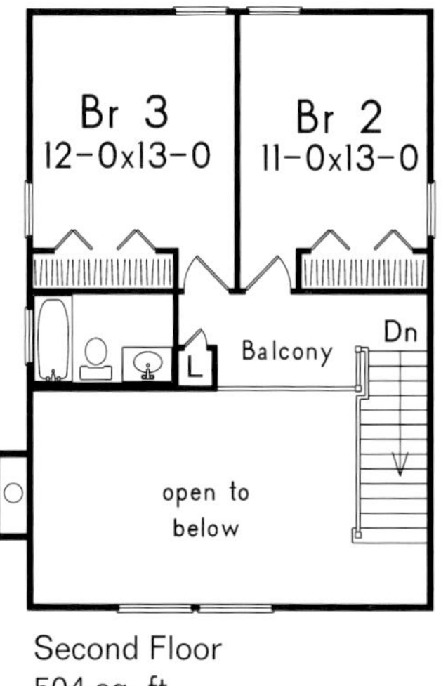

Second Floor
504 sq. ft.

PLAN NUMBER: 537-021D-0016 | PRICE CODE: B

SPECIAL FEATURES

- 1,600 total square feet of living area
- Energy efficient home with 2" x 6" exterior walls
- First floor master bedroom is accessible from two points of entry
- Master bath dressing area includes separate vanities and a mirrored makeup counter
- Second floor bedrooms have generous storage space and share a full bath
- 3 bedrooms, 2 baths, 2-car side entry garage
- Crawl space foundation, drawings also include slab foundation

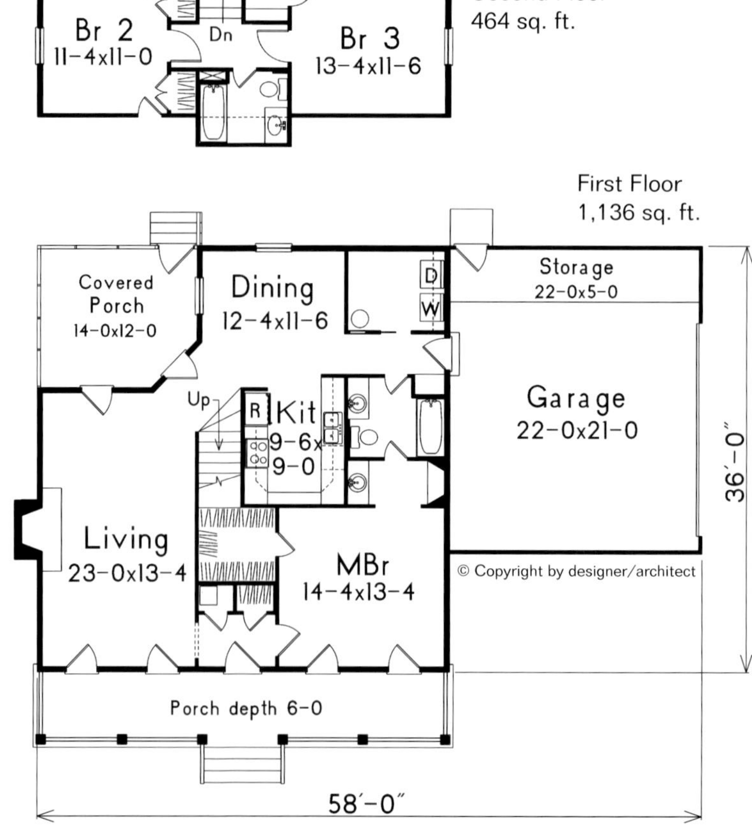

SPECIAL FEATURES

- 1,062 total square feet of living area
- Handsome appeal created by triple-gable facade
- An efficient U-shaped kitchen features a snack bar and breakfast room and is open to the living room with bay window
- Both the master bedroom, with its own private bath, and bedroom #2/study enjoy access to rear patio
- 3 bedrooms, 2 baths, 2-car garage
- Basement foundation

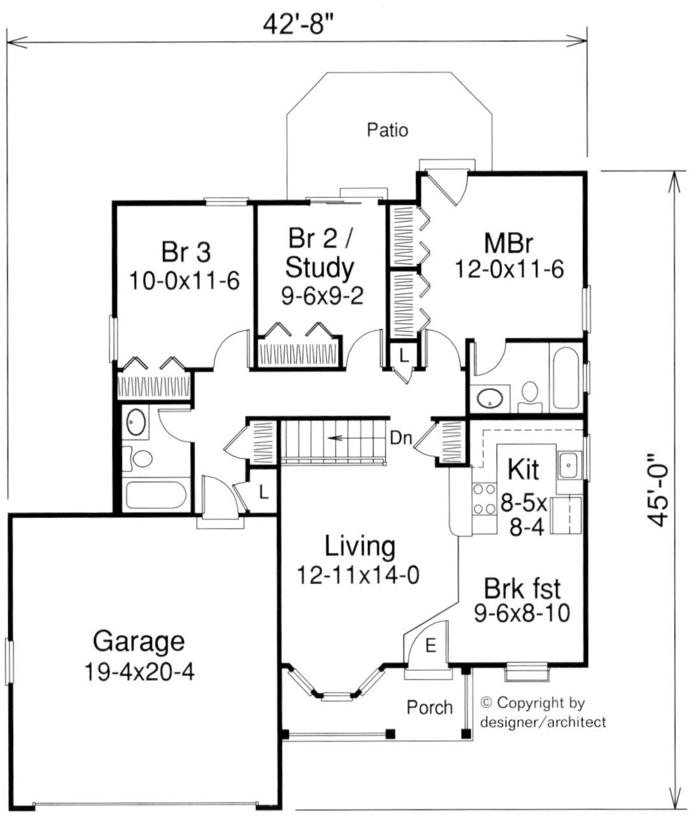

Plan Number: 537-007D-0088 | Price Code: A

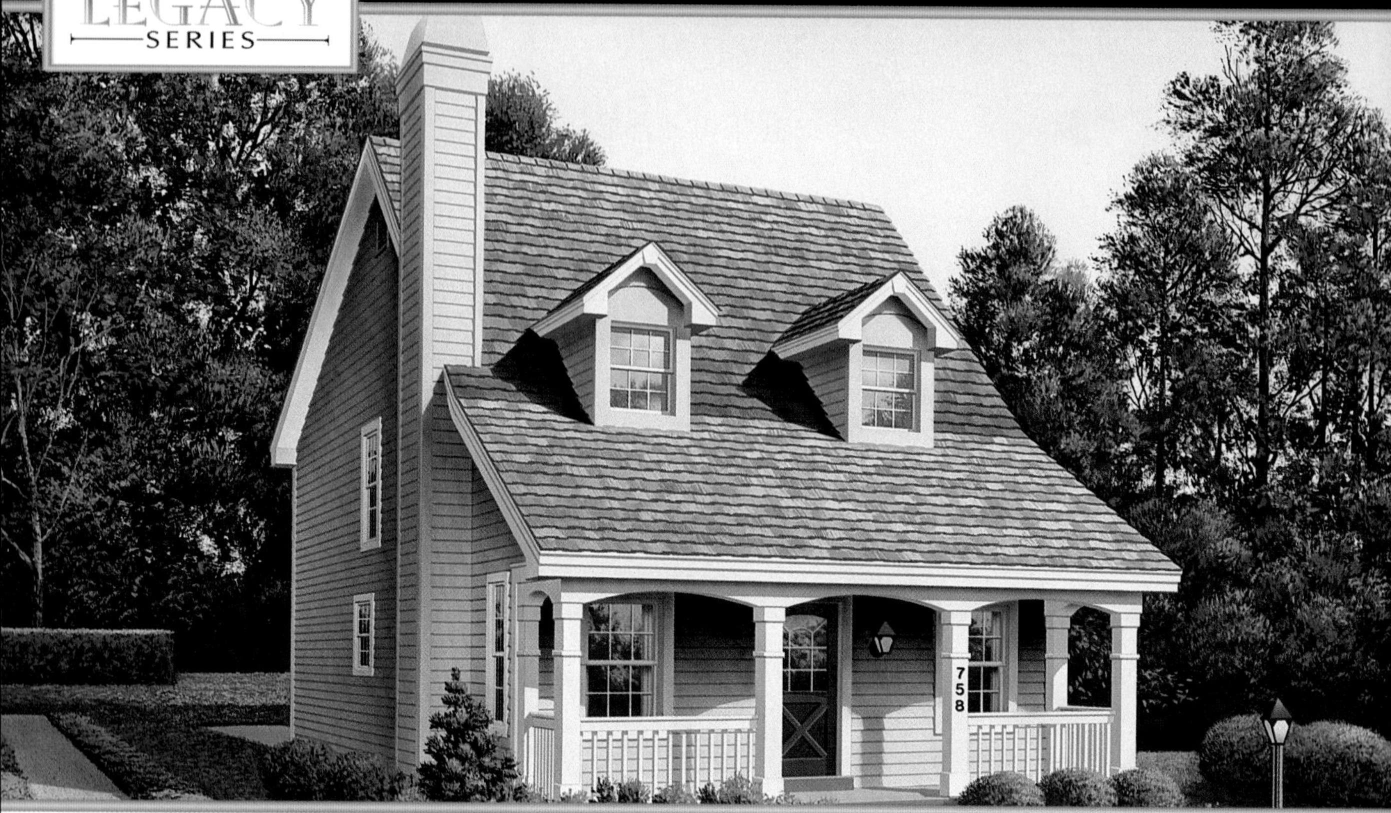

Special Features

- 1,299 total square feet of living area
- Large porch for enjoying relaxing evenings
- First floor master bedroom has a bay window, walk-in closet and roomy bath
- Two generous bedrooms with lots of closet space, a hall bath, linen closet and balcony overlook comprise the second floor
- 3 bedrooms, 2 1/2 baths
- Basement foundation

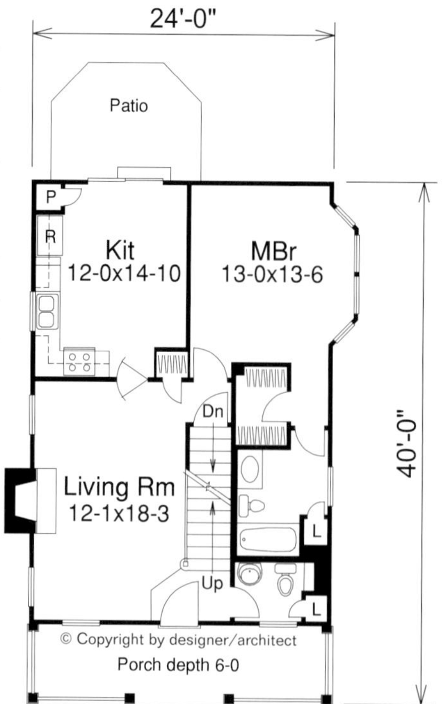

First Floor
834 sq. ft.

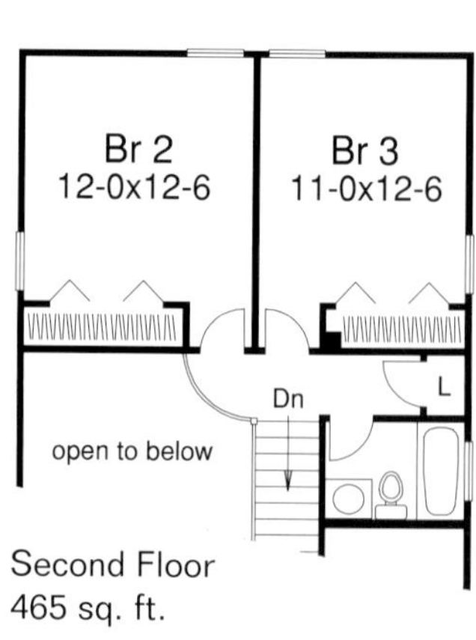

Second Floor
465 sq. ft.

SPECIAL FEATURES

- 1,239 total square feet of living area
- Master bedroom has a private bath and walk-in closet
- Convenient coat closet and pantry are located near the garage entrance
- Dining area accesses the deck
- Stairway with sloped ceiling creates an open atmosphere in the great room
- 3 bedrooms, 2 1/2 baths, 2-car garage
- Basement foundation

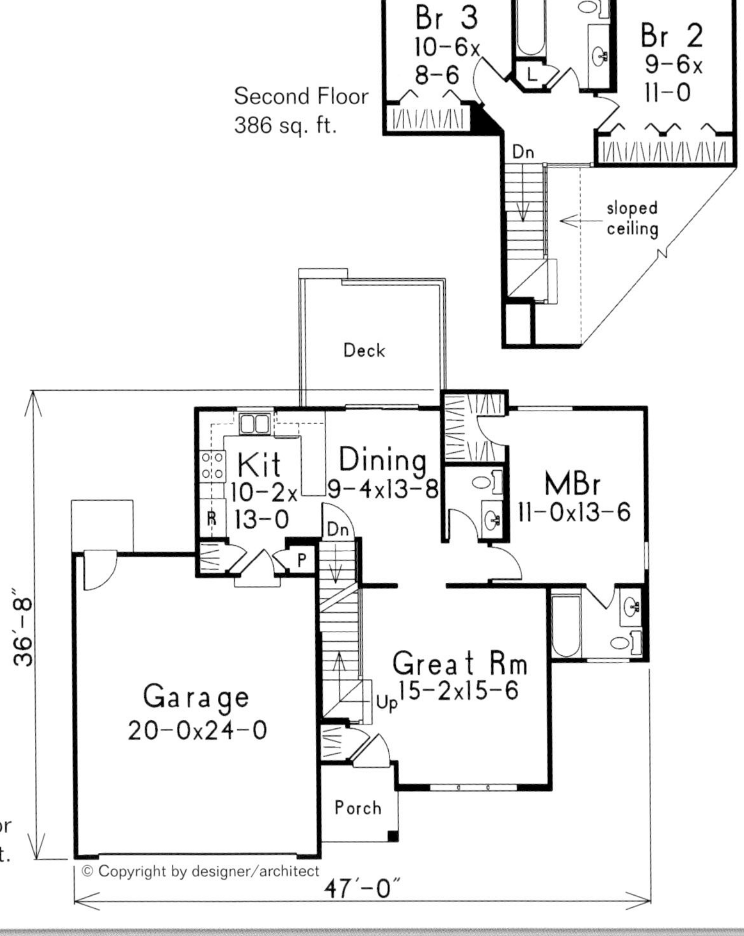

First Floor
853 sq. ft.

PLAN NUMBER: 537-040D-0026 | PRICE CODE: B

SPECIAL FEATURES

- 1,393 total square feet of living area
- L-shaped kitchen features a walk-in pantry, island cooktop and is convenient to the laundry room and dining area
- Master bedroom features a large walk-in closet and private bath with separate tub and shower
- Convenient storage/coat closet in hall
- View to the patio from the dining area
- 3 bedrooms, 2 baths, 2-car detached garage
- Crawl space foundation, drawings also include slab foundation

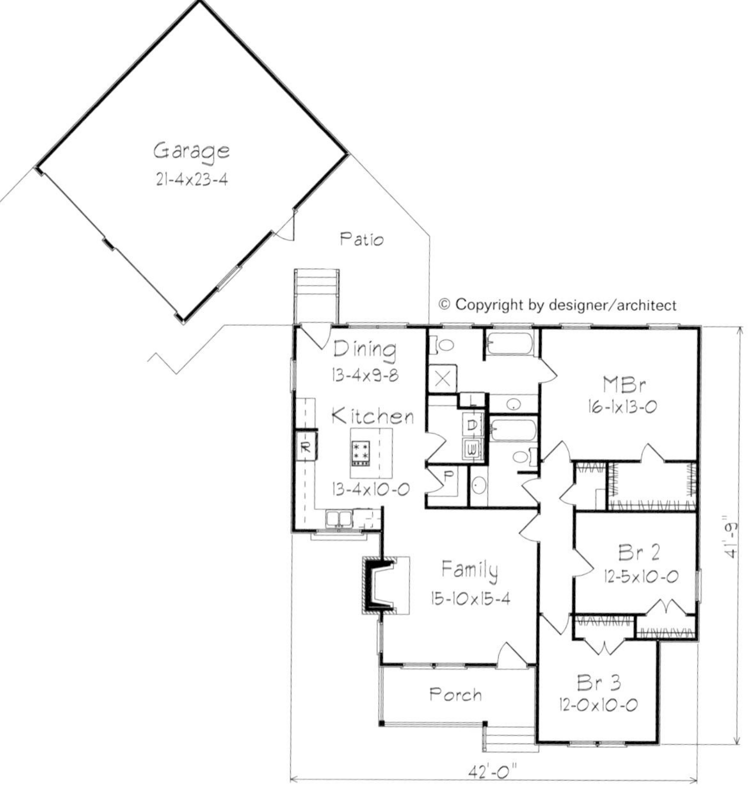

SPECIAL FEATURES

- 1,288 total square feet of living area
- Kitchen, dining area and great room join to create an open living space
- Master bedroom includes a private bath
- Secondary bedrooms enjoy ample closet space
- Hall bath features a convenient laundry closet
- Dining room accesses the outdoors
- 3 bedrooms, 2 baths
- Crawl space foundation, drawings also include basement and slab foundations

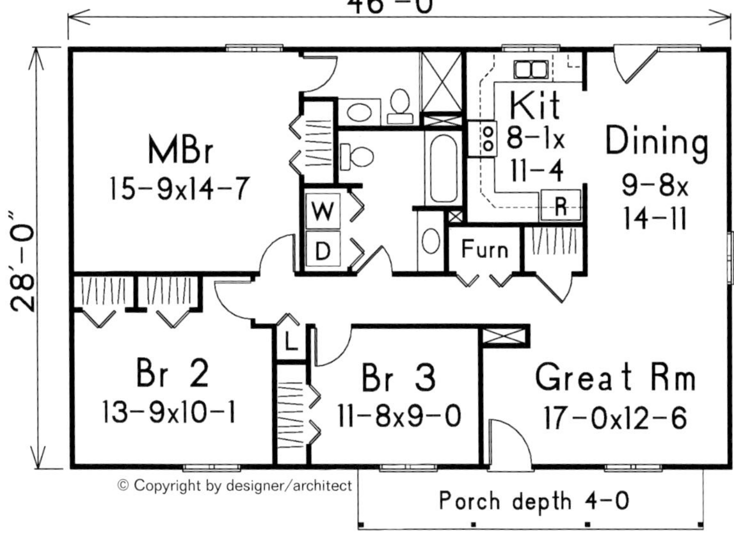

Special Features

- 1,498 total square feet of living area
- A perfect home for a narrow and sloping lot featuring both front and rear garages
- Large living room has fireplace, rear outdoor balcony and a pass-through snack bar to a spacious U-shaped kitchen with adjacent dining area
- Roomy master bedroom with luxury bath and two walk-in closets
- 2 bedrooms, 2 1/2 baths, 1-car garage and a 2-car rear entry drive under garage
- Walk-out basement foundation

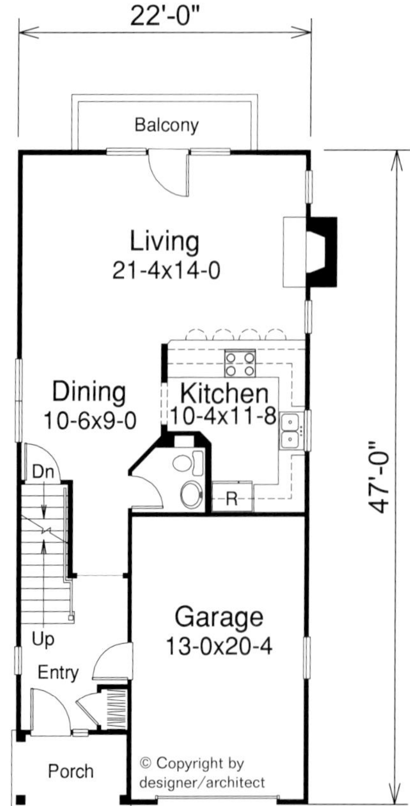

First Floor
827 sq. ft.

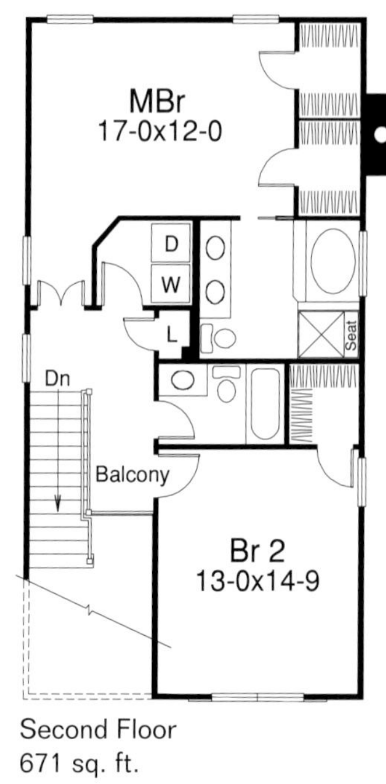

Second Floor
671 sq. ft.

SPECIAL FEATURES

- 1,610 total square feet of living area
- Attractive stone facade wraps around cozy breakfast room bay
- Roomy foyer leads to a splendid kitchen with an abundance of storage and counterspace
- The spacious living and dining room combination features access to the rear deck
- Master bedroom features a walk-in closet and compartmented bath with a luxurious garden tub
- 3 bedrooms, 2 baths
- Basement foundation, drawings also include crawl space and slab foundations

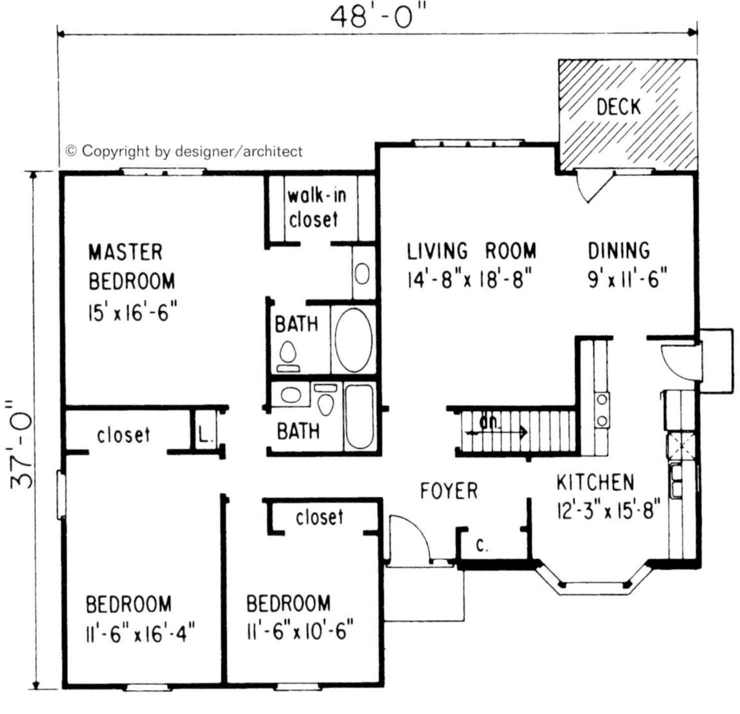

PLAN NUMBER: 537-007D-0089 | PRICE CODE: C

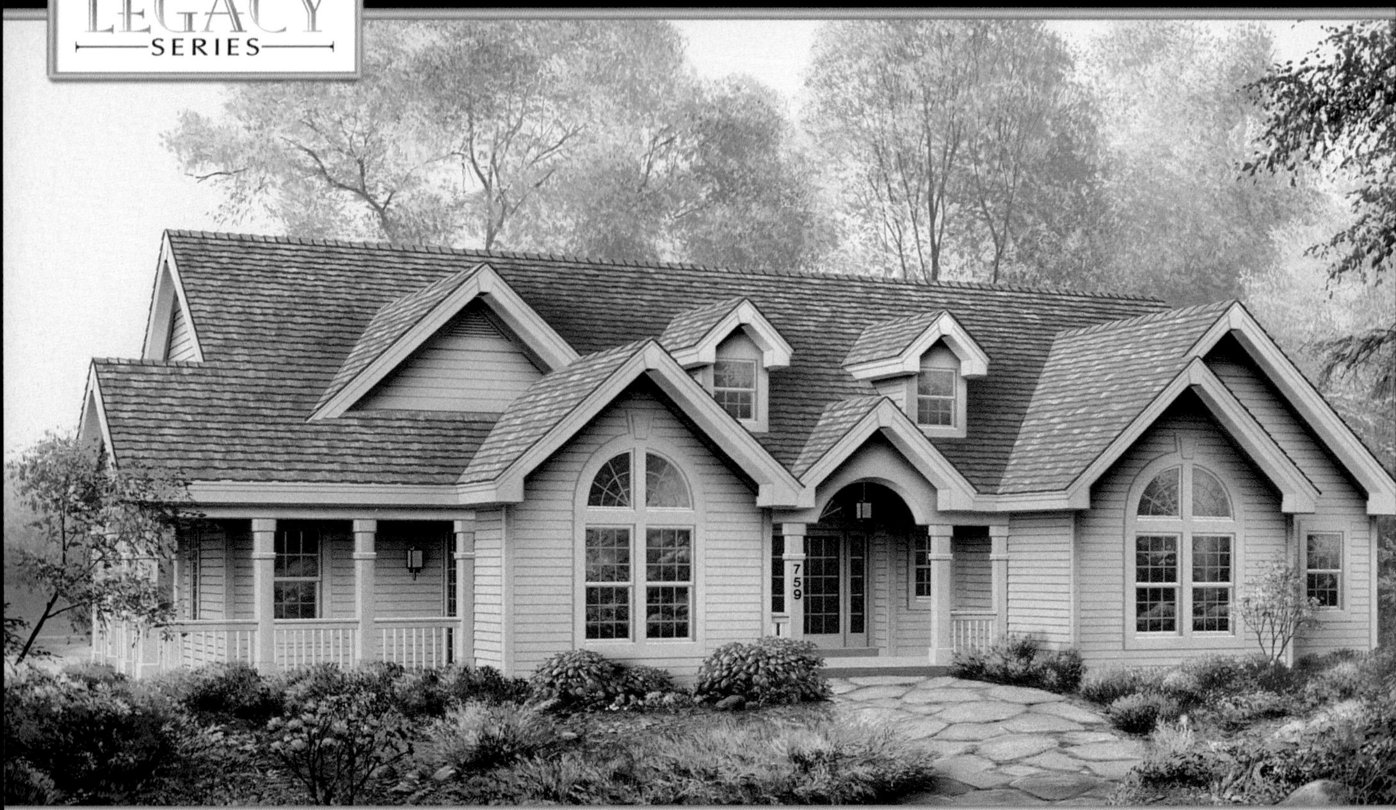

SPECIAL FEATURES

- 2,125 total square feet of living area
- A cozy porch leads to the vaulted great room with fireplace through the entry which has a walk-in closet and bath
- Large and well-arranged kitchen offers spectacular views from its cantilevered sink cabinetry through a two-story atrium window wall
- Master bedroom boasts a sitting room, large walk-in closet and bath with garden tub overhanging a brightly lit atrium
- 1,047 square feet of optional living area on the lower level featuring a study and family room with walk-in bar and full bath below the kitchen
- 3 bedrooms, 2 1/2 baths, 2-car side entry garage
- Walk-out basement foundation

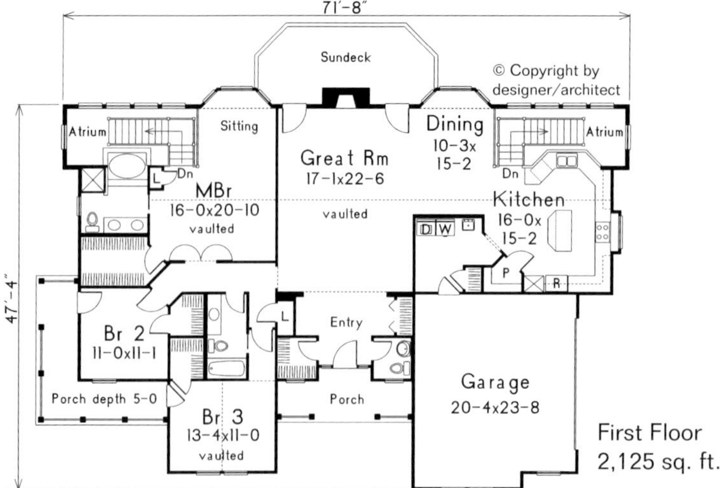

First Floor
2,125 sq. ft.

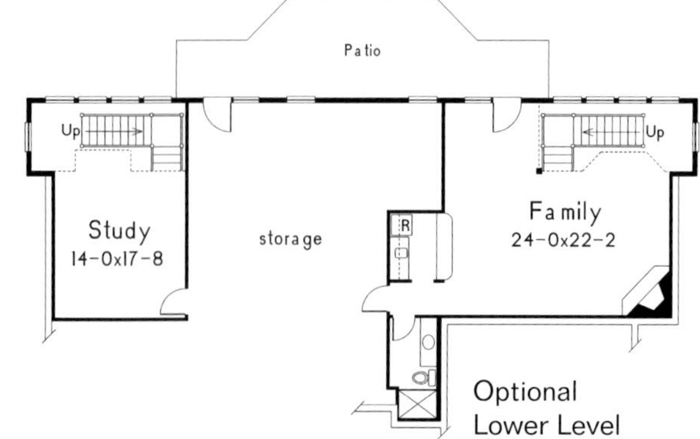

Optional
Lower Level

LOWE'S LEGACY SERIES

SPECIAL FEATURES

- 2,076 total square feet of living area
- Vaulted great room has a fireplace flanked by windows and skylights that welcome the sun
- Kitchen leads to the vaulted breakfast room and rear deck
- Study located off the foyer provides a great location for a home office
- Large bay windows grace the master bedroom and bath
- 3 bedrooms, 2 baths, 2-car garage
- Basement foundation

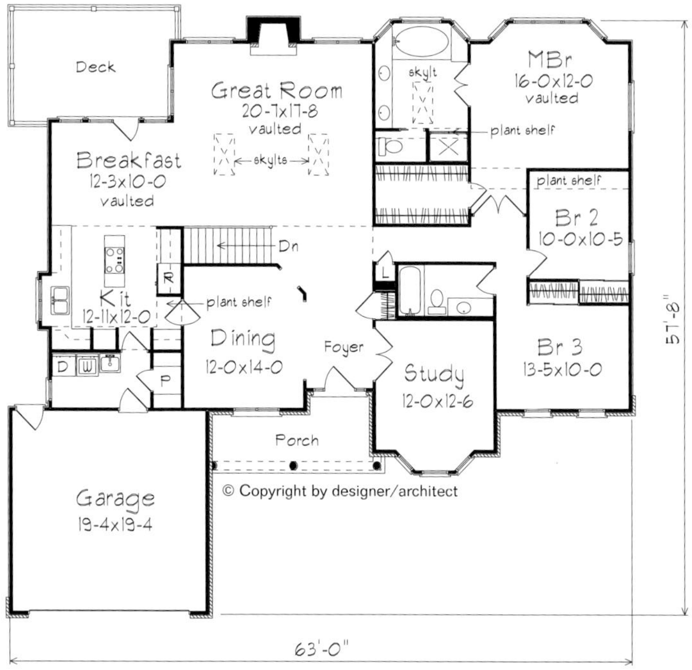

Special Features

- 1,366 total square feet of living area
- Energy efficient home with 2" x 6" exterior walls
- A delightful front porch opens into the roomy living area, perfect for family gatherings
- The kitchen features a wrap-around counter connecting to the dining room that enjoys access to the backyard
- Relax in the master bedroom suite that offers a private bath, dressing area and walk-in closet
- 2 bedrooms, 2 baths, 2-car garage
- Basement foundation

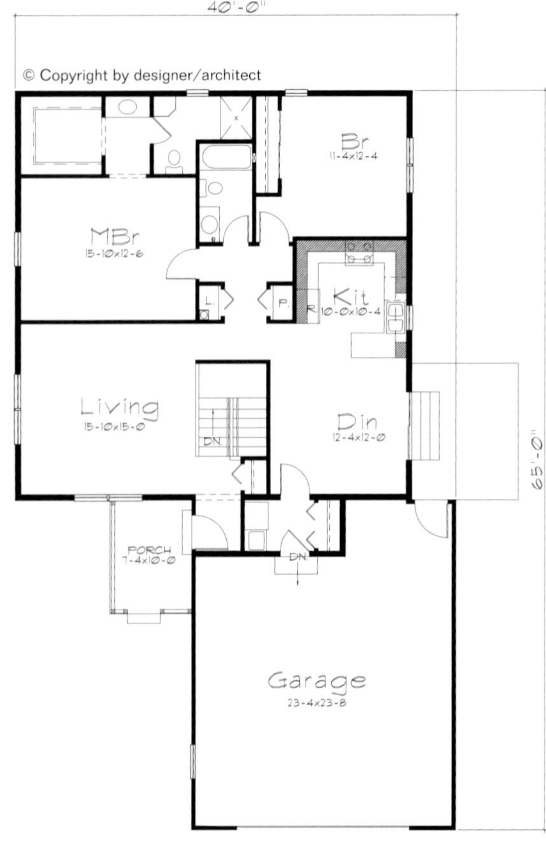

LOWE'S LEGACY SERIES

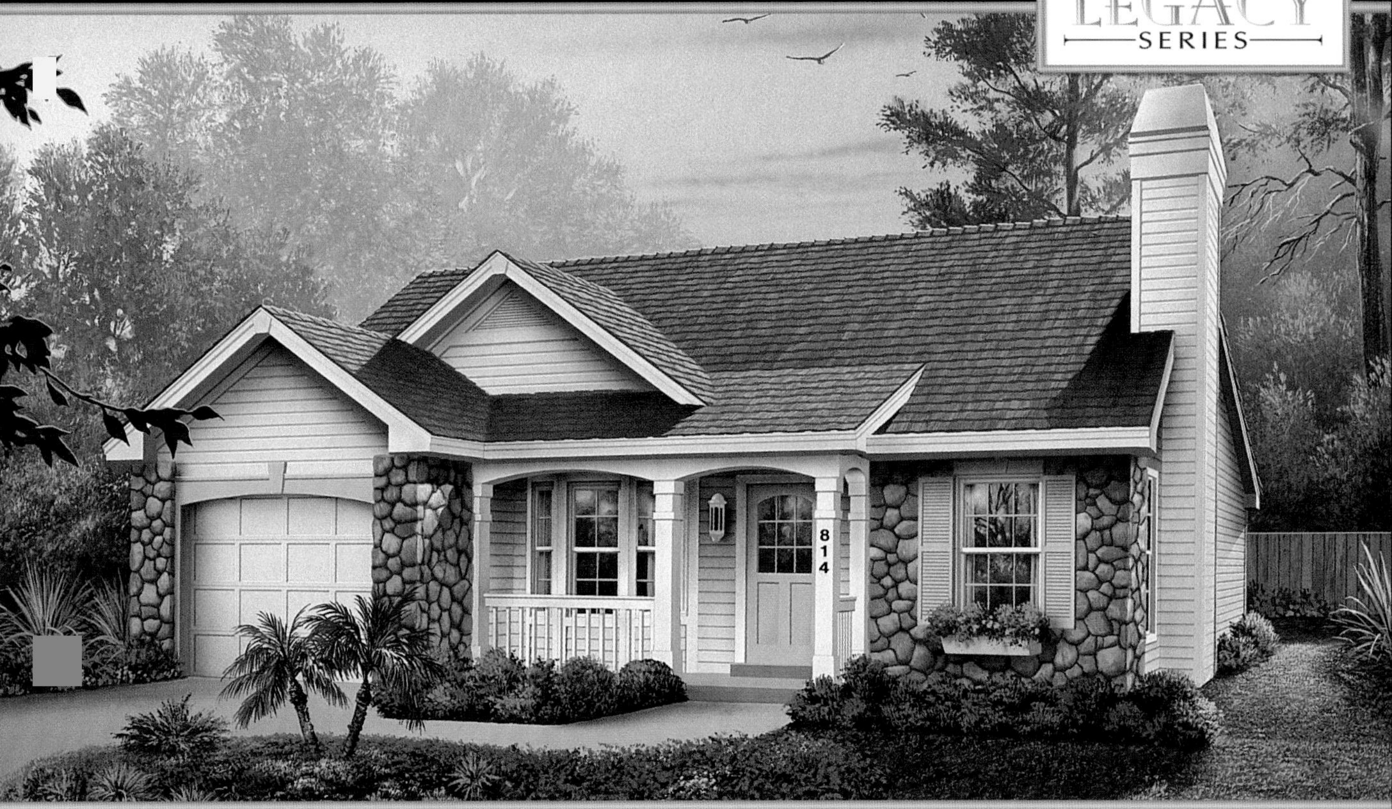

SPECIAL FEATURES

- 1,169 total square feet of living area
- Front facade features a distinctive country appeal
- Living room enjoys a wood-burning fireplace and pass-through to the kitchen
- A stylish U-shaped kitchen offers an abundance of cabinet and counterspace with a view to the living room
- A large walk-in closet, access to the rear patio and a private bath are many features of the master bedroom
- 3 bedrooms, 2 baths, 1-car garage
- Basement foundation

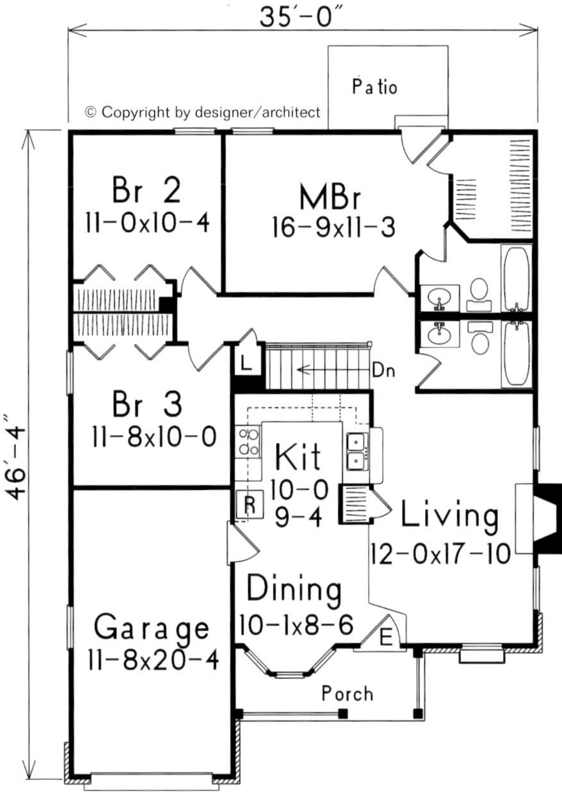

Plan Number: 537-037D-0018 | **Price Code:** AAA

Special Features

- 717 total square feet of living area
- Incline ladder leads up to a cozy loft area
- The living room features plenty of windows and a vaulted ceiling
- U-shaped kitchen includes a small bay window at the sink
- 1 bedroom, 1 bath
- Slab foundation

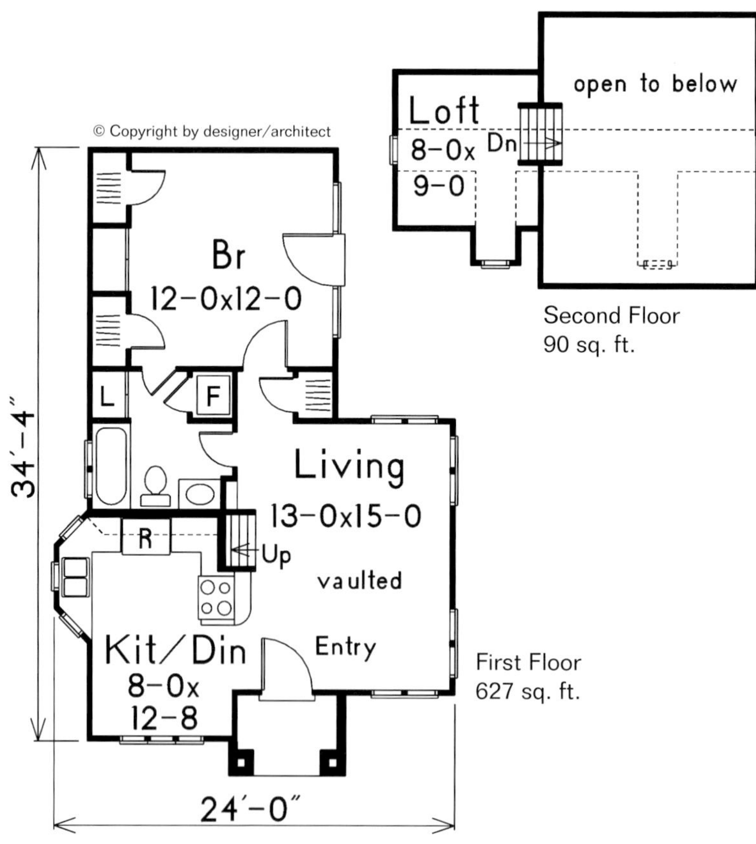

Second Floor
90 sq. ft.

First Floor
627 sq. ft.

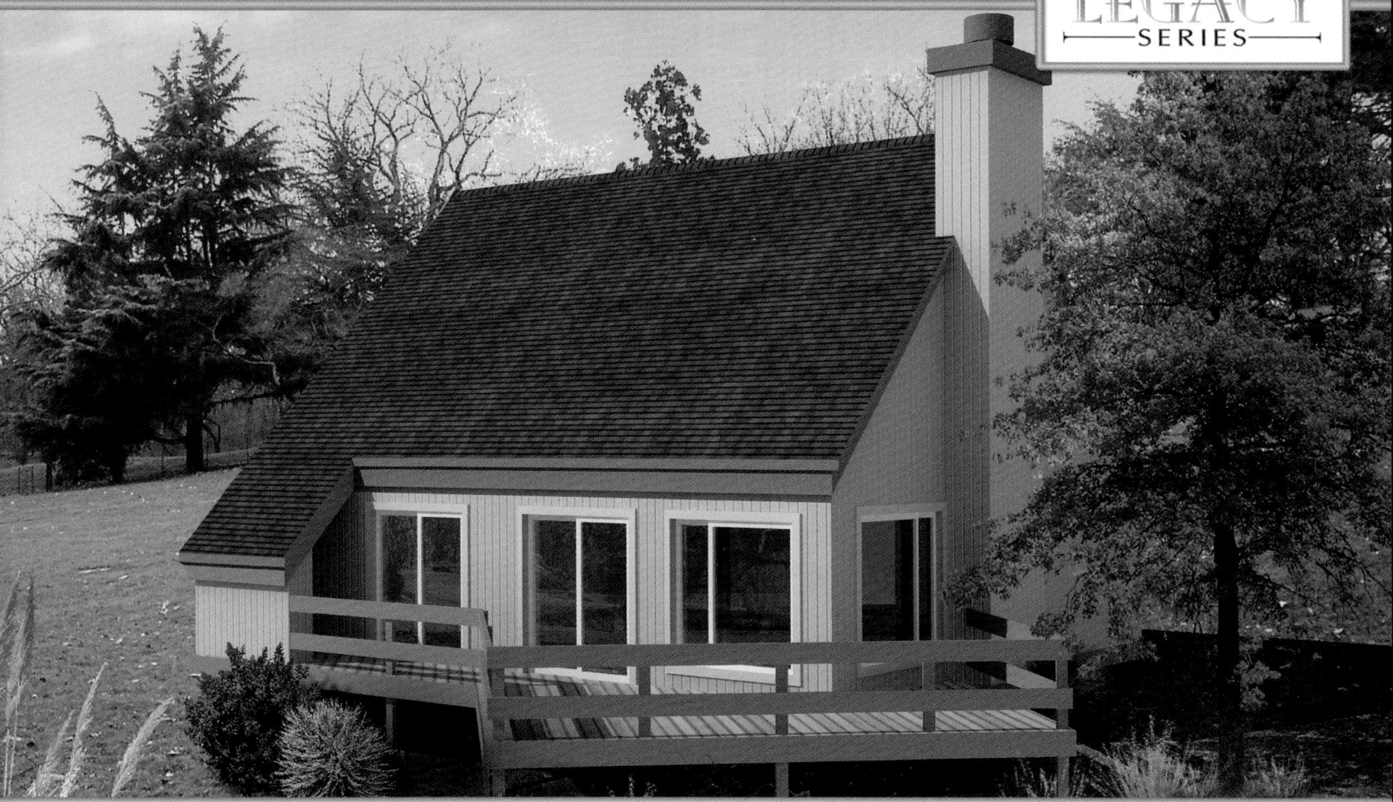

SPECIAL FEATURES

- 1,039 total square feet of living area
- Cathedral construction provides the maximum in living area openness
- Expansive glass viewing walls
- Two decks, front and back
- Charming second story loft arrangement
- Simple, low-maintenance construction
- 2 bedrooms, 1 1/2 baths
- Crawl space foundation

Second Floor
275 sq. ft.

First Floor
764 sq. ft.

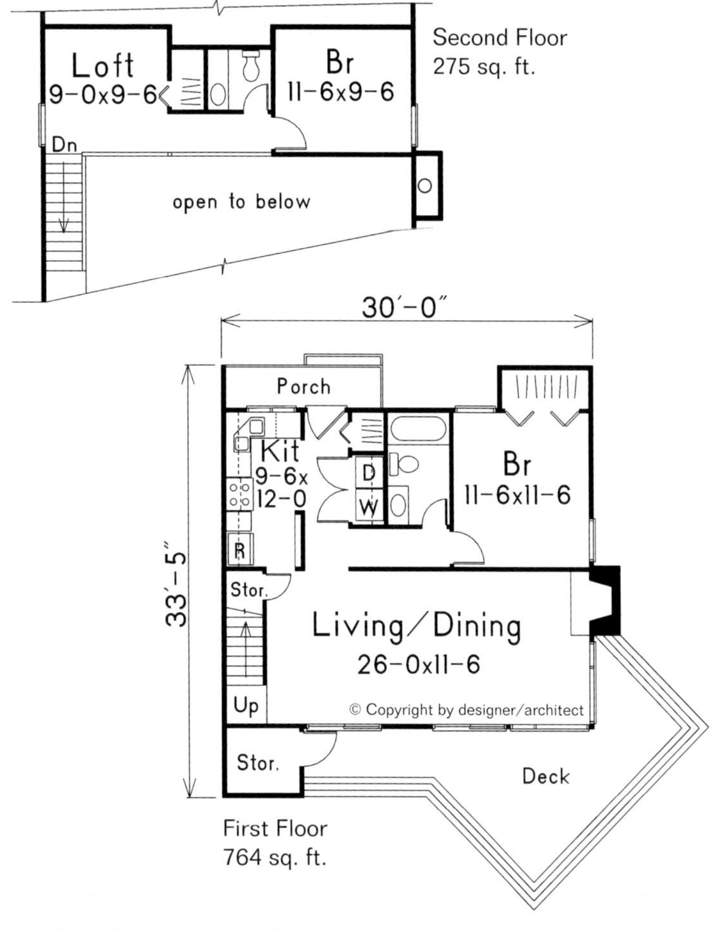

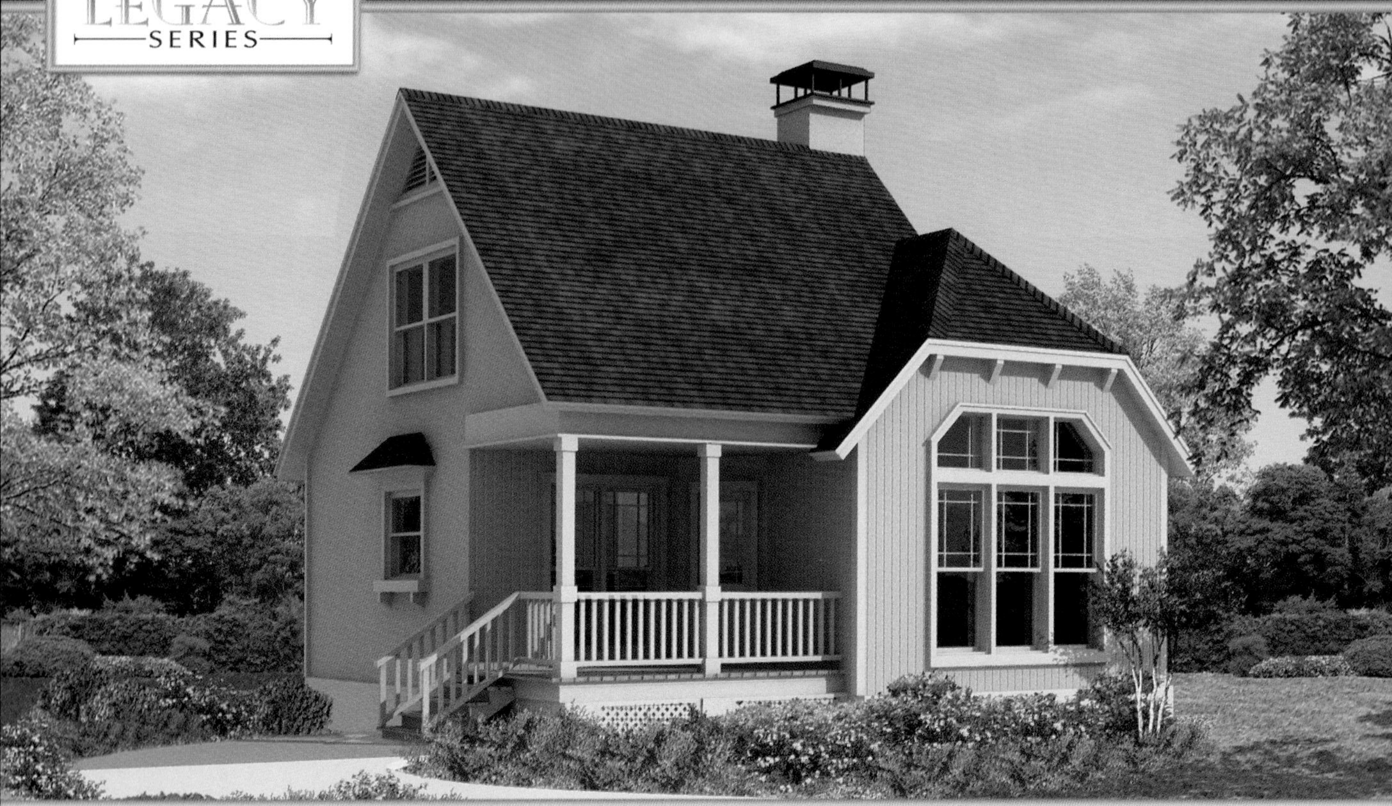

Special Features

- 828 total square feet of living area
- Vaulted ceiling in living area enhances space
- Convenient laundry room
- Sloped ceiling creates unique style in bedroom #2
- Efficient storage space under the stairs
- Covered entry porch provides a cozy sitting area and plenty of shade
- 2 bedrooms, 1 bath
- Crawl space foundation

Second Floor
168 sq. ft.

First Floor
660 sq. ft.

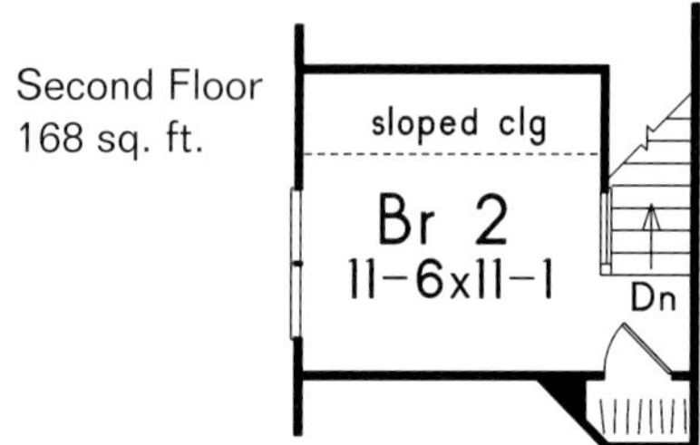

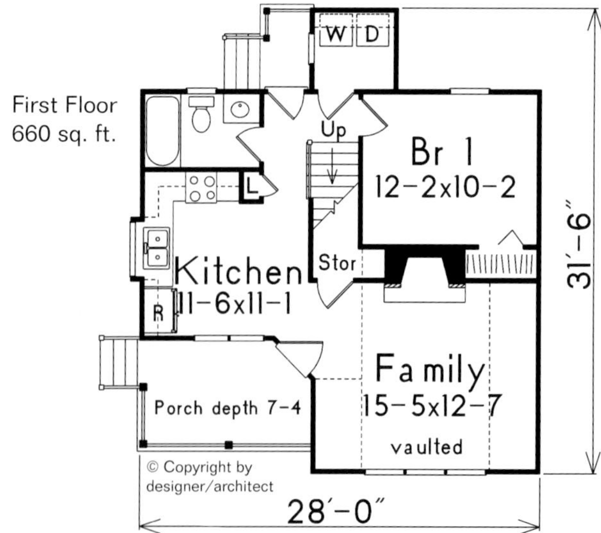

SPECIAL FEATURES

- 1,248 total square feet of living area
- Harmonious design of stonework and gables create the perfect country retreat
- Large country porch is ideal for relaxing on evenings
- Great room and dining area enjoy a vaulted ceiling, corner fireplace and views of rear patio through two sets of sliding doors
- Large walk-in pantry, U-shaped cabinetry and pass-through snack bar are a few features of the smartly designed kitchen
- 2 bedrooms, 1 1/2 baths, 2-car side entry garage
- Basement foundation, drawings also include slab foundation

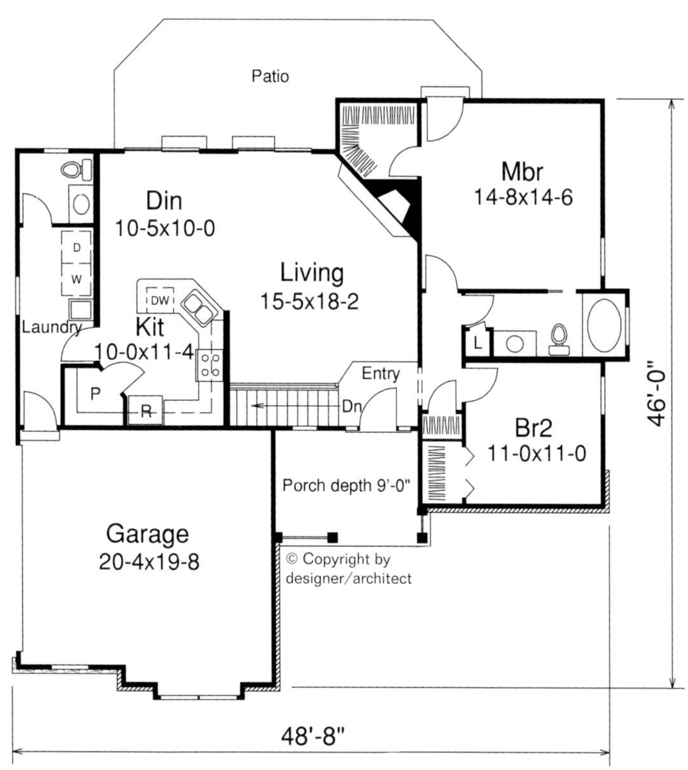

SPECIAL FEATURES

- 1,432 total square feet of living area
- Energy efficient home with 2" x 6" exterior walls
- Enter the two-story foyer from the covered porch or garage
- Living room has a square bay window with seat, glazed end wall with floor-to-ceiling windows and access to the deck
- Kitchen/dining room also opens to the deck for added convenience
- 3 bedrooms, 2 baths, 1-car garage
- Basement foundation, drawings also include slab foundation

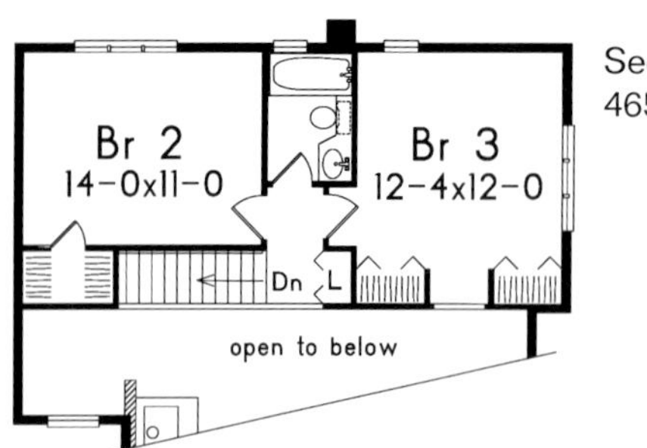

Second Floor
465 sq. ft.

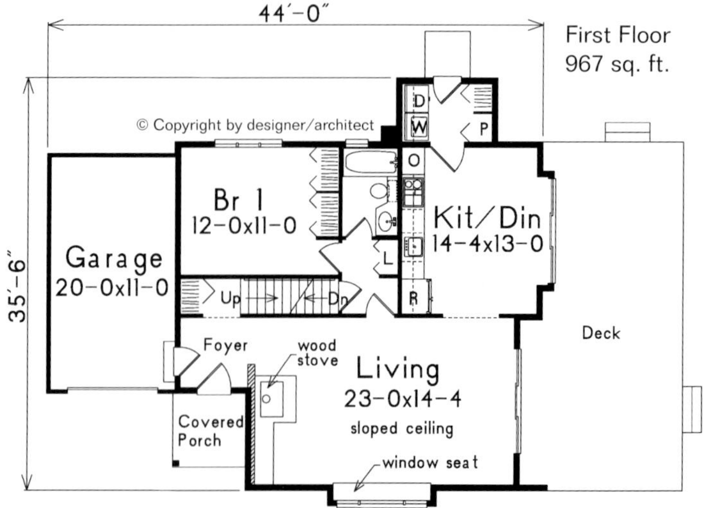

First Floor
967 sq. ft.

LOWE'S LEGACY SERIES

SPECIAL FEATURES

- 888 total square feet of living area
- Home features an eye-catching exterior and has a spacious porch
- The breakfast room with bay window is open to the living room and adjoins the kitchen with pass-through snack bar
- The bedrooms are quite roomy and feature walk-in closets
- The master bedroom has a double-door entry and access to the rear patio
- 2 bedrooms, 1 bath, 1-car garage
- Basement foundation

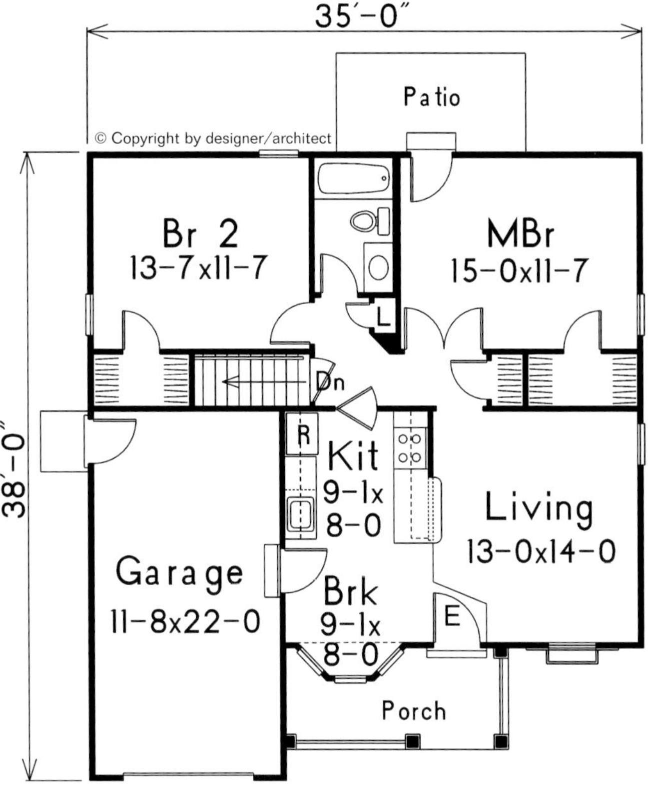

Lowe's Legacy Series

Plan Number: 537-007D-0101 | Price Code: D

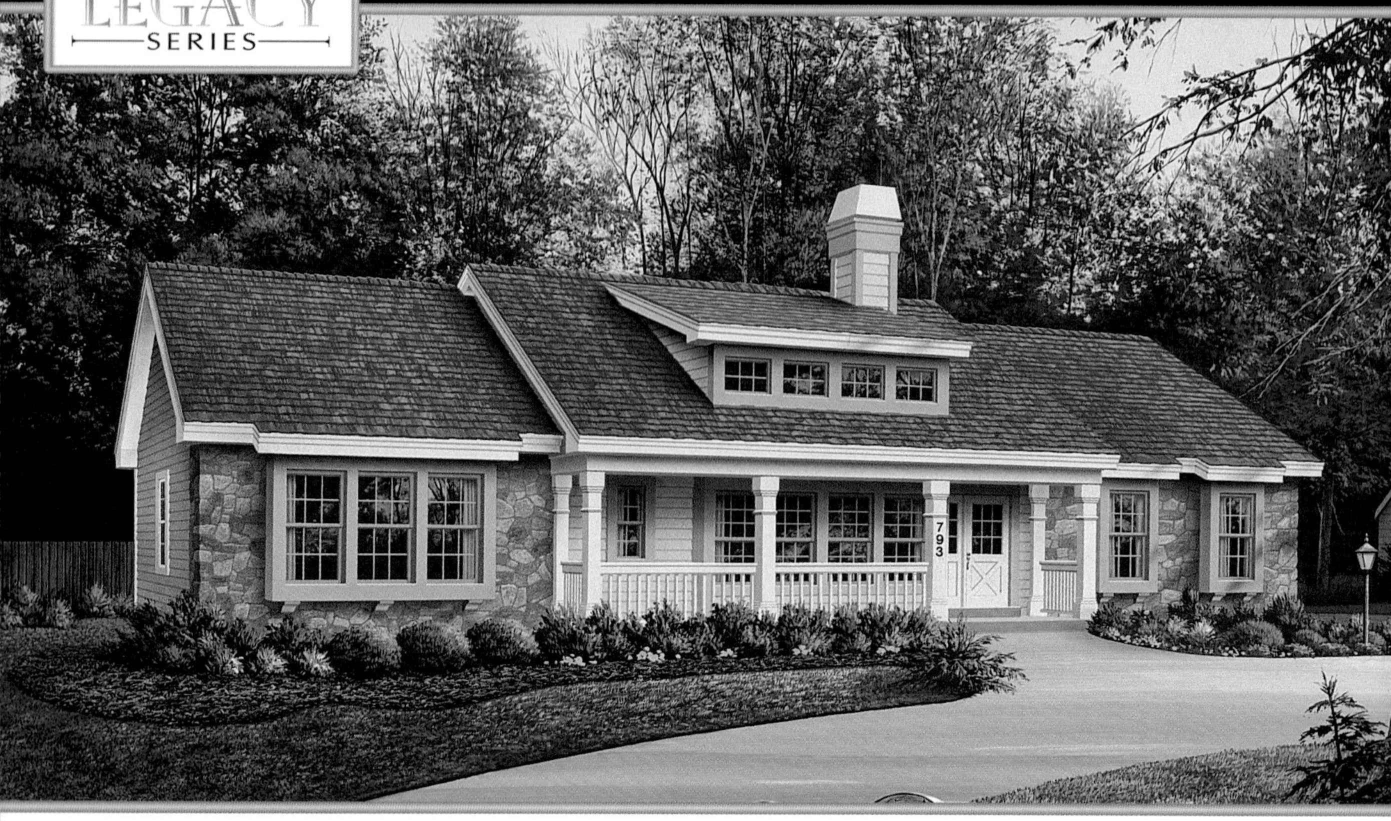

Special Features

- 2,384 total square feet of living area
- Bracketed box windows create an exterior with country charm
- Massive-sized great room features a majestic atrium, fireplace, box window wall, dining balcony and a vaulted ceiling
- An atrium balcony with large bay window off the deck is enjoyed by the spacious breakfast room
- 1,038 square feet of optional living area below with family room, wet bar, bedroom #4 and bath
- 3 bedrooms, 2 1/2 baths, 2-car side entry garage
- Walk-out basement foundation

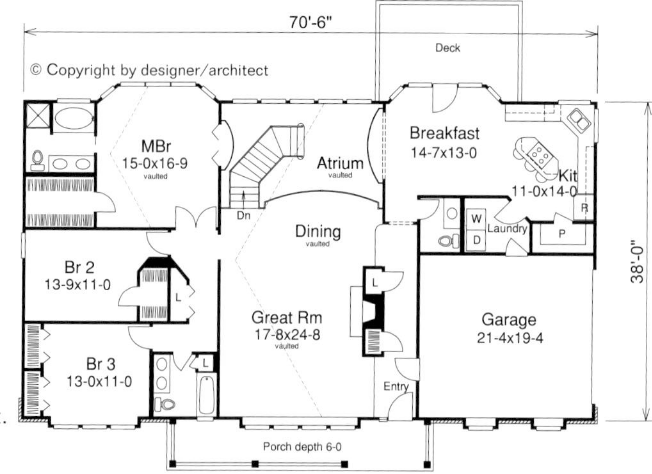

First Floor
2,384 sq. ft.

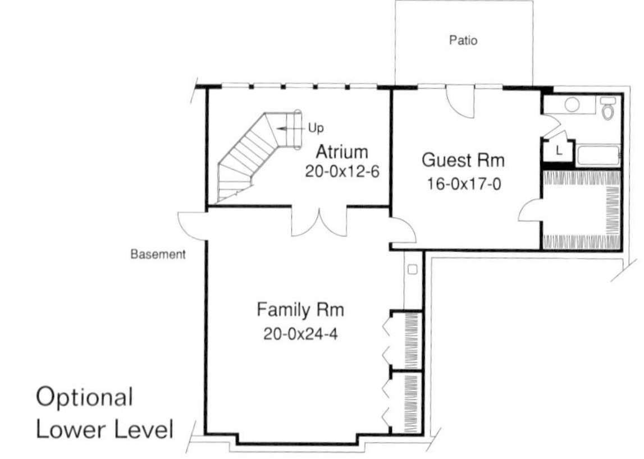

Optional
Lower Level

SPECIAL FEATURES

- 800 total square feet of living area
- Master bedroom has a walk-in closet and private access to the bath
- Large living room features a handy coat closet
- Kitchen includes side entrance, closet and convenient laundry area
- 2 bedrooms, 1 bath
- Crawl space foundation, drawings also include basement foundation

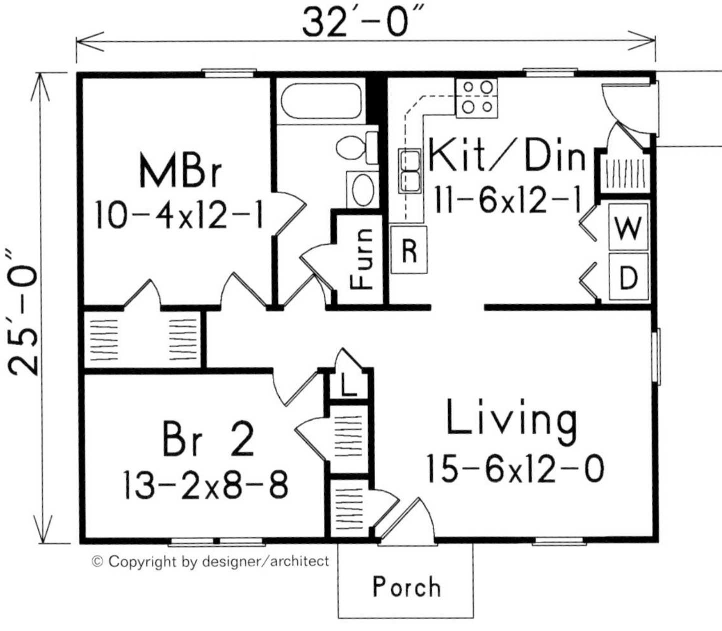

SPECIAL FEATURES

- 2,159 total square feet of living area
- Energy efficient home with 2" x 6" exterior walls
- Covered entry opens into the large foyer with a skylight and coat closet
- Master bedroom includes a private bath with angled vanity, separate spa and shower and walk-in closet
- Family and living rooms feature vaulted ceilings and sunken floors for added openness
- Kitchen features an island counter and convenient pantry
- 3 bedrooms, 2 baths, 2-car garage
- Basement foundation, drawings also include crawl space and slab foundations

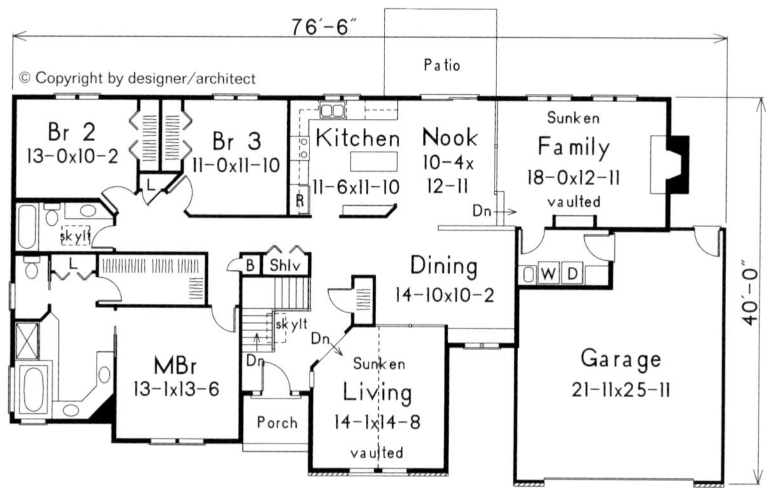

Plan Number: 537-001D-0081 | Price Code: AA

Lowe's Legacy Series

Special Features

- 1,160 total square feet of living area
- U-shaped kitchen includes breakfast bar and convenient laundry area
- Master bedroom features private half bath and large closet
- Dining room has outdoor access
- Dining and great rooms combine to create an open living atmosphere
- 3 bedrooms, 1 1/2 baths
- Crawl space foundation, drawings also include basement and slab foundations

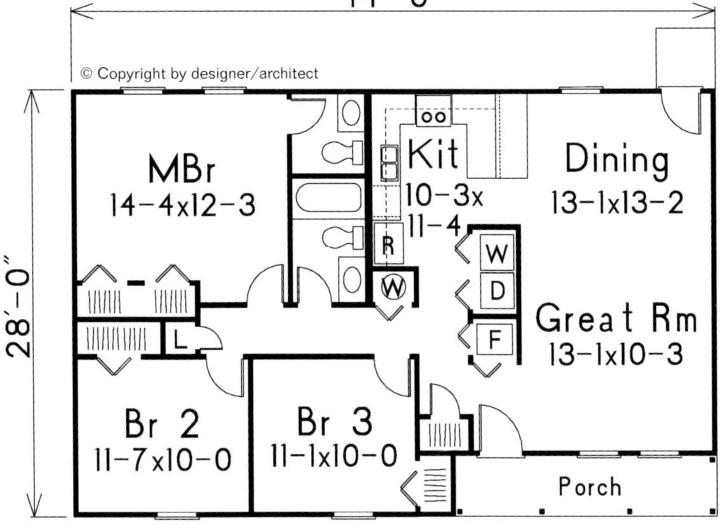

SPECIAL FEATURES

- 1,950 total square feet of living area
- Large corner kitchen with island cooktop opens to the family room
- Master bedroom features a double-door entry, raised ceiling, double-bowl vanity and walk-in closet
- Plant shelf accents hall
- 4 bedrooms, 2 baths, 3-car garage
- Crawl space foundation

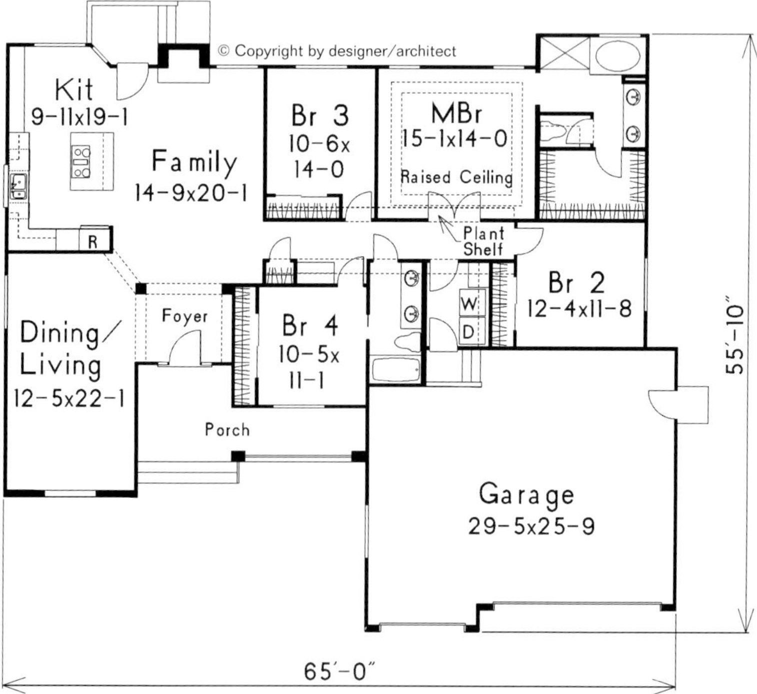

SPECIAL FEATURES

- 1,232 total square feet of living area
- Ideal porch for quiet quality evenings
- Great room opens to dining room for those large dinner gatherings
- Functional L-shaped kitchen includes broom cabinet
- Master bedroom contains a large walk-in closet and compartmented bath
- 3 bedrooms, 1 bath, optional 2-car garage
- Basement foundation, drawings also include crawl space and slab foundations

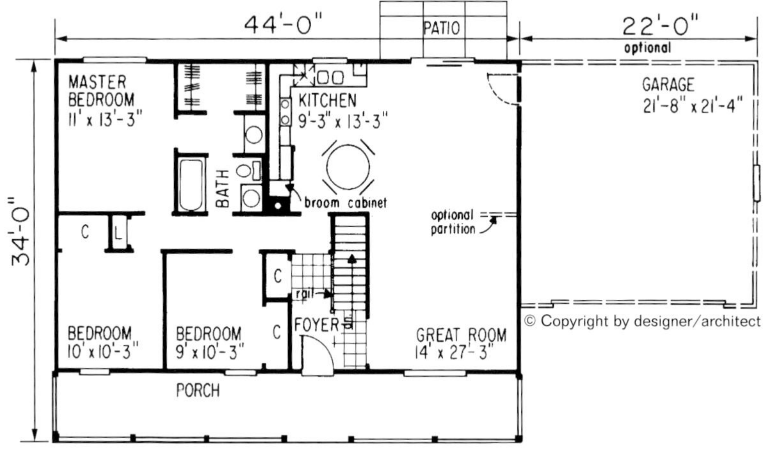

Special Features

- 2,056 total square feet of living area
- Columned foyer projects past the living and dining rooms into the family room
- Kitchen conveniently accesses the dining room and breakfast area
- Master bedroom features double-door access to the patio and a pocket door to the private bath with walk-in closet, double-bowl vanity and tub
- 4 bedrooms, 2 baths, 2-car garage
- Slab foundation, drawings also include crawl space foundation

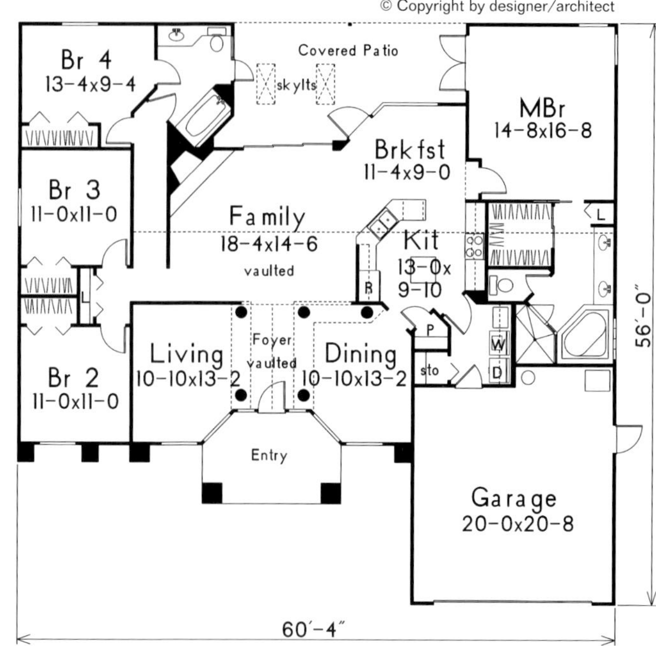

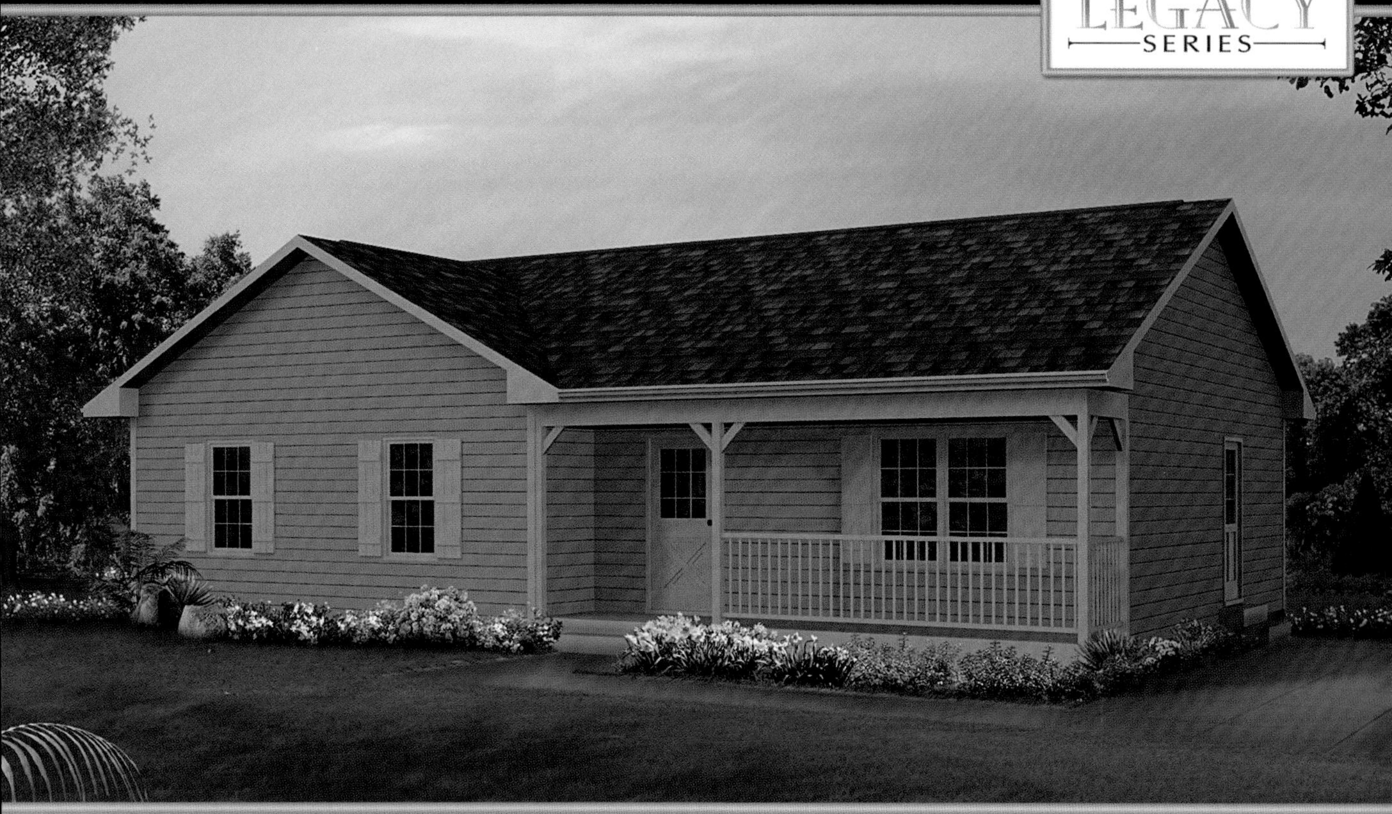

SPECIAL FEATURES

- 1,197 total square feet of living area
- U-shaped kitchen includes ample workspace, breakfast bar, laundry area and direct access to the outdoors
- Large living room has a convenient coat closet
- Bedroom #1 features a large walk-in closet
- 2" x 6" exterior walls available, please order plan #537-001D-0102
- 3 bedrooms, 1 bath
- Crawl space foundation, drawings also include basement and slab foundations

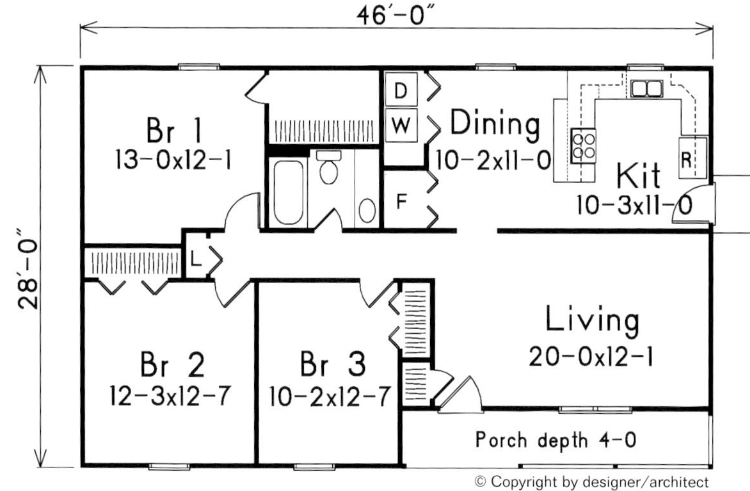

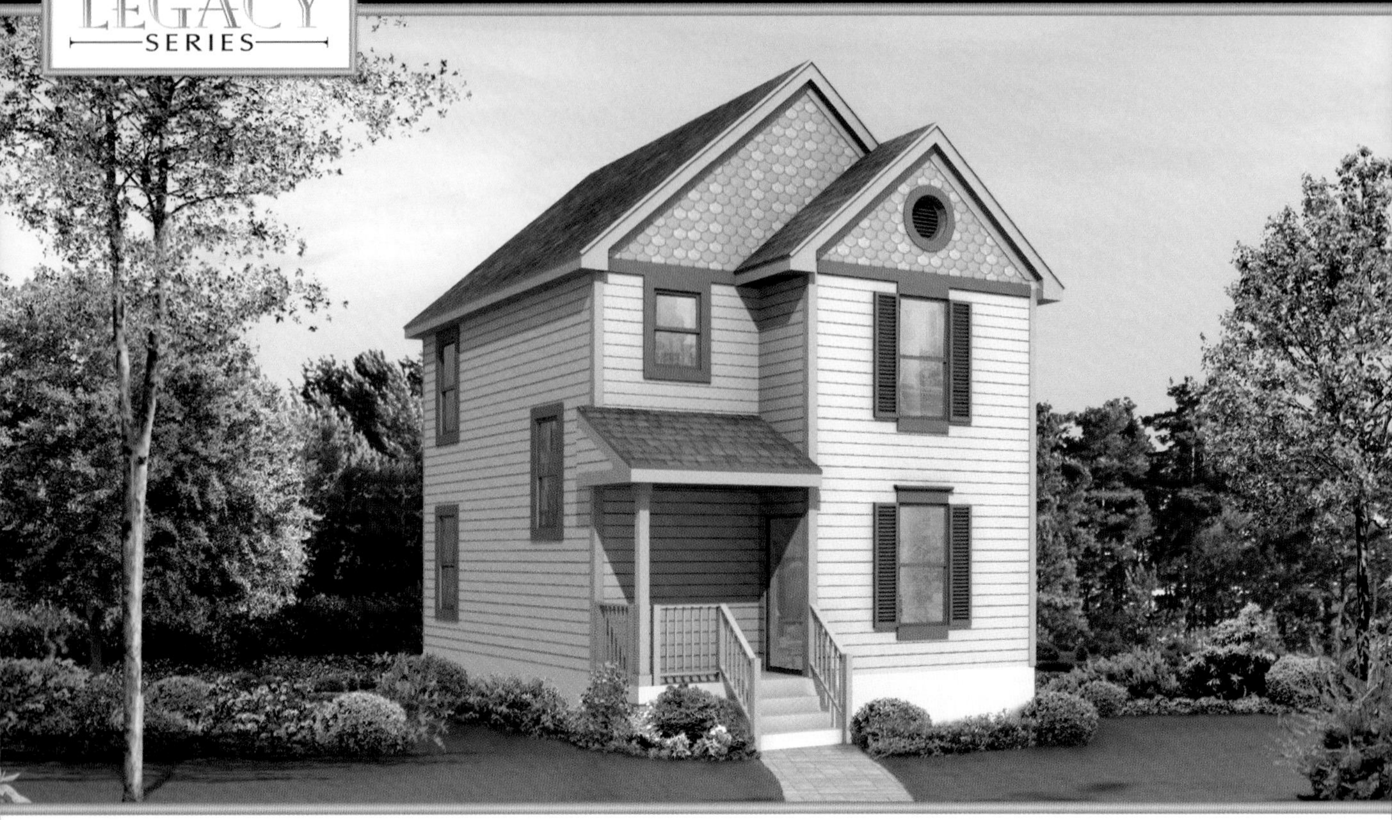

SPECIAL FEATURES

- 976 total square feet of living area
- Cozy front porch opens into the large living room
- Convenient half bath is located on the first floor
- All bedrooms are located on the second floor for privacy
- Dining room has access to the outdoors
- 3 bedrooms, 1 1/2 baths
- Basement foundation

First Floor
488 sq. ft.

Second Floor
488 sq. ft.

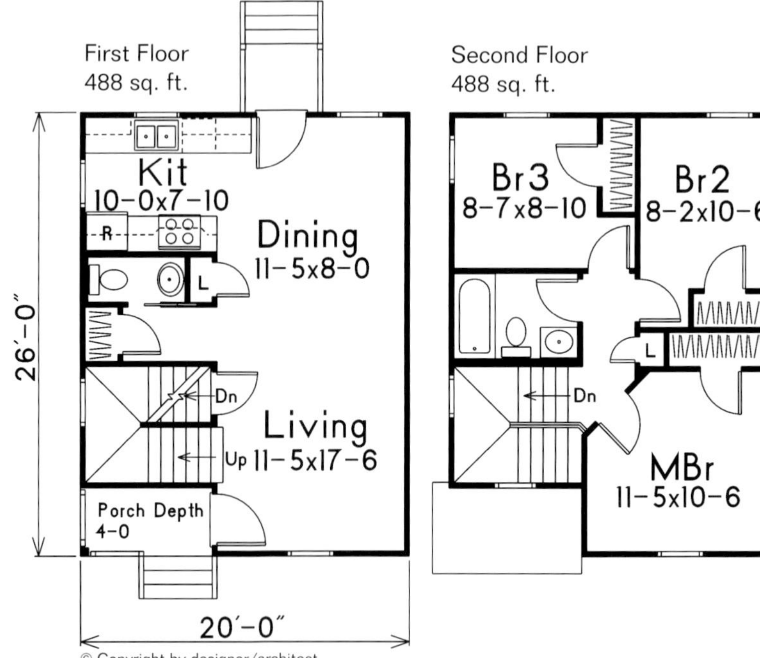

LOWE'S LEGACY SERIES

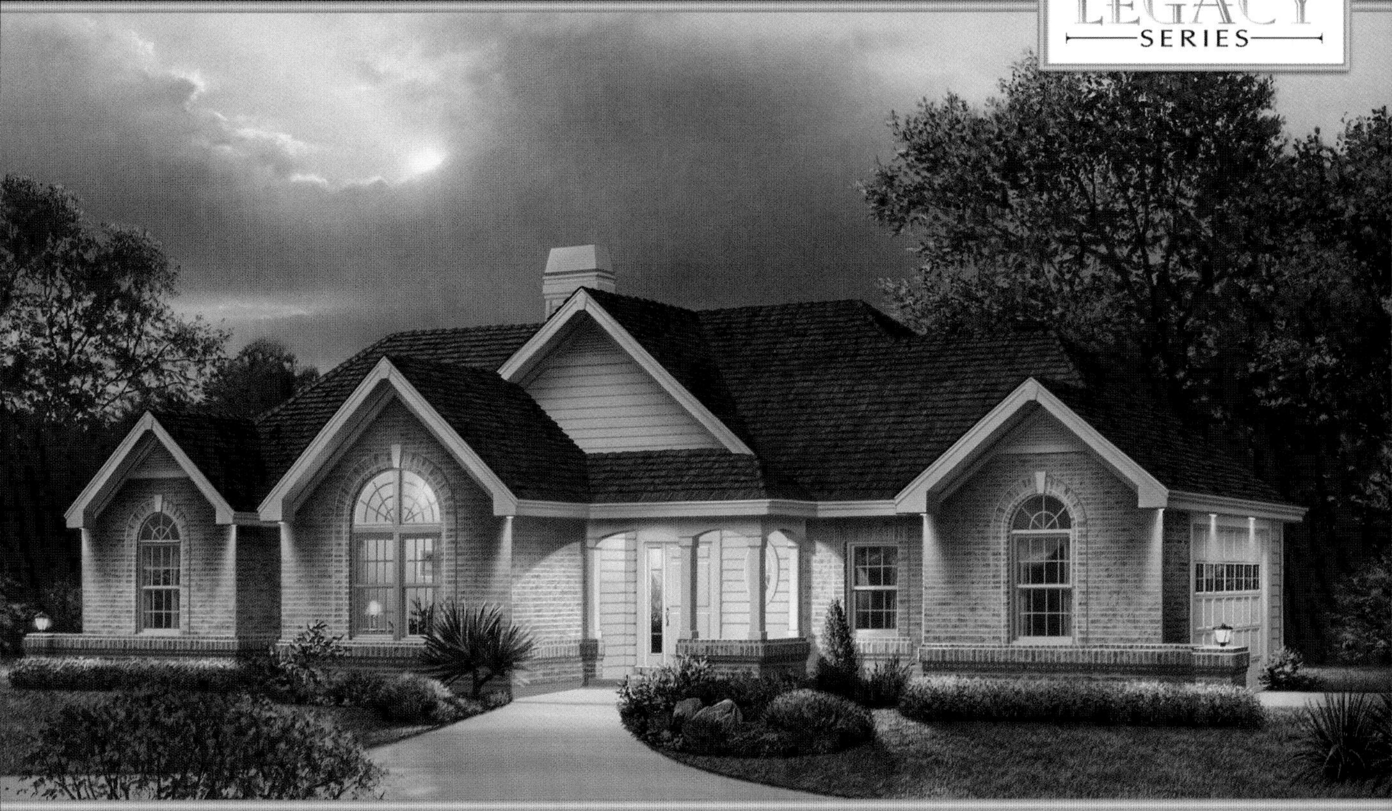

SPECIAL FEATURES

- 1,973 total square feet of living area
- The impressive great room includes a vaulted ceiling, fireplace and 10' high feature windows
- A center island, built-in pantry and corner sink with windows are a few amenities of the kitchen that has access to a large deck
- The morning/breakfast room includes a see-through fireplace and balcony overlook of the atrium and rear yard through a 13' x 14' feature window wall
- The master bedroom suite offers an expansive bay window, convenient linen closet and luxury bath
- 4 bedrooms, 2 1/2 baths, 2-car side entry garage
- Walk-out basement foundation, drawings also include slab and crawl space foundations

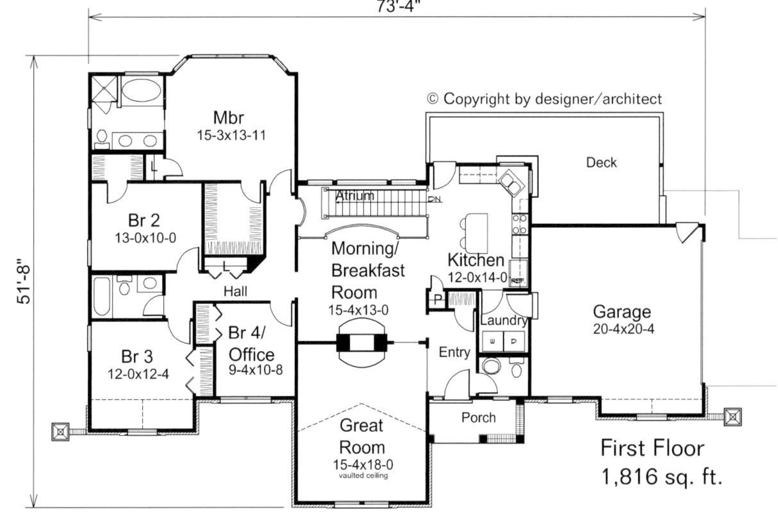

First Floor
1,816 sq. ft.

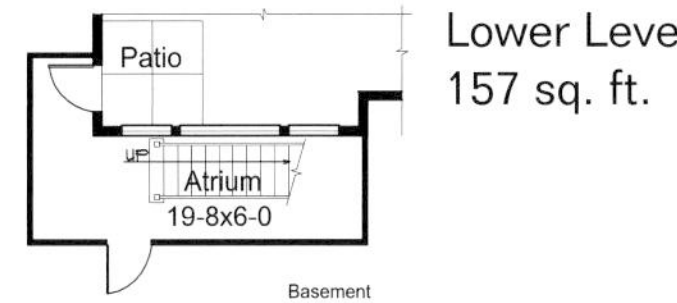

Lower Level
157 sq. ft.

PLAN NUMBER: 537-053D-0037 | PRICE CODE: A

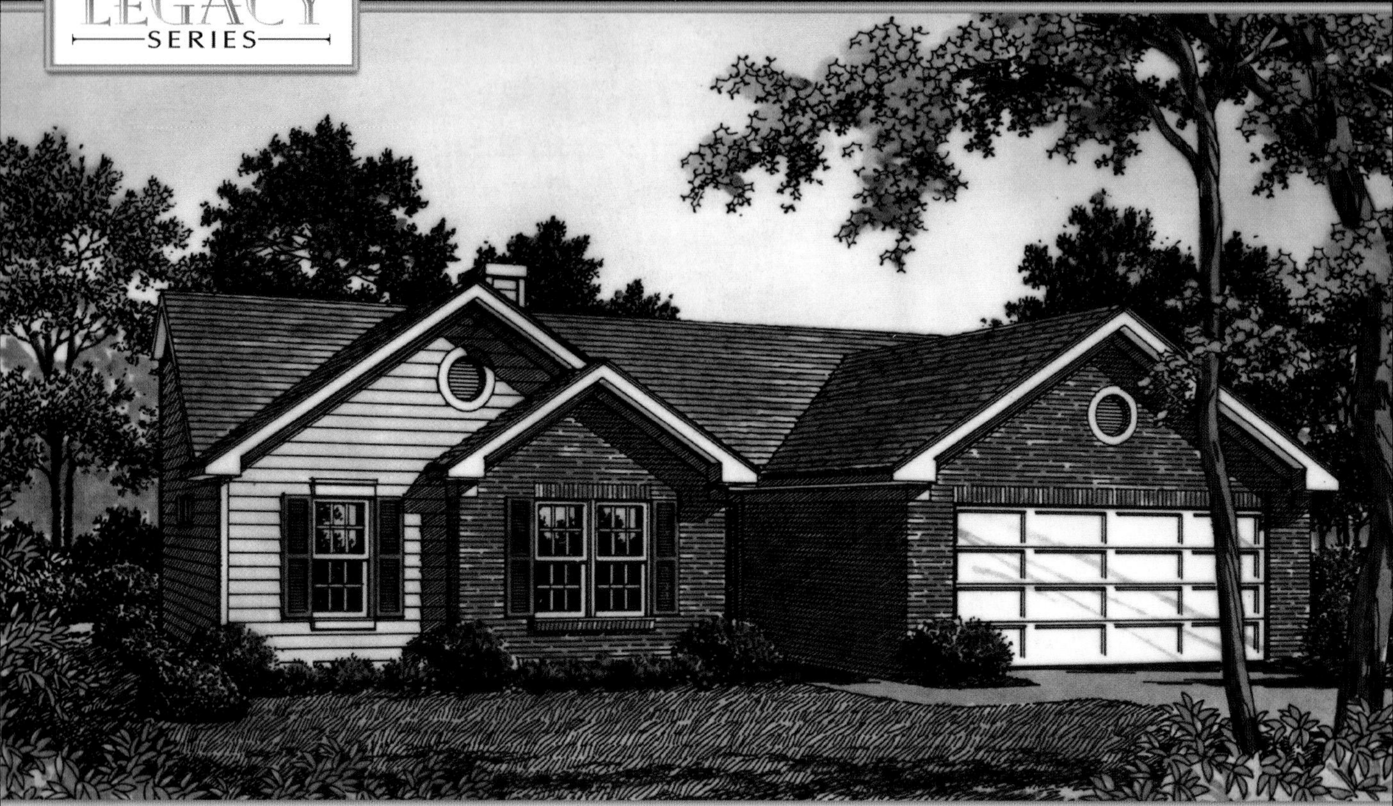

SPECIAL FEATURES

- 1,388 total square feet of living area
- Handsome see-through fireplace offers a gathering point for the kitchen, family and breakfast rooms
- Vaulted ceiling and large bay window in the master bedroom add charm to this room
- A dramatic angular wall and large windows add brightness to the kitchen and breakfast room
- Kitchen, breakfast and family rooms have vaulted ceilings, adding to this central living area
- 3 bedrooms, 2 baths, 2-car garage
- Crawl space foundation, drawings also include slab foundation

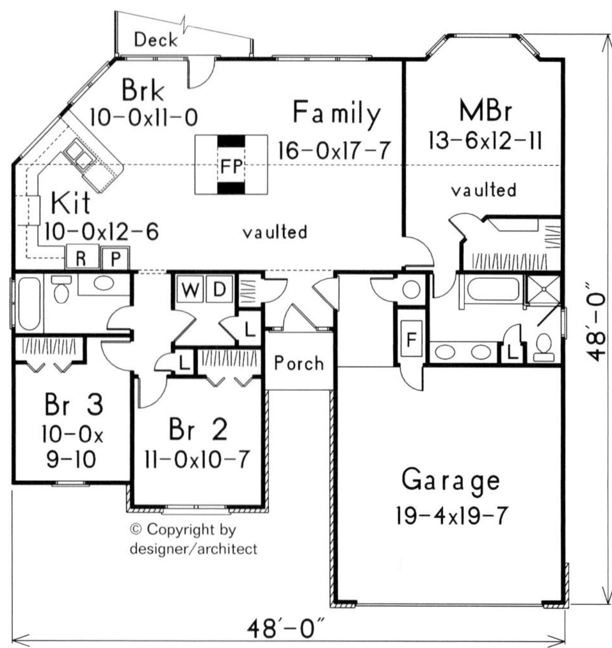

LOWE'S LEGACY SERIES

SPECIAL FEATURES

- 1,838 total square feet of living area
- Energy efficient home with 2" x 6" exterior walls
- The angled great room features a corner fireplace, French doors to the rear deck and connects to the dining room for a spacious atmosphere
- The wrap-around kitchen counter offers plenty of workspace and room for casual meals
- Retreat to the master bedroom where a deluxe bath, walk-in closet and deck access will pamper the homeowners
- 3 bedrooms, 2 baths, 2-car garage
- Crawl space foundation, drawings also include basement foundation

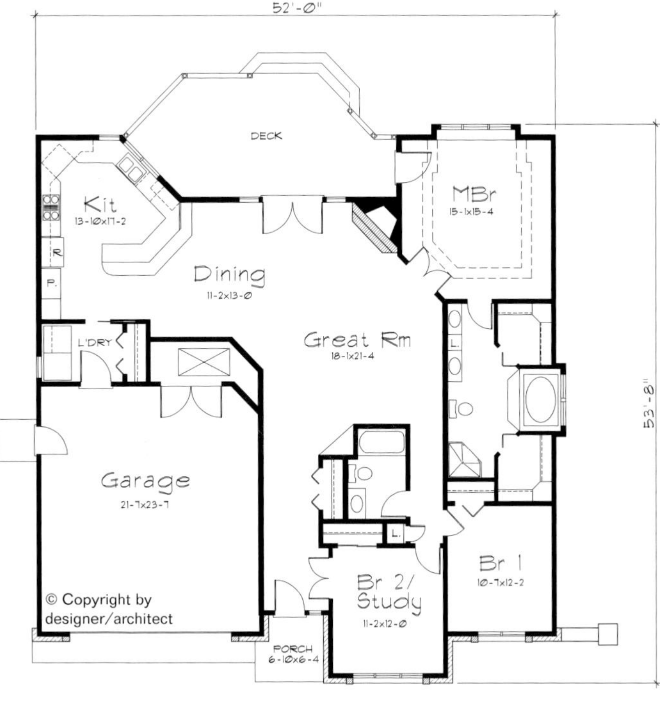

PLAN NUMBER: 537-061D-0003 | PRICE CODE: D

SPECIAL FEATURES

- 2,255 total square feet of living area
- Walk-in closets are found in all the bedrooms
- Plant shelf graces hallway
- Large functional kitchen adjoins the family room which features a fireplace and access outdoors
- Master bath comes complete with a double vanity, enclosed toilet, separate tub and shower and cozy fireplace
- Living/dining room combine for a large formal gathering room
- 4 bedrooms, 2 1/2 baths, 3-car garage
- Slab foundation

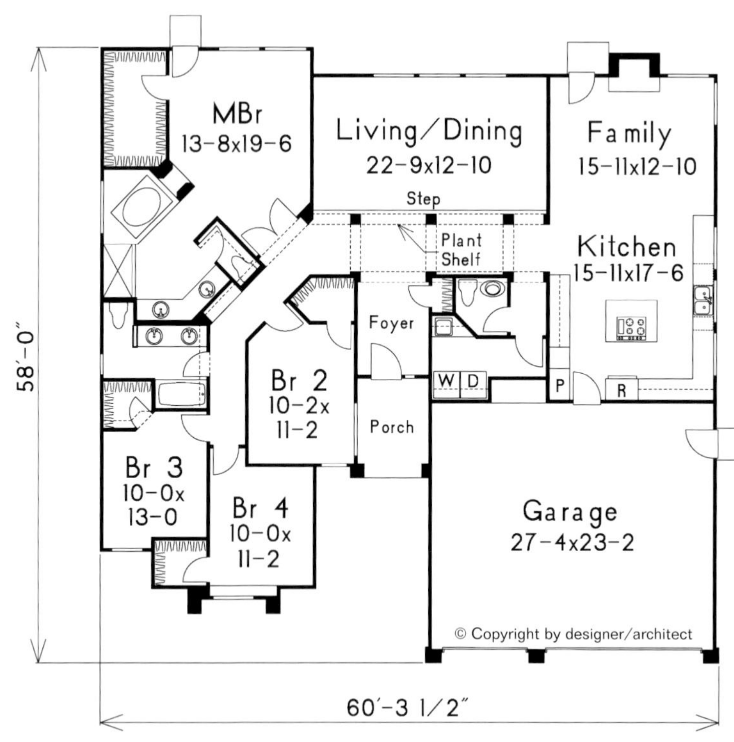

SPECIAL FEATURES

- 676 total square feet of living area
- See-through fireplace between bedroom and living area adds character
- Combined dining and living areas create an open feeling
- Full-length front covered porch is perfect for enjoying the outdoors
- Additional storage is available in the utility room
- 2" x 6" exterior walls available, please order plan #537-058D-0074
- 1 bedroom, 1 bath
- Crawl space foundation

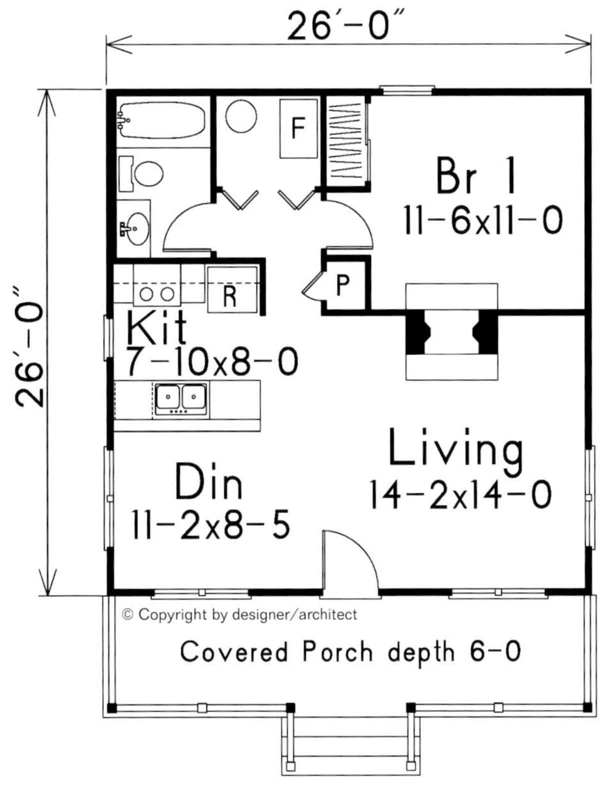

SPECIAL FEATURES

- 1,433 total square feet of living area
- Vaulted living room includes a cozy fireplace and an oversized entertainment center
- Bedrooms #2 and #3 share a full bath
- Master bedroom has a full bath and large walk-in closet
- 3 bedrooms, 2 baths, 2-car garage
- Basement foundation, drawings also include crawl space and slab foundations

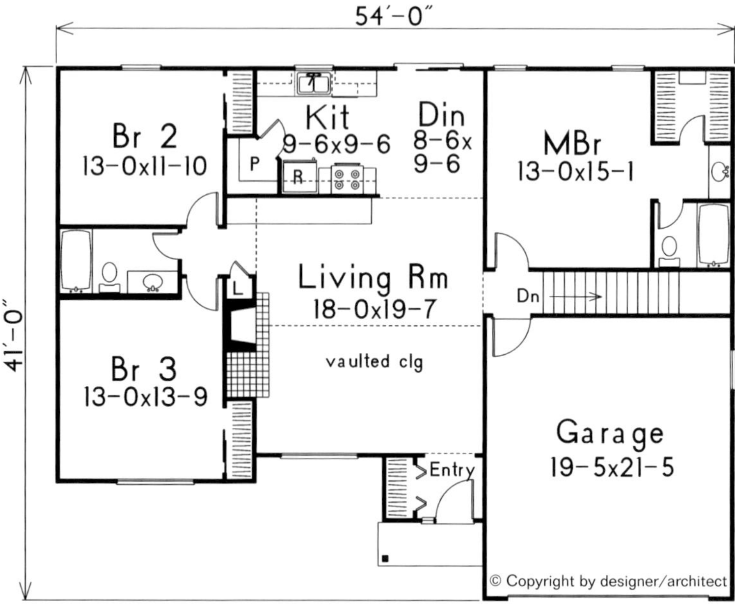

LOWE'S LEGACY SERIES

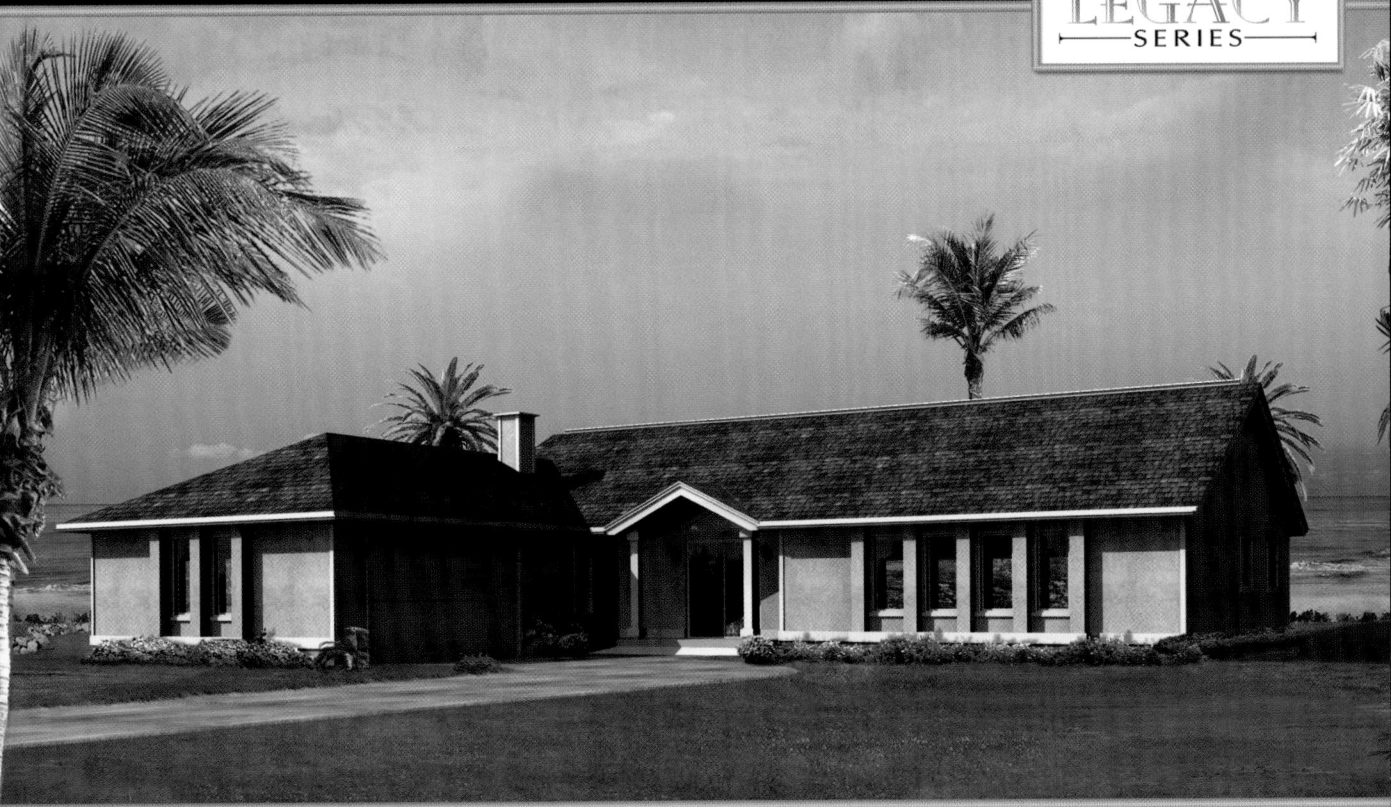

SPECIAL FEATURES

- 1,960 total square feet of living area
- Comforts abound in this well-designed ranch
- Sunlit entryway leads to activity area with corner fireplace at rear of home
- U-shaped kitchen with built-in pantry and desk is adjacent to the dining room with an optional deck
- Large laundry room with a half bath is conveniently located adjacent to the garage and just off the kitchen
- Master bedroom features a large walk-in closet, dressing area with makeup vanity and compartmented bath with shower and raised tub
- Two additional bedrooms are served with a full bath
- 3 bedrooms, 2 1/2 baths, 2-car side entry garage
- Slab foundation

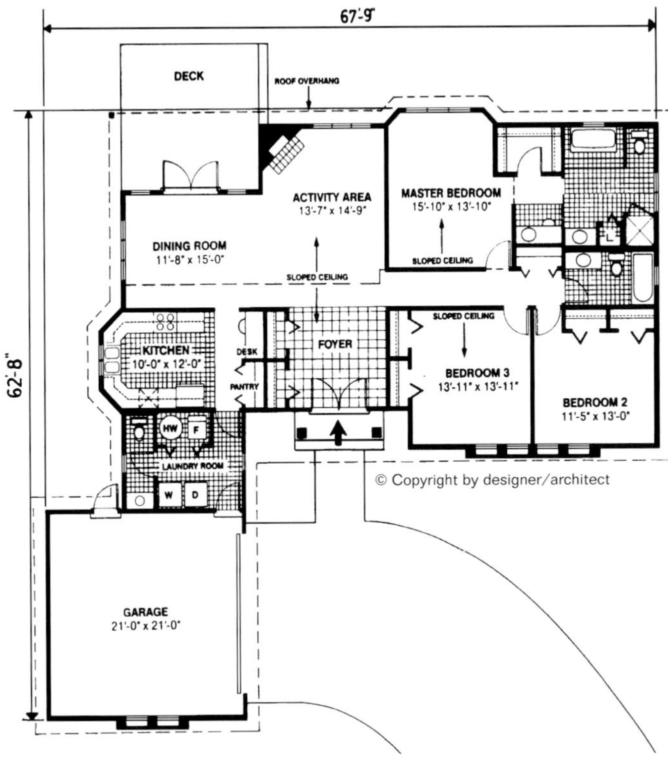

Plan Number: 537-007D-0192 | Price Code: B

Special Features

- 1,420 total square feet of living area
- The exterior features fancy brickwork, attractive roof dormers and a porch large enough for outdoor furniture
- The large living room includes a private entry with guest closet and a fireplace with adjacent shelving
- A big dining area with huge built-in pantry is open to a spacious U-shaped kitchen while both enjoy views of the rear patio through glass sliding doors
- 3 bedrooms, 2 baths, 2-car garage
- Basement foundation, drawings also include slab and crawl space foundations

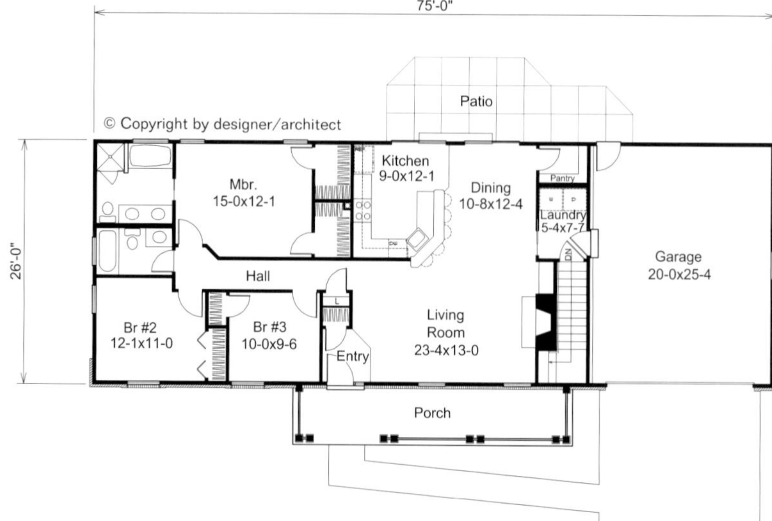

Plan Number: 537-057D-0023 | Price Code: B

Lowe's Legacy Series

Special Features

- 1,674 total square feet of living area
- Energy efficient home with 2" x 6" exterior walls
- Covered entrance opens to find open living and dining rooms that are designed for entertaining
- A quiet study could also be used as a guest bedroom
- The master bedroom is secluded on the first floor while two additional bedrooms share the second floor
- 3 bedrooms, 2 baths
- Basement foundation

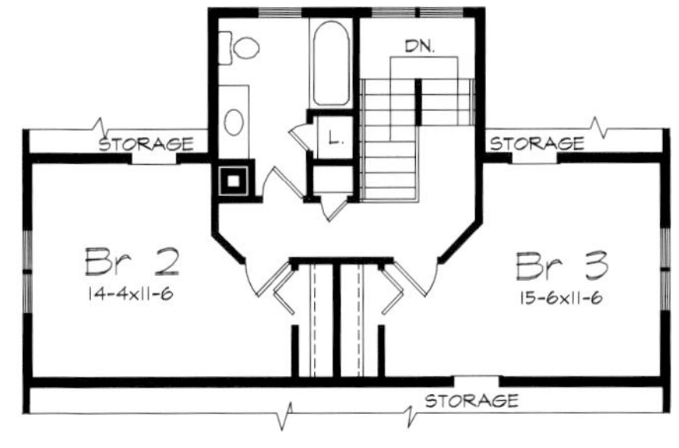

Second Floor
570 sq. ft.

First Floor
1,104 sq. ft.

Special Features

- 1,416 total square feet of living area
- Excellent floor plan eases traffic
- Master bedroom features a private bath
- Foyer opens to both a formal living room and an informal great room
- Great room has access to the outdoors through sliding doors
- 3 bedrooms, 2 baths, 2-car garage
- Crawl space foundation, drawings also include basement foundation

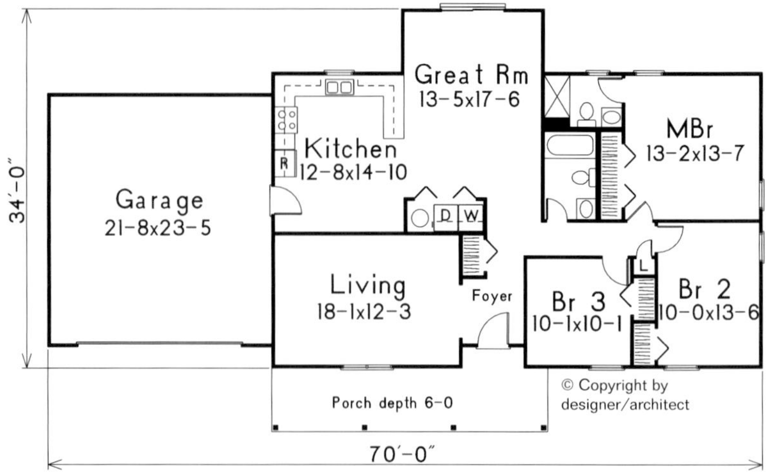

LOWE'S LEGACY SERIES

SPECIAL FEATURES

- 1,345 total square feet of living area
- Brick front details add a touch of elegance
- Master bedroom has a private full bath
- Great room combines with the dining area creating a sense of spaciousness
- Garage includes a handy storage area which could easily convert to a workshop space
- 3 bedrooms, 2 baths, 2-car side entry garage
- Basement foundation, drawings also include crawl space and slab foundations

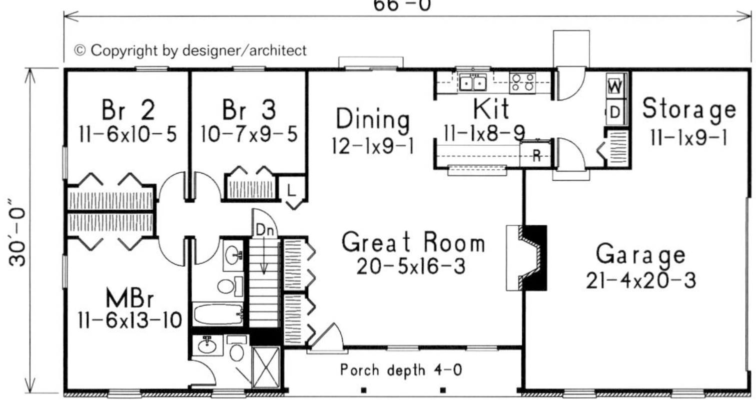

SPECIAL FEATURES

- 1,117 total square feet of living area
- Energy efficient home with 2" x 6" exterior walls
- A wide deck opens to the combined living room and kitchen/breakfast area that span two-stories high
- Windows flood this vacation home with an abundance of light, keeping the area bright and cheerful
- The second floor loft offers a spacious area perfect for a play room or home theater
- 2 bedrooms, 1 bath
- Basement foundation

Second Floor
327 sq. ft.

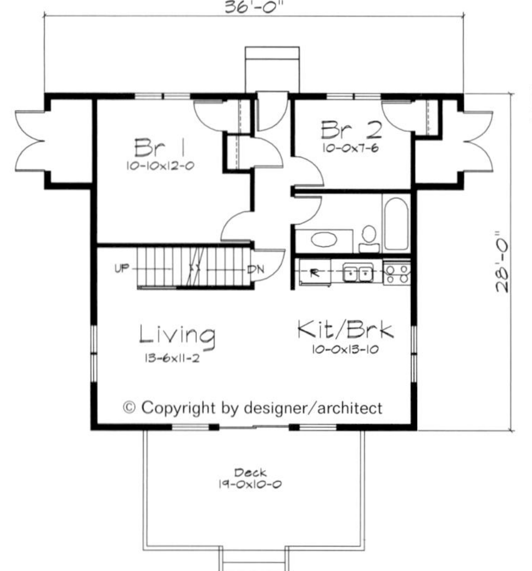

First Floor
790 sq. ft.

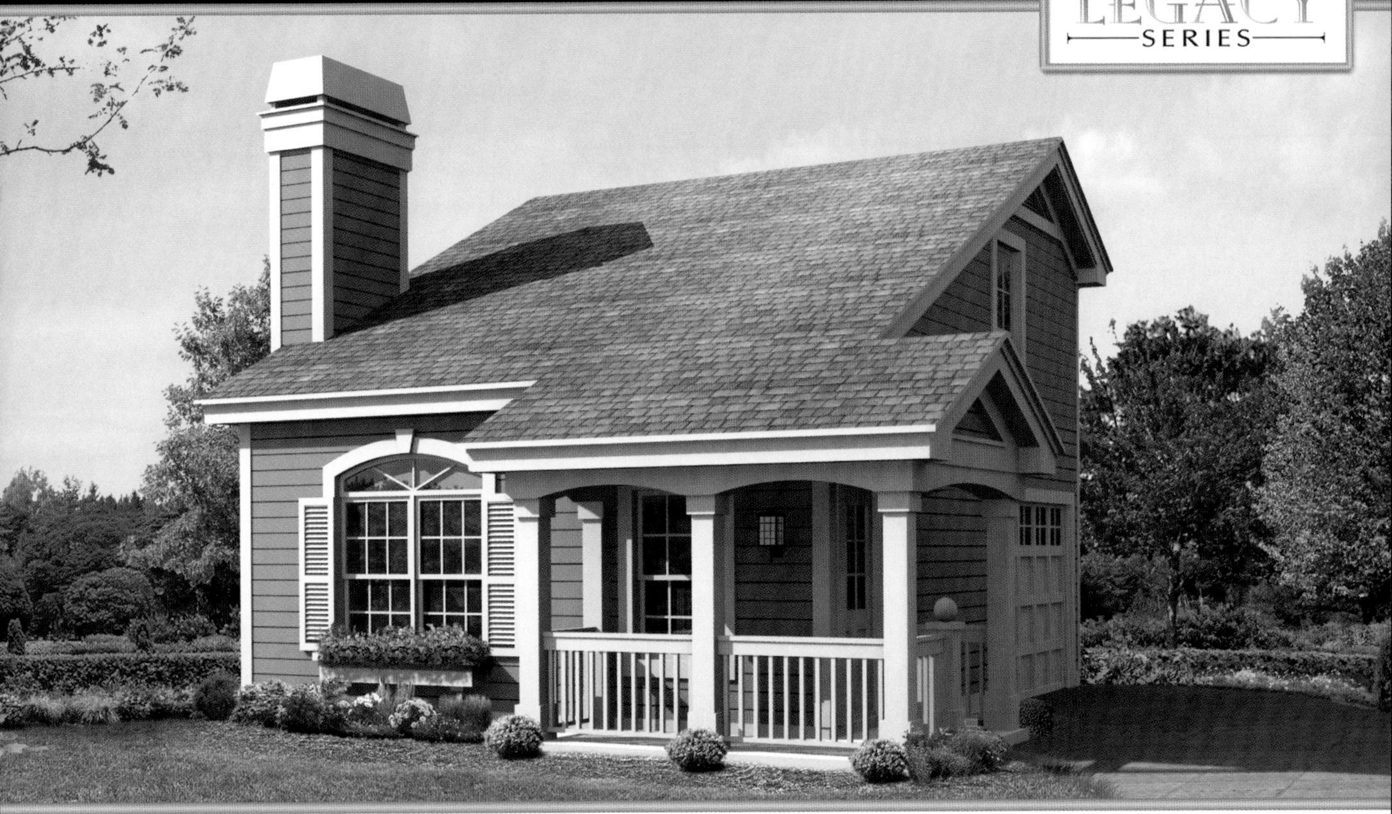

SPECIAL FEATURES

641 total square feet of living area

Charming exterior enjoys a wrap-around porch and a large feature window with arch and planter box

The living room features a kitchenette, fireplace, vaulted ceiling with plant shelf, separate entry with coat closet and access to adjacent powder room and garage

The stair leads to a spacious second floor bedroom complete with bath, walk-in closet and a unique opening with louvered doors for an overview of the living room below

1 bedroom, 1 1/2 baths, 1-car side entry garage

Slab foundation

Second Floor
311 sq. ft.

First Floor
330 sq. ft.

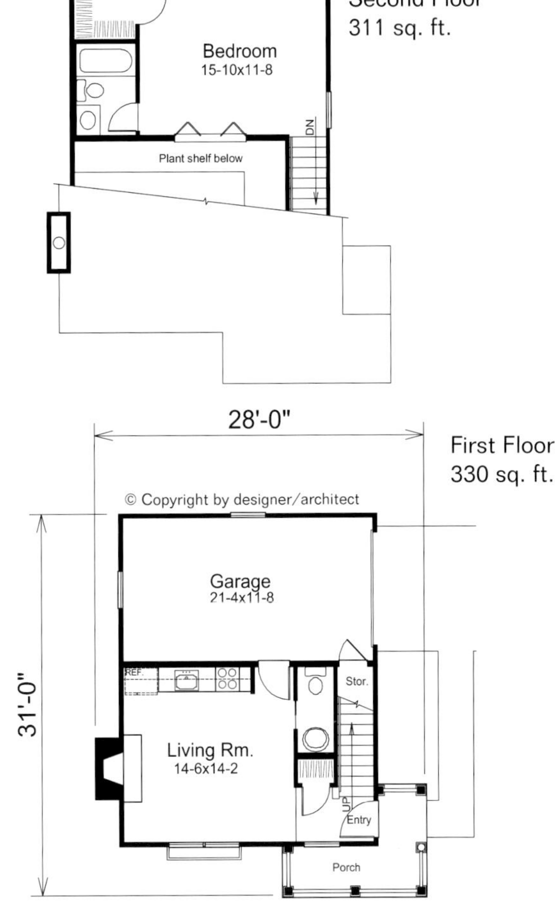

SPECIAL FEATURES

- 1,668 total square feet of living area
- Simple, but attractively styled ranch home is perfect for a narrow lot
- Front entry porch flows into the foyer which connects to the living room
- Garage entrance to home leads to the kitchen through the mud room/laundry area
- U-shaped kitchen opens to the dining area and family room
- Three bedrooms are situated at the rear of the home with two full baths
- Master bedroom has a walk-in closet
- 3 bedrooms, 2 baths, 2-car garage
- Partial basement/crawl space foundation, drawings also include crawl space and slab foundations

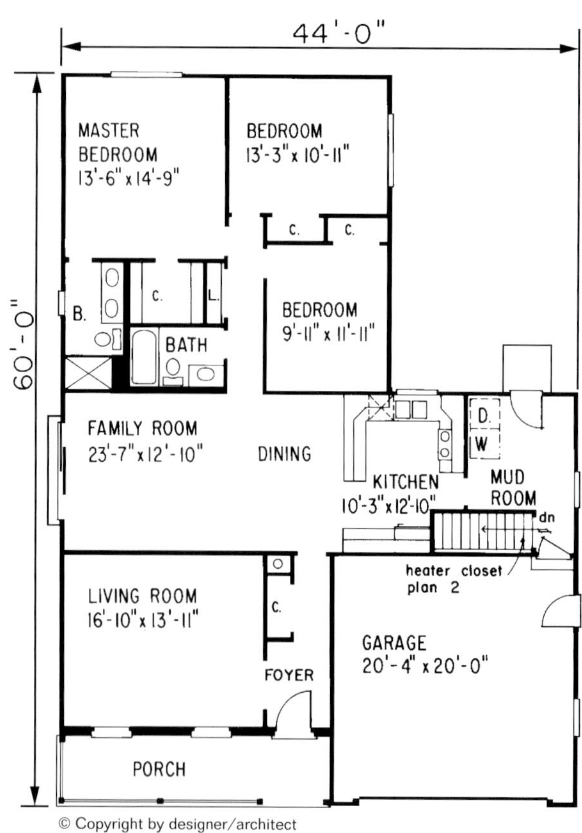

SPECIAL FEATURES

- 1,559 total square feet of living area
- Energy efficient home with 2" x 6" exterior walls
- This stylish earth berm design features stunning planter boxes surrounding the home
- Enjoy the spacious atmosphere created with the combined kitchen, living and dining rooms
- Retreat to the master bedroom to find a dressing area with two closets and a private bath with double-bowl vanity
- 3 bedrooms, 2 baths
- Slab foundation

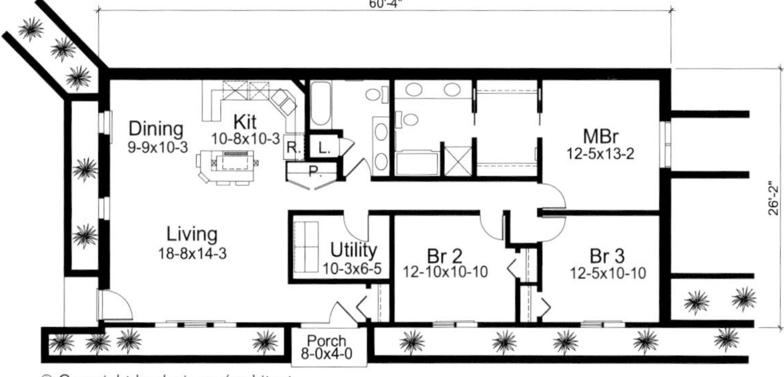

Plan Number: 537-008D-0010 | Price Code: A

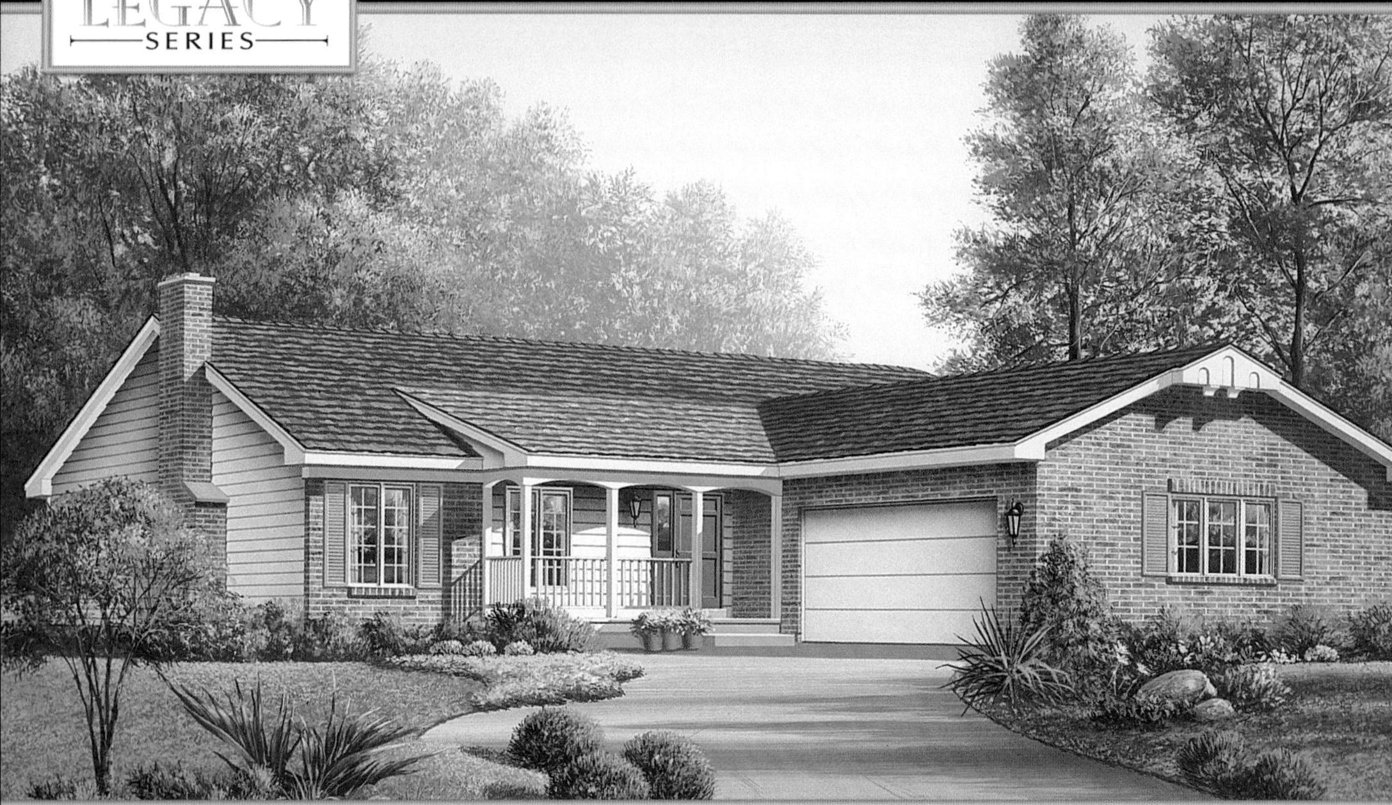

Special Features

- 1,440 total square feet of living area
- Foyer adjoins massive-sized great room with sloping ceiling and tall masonry fireplace
- The kitchen connects to the spacious dining room and features a pass-through to the breakfast bar
- Master bedroom enjoys a private bath and two closets
- An oversized two-car side entry garage offers plenty of storage for bicycles, lawn equipment, etc.
- 3 bedrooms, 2 baths, 2-car side entry garage
- Basement foundation, drawings also include crawl space and slab foundations

To Order See Page 288

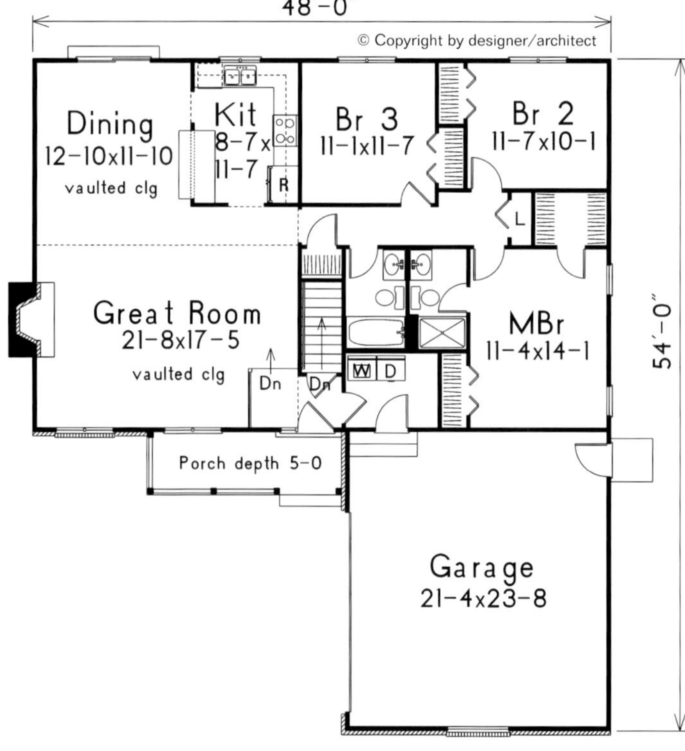

SPECIAL FEATURES

- 1,826 total square feet of living area
- An arched opening with columns invites you into a beautiful great room with fireplace, wet bar and vaulted ceiling
- A double-door entry leads into a large vaulted dining room with a fireplace, plant shelves and great view of the rear patio through a sweeping bay window
- Every bedroom enjoys private zoning with lots of closet space
- 3 bedrooms, 2 baths, 2-car garage
- Basement foundation

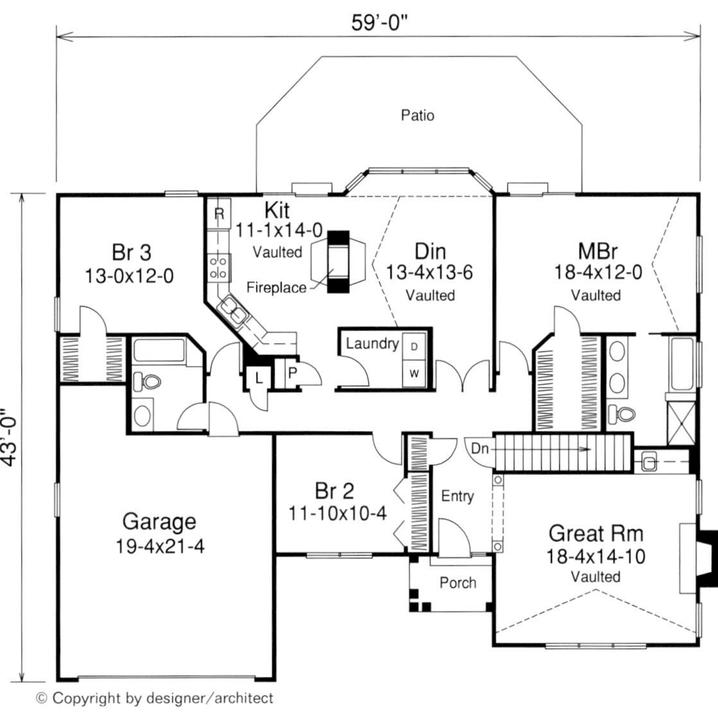

LOWE'S LEGACY SERIES

PLAN NUMBER: 537-053D-0040 | PRICE CODE: A

SPECIAL FEATURES

- 1,407 total square feet of living area
- Large living room has a fireplace and access to the rear deck
- Kitchen and dining area combine to create an open gathering area
- Convenient laundry room and broom closet
- Master bedroom includes a private bath with large vanity and separate tub and shower
- 3 bedrooms, 2 baths, 2-car drive under garage
- Basement foundation

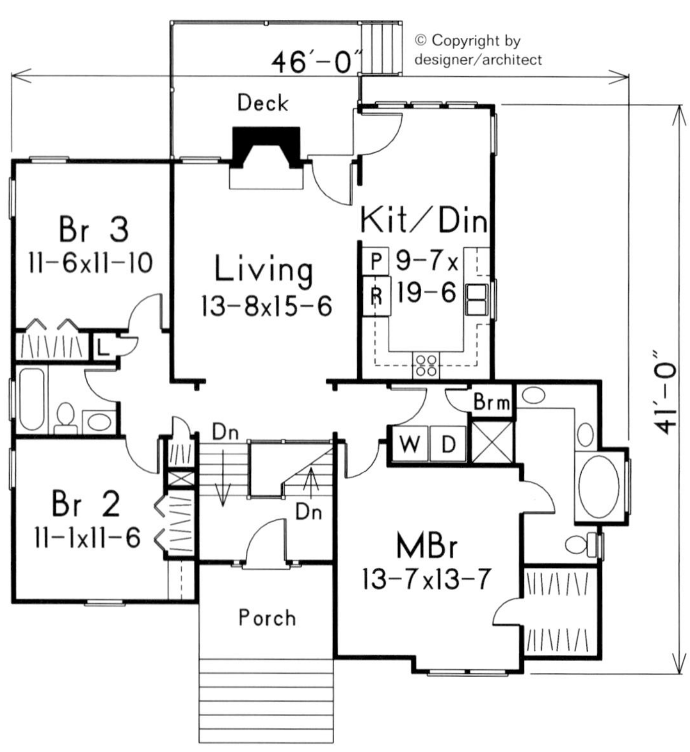

TO ORDER SEE PAGE 288 | CALL TOLL-FREE 1-877-379-3420

SPECIAL FEATURES

- 1,584 total square feet of living area
- Master bedroom includes dressing area, private bath and walk-in closet
- Secondary bedrooms feature large walk-in closets
- Large living room enjoys access to the rear patio
- U-shaped kitchen features pantry, outdoor access and convenient laundry closet
- 2" x 6" exterior walls available, please order plan #537-001D-0123
- 3 bedrooms, 2 baths
- Crawl space foundation, drawings also include basement and slab foundations

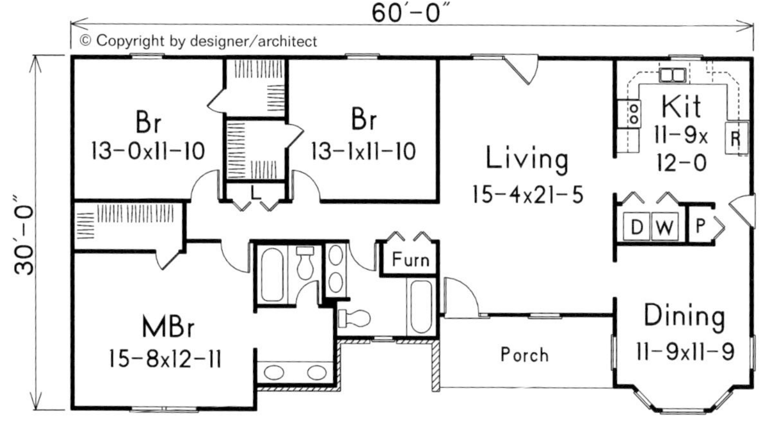

LOWE'S LEGACY SERIES

PLAN NUMBER: 537-008D-0045 | PRICE CODE: B

SPECIAL FEATURES

- 1,540 total square feet of living area
- Porch entrance into foyer leads to an impressive dining area with a full window and a half-circle window above
- Kitchen/breakfast room features a center island and cathedral ceiling
- Great room with cathedral ceiling and exposed beams is accessible from the foyer
- Master bedroom includes a full bath and walk-in closet
- Two additional bedrooms share a full bath
- 3 bedrooms, 2 baths, 2-car garage
- Basement foundation, drawings also include crawl space and slab foundations

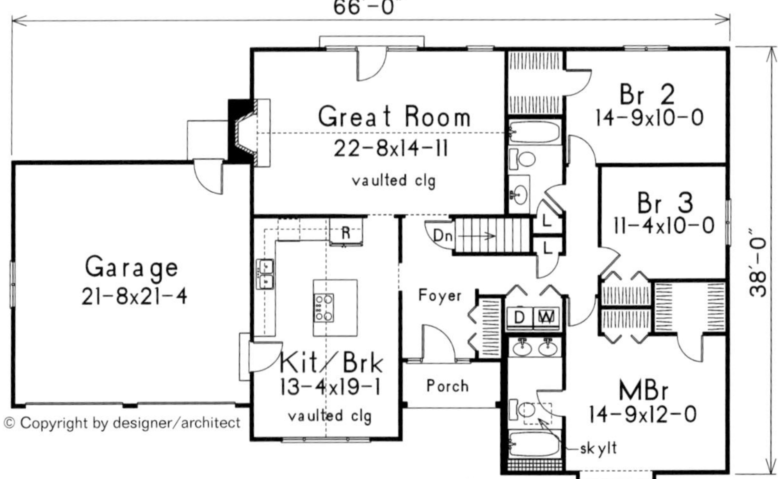

SPECIAL FEATURES

- 1,072 total square feet of living area
- Integrated open and screened front porches guarantee comfortable summer enjoyment
- Oversized garage includes area for shop and miscellaneous storage
- U-shaped kitchen and breakfast nook are adjacent to the vaulted living room and have access to the screened porch through sliding glass doors
- 345 square feet of optional living area on the lower level including a third bedroom and a bath
- 2 bedrooms, 2 baths, 2-car side entry garage
- Basement foundation

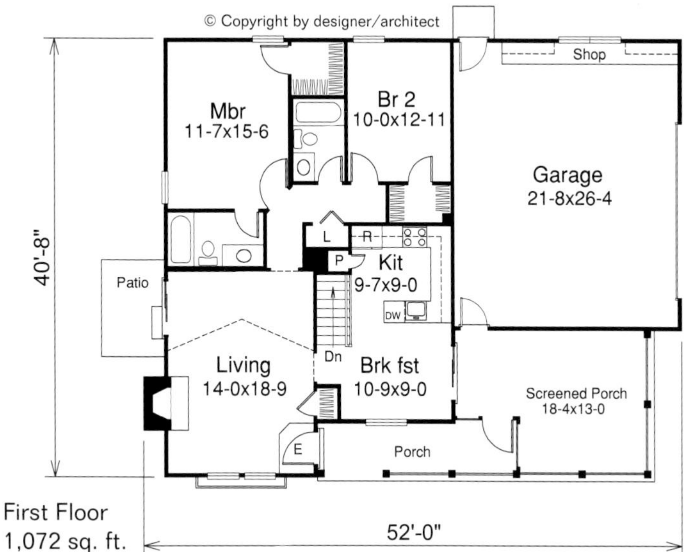

First Floor
1,072 sq. ft.

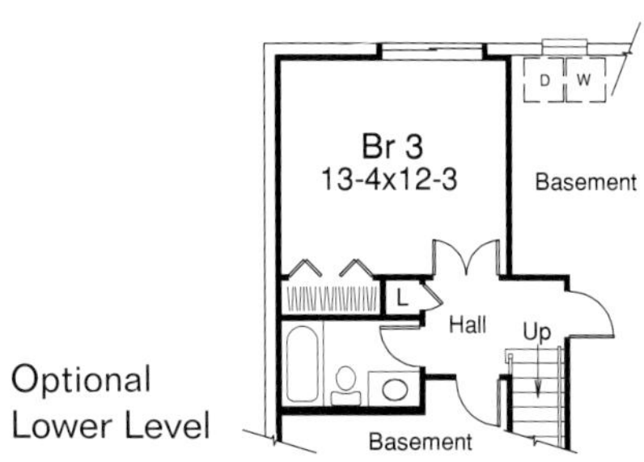

Optional
Lower Level

SPECIAL FEATURES

- 1,832 total square feet of living area
- Distinctive master bedroom is enhanced by skylights, a garden tub, separate shower and a walk-in closet
- U-shaped kitchen features a convenient pantry, laundry area and full view to breakfast room
- Large front porch creates enjoyable outdoor living
- 2" x 6" exterior walls available, please order plan #537-001D-0127
- 3 bedrooms, 2 baths, 2-car detached garage
- Crawl space foundation, drawings also include basement and slab foundations

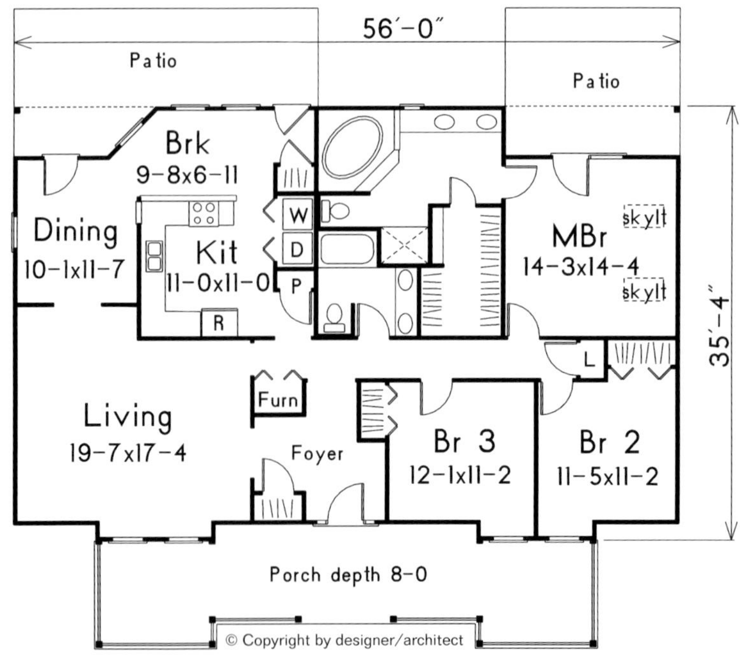

SPECIAL FEATURES

- 1,280 total square feet of living area
- Attention to architectural detail has created the look of an authentic Swiss cottage
- Spacious living room, adjacent kitchenette and dining area all enjoy views to the front deck
- Hall bath shared by two sizable bedrooms is included on the first and second floors
- 4 bedrooms, 2 baths
- Crawl space foundation, drawings also include basement foundation

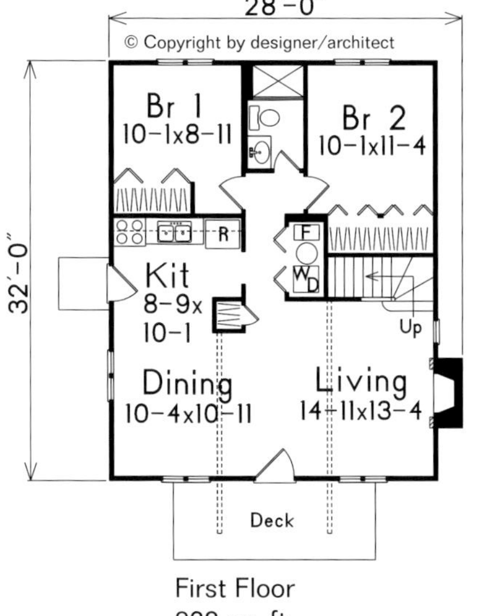

First Floor
832 sq. ft.

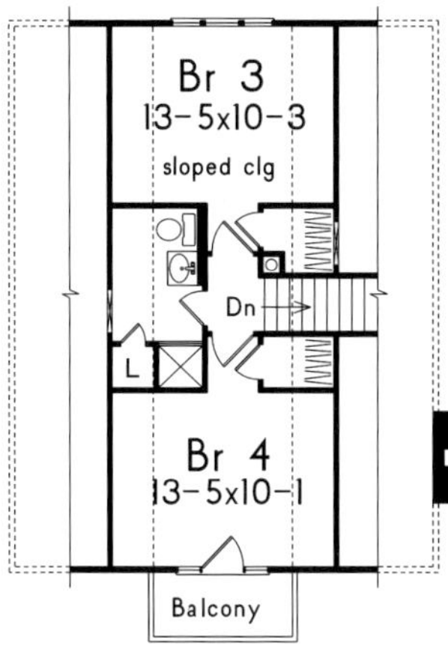

Br 3
13-5x10-3
sloped clg
Dn
L
Br 4
13-5x10-1
Balcony

Second Floor
448 sq. ft.

LOWE'S LEGACY SERIES

PLAN NUMBER: 537-001D-0089 | PRICE CODE: AA

SPECIAL FEATURES

- 1,000 total square feet of living area
- Master bedroom has double closets and an adjacent bath
- L-shaped kitchen includes side entrance, closet and convenient laundry area
- Living room features handy coat closet
- 3 bedrooms, 1 bath
- Crawl space foundation, drawings also include basement and slab foundations

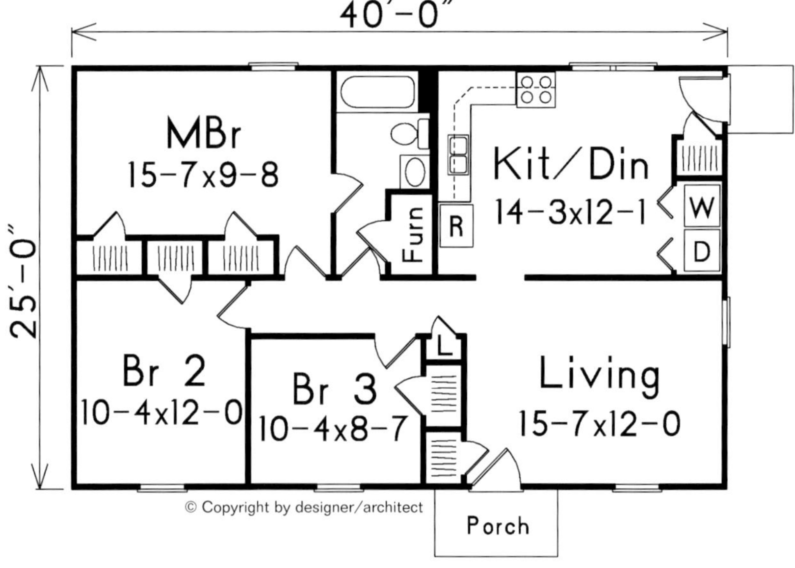

SPECIAL FEATURES

- 983 total square feet of living area
- Spacious front porch leads you into the living and dining areas open to a pass-through kitchen
- A small patio with privacy fence creates exterior access from the living room
- The master bedroom includes a large walk-in closet and its own private full bath
- 3 bedrooms, 2 baths, 2-car garage
- Crawl space foundation, drawings also include slab foundation

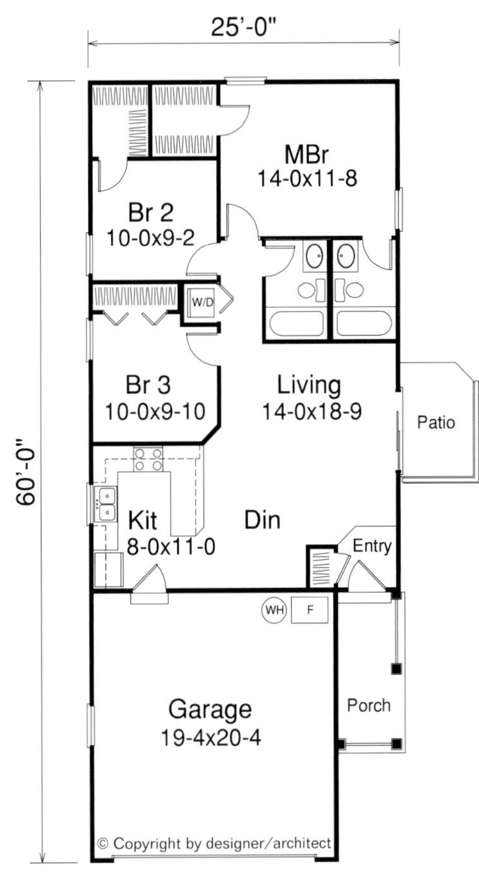

SPECIAL FEATURES

- 768 total square feet of living area
- Great room has an attractive box window for enjoying views
- The compact, yet efficient kitchen is open to the great room
- Six closets provide great storage for a compact plan
- Plans include optional third bedroom with an additional 288 square feet of living area
- 2 bedrooms, 1 bath
- Basement foundation, drawings also include crawl space and slab foundations

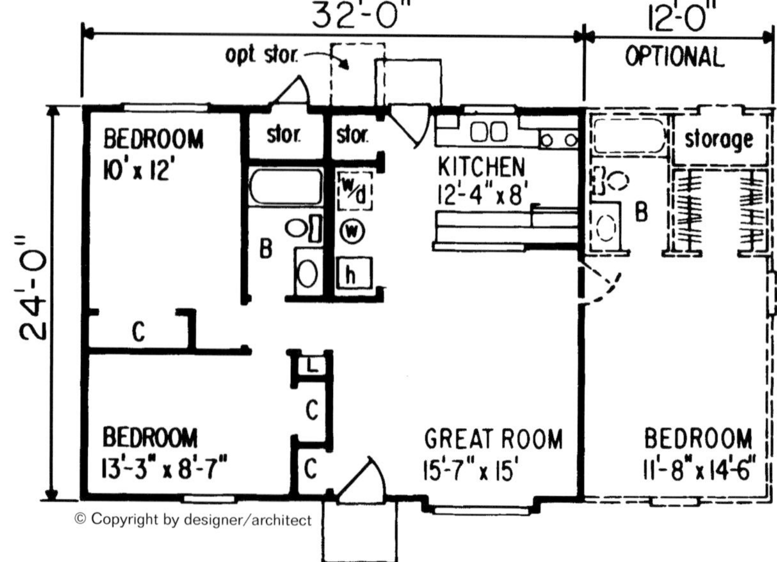

Plan Number: 537-057D-0021 | Price Code: B

Lowe's Legacy Series

Special Features

- 1,699 total square feet of living area
- Energy efficient home with 2" x 6" exterior walls
- An elegant fireplace warms the adjoining living and dining rooms, adding style and comfort
- Sliding glass doors in the dining room access a lovely greenhouse that can be used as a sunroom
- A casual family room is located on the second floor and is perfect for a home theater or game room
- 2 bedrooms, 2 1/2 baths, 2-car garage
- Basement foundation

Second Floor
620 sq. ft.

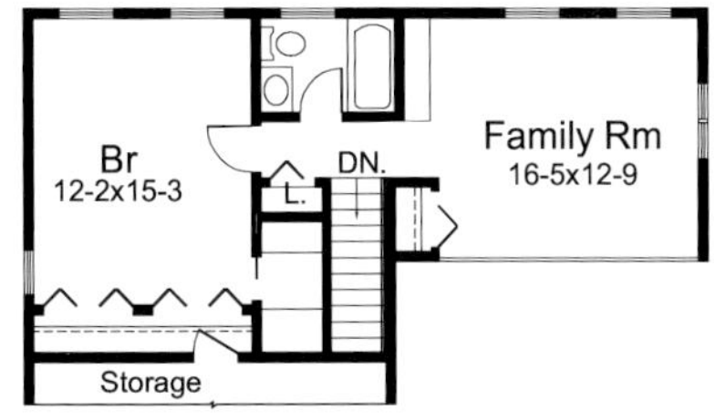

First Floor
1,079 sq. ft.

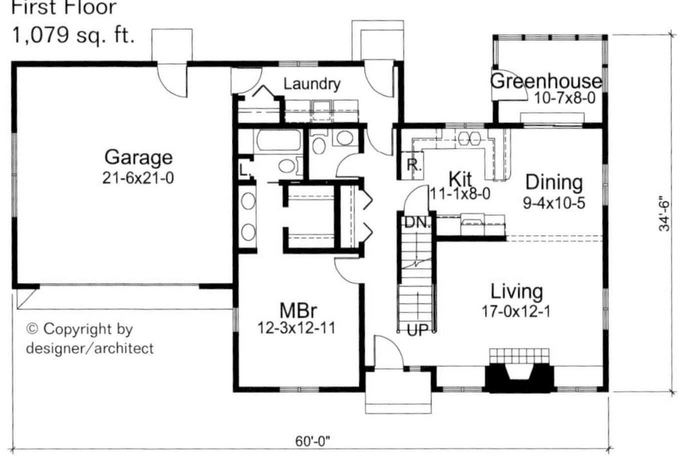

SPECIAL FEATURES

- 1,550 total square feet of living area
- Convenient mud room between the garage and kitchen
- Oversized dining area allows plenty of space for entertaining
- Master bedroom has a private bath and ample closet space
- Large patio off the family room brings the outdoors in
- 3 bedrooms, 2 baths, 2-car side entry garage
- Basement foundation, drawings also include crawl space or slab foundations

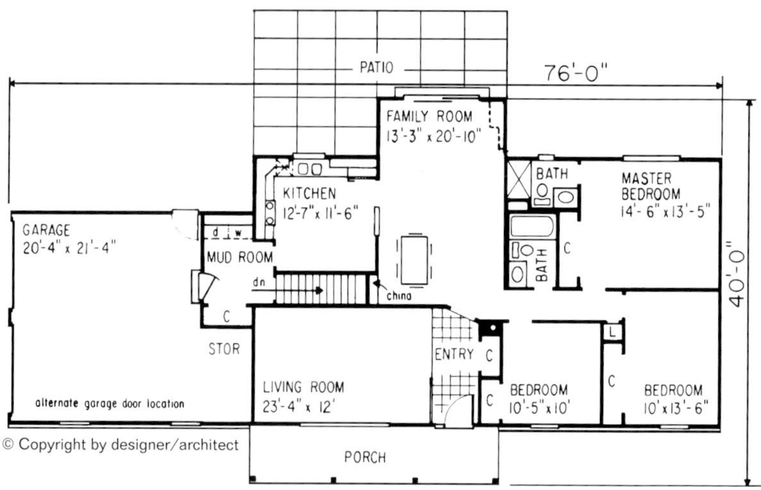

Plan Number: 537-001D-0055 | Price Code: B

Lowe's Legacy Series

Special Features

- 1,705 total square feet of living area
- Two bedrooms on the first floor for convenience and two bedrooms on the second for privacy
- L-shaped kitchen adjacent to dining room accesses the outdoors
- 2" x 6" exterior walls available, please order plan #537-001D-0110
- 4 bedrooms, 2 baths
- Crawl space foundation, drawings also include basement and slab foundations

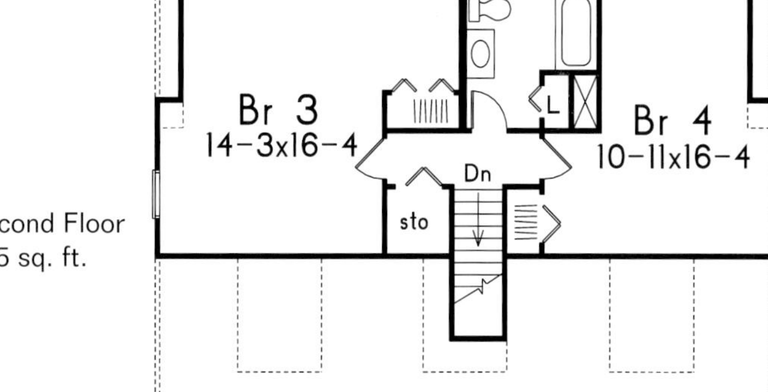

Second Floor
665 sq. ft.

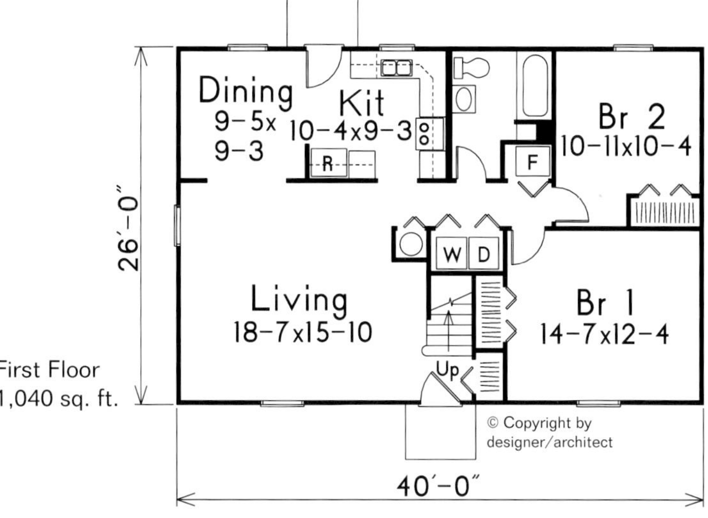

First Floor
1,040 sq. ft.

Plan Number: 537-008D-0004 | Price Code: B

Special Features

- 1,643 total square feet of living area
- An attractive front entry porch gives this ranch a country accent
- Spacious family/dining room is the focal point of this design
- Kitchen and utility room are conveniently located near gathering areas
- Formal living room in the front of the home provides area for quiet and privacy
- Master bedroom has view to the rear of the home and a generous walk-in closet
- 3 bedrooms, 2 baths, 2-car garage
- Basement foundation, drawings also include crawl space and slab foundations

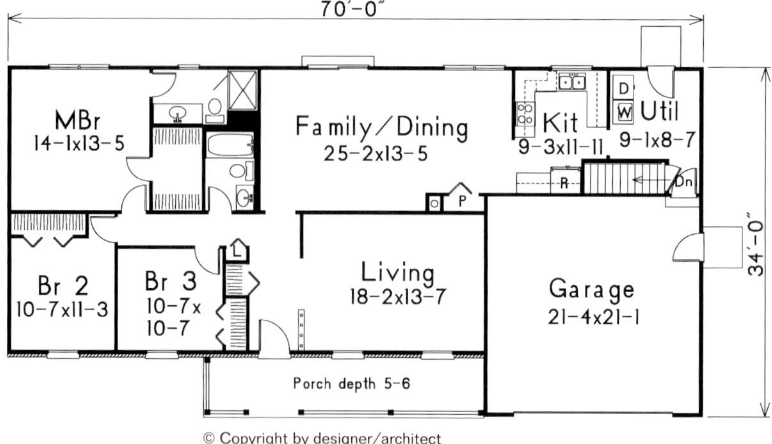

Plan Number: 537-053D-0044 | Price Code: A

Lowe's Legacy Series

Special Features

- 1,340 total square feet of living area
- Master bedroom has a private bath and walk-in closet
- Recessed entry leads to the vaulted family room that shares a see-through fireplace with the kitchen/dining area
- Garage includes a handy storage area
- Convenient laundry closet is located in the kitchen
- 3 bedrooms, 2 baths, 2-car side entry garage
- Slab foundation, drawings also include crawl space foundation

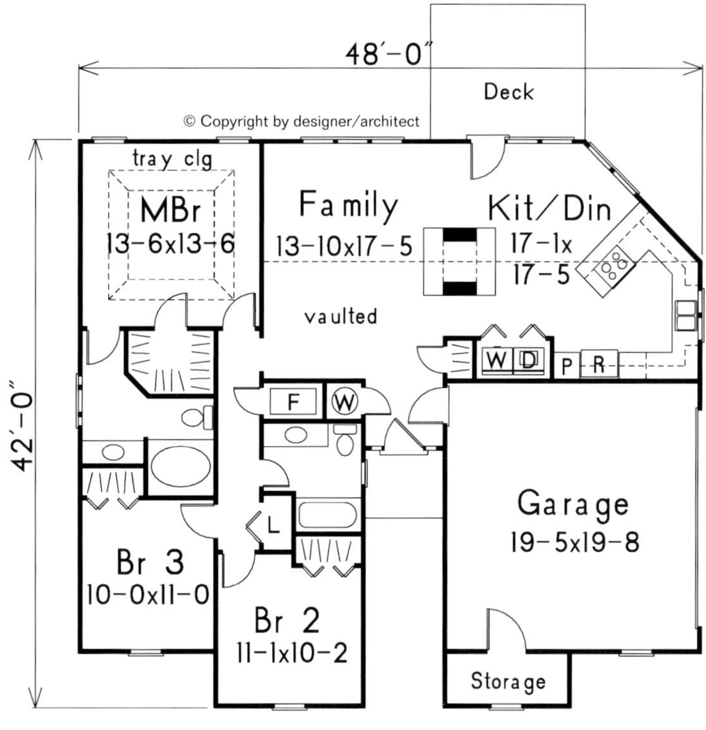

SPECIAL FEATURES

- 1,476 total square feet of living area
- Energy efficient home with 2" x 6" exterior walls
- Living room is made more spacious by a vaulted ceiling
- Laundry/mud room has a large pantry and accesses the dining area, garage, stairs and the outdoors
- Master bedroom features a bath and private deck
- Dining room is defined by columns and a large bow window
- 3 bedrooms, 2 baths, 2-car side entry garage
- Basement foundation, drawings also include slab foundation

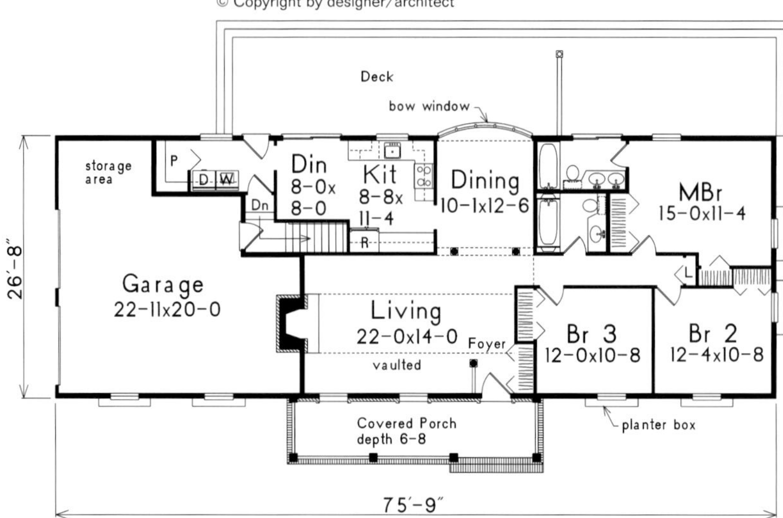

SPECIAL FEATURES

- 1,391 total square feet of living area
- Large living room with masonry fireplace features a soaring vaulted ceiling
- A spiral staircase in the hall leads to a huge loft area overlooking the living room below
- Two first floor bedrooms share a full bath
- 2 bedrooms, 1 bath
- Pier foundation, drawings also include crawl space foundation

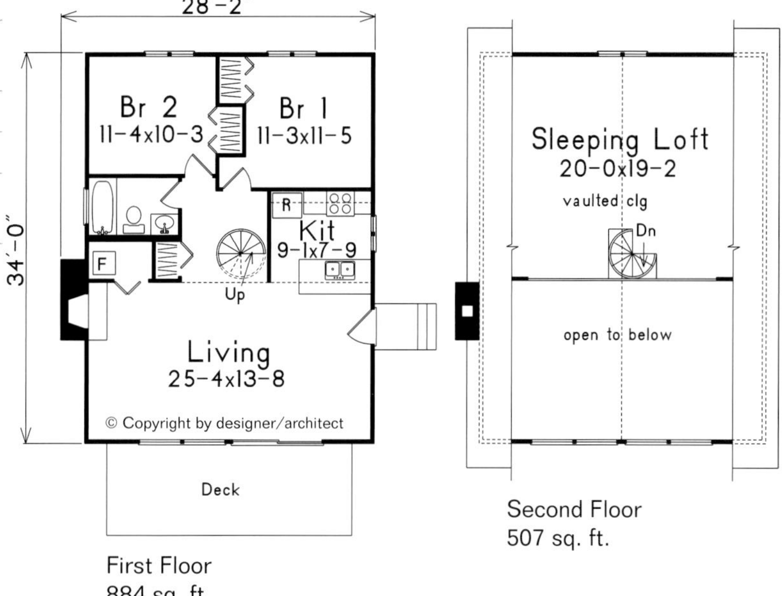

First Floor
884 sq. ft.

Second Floor
507 sq. ft.

SPECIAL FEATURES

1,131 total square feet of living area

Inviting porch and roof dormer create a charming exterior

The spacious area on the first floor is perfect for a large shop, private studio, office or cottage great room and includes a fireplace, kitchenette and half bath

Two bedrooms, a full bath and attic storage comprise the second floor which has its own private entrance and wide sunny hallway

2 bedrooms, 1 1/2 baths

Slab foundation

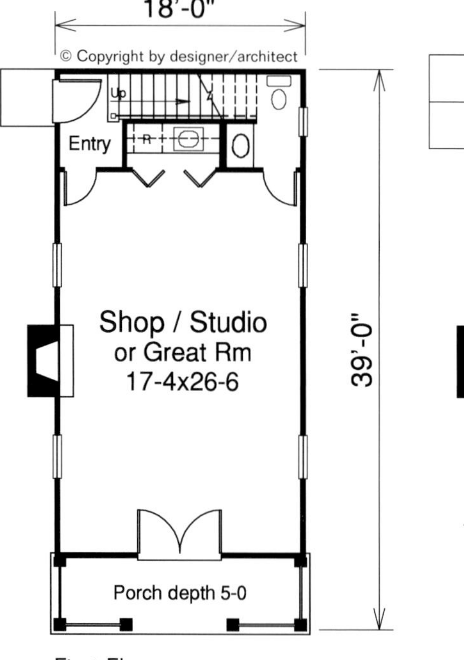

First Floor
612 sq. ft.

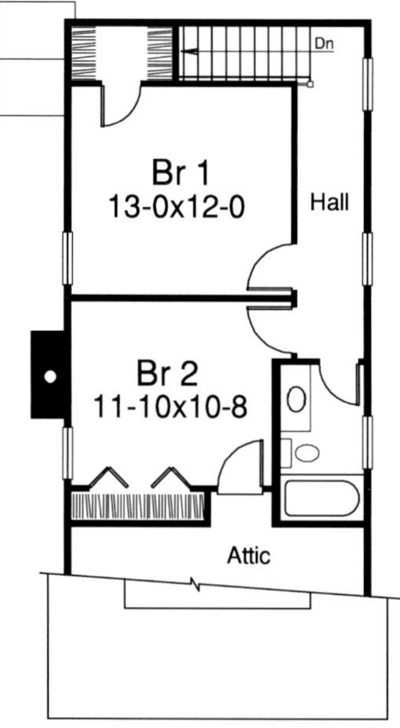

Second Floor
519 sq. ft.

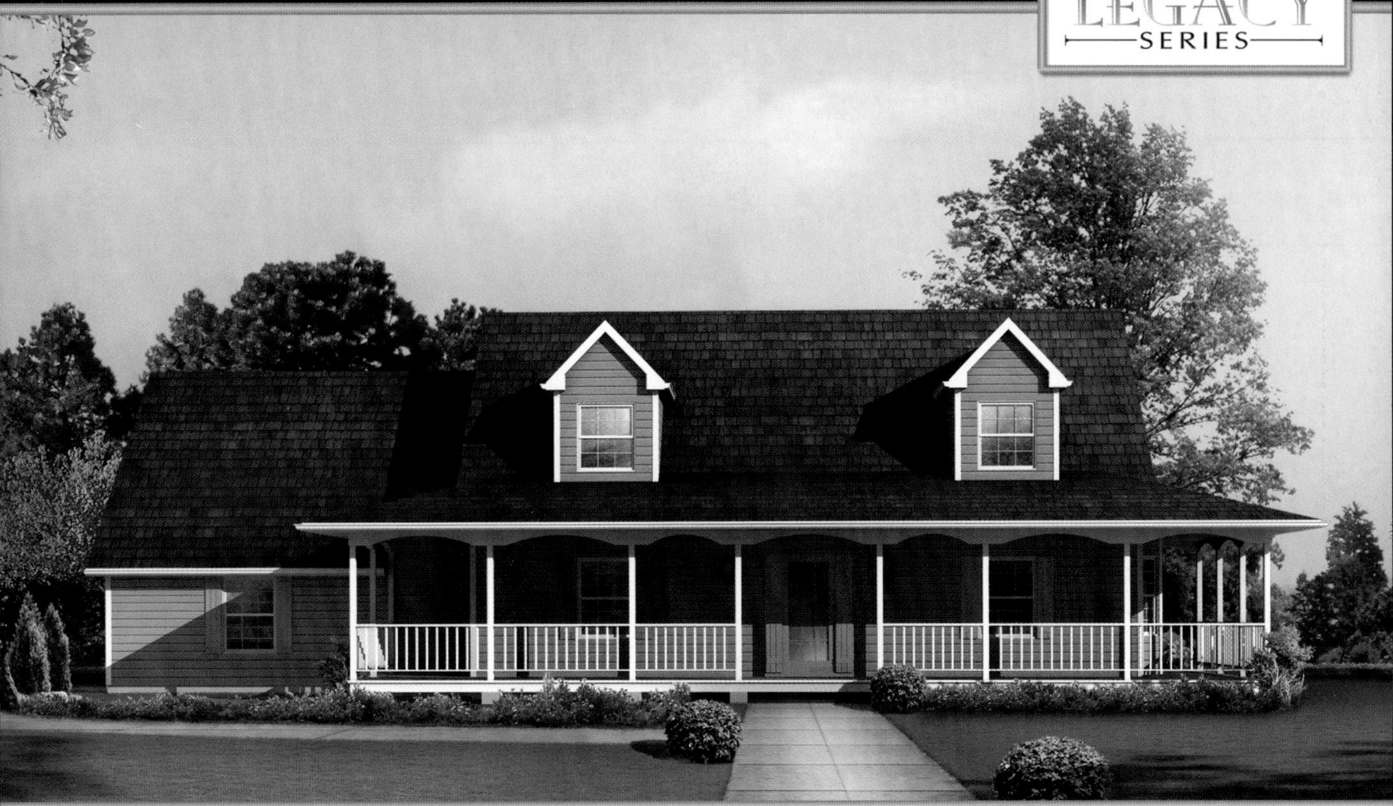

SPECIAL FEATURES

- 1,875 total square feet of living area
- Country-style exterior with wrap-around porch and dormers
- Large second floor bedrooms share a dressing area and bath
- Master bedroom includes a bay window, walk-in closet, dressing area and bath
- 2" x 6" exterior walls available, please order plan #537-001D-0114
- 3 bedrooms, 2 baths, 2-car side entry garage
- Crawl space foundation, drawings also include basement and slab foundations

Second Floor
820 sq. ft.

First Floor
1,055 sq. ft.

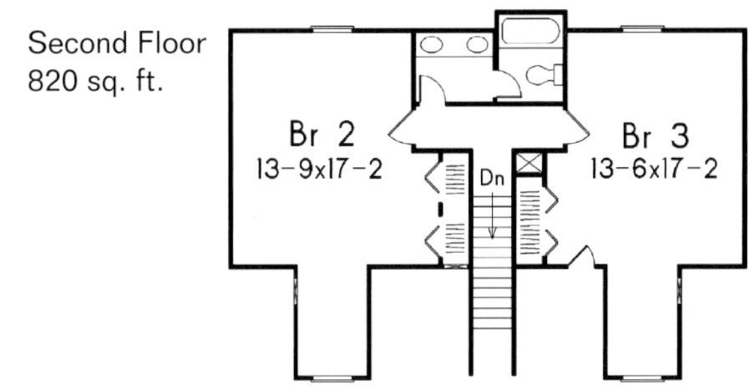

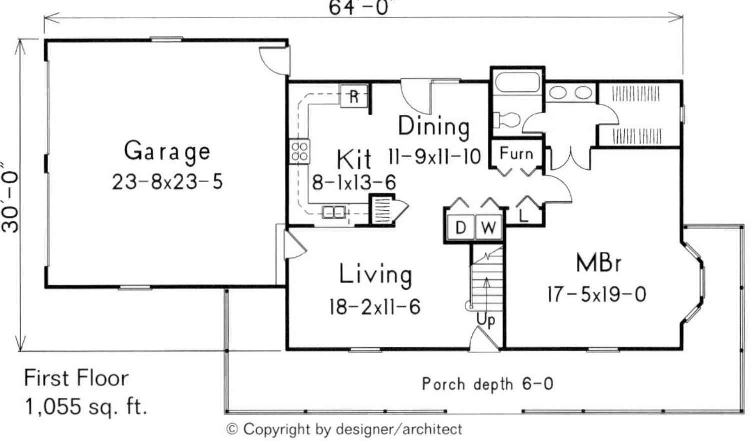

PLAN NUMBER: 537-058D-0012 | PRICE CODE: AA

SPECIAL FEATURES

- 1,143 total square feet of living area
- Enormous stone fireplace in the family room adds warmth and character
- Spacious kitchen with breakfast bar overlooks the family room
- Separate dining area is great for entertaining
- Vaulted family room and kitchen create an open atmosphere
- 2" x 6" exterior walls available, please order plan #537-058D-0075
- 2 bedrooms, 1 bath
- Crawl space foundation

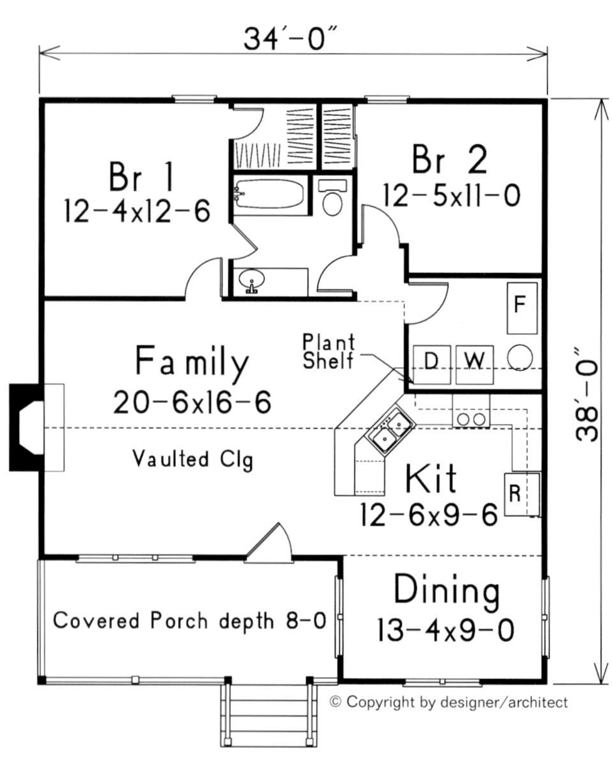

SPECIAL FEATURES

- 1,400 total square feet of living area
- Front porch offers warmth and welcome
- Large great room opens into the dining room creating an open living atmosphere
- Kitchen features convenient laundry area, pantry and breakfast bar
- 2" x 6" exterior walls available, please order plan #537-001D-0103
- 3 bedrooms, 2 baths, 2-car garage
- Crawl space foundation, drawings also include basement and slab foundations

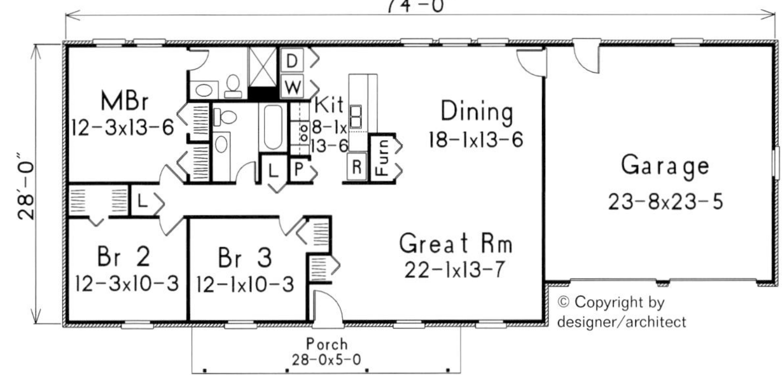

SPECIAL FEATURES

- 1,593 total square feet of living area
- A welcoming porch invites you into a spacious living room
- Kitchen and dining room is open to family room through wood balustrade
- Master bedroom offers private bath and two closets
- Laundry/mud room located directly off garage with convenient access to the outdoors
- 3 bedrooms, 2 baths, 2-car garage
- Basement foundation, drawings also include crawl space and slab foundations

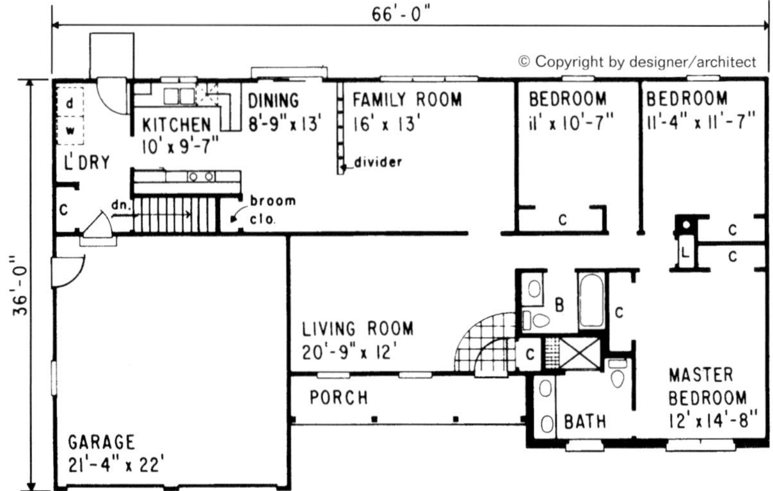

Plan Number: 537-007D-0181 | Price Code: AA

Lowe's Legacy Series

Special Features

- 1,140 total square feet of living area
- Delightful appearance with a protective porch
- The entry, with convenient stairs to the basement, leads to spacious living and dining rooms open to the adjacent kitchen
- The master bedroom enjoys a double-door entry, walk-in closet and a private bath with its own linen closet
- 3 bedrooms, 2 baths, 2-car garage
- Basement foundation, drawings also include slab and crawl space foundations

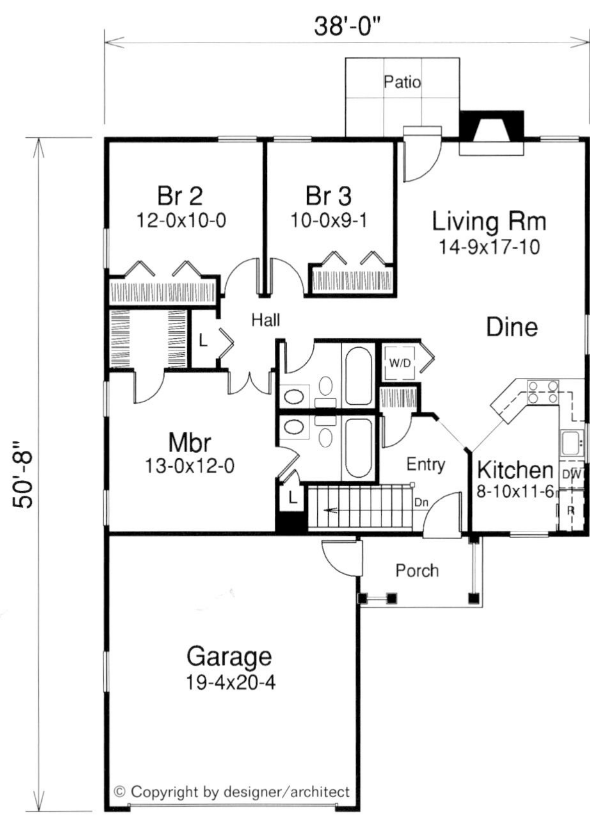

SPECIAL FEATURES

- 1,261 total square feet of living area
- Great room, brightened by windows and doors, features a vaulted ceiling, fireplace and access to the deck
- Vaulted master bedroom enjoys a private bath
- Split-level foyer leads to the living space or basement
- Centrally located laundry area is near the bedrooms
- 3 bedrooms, 2 baths, 2-car drive under garage
- Basement foundation

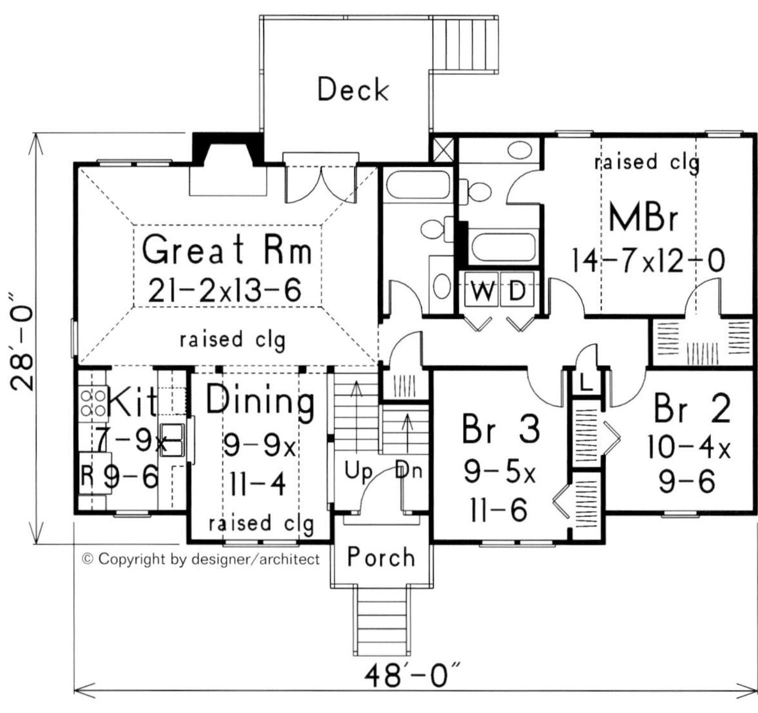

SPECIAL FEATURES

- 1,102 total square feet of living area
- Attractive exterior features a cozy porch, palladian windows and a decorative planter box
- The vaulted great room has a fireplace, view to rear patio and dining area with feature window
- Open to the great room is a U-shaped kitchen which includes all the necessities and a breakfast bar
- The master bedroom offers a vaulted ceiling, private bath, walk-in closet and sliding doors to the rear patio
- 3 bedrooms, 2 baths, 2-car garage
- Basement foundation, drawings also include slab and crawl space foundations

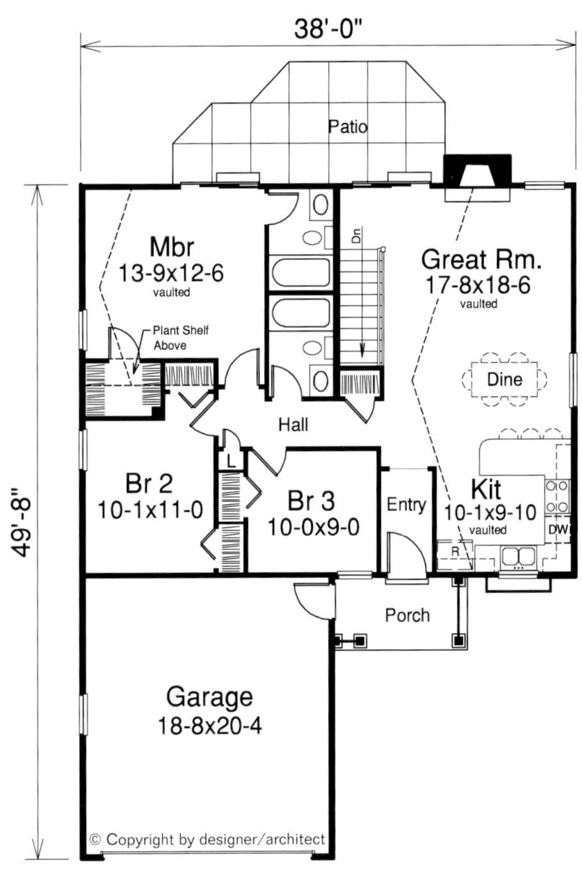

LOWE'S LEGACY SERIES

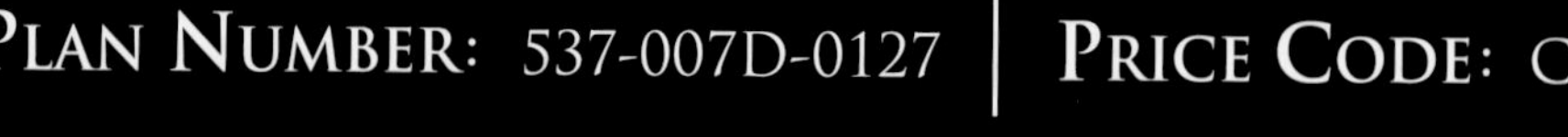

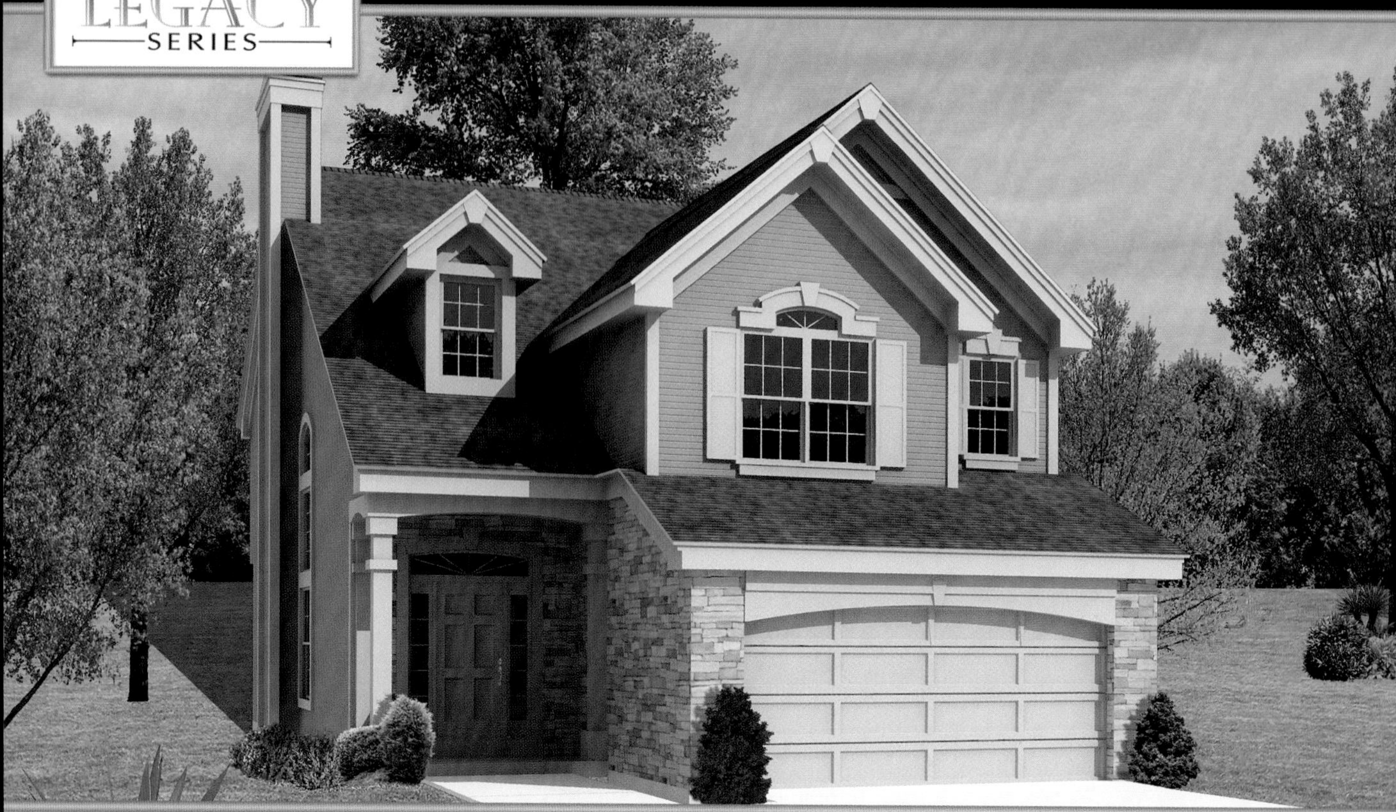

SPECIAL FEATURES

- 2,158 total square feet of living area
- Vaulted entry has a coat closet and built-in shelves with plant shelf above
- The two-story living room has tall dramatic windows flanking the fireplace and a full-length second floor balcony
- A laundry and half bath are located near the kitchen which has over 30' of counterspace
- Vaulted master bedroom has window seat entry, two walk-in closets and a luxury bath
- 3 bedrooms, 2 1/2 baths, 2-car garage
- Basement foundation

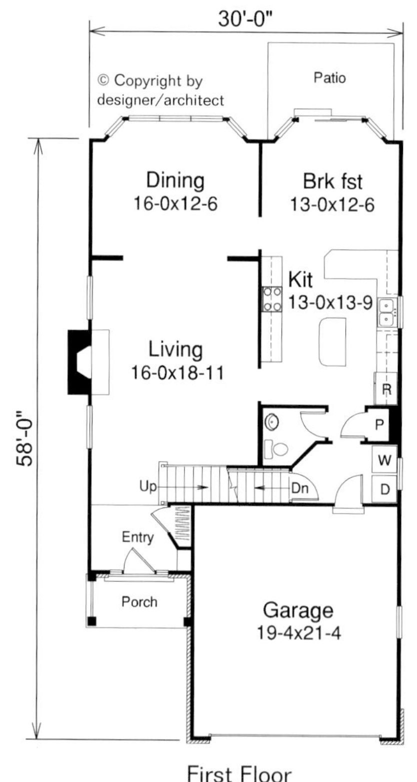

First Floor
1,125 sq. ft.

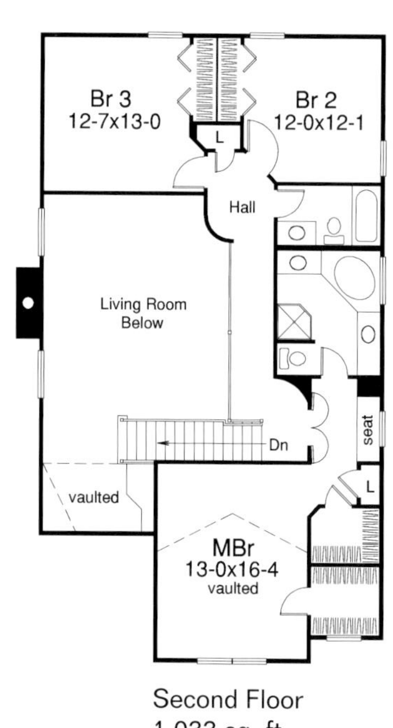

Second Floor
1,033 sq. ft.

Lowe's Special Rebate Offer

Purchase any plan package featured in this book PLUS at least $15,000 of your materials from Lowe's and receive a gift card for the purchase price of your plans.

To receive the rebate:

1. Purchase any of the plan packages in this publication PLUS at least $15,000 of the materials to build your home at Lowe's before 12/31/09. Requests must be postmarked by 1/31/10. Claims postmarked after this date will not be honored.
2. Limit one gift card per set of plans.
3. Please allow 3-4 weeks for processing. If you do not receive a gift card after 4 weeks, visit www.lowes.com/rebates, or you may call 1-877-204-1223.
4. Please keep a copy of all materials submitted for your records.
5. Copy the entire sale receipt(s), including store name, location, purchase date, and invoice number, showing blueprint purchase and total amount spent.
6. Mail this complete page with your name, address and other information below, along with a copy of the receipt(s).

Name ______________________________

Street Address ______________________________

City ______________________________

State/Zip ______________________________

Daytime phone number (_____) - ______________________________

E-mail address ______________________________

Plan number purchased 537- ______________________________

I purchased a

- ☐ One-Set Plan Package
- ☐ Five-Set Plan Package
- ☐ Eight-Set Plan Package
- ☐ Reproducible Masters
- ☐ Builder's CAD Package

MAIL TO:
Lowe's Free Gift Card Offer
P.O. Box 3029
Young America, MN 55558-3029

Check the status of your rebate at www.lowes.com/rebates

Other terms and conditions. Requests from groups will not be honored. Fraudulent submission of multiple requests could result in federal prosecution under the U.S. Mail Fraud Statutes (18 USC, Section 1341 and 1342). Offer good in the U.S.A. only. Void where prohibited, taxed or restricted by law. If you do not receive your rebate within 3-4 weeks, please call 1-877-204-1223 or visit www.lowes.com/rebates. This page may not be reproduced, traded or sold. Please keep a copy for future reference.

Our Blueprint Packages Include...

Quality plans for building your future, with extras that provide unsurpassed value, ensure good construction and long-term enjoyment.

Cover Sheet

Included with many of the plans, the cover sheet is the artist's rendering of the exterior of the home. It will give you an idea of how your home will look when completed and landscaped.

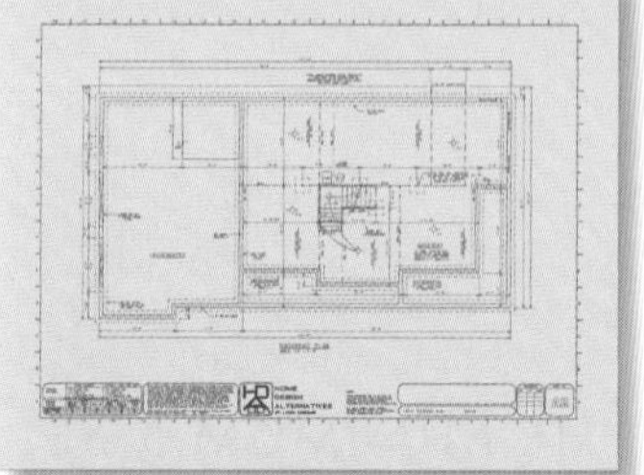

Foundation

The foundation plan shows the layout of the basement, walk-out basement, crawl space, slab or pier foundation. All necessary notations and dimensions are included. See plan page for the foundation types included. If the home plan you choose does not have your desired foundation type, our Customer Service Representatives can advise you on how to customize your foundation to suit your specific needs or site conditions.

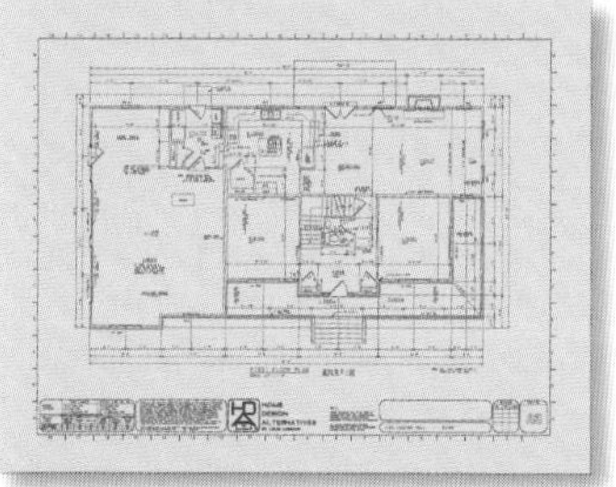

Floor Plans

The floor plans show the placement of walls, doors, closets, plumbing fixtures, electrical outlets, columns, and beams for each level of the home.

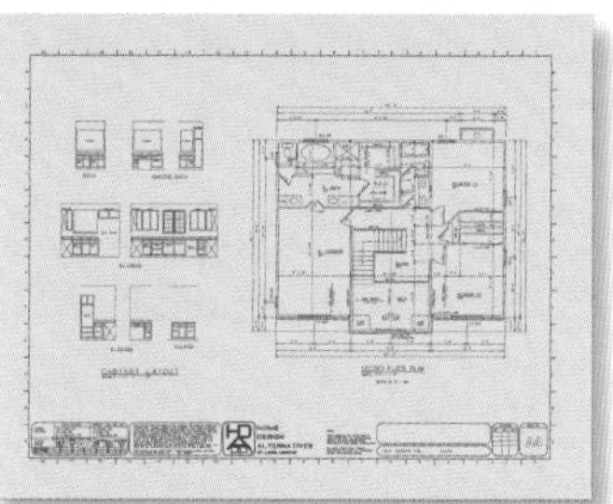

Interior Elevations

Interior elevations provide views of special interior elements such as fireplaces, kitchen cabinets, built-in units and other features of the home.

Exterior Elevations

Exterior elevations illustrate the front, rear and both sides of the house, with all details of exterior materials and the required dimensions.

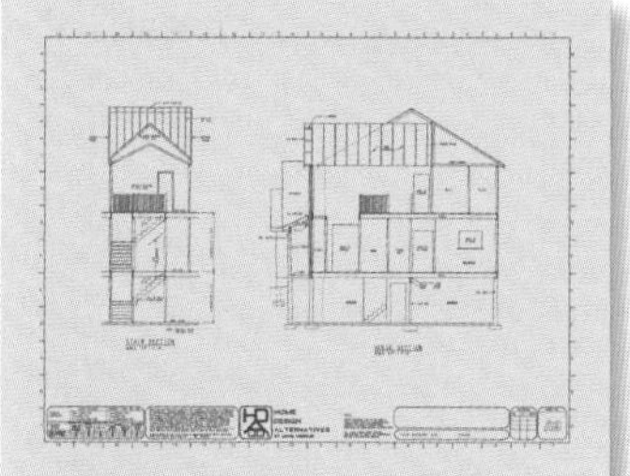

Sections

Show detail views of the home or portions of the home as if it were sliced from the roof to the foundation. This sheet shows important areas such as load-bearing walls, stairs, joists, trusses and other structural elements, which are critical for proper construction.

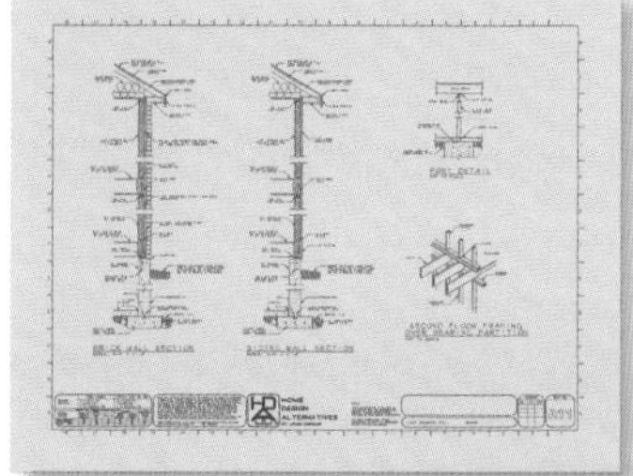

Details

Show how to construct certain components of your home, such as the roof system, stairs, deck, etc.

What Kind Of Plan Package Do You Need?

Now that you've found the home you've been looking for, here are some suggestions on how to make your Dream Home a reality. To get started, order the type of plans that fit your particular situation.

Your Choices

The One-Set Study Package -

We offer a One-set plan package so you can study your home in detail. This one set is considered a study set and is marked "not for construction." It is a copyright violation to reproduce blueprints.

The Minimum 5-Set Package -

If you're ready to start the construction process, this 5-set package is the minimum number of blueprint sets you will need. It will require keeping close track of each set so they can be used by multiple subcontractors and tradespeople.

The Standard 8-Set Package -

For best results in terms of cost, schedule and quality of construction, we recommend you order eight (or more) sets of blueprints. Besides one set for yourself, additional sets of blueprints will be required by your mortgage lender, local building department, general contractor and all subcontractors working on foundation, electrical, plumbing, heating/air conditioning, carpentry work, etc.

Reproducible Masters -

If you wish to make some minor design changes, you'll want to order reproducible masters. These drawings contain the same information as the blueprints but are printed on reproducible paper that is easy to alter and clearly indicates your right to copy or reproduce. This will allow your builder or a local design professional to make the necessary drawing changes without the major expense of redrawing the plans. This package also allows you to print copies of the modified plans as needed. The right of building only one structure from these plans is licensed exclusively to the buyer. You may not use this design to build a second or multiple dwelling(s) without purchasing another blueprint. Each violation of the Copyright Law is punishable in a fine.

Mirror Reverse Sets -

Plans can be printed in mirror reverse. These plans are useful when the house would fit your site better if all the rooms were on the opposite side than shown. They are simply a mirror image of the original drawings causing the lettering and dimensions to read backwards. Therefore, when ordering mirror reverse drawings, you must purchase at least one set of right-reading plans. Some of our plans are offered mirror reverse right-reading. This means the plan, lettering and dimensions are flipped but read correctly. See the Home Plans Index on pages 285-286 for availability

CAD Packages -

A CAD package is a complete set of construction drawings in an electronic file format. They are beneficial if you have a significant amount of changes to make to the home plan or if you need to make the home plan fit your local codes. If you purchase a CAD Package, you can take the plan to a local design professional who uses AutoCAD or DataCAD and they can modify the design much quicker than with a paper-based drawing, which will help save you time and money. Just like our reproducible masters, with a CAD package you will receive a one-time build copyright release that allows you to make changes and the necessary copies needed to build your home. For more information and availability, please call our Customer Service Department at 1-877-379-3420.

More Helpful Building Aids

Your Blueprint Package will contain the necessary construction information to build your home. We also offer the following products and services to save you time and money in the building process.

Material List

Material lists are available for all of the plans in this book. Each list gives you the quantity, dimensions and description of the building materials necessary to construct your home. You'll get faster and more accurate bids from your contractor while saving money by paying for only the materials you need. **Cost: $125.00**

Note: Material lists are not refundable.

Express Delivery

Most orders are processed within 24 hours of receipt. Please allow 7-10 business days for delivery. If you need to place a rush order, please call us by 11:00 a.m. Monday-Friday CST and ask for express service (allow 1-2 business days).

Technical Assistance

If you have questions, call our technical support line at 1-314-770-2228 between 8:00 a.m. and 5:00 p.m. Monday-Friday CST. Whether it involves design modifications or field assistance, our designers are extremely familiar with all of our designs and will be happy to help you. We want your home to be everything you expect it to be.

Other Great Products

The Legal Kit -

Avoid many legal pitfalls and build your home with confidence using the forms and contract featured in this kit. Included are request for proposal documents, various fixed price and cost plus contracts, instructions on how and when to use each form, warranty statements and more. Save time and money before you break ground on your new home or start a remodeling project. All forms are reproducible. The kit is ideal for homebuilders and contractors. **Cost: $35.00**

Detail Plan Packages -

Electrical, Plumbing and Framing Packages

Three separate packages offer homebuilders details for constructing various foundations; numerous floor, wall and roof framing techniques; simple to complex residential wiring; sump and water softener hookups; plumbing connection methods; installation of septic systems, and more. Each package includes three dimensional illustrations and a glossary of terms. Purchase one or all three. Note: These drawings do not pertain to a specific home plan.

Cost: $20.00 each or all three for $40.00

Exchange Policies

Since blueprints are printed in response to your order, we cannot honor requests for refunds. However, if for some reason you find that the plan you have purchased does not meet your requirements, you may exchange that plan for another plan in our collection within 90 days of purchase. At the time of the exchange, you will be charged a processing fee of 25% of your original plan package price, plus the difference in price between the plan packages (if applicable) and the cost to ship the new plans to you. Please note: Reproducible drawings can only be exchanged if the package is unopened.

Building Codes & Requirements

At the time the construction drawings were prepared, every effort was made to ensure that these plans and specifications meet nationally recognized codes. Our plans conform to most national building codes. Because building codes vary from area to area, some drawing modifications and/or the assistance of a professional designer or architect may be necessary to comply with your local codes or to accommodate specific building site conditions. We advise you to consult with your local building official for information regarding codes governing your area.

Additional Sets*

Additional sets of the plan ordered are available for an additional cost of $45.00 each. Five-set, eight-set, and reproducible packages offer considerable savings.

Mirror Reverse Plans*

Available for an additional $15.00 per set, these plans are simply a mirror image of the original drawings causing the dimensions and lettering to read backwards. Therefore, when ordering mirror reverse plans, you must purchase at least one set of right-reading plans. Some of our plans are offered mirror reverse right-reading. This means the plan, lettering and dimensions are flipped but read correctly. To purchase a mirror reverse right-reading set, the cost is an additional $150.00. See the Home Plans Index on pages 285-286 for availability.

One-Set Study Package

We offer a one-set plan package so you can study your home in detail. This one set is considered a study set and is marked "not for construction." It is a copyright violation to reproduce blueprints.

*Available only within 90 days after purchase of plan package or reproducible masters of same plan.

BLUEPRINT PRICE SCHEDULE

BEST VALUE

Price Code	1-Set	Save $80 5-Sets	Save $115 8-Sets	Reproducible Masters
AAA	$310	$410	$510	$610
AA	$410	$510	$610	$710
A	$470	$570	$670	$770
B	$530	$630	$730	$830
C	$585	$685	$785	$885
D	$635	$735	$835	$935
E	$695	$795	$895	$995
F	$750	$850	$950	$1050
G	$1000	$1100	$1200	$1300
H	$1100	$1200	$1300	$1400

Plan prices are subject to change without notice.
Please note that plans and material lists are not refundable.

SHIPPING & HANDLING CHARGES

US SHIPPING (AK and HI express only)	1-4 Sets	5-7 Sets	8 Sets or Reproducibles
Regular (allow 7-10 business days)	$15.00	$17.50	$25.00
Priority (allow 3-5 business days)	$25.00	$30.00	$35.00
Express* (allow 1-2 business days)	$40.00	$45.00	$50.00

CANADA SHIPPING**	1-4 Sets	5-7 Sets	8 Sets or Reproducibles
Standard (allow 8-12 business days)	$35.00	$40.00	$45.00
Express* (allow 3-5 business days)	$65.00	$75.00	$85.00

*For express delivery please call us by 11:00 a.m. Monday-Friday CST
Overseas Shipping/International - Call, fax, or e-mail (plans@hdainc.com) for shipping costs

**Orders may be subject to custom's fees and or duties/taxes

CAD FORMAT PLANS Many of our plans are available in CAD. For availability, please call our Customer Service Number below.

1-877-379-3420

How To Order

1.) **CALL** toll-free 1-877-379-3420 for credit card orders

2.) **FAX** your order to 1-314-770-2226

3.) **MAIL** the Order Form to: *HDA , Inc.*
944 Anglum Road
St. Louis, MO 63042
ATTN: Customer Service Dept.

For fastest service, Call Toll-Free
1-877-379-3420 day or night

Order Form

Please send me -

PLAN NUMBER 537-__________________

PRICE CODE _____ (see pages 285-286)

Specify Foundation Type (see plan page for availability)

☐ Slab ☐ Crawl space ☐ Pier

☐ Basement ☐ Walk-out basement

☐ Reproducible Masters $________

☐ Eight-Set Plan Package $________

☐ Five-Set Plan Package $________

☐ One-Set Study Package (no mirror reverse) $________

Additional Plan Sets*

☐ ____ (Qty.) at $45.00 each $________

Mirror Reverse*

☐ Right-reading $150 one-time charge $________
(see index on pages 285-286 for availability)

☐ Print in Mirror Reverse (where right-reading is not available) $________

____ (Qty.) at $15.00 each

☐ Material List* $125 $________

☐ Legal Kit (see page 284) (002D-9991) $________

Detail Plan Packages: (see page 284)

☐ Framing (002D-9992) ☐ Electrical (002D-9993) ☐ Plumbing (002D-9994) $________

☐ CAD Packages (call for availability and pricing) $________

SUBTOTAL $________

Sales Tax (MO residents add 7%) $________

☐ Shipping / Handling (see chart on page 287) $________

TOTAL (US funds only - sorry no CODs) $________

* Available only within 90 days after purchase of plan package or reproducible masters of the same plan.

I hereby authorize HDA, Inc. to charge this purchase to my credit card account (check one):

☐ MasterCard ☐ VISA ☐ Discover ☐ American Express Cards

Prices are subject to change without notice.
Please note plans and material lists are not refundable.

Credit Card number __________________

Expiration date __________________

Signature __________________

Name __________________
(Please print or type)

Street Address __________________
(Please do not use a PO Box)

____

City __________________

State __________________

Zip __________________

Daytime phone number (____) - __________

E-mail address __________________

I am a ☐ Builder/Contractor
☐ Homeowner
☐ Renter

I ☐ have ☐ have not selected my general contractor.

Thank you for your order!